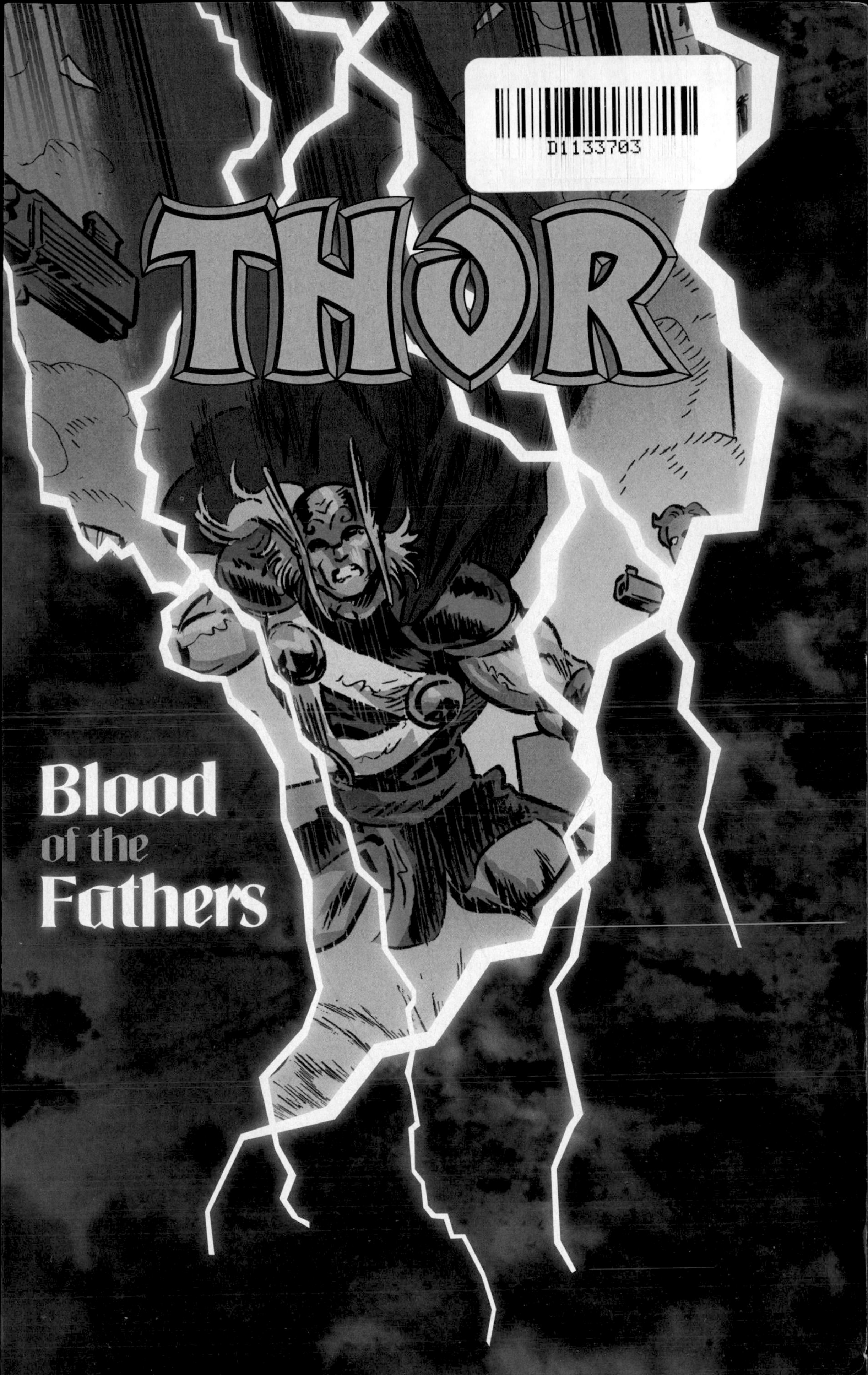
THOR
Blood of the Fathers

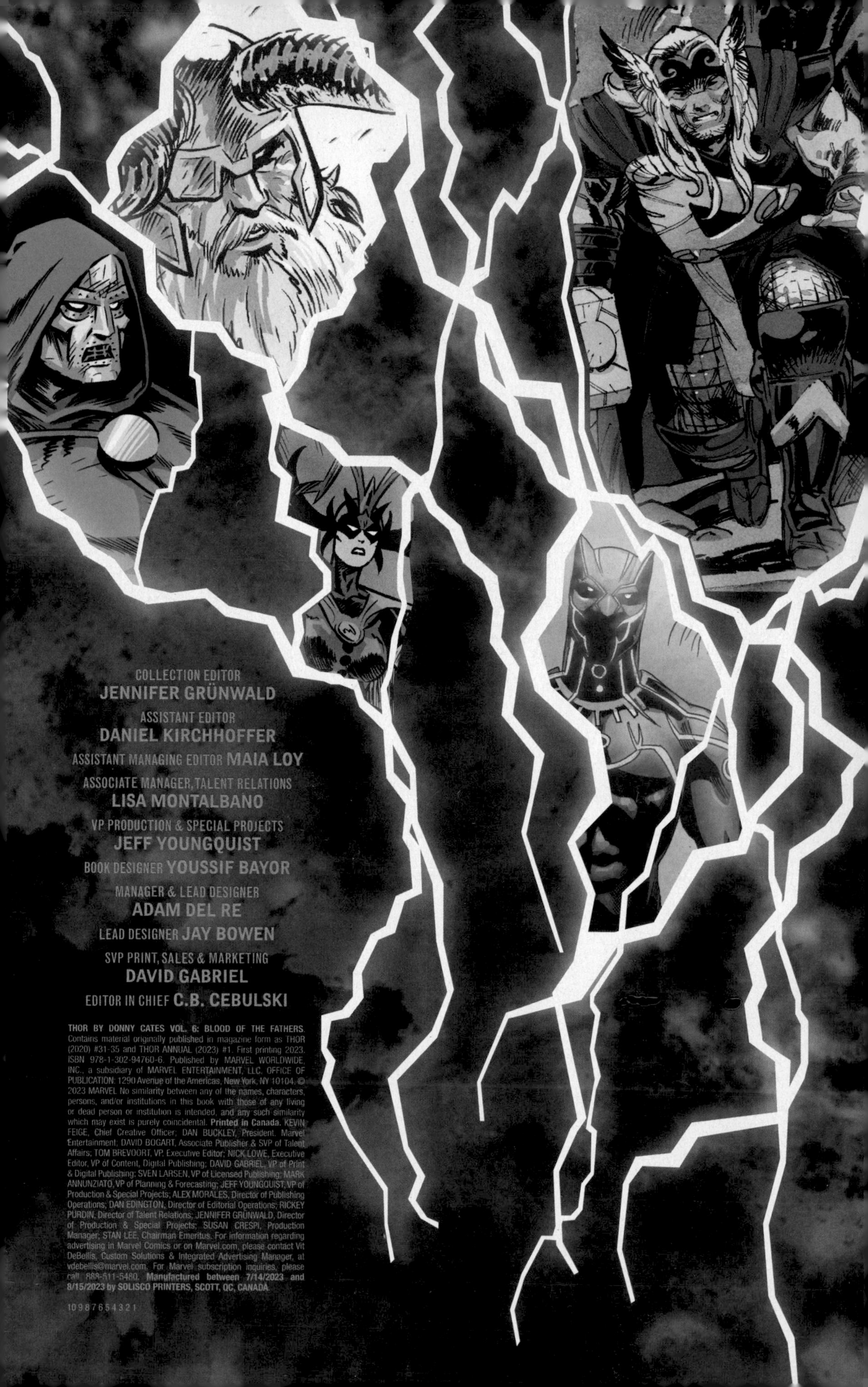

COLLECTION EDITOR **JENNIFER GRÜNWALD**

ASSISTANT EDITOR **DANIEL KIRCHHOFFER**

ASSISTANT MANAGING EDITOR **MAIA LOY**

ASSOCIATE MANAGER, TALENT RELATIONS **LISA MONTALBANO**

VP PRODUCTION & SPECIAL PROJECTS **JEFF YOUNGQUIST**

BOOK DESIGNER **YOUSSIF BAYOR**

MANAGER & LEAD DESIGNER **ADAM DEL RE**

LEAD DESIGNER **JAY BOWEN**

SVP PRINT, SALES & MARKETING **DAVID GABRIEL**

EDITOR IN CHIEF **C.B. CEBULSKI**

THOR BY DONNY CATES VOL. 6: BLOOD OF THE FATHERS. Contains material originally published in magazine form as THOR (2020) #31-35 and THOR ANNUAL (2023) #1. First printing 2023. ISBN 978-1-302-94760-6. Published by MARVEL WORLDWIDE, INC., a subsidiary of MARVEL ENTERTAINMENT, LLC. OFFICE OF PUBLICATION: 1290 Avenue of the Americas, New York, NY 10104. **Printed in Canada.** KEVIN FEIGE, Chief Creative Officer; DAN BUCKLEY, President, Marvel Entertainment; DAVID BOGART, Associate Publisher & SVP of Talent Affairs; TOM BREVOORT, VP, Executive Editor; NICK LOWE, Executive Editor, VP of Content, Digital Publishing; DAVID GABRIEL, VP of Print & Digital Publishing; SVEN LARSEN, VP of Licensed Publishing; MARK ANNUNZIATO, VP of Planning & Forecasting; JEFF YOUNGQUIST, VP of Production & Special Projects; ALEX MORALES, Director of Publishing Operations; DAN EDINGTON, Director of Editorial Operations; RICKEY PURDIN, Director of Talent Relations; JENNIFER GRUNWALD, Director of Production & Special Projects; SUSAN CRESPI, Production Manager; STAN LEE, Chairman Emeritus. For information regarding advertising in Marvel Comics or on Marvel.com, please contact Vit DeBellis, Custom Solutions & Integrated Advertising Manager, at vdebellis@marvel.com. For Marvel subscription inquiries, please call 888-511-5480. **Manufactured between 7/14/2023 and 8/15/2023 by SOLISCO PRINTERS, SCOTT, QC, CANADA.**

10 9 8 7 6 5 4 3 2 1

Cates, Donny,
Thor. Vol 6, Blood of the
fathers /
2023.
33305256984687
ca   09/28/23

...F THANOS--**CORVUS GLAIVE**--KIDNAPPED
...DINSDOTTIR--AND DRAGGED HER AWAY
...MAGIC UNTOUCHED SINCE THE DAYS OF
...HOR PURSUED THEM, HE LEARNED HIS
...WAGED WAR ON THOSE SAME LANDS FOR
...N ANCIENT WEAPON.

AFTER, BOR HAD SEALED THE WEAPON BEHIND A VAULT THAT COULD BE
OPENED ONLY WITH HIS BLOOD. THOR AND **RÚNA** RESCUED LAUSSA BEFORE
CORVUS COULD USE HER BLOOD AS THE KEY, BUT THOR REFUSED TO LEAVE
WITHOUT KNOWING WHAT SECRETS LAY BEHIND THAT DOOR...NOT KNOWING
THAT SOMEONE ELSE WAS WATCHING: **DOCTOR DOOM.**

THOR
Blood of the Fathers

THOR #31	THOR #32-35	THOR ANNUAL #1
Torunn Grønbekk & **Donny Cates** WRITERS	**Torunn Grønbekk** WRITER	**Collin Kelly &** **Jackson Lanzing** WRITERS
Nic Klein ARTIST	**Juan Gedeon** (#32-35) & **Sergio Dávila** (#34-35) PENCILERS	**Ibraim Roberson** ARTIST
Matthew Wilson COLOR ARTIST	**Juan Gedeon** (#32-35) & **Sean Parsons** (#34-35) INKERS	**Dan Brown** COLOR ARTIST
Nic Klein COVER ART	**Matthew Wilson** COLOR ARTIST	**Adam Kubert &** **Matt Milla** COVER ART
	Nic Klein COVER ART	

"When One Door Closes"
CHERYL LYNN EATON WRITER
CHRISCROSS ARTIST
ANDREW DALHOUSE
COLOR ARTIST

VC's Joe Sabino LETTERER	**Michelle Marchese** ASSISTANT EDITOR	**Wil Moss** EDITOR

THOR CREATED BY **Stan Lee, Larry Lieber & Jack Kirby**

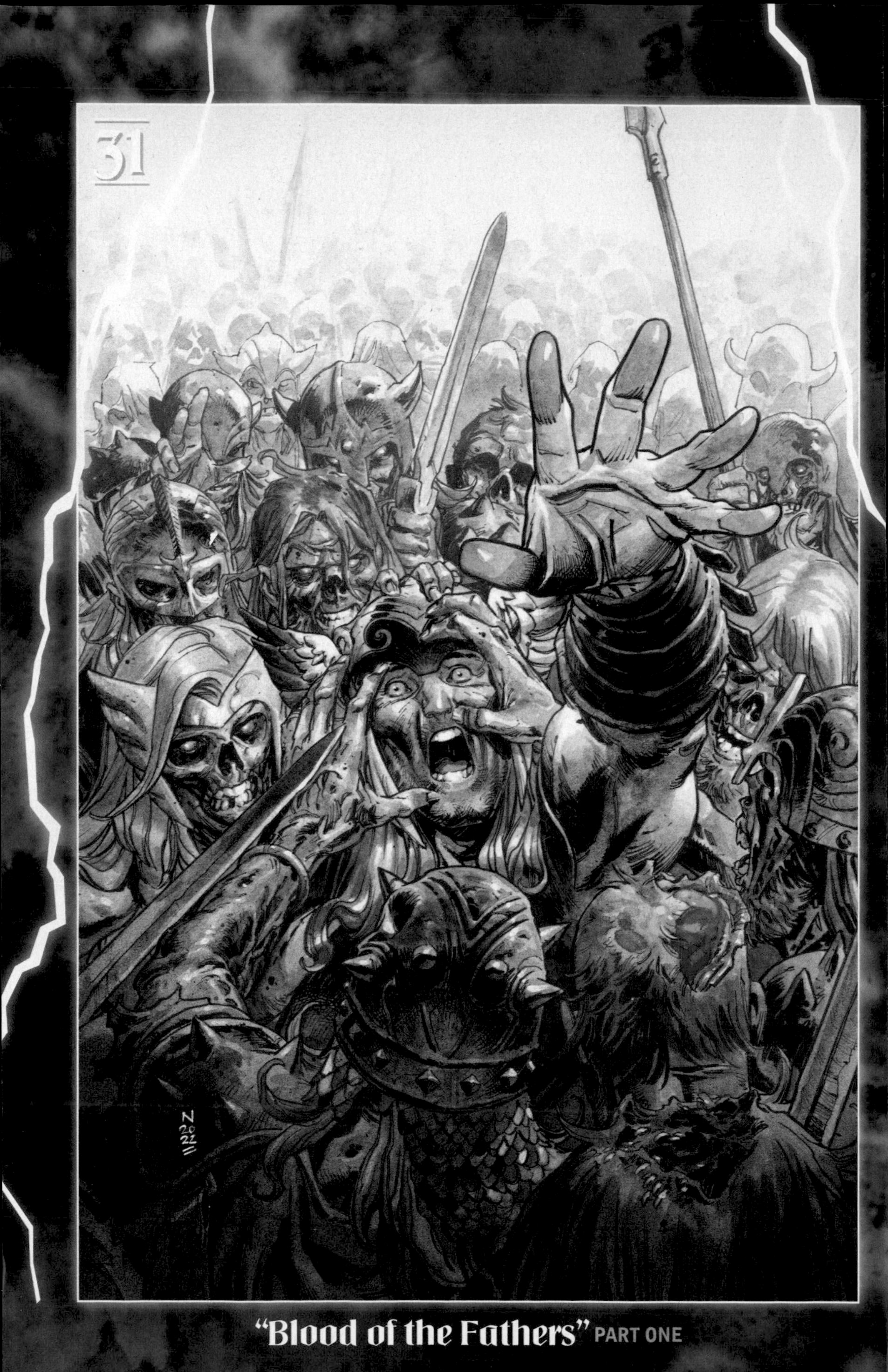
31

"Blood of the Fathers" PART ONE

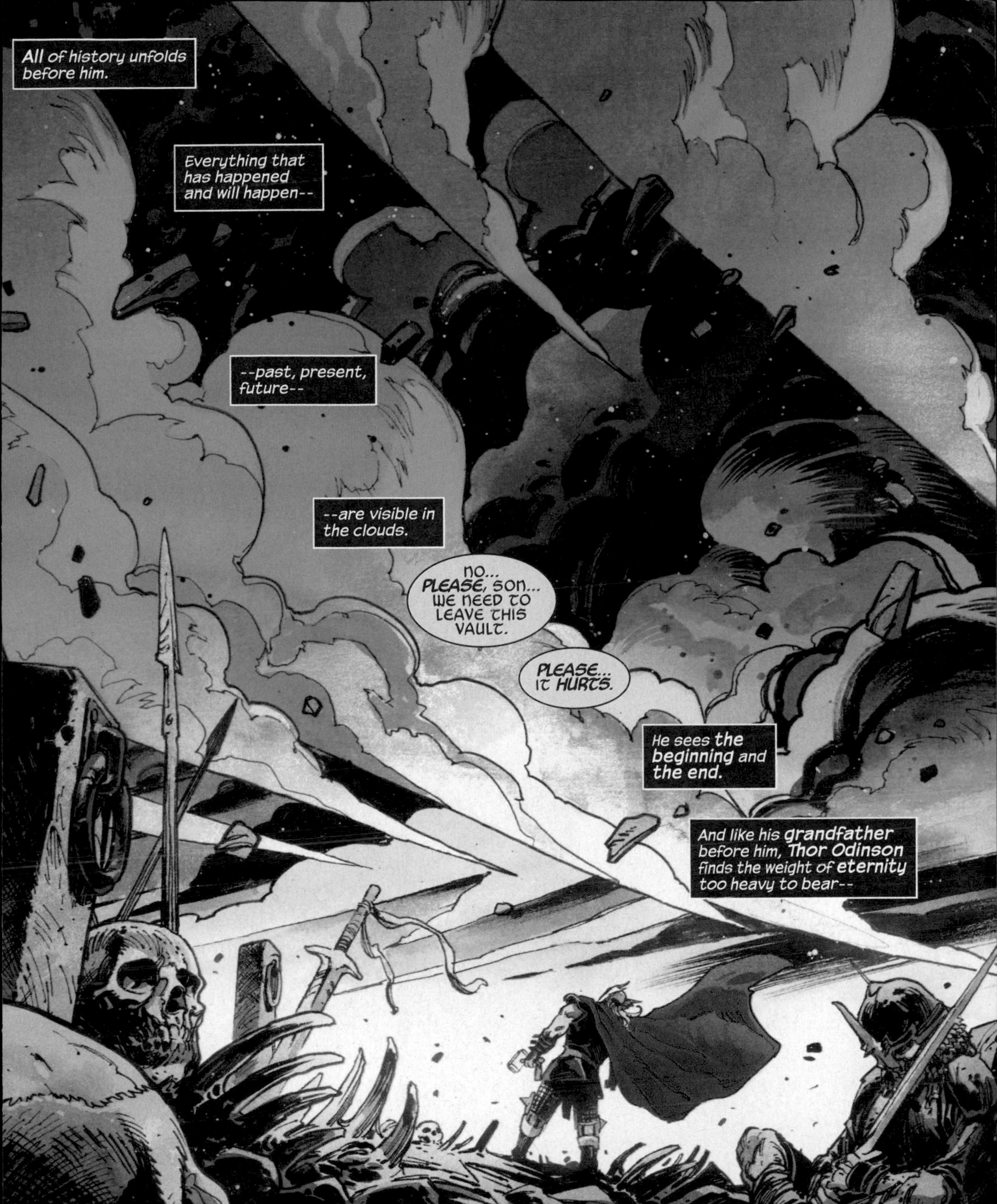
All of history unfolds before him.
Everything that has happened and will happen--
--past, present, future--
--are visible in the clouds.
NO... PLEASE, SON... WE NEED TO LEAVE THIS VAULT.
PLEASE... IT HURTS.
He sees the beginning and the end.
And like his grandfather before him, Thor Odinson finds the weight of eternity too heavy to bear--

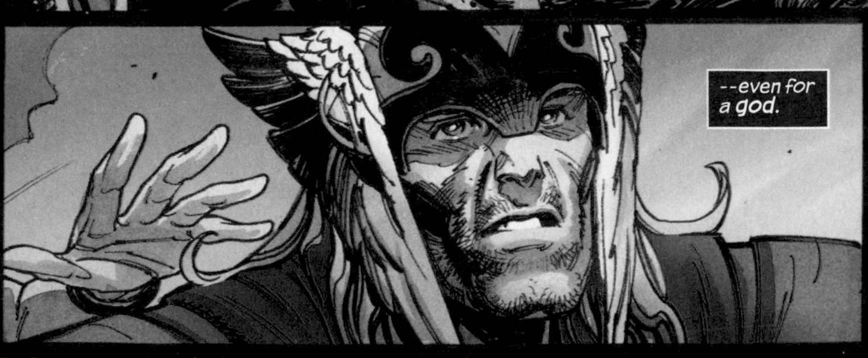
--even for a god.

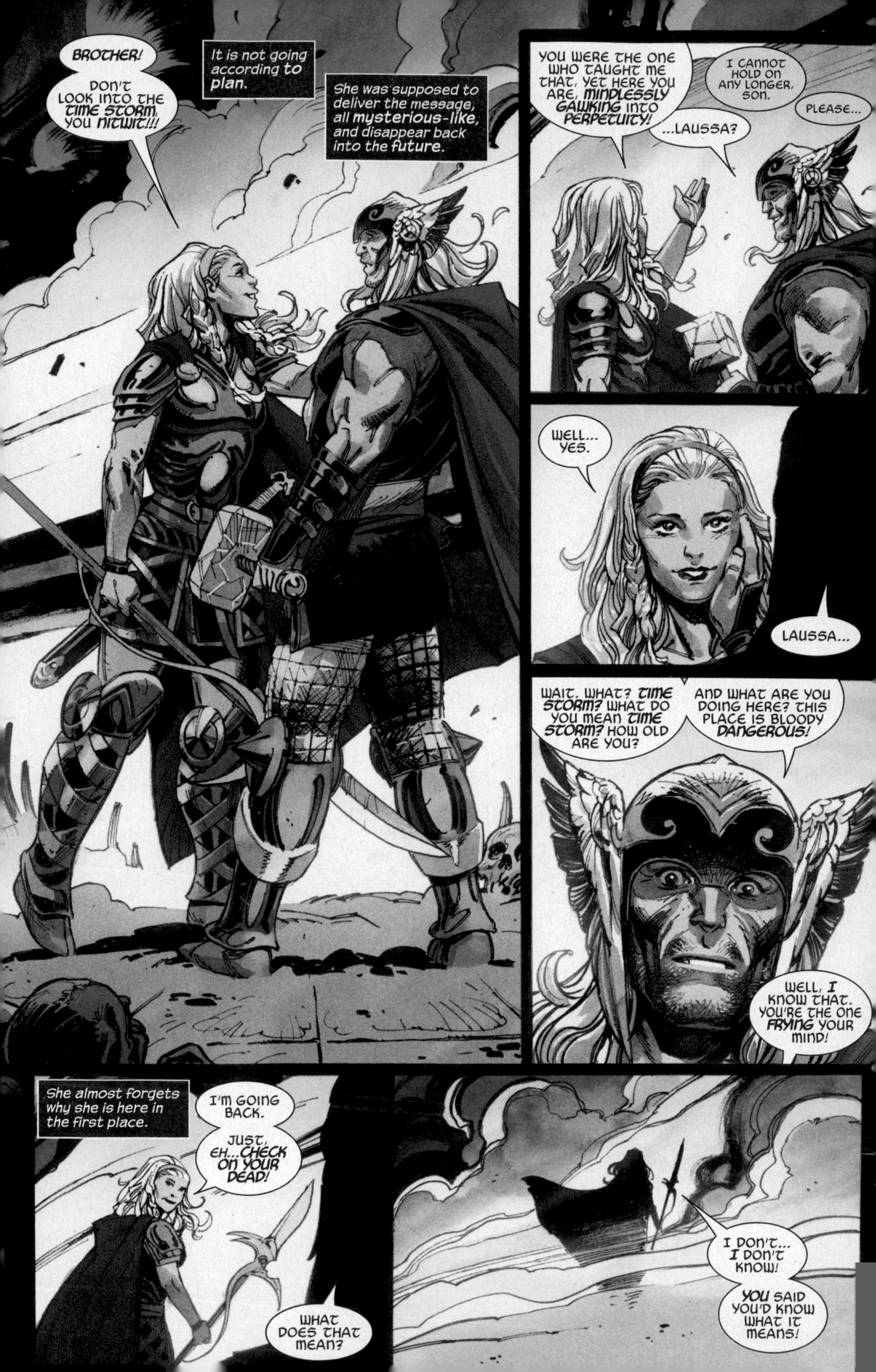
BROTHER!
DON'T LOOK INTO THE TIME STORM, YOU NITWIT!!!
It is not going according to plan.
She was supposed to deliver the message, all mysterious-like, and disappear back into the future.
YOU WERE THE ONE WHO TAUGHT ME THAT, YET HERE YOU ARE, MINDLESSLY GAWKING INTO PERPETUITY!
...LAUSSA?
I CANNOT HOLD ON ANY LONGER, SON.
PLEASE...
WELL... YES.
LAUSSA...
WAIT. WHAT? TIME STORM? WHAT DO YOU MEAN TIME STORM? HOW OLD ARE YOU?
AND WHAT ARE YOU DOING HERE? THIS PLACE IS BLOODY DANGEROUS!
WELL, I KNOW THAT. YOU'RE THE ONE FRYING YOUR MIND!
She almost forgets why she is here in the first place.
I'M GOING BACK.
JUST, EH...CHECK ON YOUR DEAD!
WHAT DOES THAT MEAN?
I DON'T... I DON'T KNOW!
YOU SAID YOU'D KNOW WHAT IT MEANS!

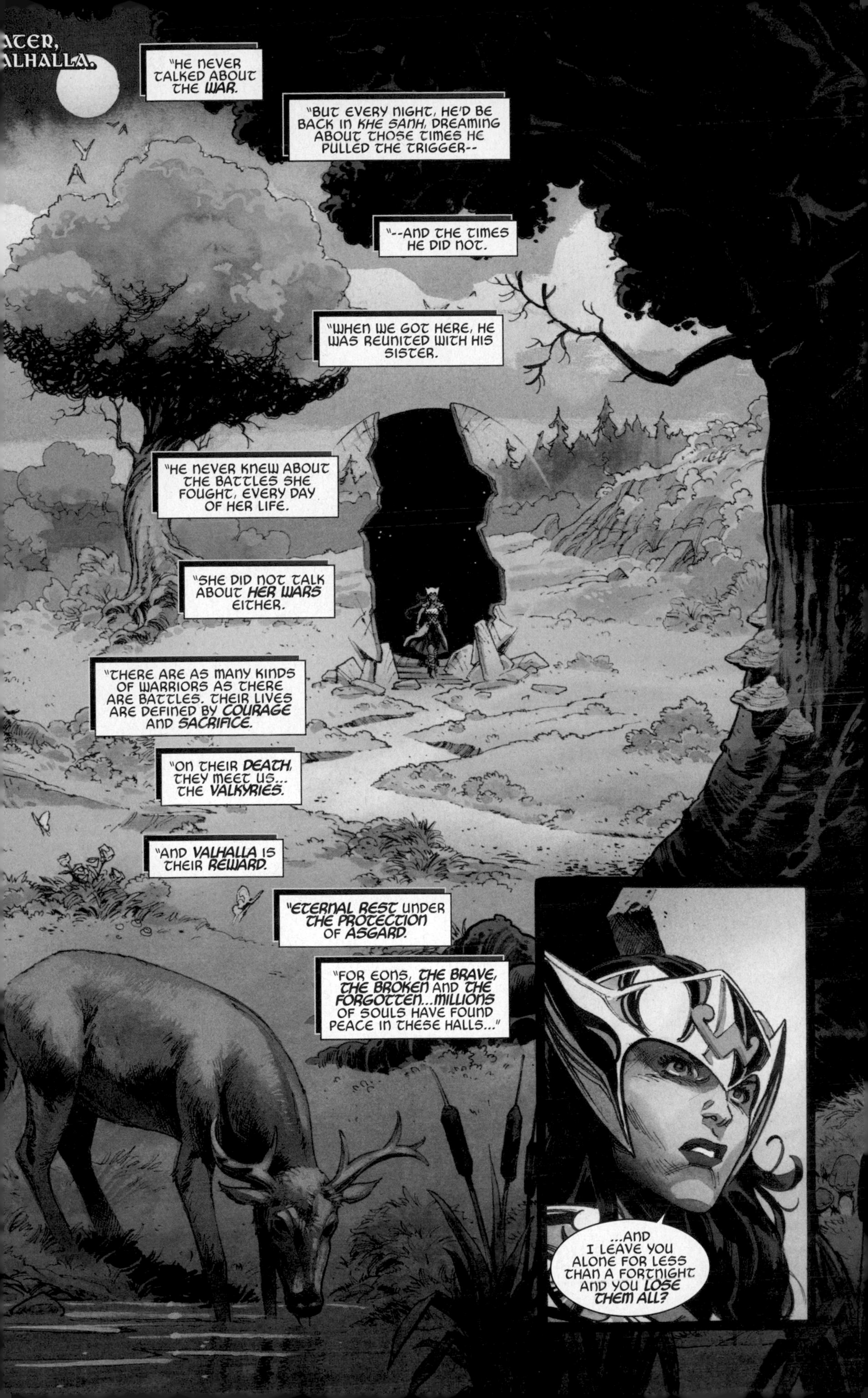

ATER,
ALHALLA.
"HE NEVER TALKED ABOUT THE WAR.
"BUT EVERY NIGHT, HE'D BE BACK IN KHE SANH, DREAMING ABOUT THOSE TIMES HE PULLED THE TRIGGER--
"--AND THE TIMES HE DID NOT.
"WHEN WE GOT HERE, HE WAS REUNITED WITH HIS SISTER.
"HE NEVER KNEW ABOUT THE BATTLES SHE FOUGHT, EVERY DAY OF HER LIFE.
"SHE DID NOT TALK ABOUT HER WARS EITHER.
"THERE ARE AS MANY KINDS OF WARRIORS AS THERE ARE BATTLES. THEIR LIVES ARE DEFINED BY COURAGE AND SACRIFICE.
"ON THEIR DEATH, THEY MEET US... THE VALKYRIES.
"AND VALHALLA IS THEIR REWARD.
"ETERNAL REST UNDER THE PROTECTION OF ASGARD.
"FOR EONS, THE BRAVE, THE BROKEN AND THE FORGOTTEN...MILLIONS OF SOULS HAVE FOUND PEACE IN THESE HALLS..."
...AND I LEAVE YOU ALONE FOR LESS THAN A FORTNIGHT AND YOU LOSE THEM ALL?

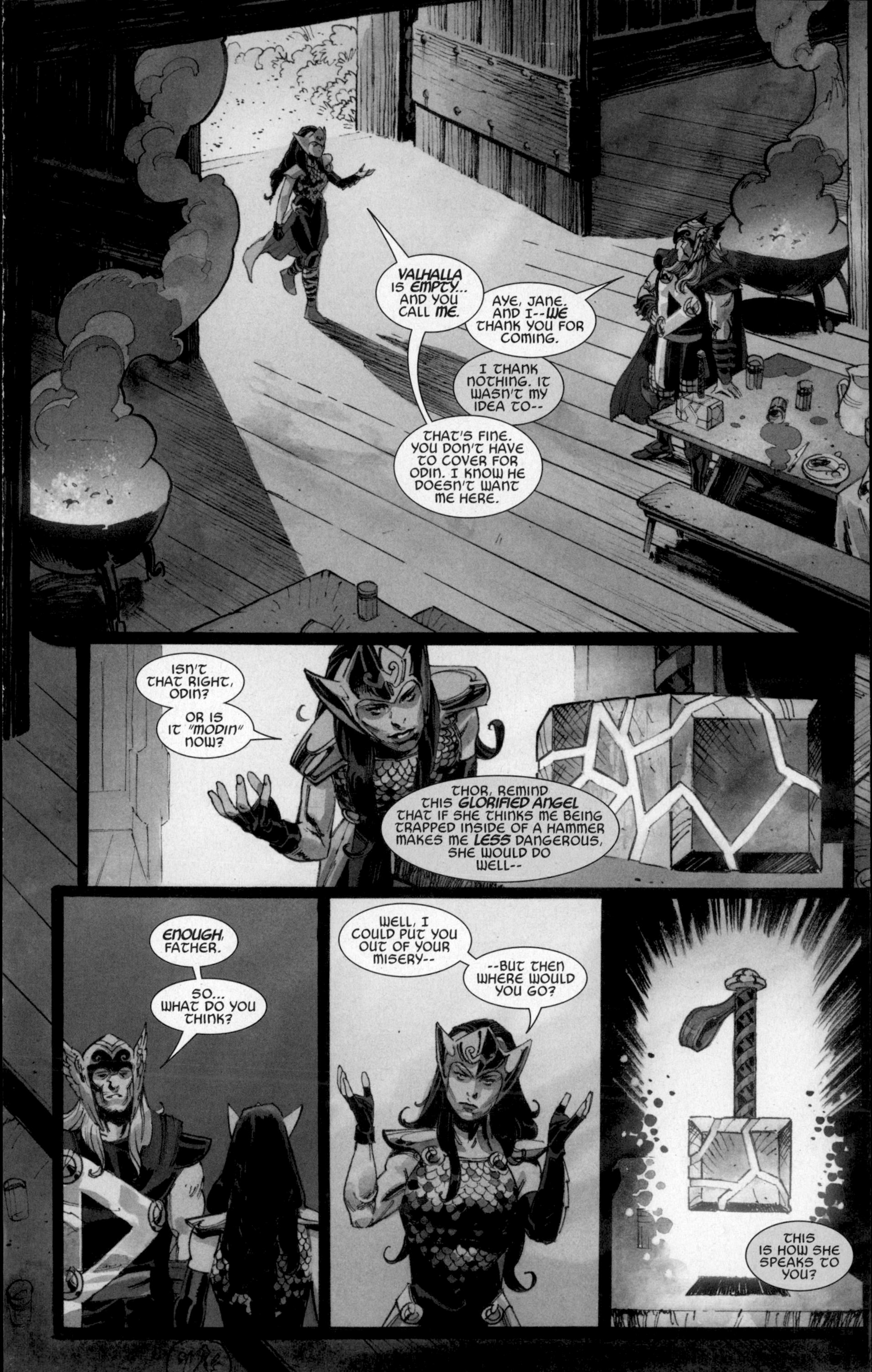
VALHALLA IS EMPTY... AND YOU CALL ME.
AYE, JANE. AND I--WE THANK YOU FOR COMING.
I THANK NOTHING. IT WASN'T MY IDEA TO--
THAT'S FINE. YOU DON'T HAVE TO COVER FOR ODIN. I KNOW HE DOESN'T WANT ME HERE.
ISN'T THAT RIGHT, ODIN?
OR IS IT "MODIN" NOW?
THOR, REMIND THIS GLORIFIED ANGEL THAT IF SHE THINKS ME BEING TRAPPED INSIDE OF A HAMMER MAKES ME LESS DANGEROUS, SHE WOULD DO WELL--
ENOUGH, FATHER.
SO... WHAT DO YOU THINK?
WELL, I COULD PUT YOU OUT OF YOUR MISERY--
--BUT THEN WHERE WOULD YOU GO?
THIS IS HOW SHE SPEAKS TO YOU?

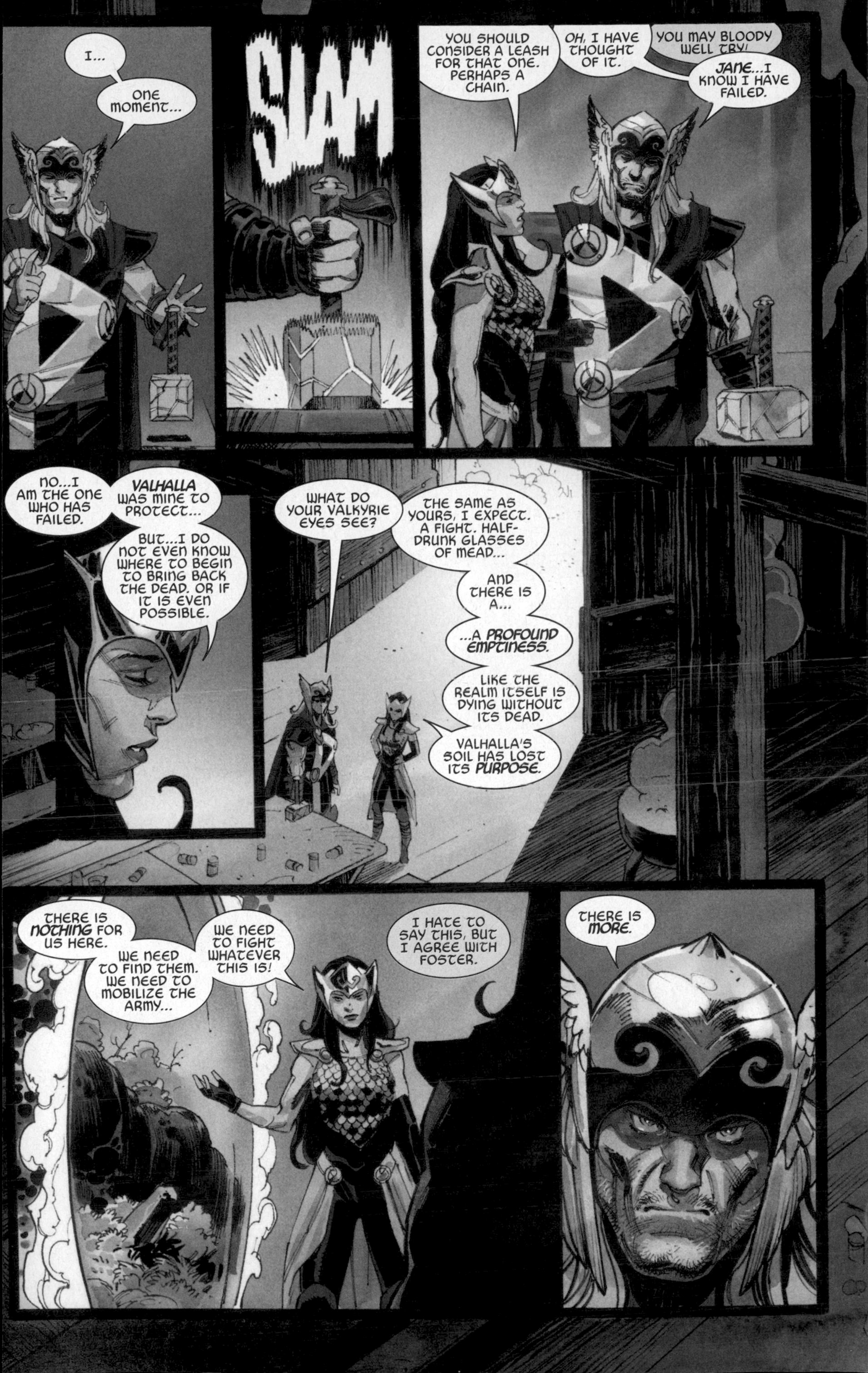
I...
ONE MOMENT...
SLAM
YOU SHOULD CONSIDER A LEASH FOR THAT ONE. PERHAPS A CHAIN.
OH, I HAVE THOUGHT OF IT.
YOU MAY BLOODY WELL TRY!
JANE...I KNOW I HAVE FAILED.
NO...I AM THE ONE WHO HAS FAILED.
VALHALLA WAS MINE TO PROTECT...
BUT...I DO NOT EVEN KNOW WHERE TO BEGIN TO BRING BACK THE DEAD. OR IF IT IS EVEN POSSIBLE.
WHAT DO YOUR VALKYRIE EYES SEE?
THE SAME AS YOURS, I EXPECT. A FIGHT. HALF-DRUNK GLASSES OF MEAD...
AND THERE IS A...
...A PROFOUND EMPTINESS.
LIKE THE REALM ITSELF IS DYING WITHOUT ITS DEAD.
VALHALLA'S SOIL HAS LOST ITS PURPOSE.
THERE IS NOTHING FOR US HERE.
WE NEED TO FIND THEM. WE NEED TO MOBILIZE THE ARMY...
WE NEED TO FIGHT WHATEVER THIS IS!
I HATE TO SAY THIS, BUT I AGREE WITH FOSTER.
THERE IS MORE.

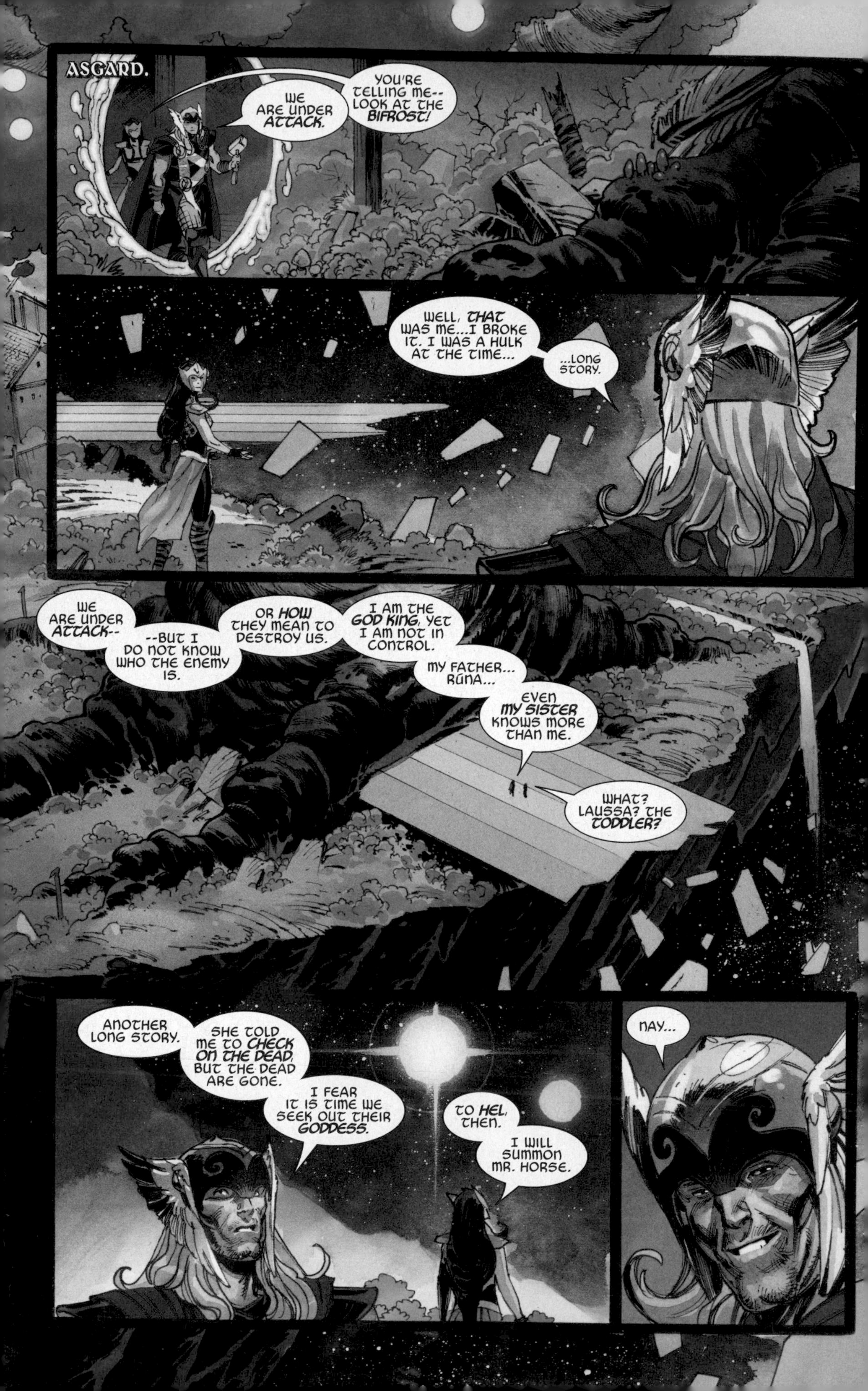
ASGARD.
WE ARE UNDER ATTACK.
YOU'RE TELLING ME-- LOOK AT THE BIFROST!
WELL, THAT WAS ME...I BROKE IT. I WAS A HULK AT THE TIME...
...LONG STORY.
WE ARE UNDER ATTACK--
--BUT I DO NOT KNOW WHO THE ENEMY IS.
OR HOW THEY MEAN TO DESTROY US.
I AM THE GOD KING, YET I AM NOT IN CONTROL.
MY FATHER... RŪNA...
EVEN MY SISTER KNOWS MORE THAN ME.
WHAT? LAUSSA? THE TODDLER?
ANOTHER LONG STORY.
SHE TOLD ME TO CHECK ON THE DEAD, BUT THE DEAD ARE GONE.
I FEAR IT IS TIME WE SEEK OUT THEIR GODDESS.
TO HEL, THEN.
I WILL SUMMON MR. HORSE.
NAY...

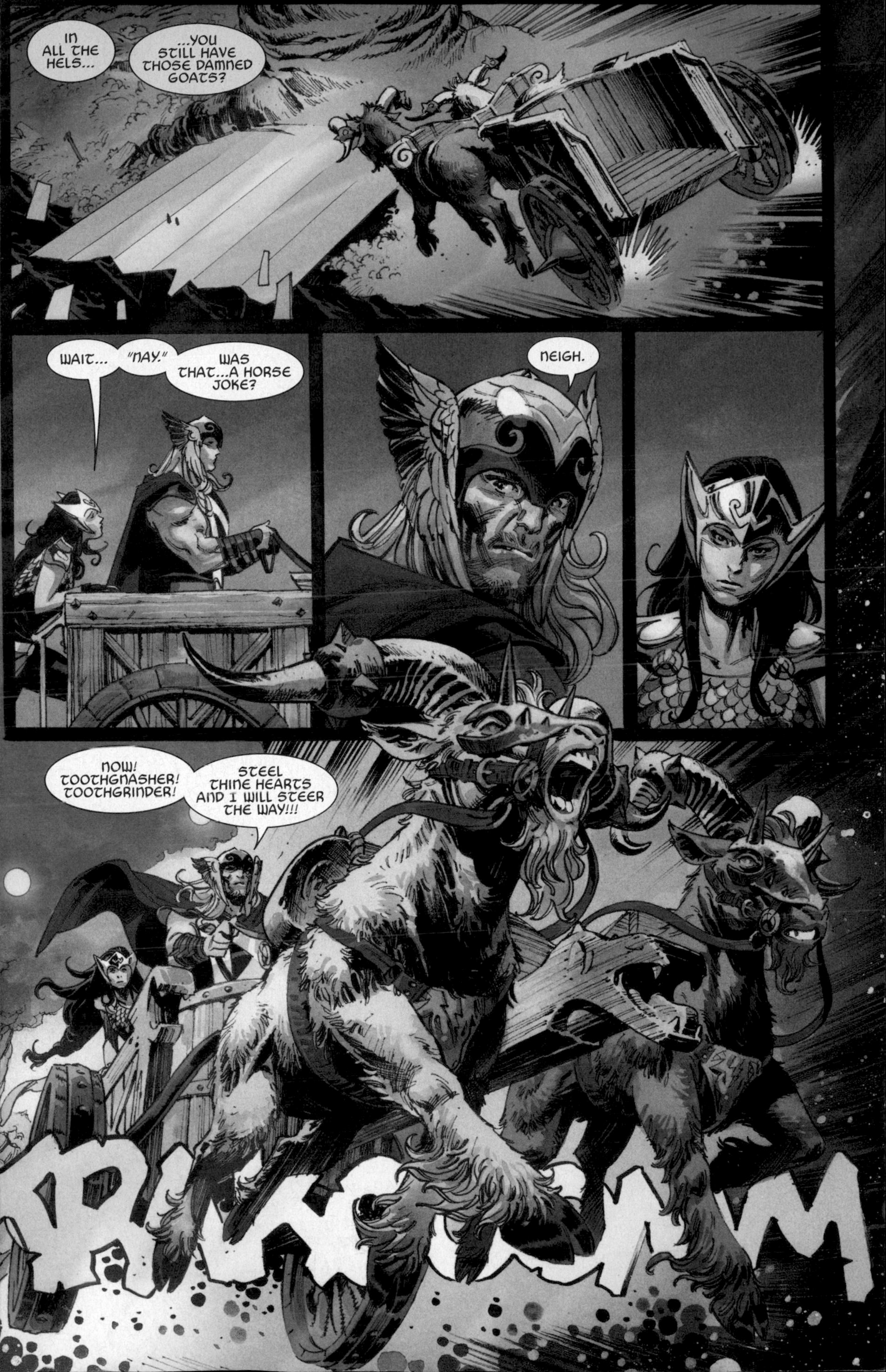
IN ALL THE HELS...
...YOU STILL HAVE THOSE DAMNED GOATS?
WAIT...
"NAY."
WAS THAT...A HORSE JOKE?
NEIGH.
NOW! TOOTHGNASHER! TOOTHGRINDER!
STEEL THINE HEARTS AND I WILL STEER THE WAY!!!

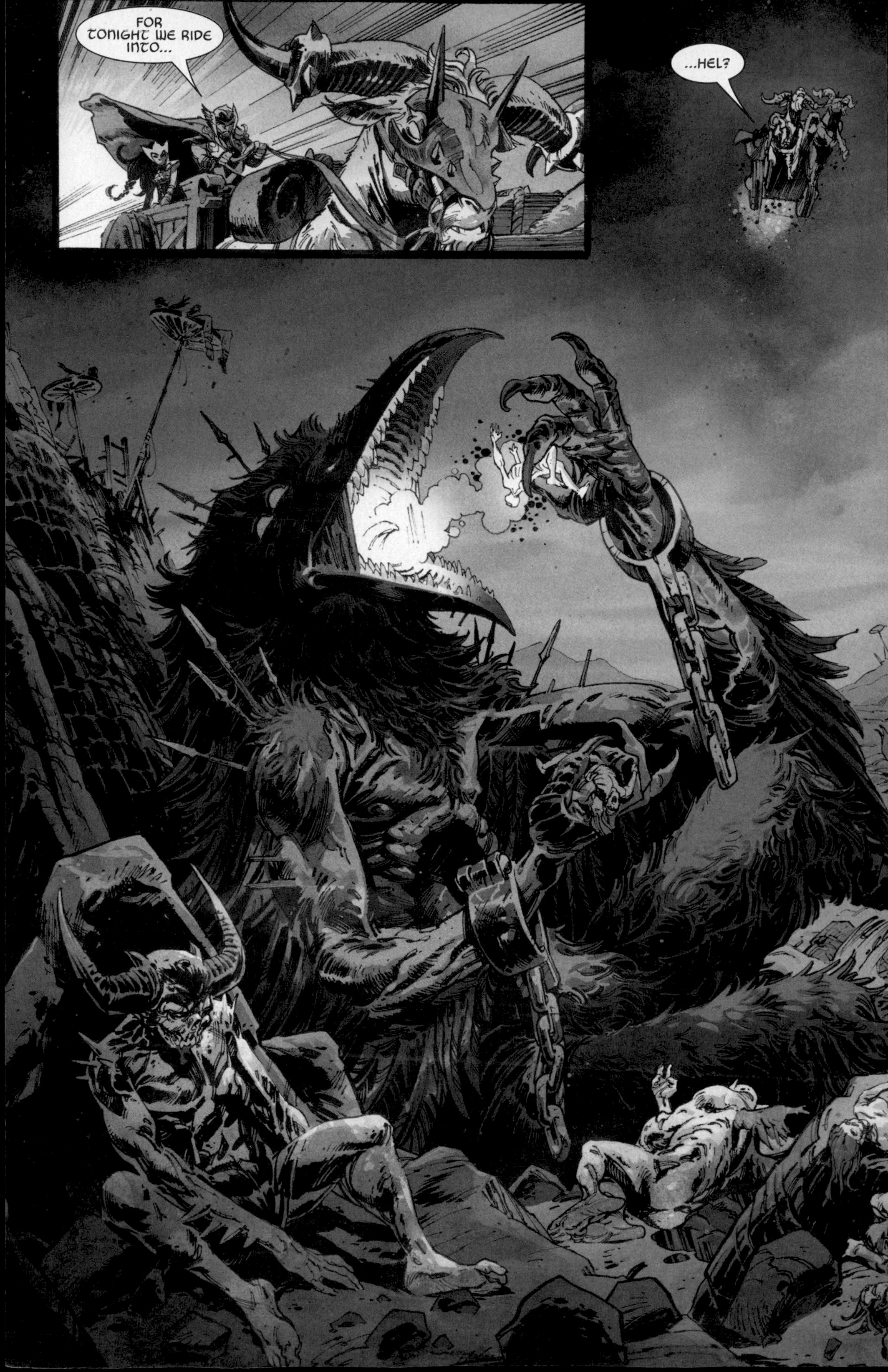
FOR TONIGHT WE RIDE INTO...
...HEL?

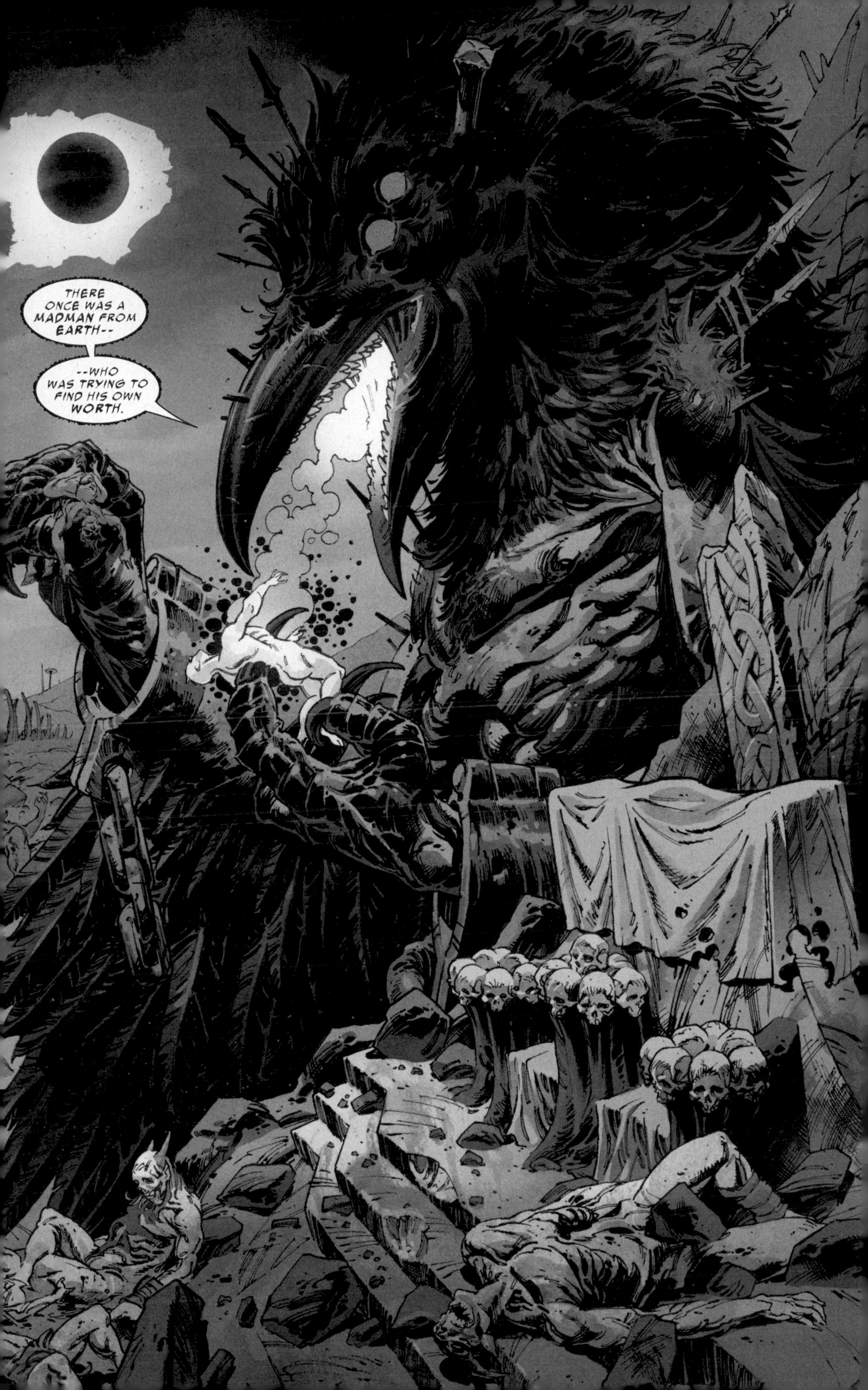
THERE ONCE WAS A MADMAN FROM EARTH--
--WHO WAS TRYING TO FIND HIS OWN WORTH.

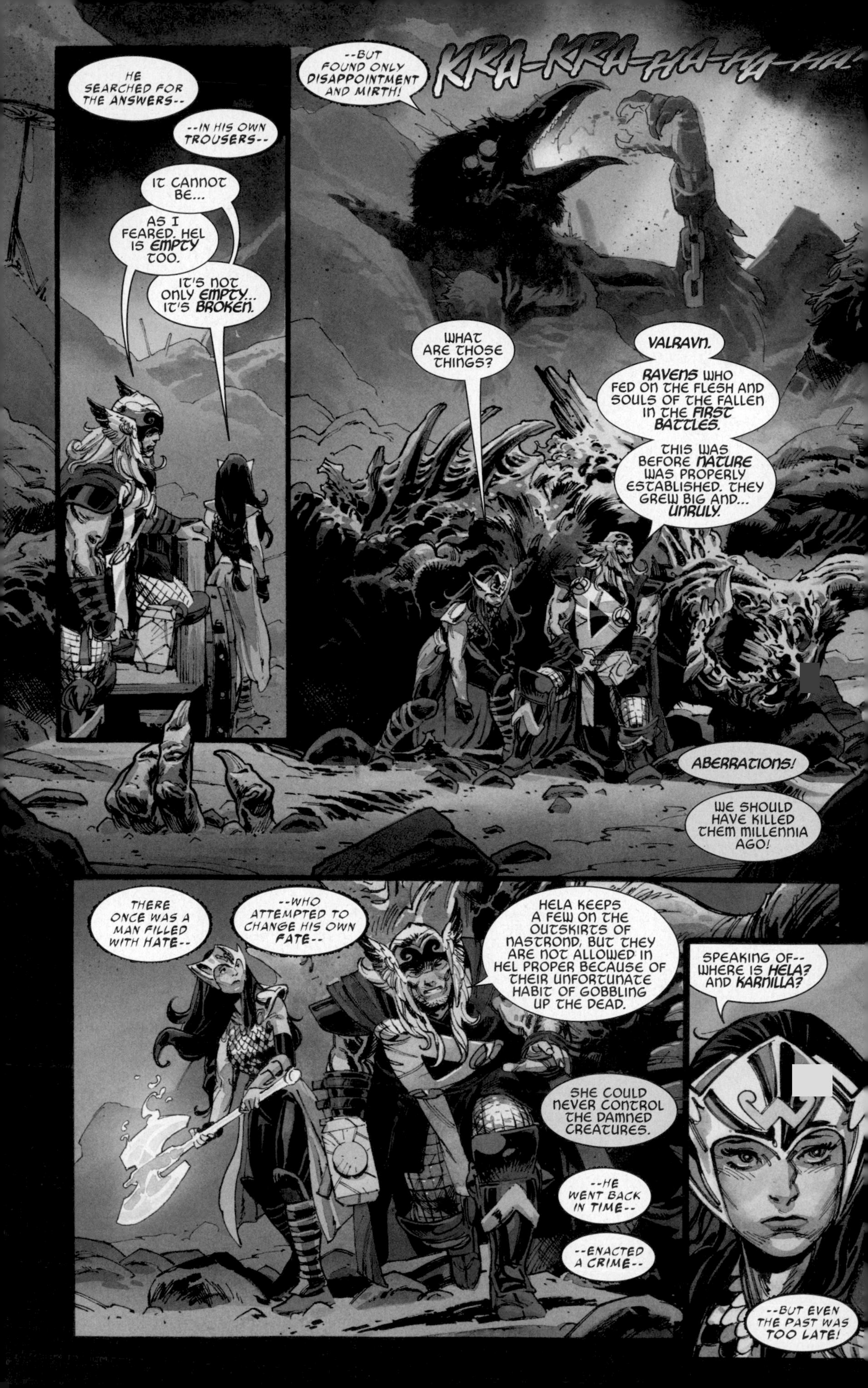

HE SEARCHED FOR THE ANSWERS--
--IN HIS OWN TROUSERS--
--BUT FOUND ONLY DISAPPOINTMENT AND MIRTH!
KRA-KRA-HA-HA-HA
IT CANNOT BE...
AS I FEARED. HEL IS EMPTY TOO.
IT'S NOT ONLY EMPTY... IT'S BROKEN.
WHAT ARE THOSE THINGS?
VALRAVN.
RAVENS WHO FED ON THE FLESH AND SOULS OF THE FALLEN IN THE FIRST BATTLES.
THIS WAS BEFORE NATURE WAS PROPERLY ESTABLISHED. THEY GREW BIG AND... UNRULY.
ABERRATIONS!
WE SHOULD HAVE KILLED THEM MILLENNIA AGO!
THERE ONCE WAS A MAN FILLED WITH HATE--
--WHO ATTEMPTED TO CHANGE HIS OWN FATE--
HELA KEEPS A FEW ON THE OUTSKIRTS OF NASTROND, BUT THEY ARE NOT ALLOWED IN HEL PROPER BECAUSE OF THEIR UNFORTUNATE HABIT OF GOBBLING UP THE DEAD.
SHE COULD NEVER CONTROL THE DAMNED CREATURES.
--HE WENT BACK IN TIME--
--ENACTED A CRIME--
SPEAKING OF-- WHERE IS HELA? AND KARNILLA?
--BUT EVEN THE PAST WAS TOO LATE!

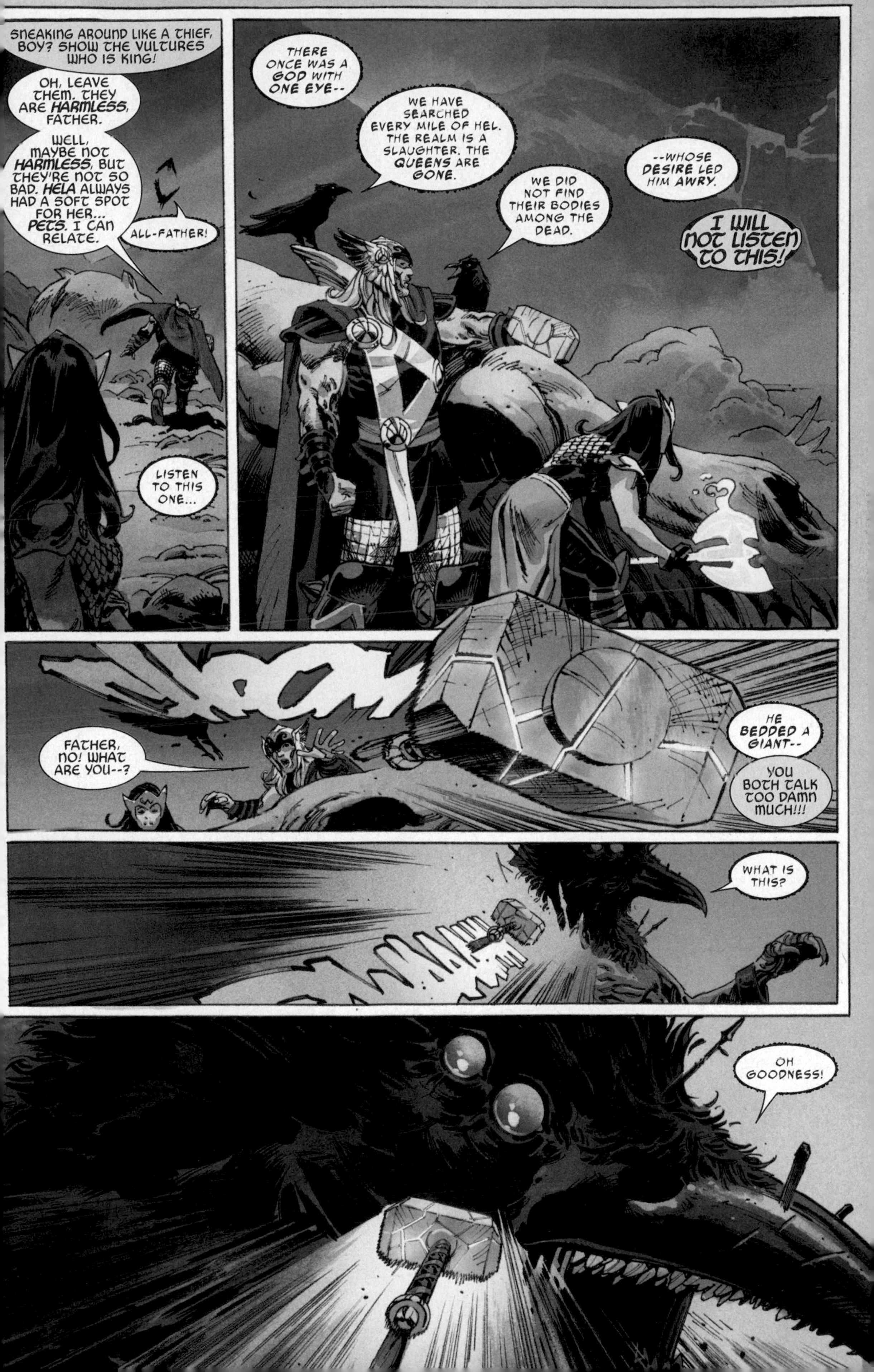
SNEAKING AROUND LIKE A THIEF, BOY? SHOW THE VULTURES WHO IS KING!
OH, LEAVE THEM. THEY ARE HARMLESS, FATHER.
WELL, MAYBE NOT HARMLESS, BUT THEY'RE NOT SO BAD. HELA ALWAYS HAD A SOFT SPOT FOR HER... PETS. I CAN RELATE.
ALL-FATHER!
LISTEN TO THIS ONE...
THERE ONCE WAS A GOD WITH ONE EYE--
WE HAVE SEARCHED EVERY MILE OF HEL. THE REALM IS A SLAUGHTER. THE QUEENS ARE GONE.
WE DID NOT FIND THEIR BODIES AMONG THE DEAD.
--WHOSE DESIRE LED HIM AWRY.
I WILL NOT LISTEN TO THIS!
FATHER, NO! WHAT ARE YOU--?
HE BEDDED A GIANT--
YOU BOTH TALK TOO DAMN MUCH!!!
WHAT IS THIS?
OH GOODNESS!

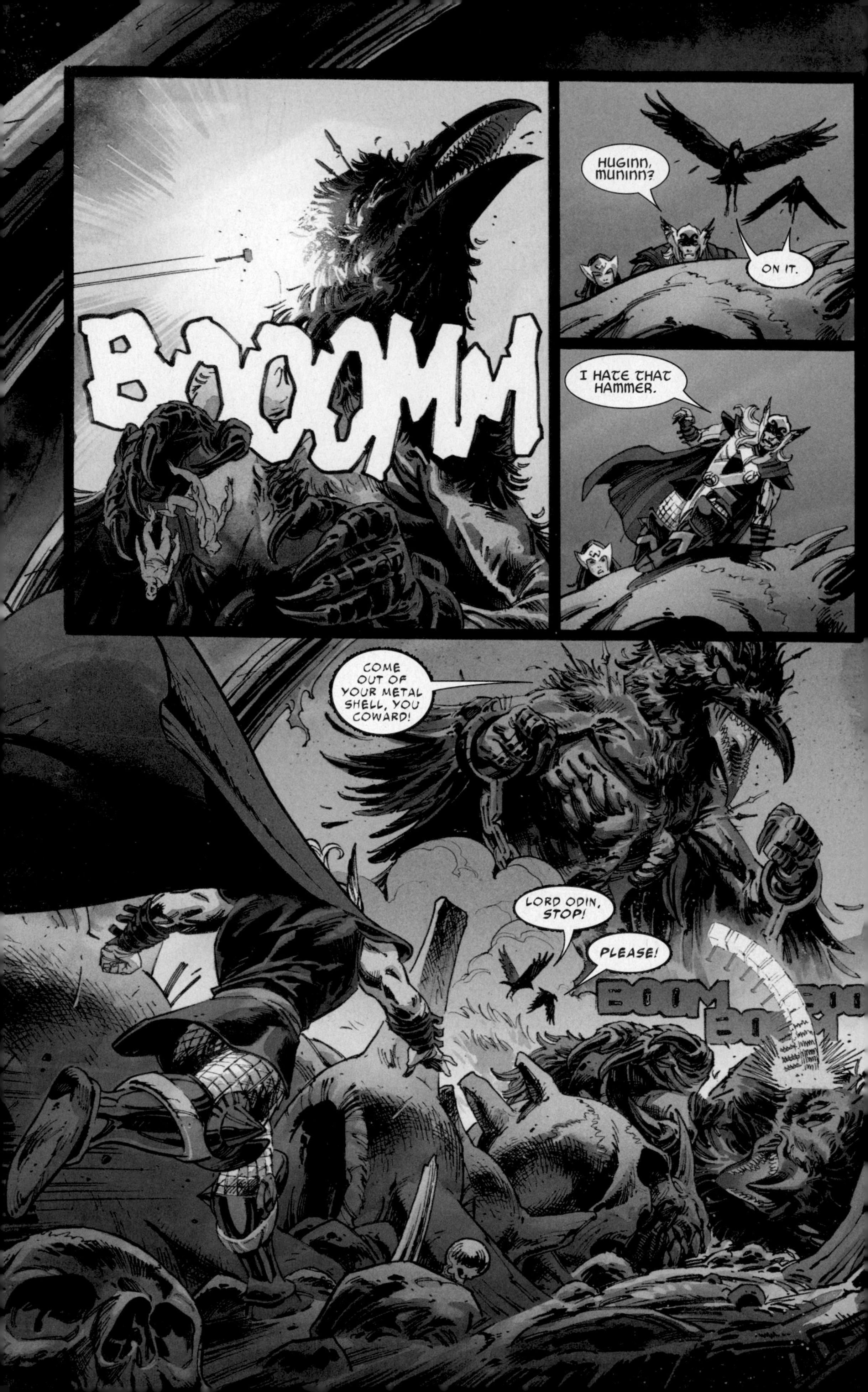

BOOOMM
HUGINN, MUNINN?
ON IT.
I HATE THAT HAMMER.
COME OUT OF YOUR METAL SHELL, YOU COWARD!
LORD ODIN, STOP!
PLEASE!
BOOM

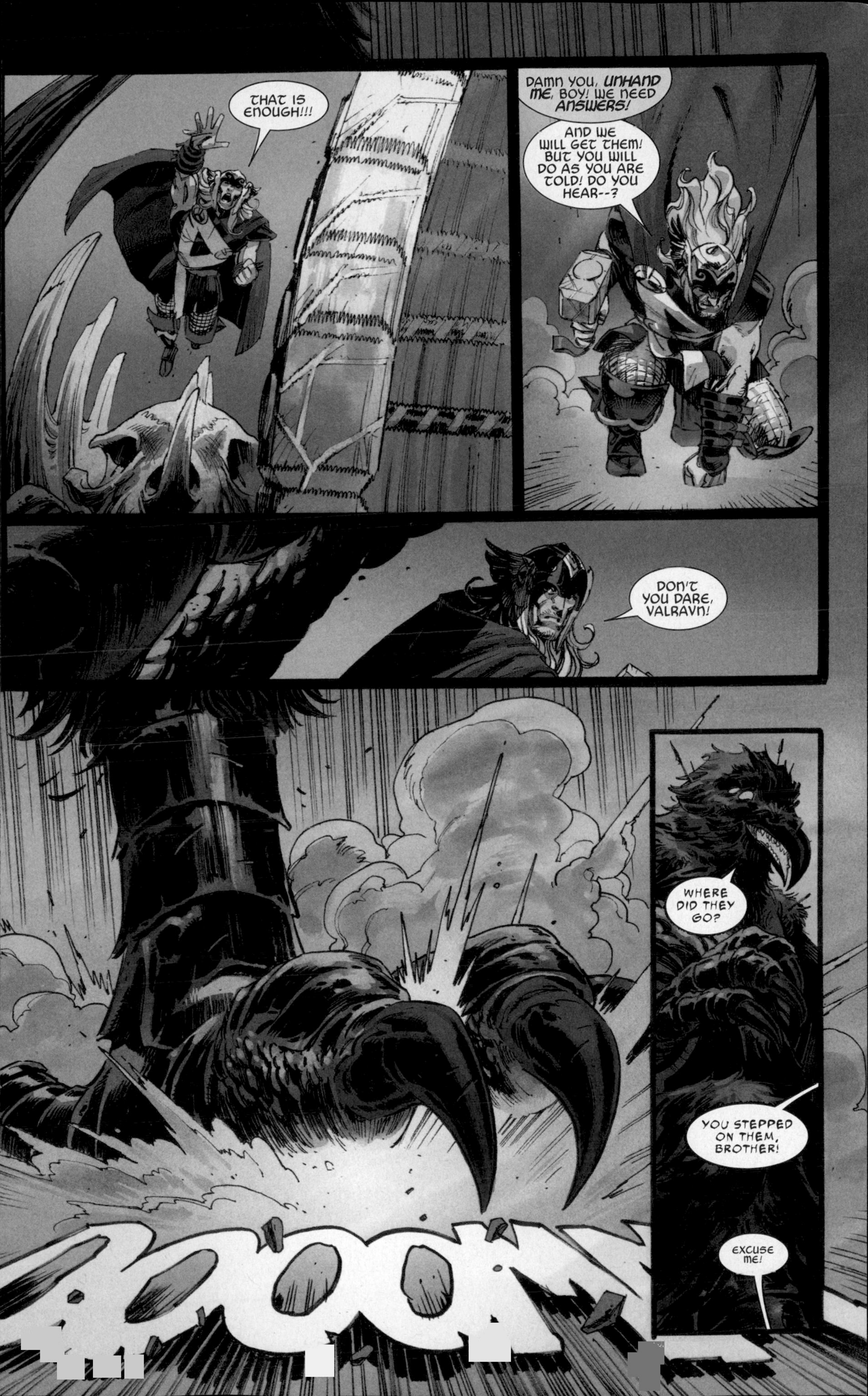
THAT IS ENOUGH!!!
DAMN YOU, UNHAND ME, BOY! WE NEED ANSWERS!
AND WE WILL GET THEM! BUT YOU WILL DO AS YOU ARE TOLD! DO YOU HEAR--?
DON'T YOU DARE, VALRAVN!
WHERE DID THEY GO?
YOU STEPPED ON THEM, BROTHER!
EXCUSE ME!

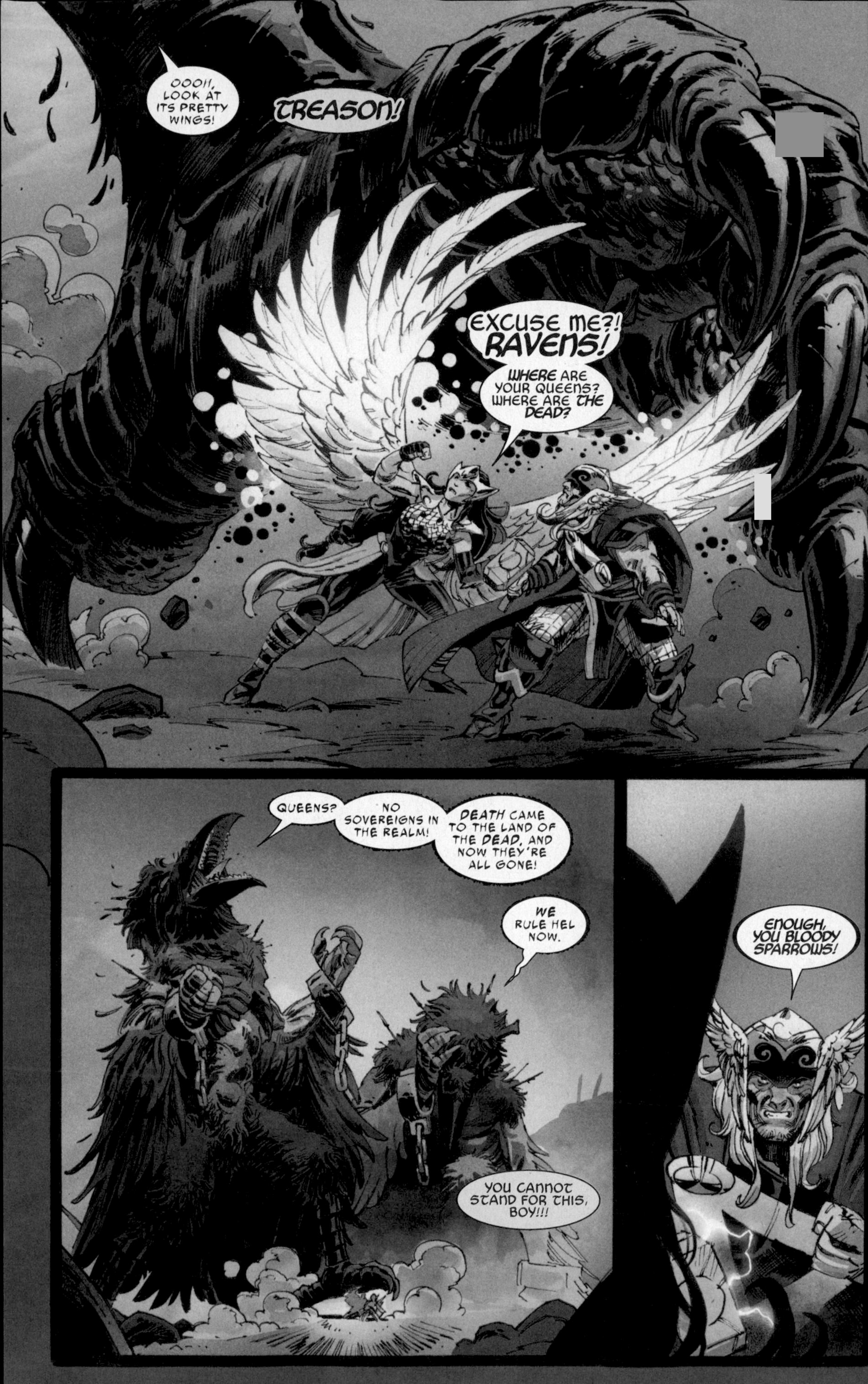
OOOH, LOOK AT ITS PRETTY WINGS!
TREASON!
EXCUSE ME?! RAVENS!
WHERE ARE YOUR QUEENS? WHERE ARE THE DEAD?
QUEENS?
NO SOVEREIGNS IN THE REALM!
DEATH CAME TO THE LAND OF THE DEAD, AND NOW THEY'RE ALL GONE!
WE RULE HEL NOW.
YOU CANNOT STAND FOR THIS, BOY!!!
ENOUGH, YOU BLOODY SPARROWS!

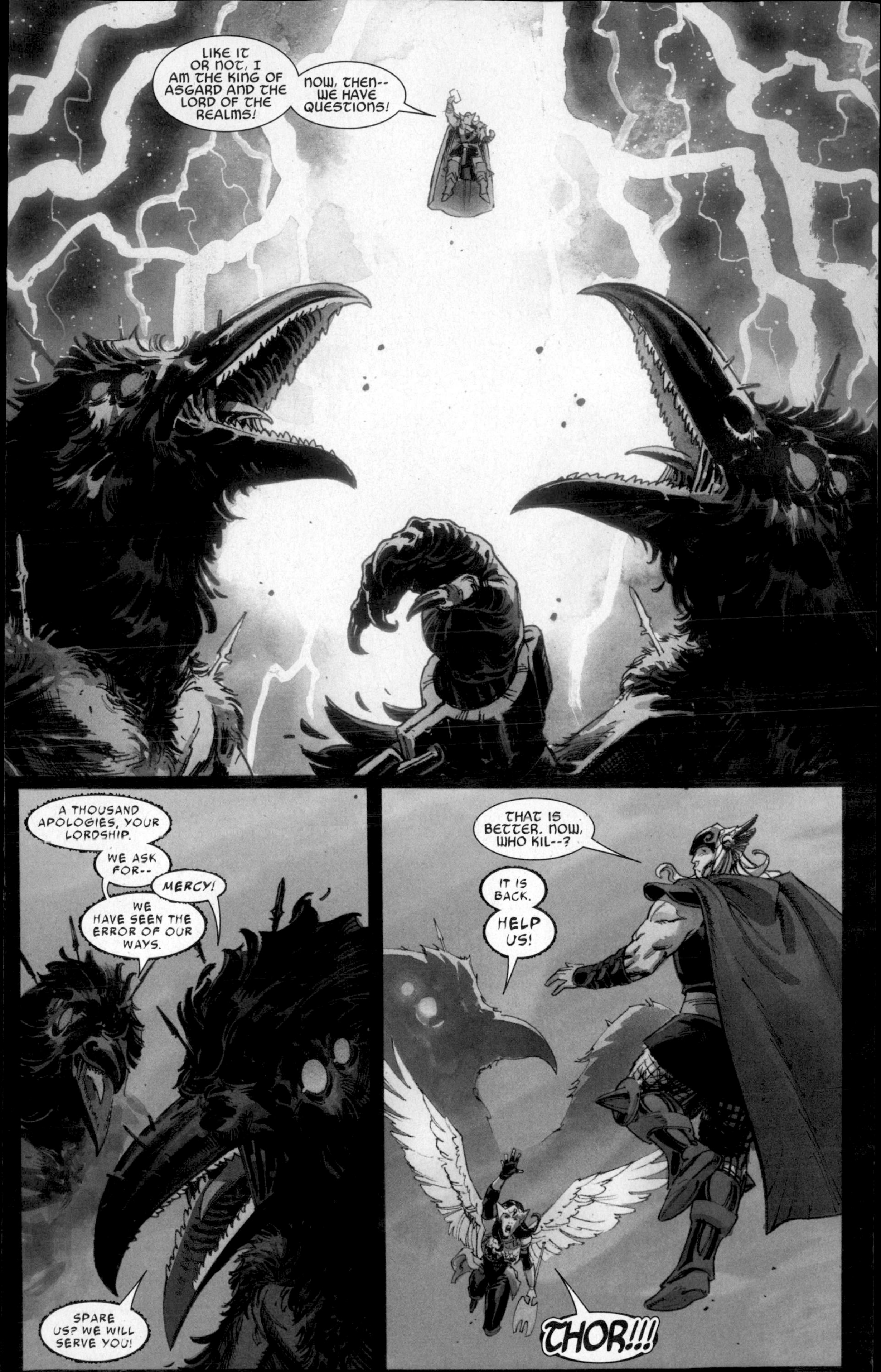
LIKE IT OR NOT, I AM THE KING OF ASGARD AND THE LORD OF THE REALMS!
NOW, THEN-- WE HAVE QUESTIONS!
A THOUSAND APOLOGIES, YOUR LORDSHIP.
WE ASK FOR--
MERCY!
WE HAVE SEEN THE ERROR OF OUR WAYS.
SPARE US? WE WILL SERVE YOU!
THAT IS BETTER. NOW, WHO KIL--?
IT IS BACK.
HELP US!
THOR!!!

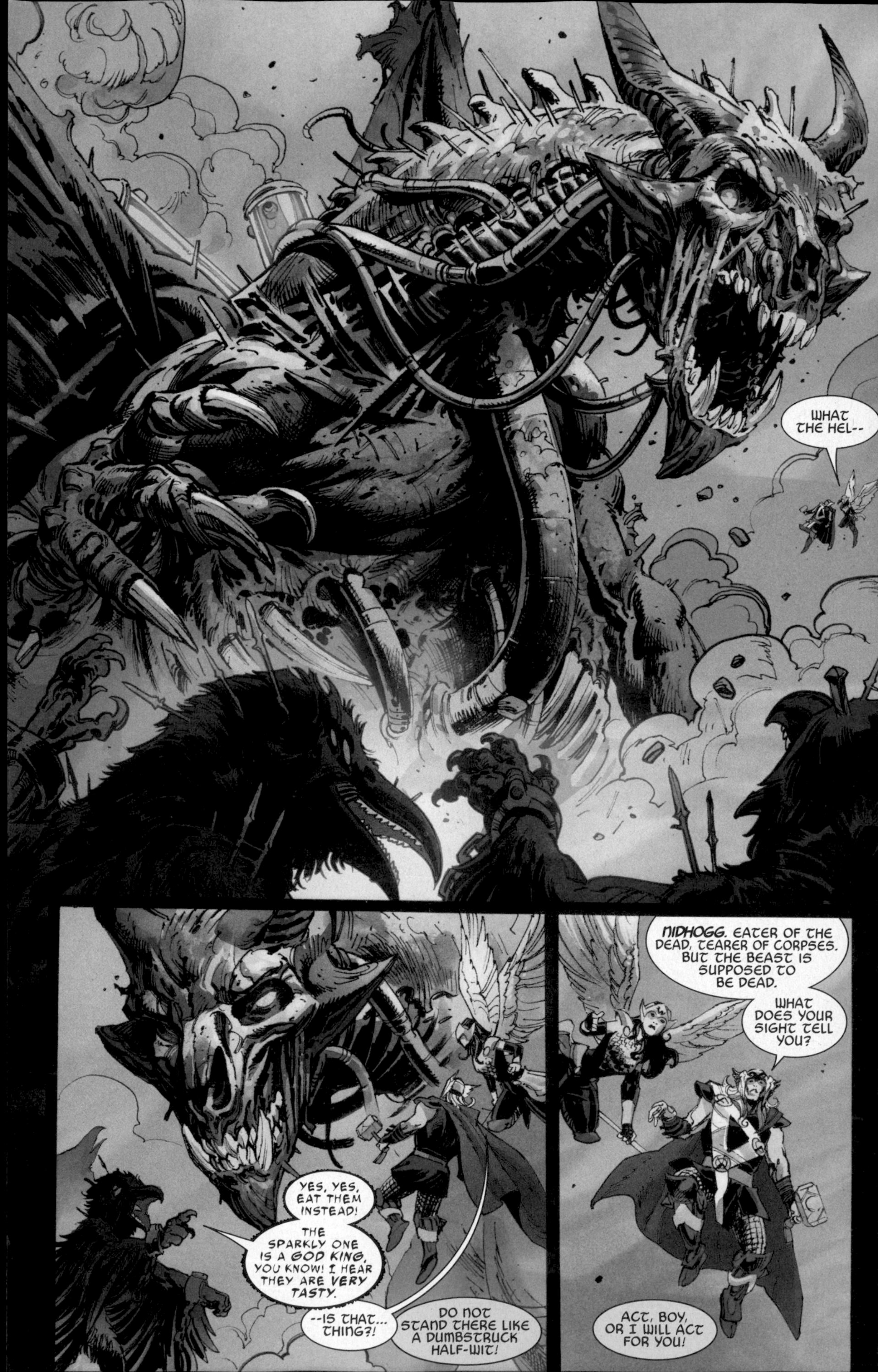
WHAT THE HEL--
YES, YES, EAT THEM INSTEAD!
THE SPARKLY ONE IS A GOD KING, YOU KNOW! I HEAR THEY ARE VERY TASTY.
--IS THAT... THING?!
DO NOT STAND THERE LIKE A DUMBSTRUCK HALF-WIT!
NIDHOGG. EATER OF THE DEAD, TEARER OF CORPSES. BUT THE BEAST IS SUPPOSED TO BE DEAD.
WHAT DOES YOUR SIGHT TELL YOU?
ACT, BOY, OR I WILL ACT FOR YOU!

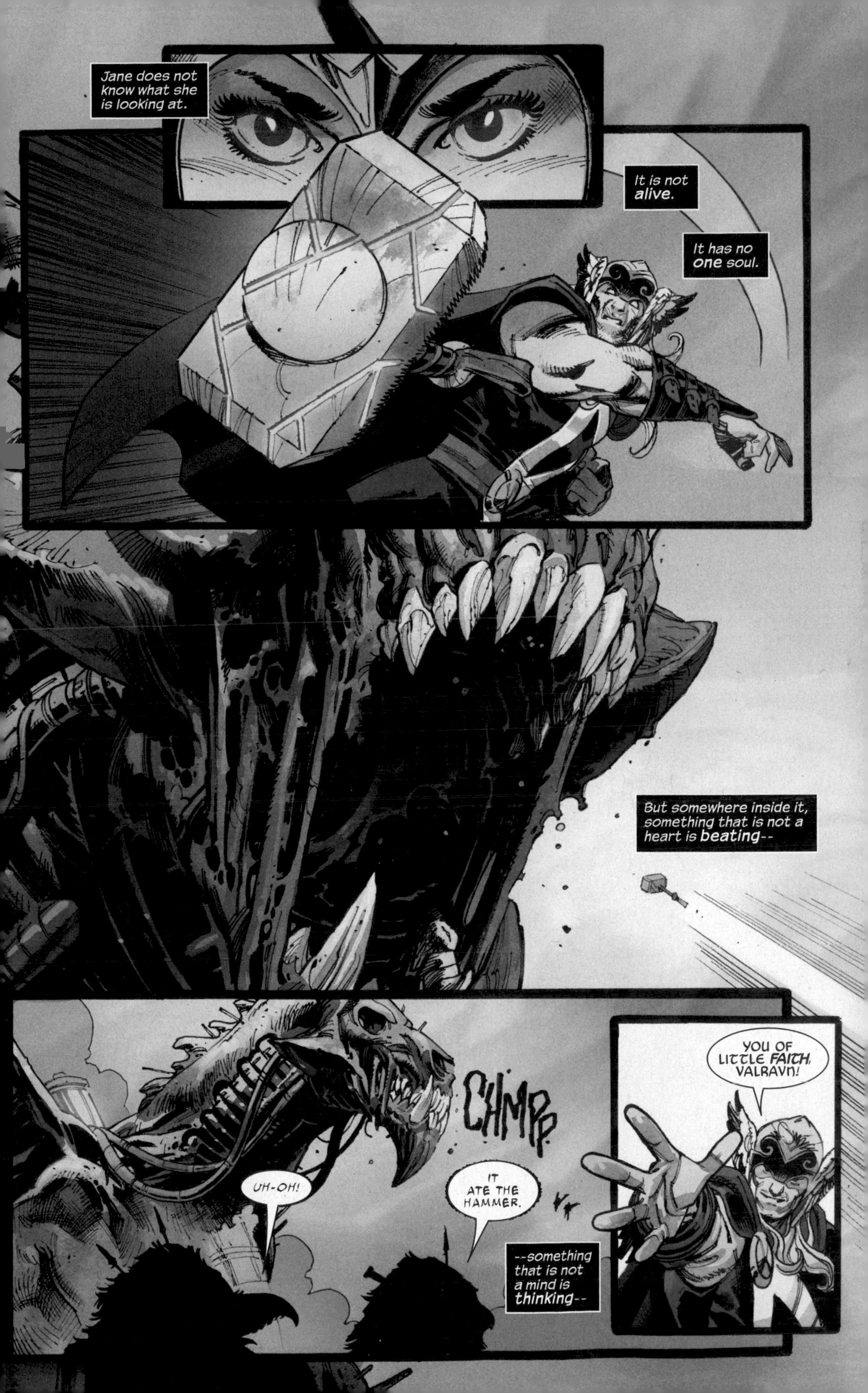
Jane does not know what she is looking at.
It is not **alive.**
It has no **one** soul.
But somewhere inside it, something that is not a heart is **beating**--
CHMPP
UH-OH!
IT ATE THE HAMMER.
--something that is not a mind is **thinking**--
YOU OF LITTLE FAITH, VALRAVN!

--something that is not a soul is screaming.
BOOOMMM
SORRY ABOUT THE SNAKE GOO, FATHER.
THMMPP
...F-FATHER?
"IT IS NOT THE BEGINNING OF THE END..."

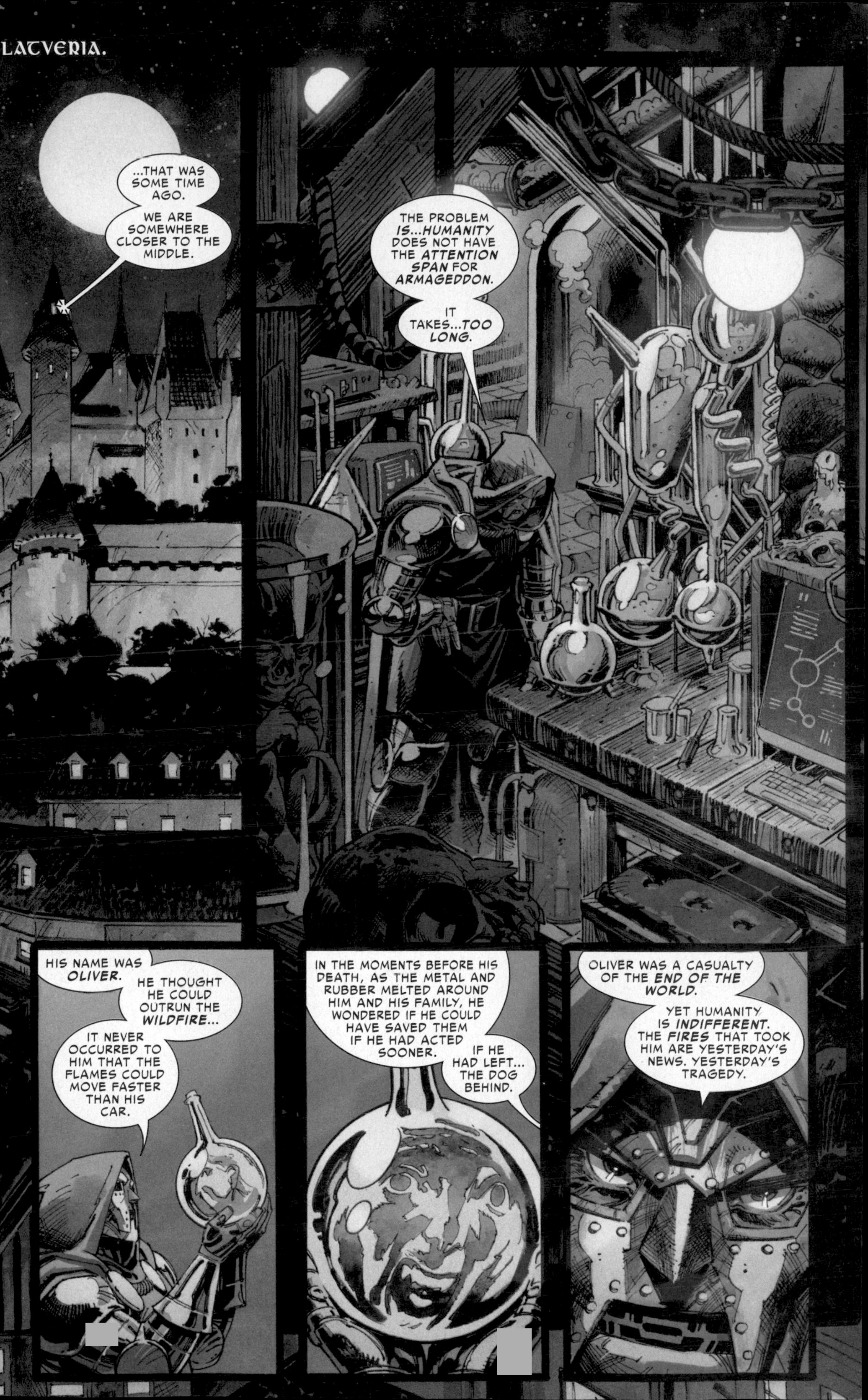

LATVERIA.
...THAT WAS SOME TIME AGO.
WE ARE SOMEWHERE CLOSER TO THE MIDDLE.
THE PROBLEM IS...HUMANITY DOES NOT HAVE THE ATTENTION SPAN FOR ARMAGEDDON.
IT TAKES...TOO LONG.
HIS NAME WAS OLIVER.
HE THOUGHT HE COULD OUTRUN THE WILDFIRE...
IT NEVER OCCURRED TO HIM THAT THE FLAMES COULD MOVE FASTER THAN HIS CAR.
IN THE MOMENTS BEFORE HIS DEATH, AS THE METAL AND RUBBER MELTED AROUND HIM AND HIS FAMILY, HE WONDERED IF HE COULD HAVE SAVED THEM IF HE HAD ACTED SOONER.
IF HE HAD LEFT... THE DOG BEHIND.
OLIVER WAS A CASUALTY OF THE END OF THE WORLD.
YET HUMANITY IS INDIFFERENT. THE FIRES THAT TOOK HIM ARE YESTERDAY'S NEWS. YESTERDAY'S TRAGEDY.

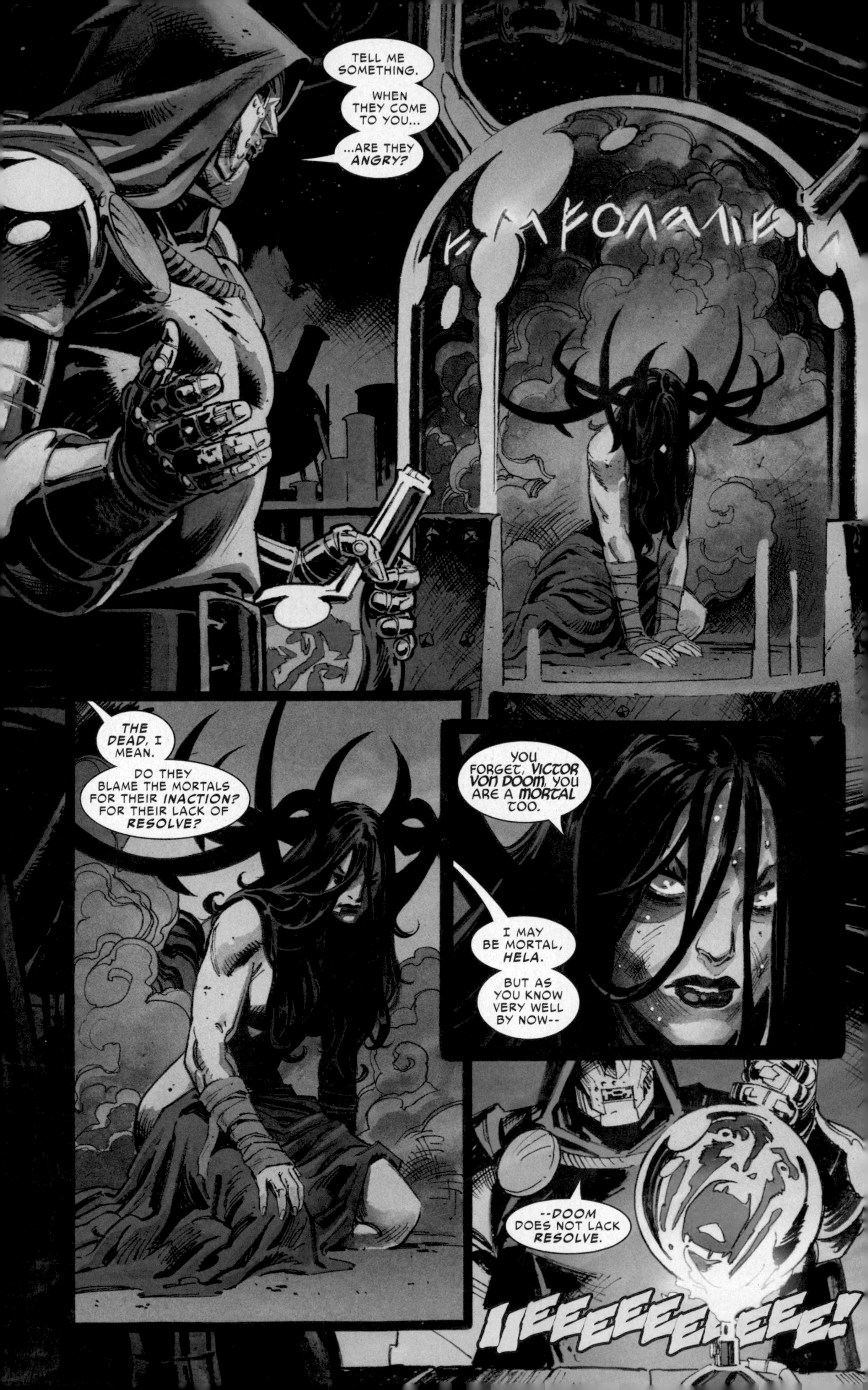
TELL ME SOMETHING.
WHEN THEY COME TO YOU...
...ARE THEY ANGRY?
THE DEAD, I MEAN.
DO THEY BLAME THE MORTALS FOR THEIR INACTION? FOR THEIR LACK OF RESOLVE?
YOU FORGET, VICTOR VON DOOM, YOU ARE A MORTAL TOO.
I MAY BE MORTAL, HELA.
BUT AS YOU KNOW VERY WELL BY NOW--
--DOOM DOES NOT LACK RESOLVE.
IIEEEEEEEEEE!

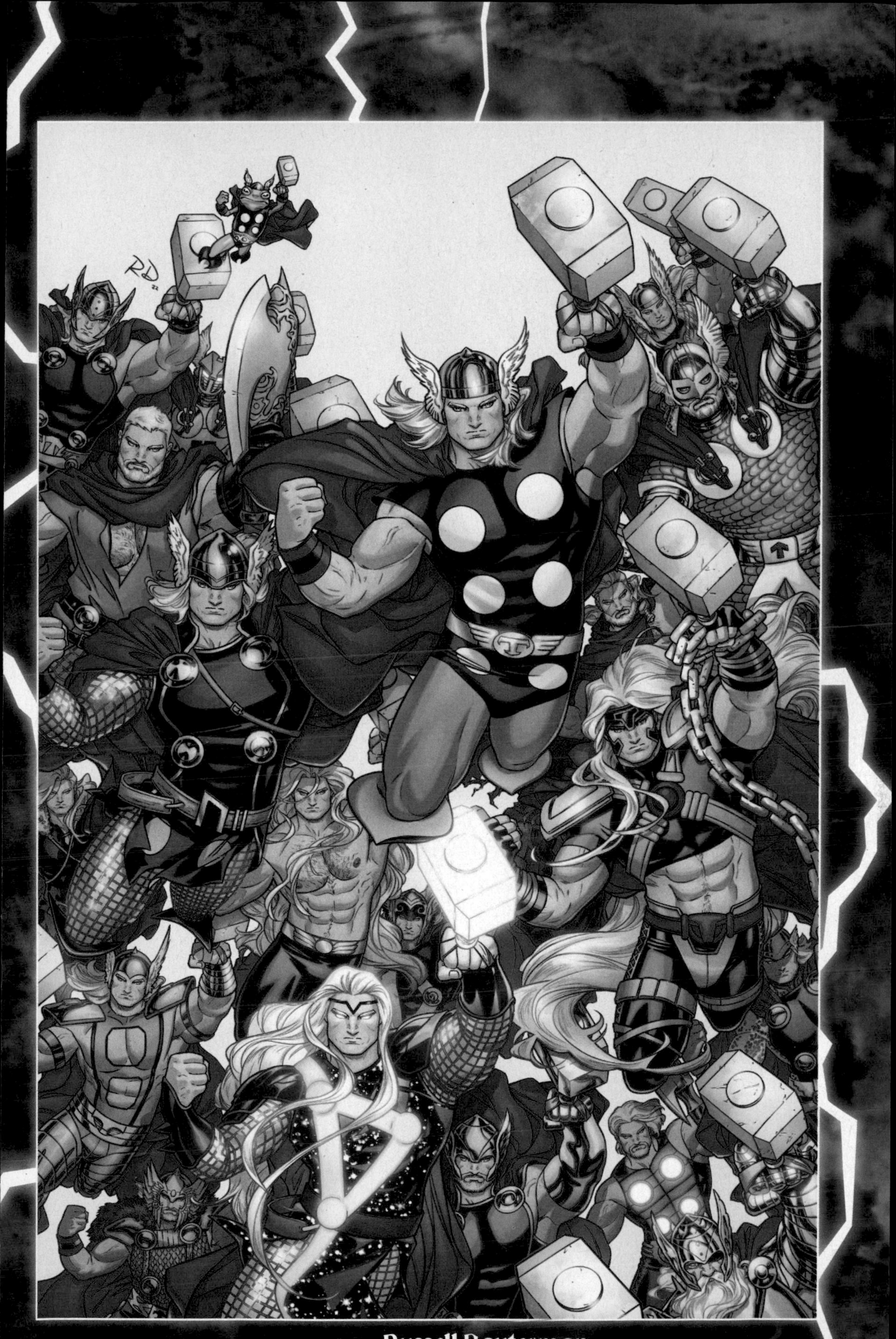

#31 VARIANT BY **Russell Dauterman**

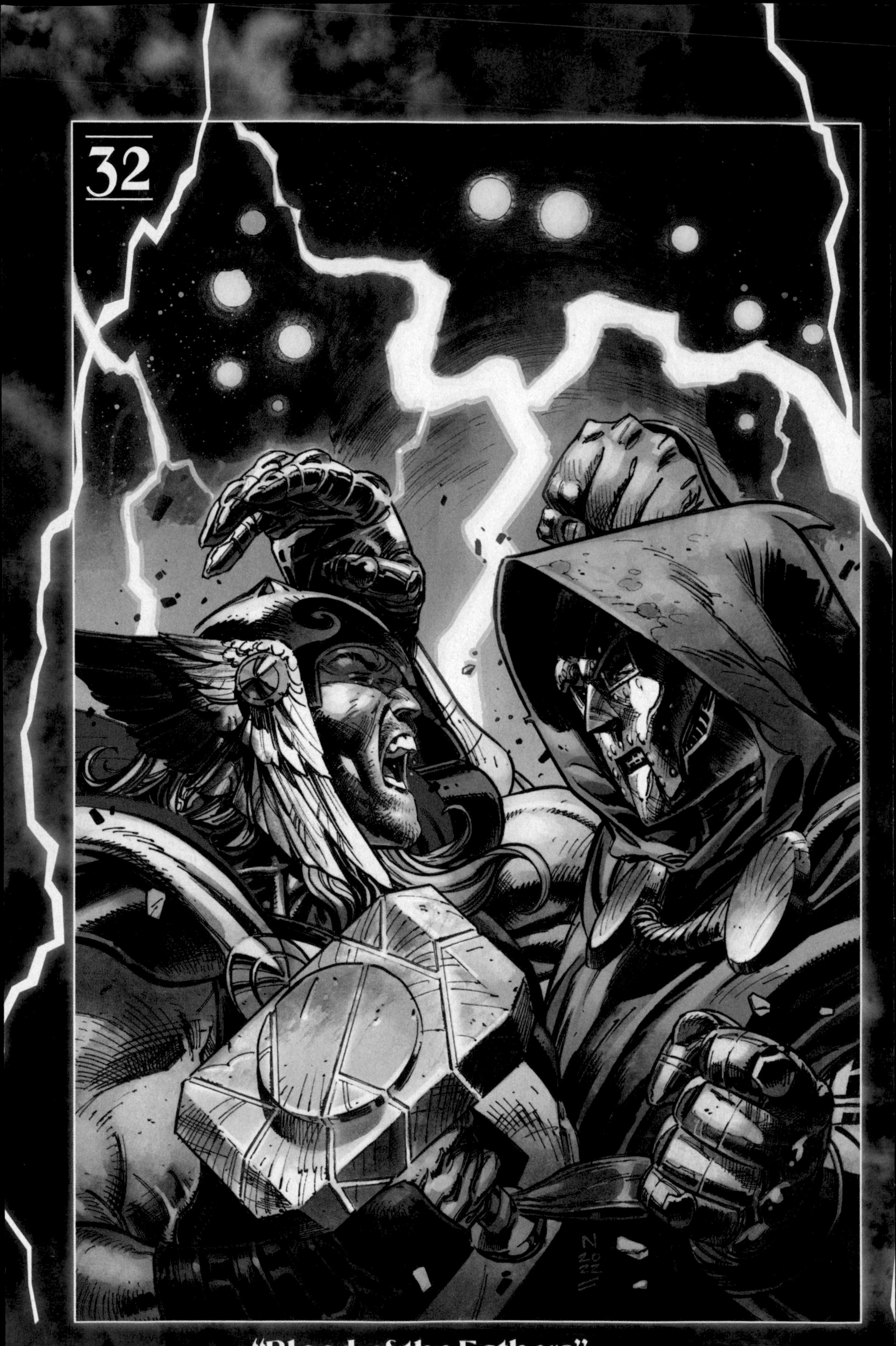
32

"Blood of the Fathers" PART TWO

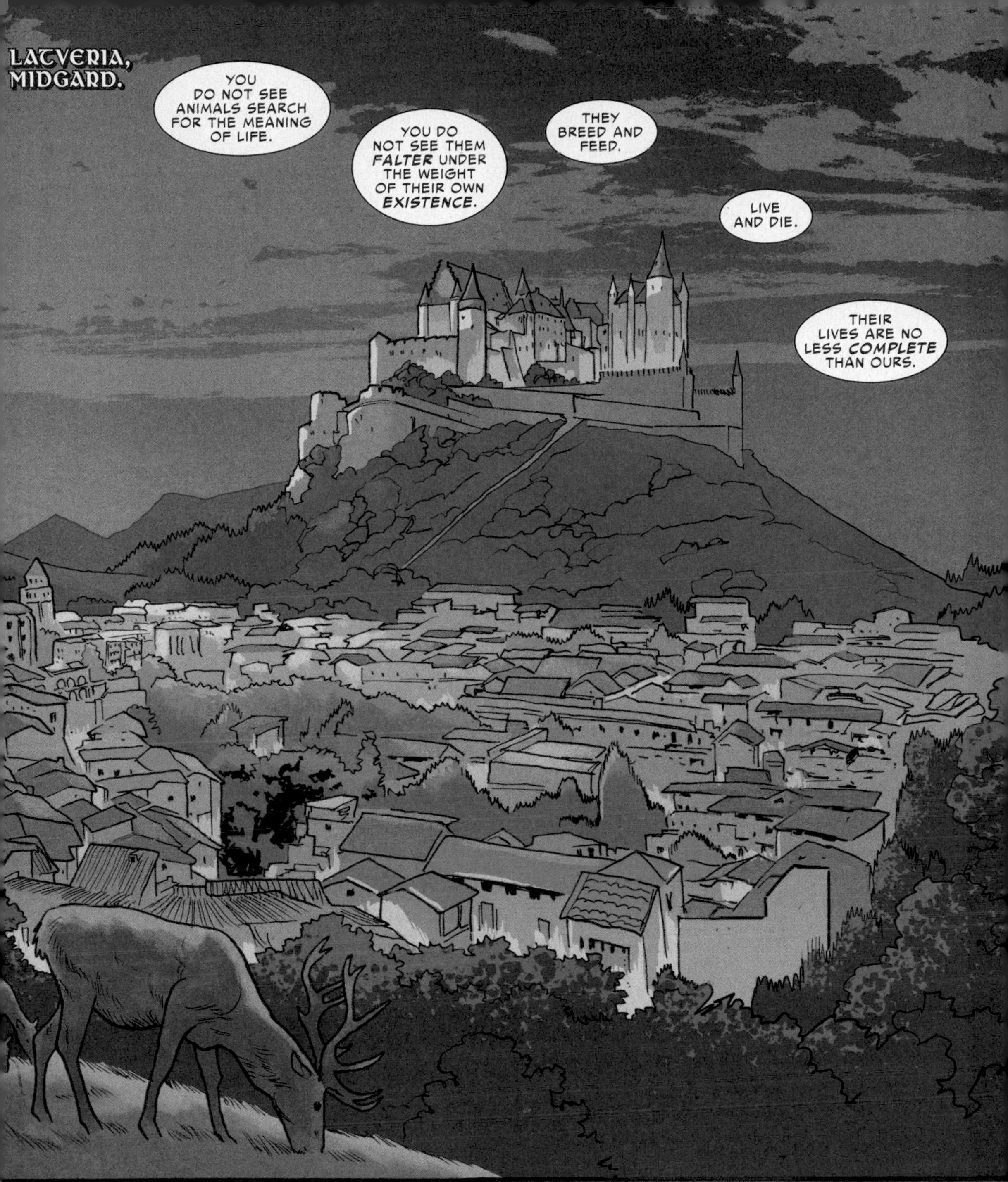
LATVERIA, MIDGARD.
YOU DO NOT SEE ANIMALS SEARCH FOR THE MEANING OF LIFE.
YOU DO NOT SEE THEM FALTER UNDER THE WEIGHT OF THEIR OWN EXISTENCE.
THEY BREED AND FEED.
LIVE AND DIE.
THEIR LIVES ARE NO LESS COMPLETE THAN OURS.
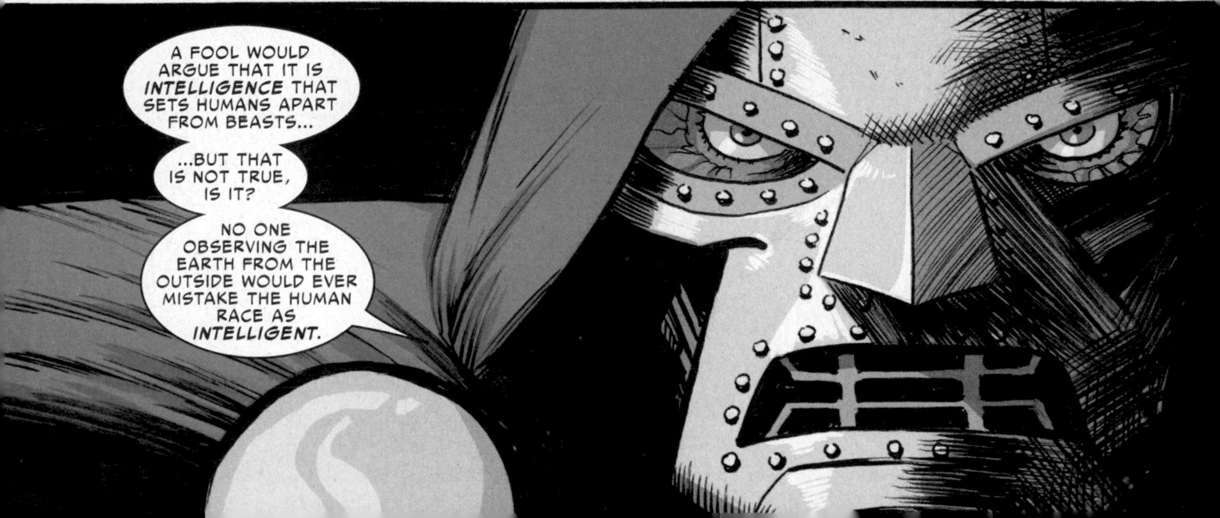
A FOOL WOULD ARGUE THAT IT IS INTELLIGENCE THAT SETS HUMANS APART FROM BEASTS...
...BUT THAT IS NOT TRUE, IS IT?
NO ONE OBSERVING THE EARTH FROM THE OUTSIDE WOULD EVER MISTAKE THE HUMAN RACE AS INTELLIGENT.

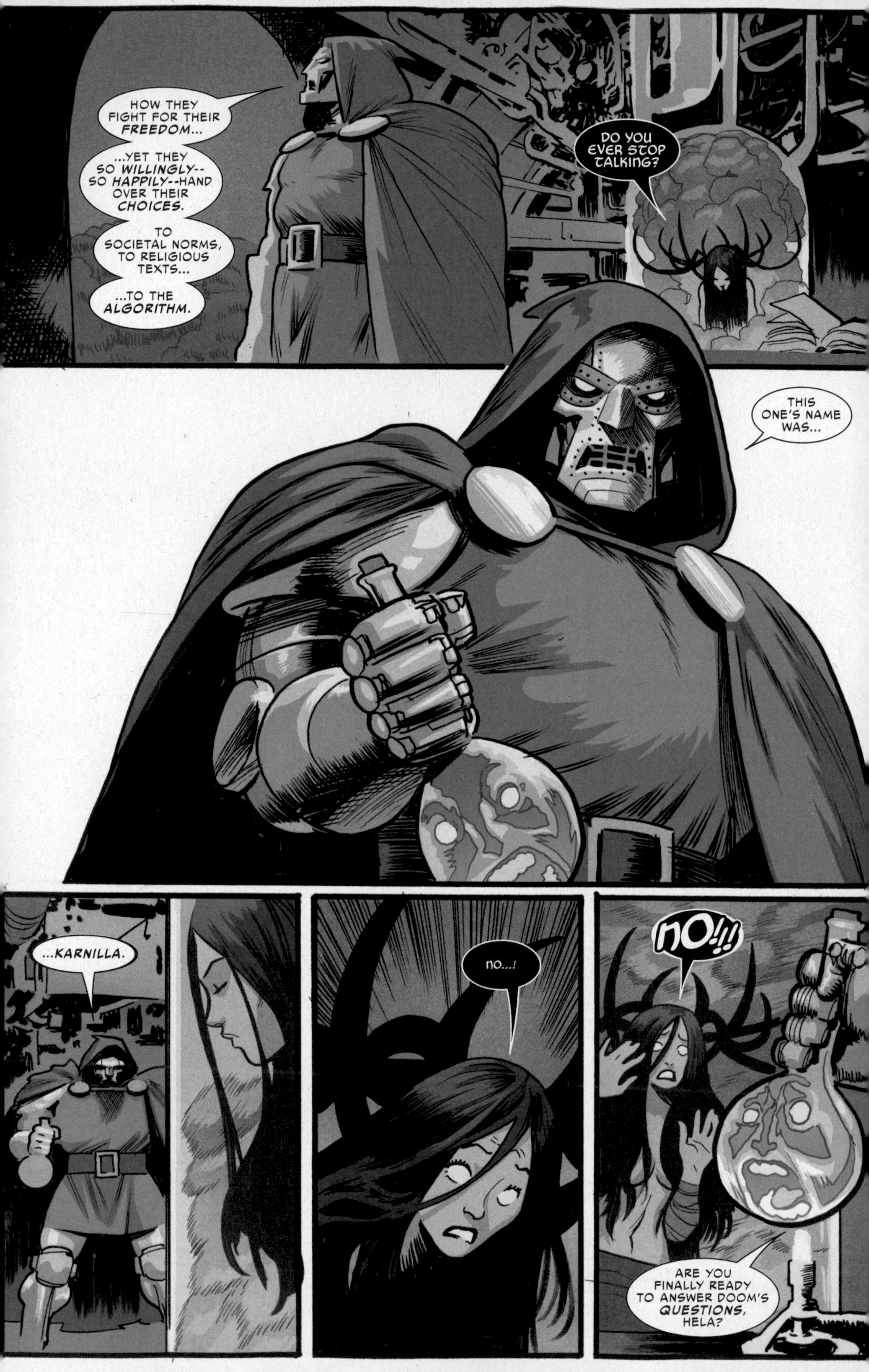

HOW THEY FIGHT FOR THEIR FREEDOM...
...YET THEY SO WILLINGLY--SO HAPPILY--HAND OVER THEIR CHOICES.
TO SOCIETAL NORMS, TO RELIGIOUS TEXTS...
...TO THE ALGORITHM.
DO YOU EVER STOP TALKING?
THIS ONE'S NAME WAS...
...KARNILLA.
no...!
NO!!!
ARE YOU FINALLY READY TO ANSWER DOOM'S QUESTIONS, HELA?

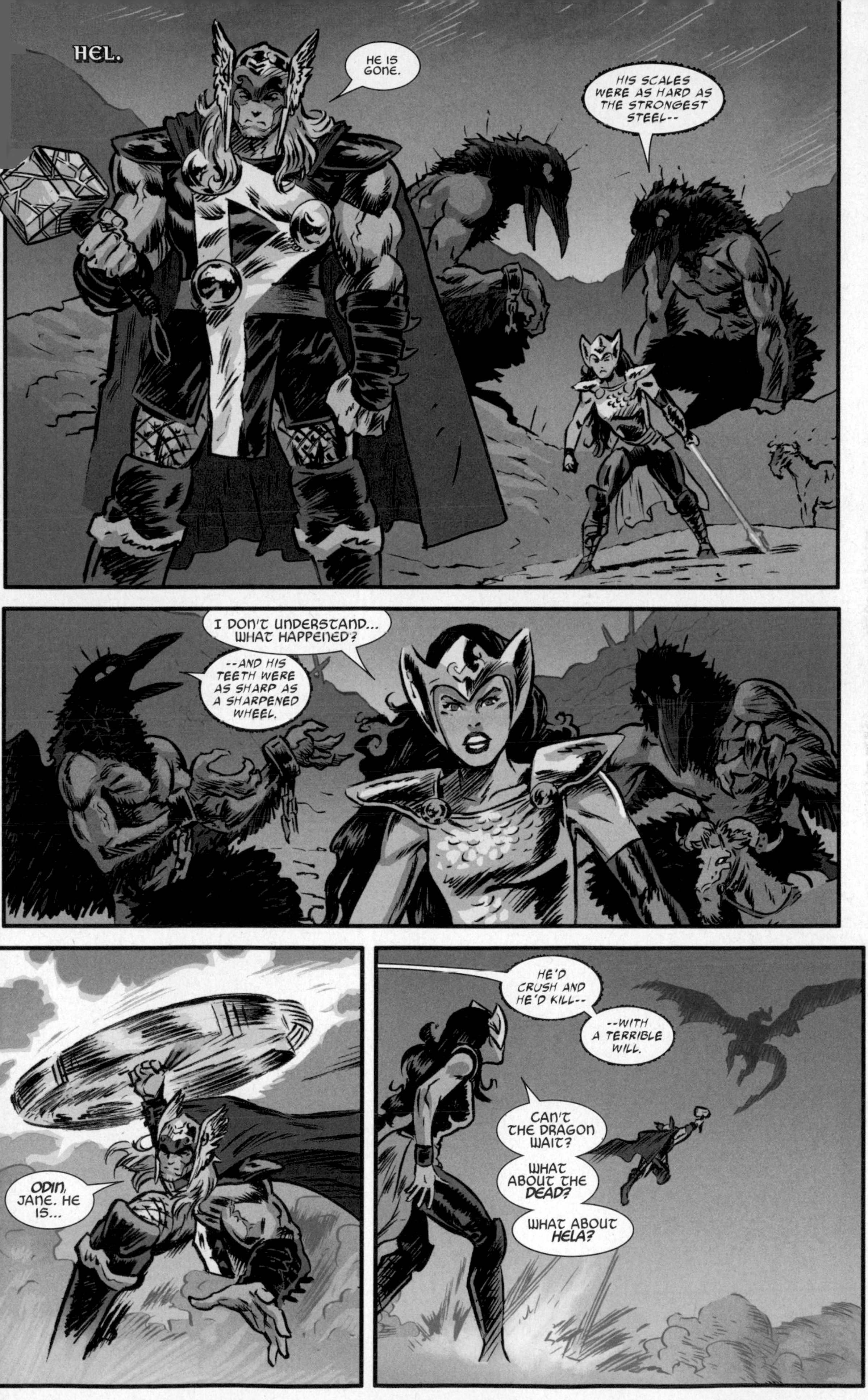
HEL.
HE IS GONE.
HIS SCALES WERE AS HARD AS THE STRONGEST STEEL--
I DON'T UNDERSTAND... WHAT HAPPENED?
--AND HIS TEETH WERE AS SHARP AS A SHARPENED WHEEL.
ODIN, JANE. HE IS...
HE'D CRUSH AND HE'D KILL--
--WITH A TERRIBLE WILL.
CAN'T THE DRAGON WAIT?
WHAT ABOUT THE DEAD?
WHAT ABOUT HELA?

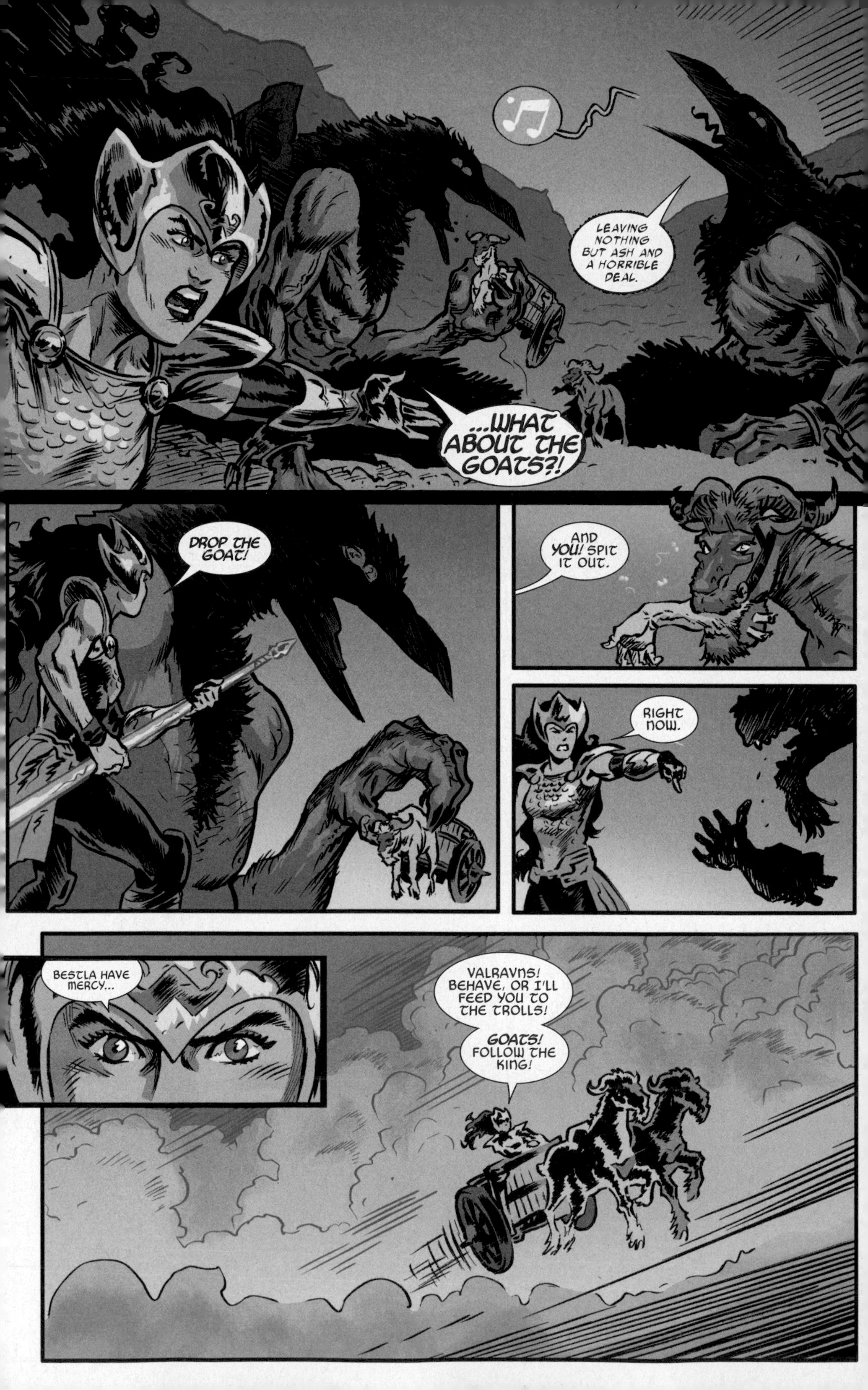
LEAVING NOTHING BUT ASH AND A HORRIBLE DEAL.
...WHAT ABOUT THE GOATS?!
DROP THE GOAT!
AND YOU! SPIT IT OUT.
RIGHT NOW.
BESTLA HAVE MERCY...
VALRAVNS! BEHAVE, OR I'LL FEED YOU TO THE TROLLS!
GOATS! FOLLOW THE KING!

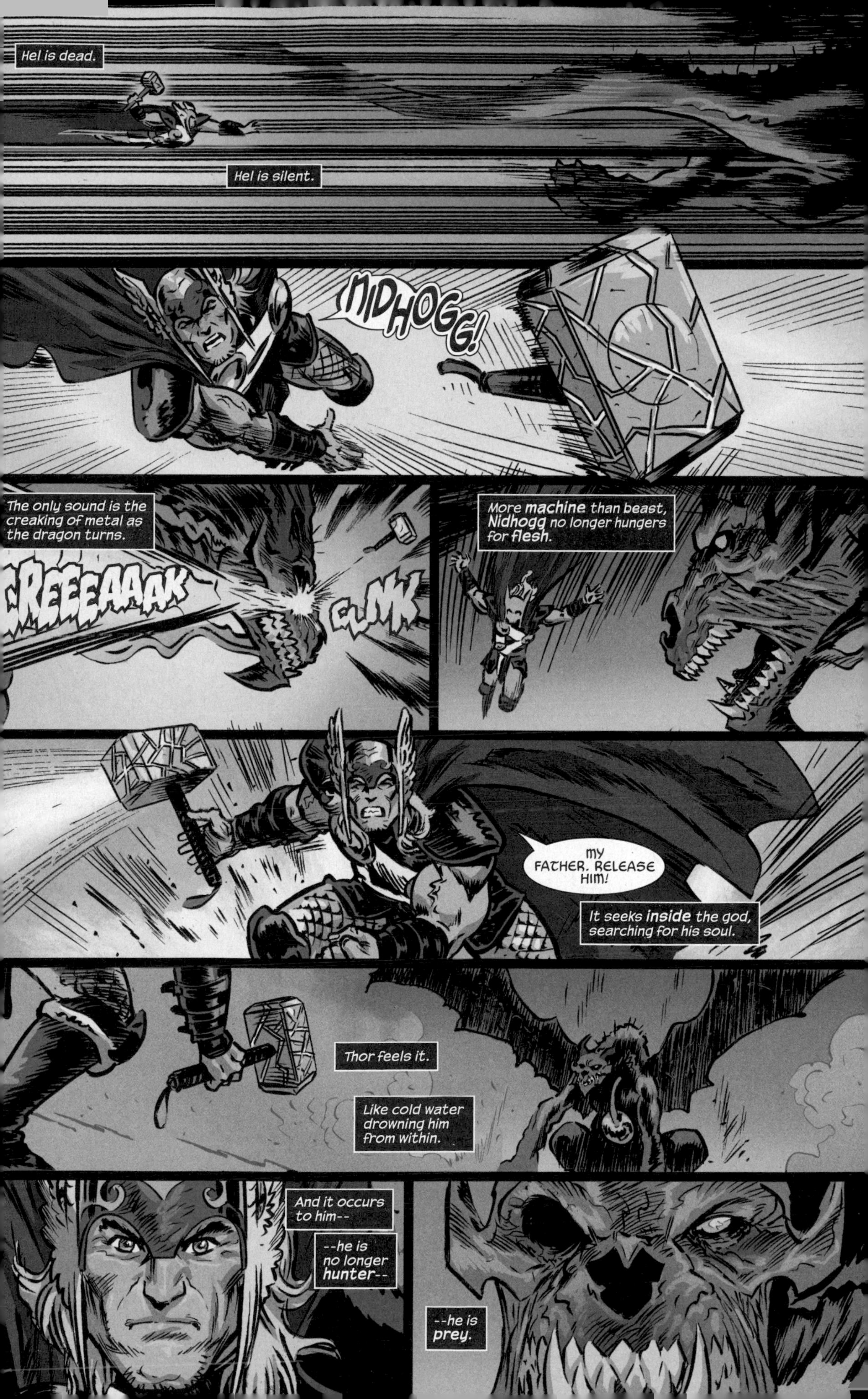
Hel is dead.
Hel is silent.
NIDHOGG!
The only sound is the creaking of metal as the dragon turns.
CREEEAAAK
CLUNK
More machine than beast, Nidhogg no longer hungers for flesh.
MY FATHER. RELEASE HIM!
It seeks inside the god, searching for his soul.
Thor feels it.
Like cold water drowning him from within.
And it occurs to him--
--he is no longer hunter--
--he is prey.

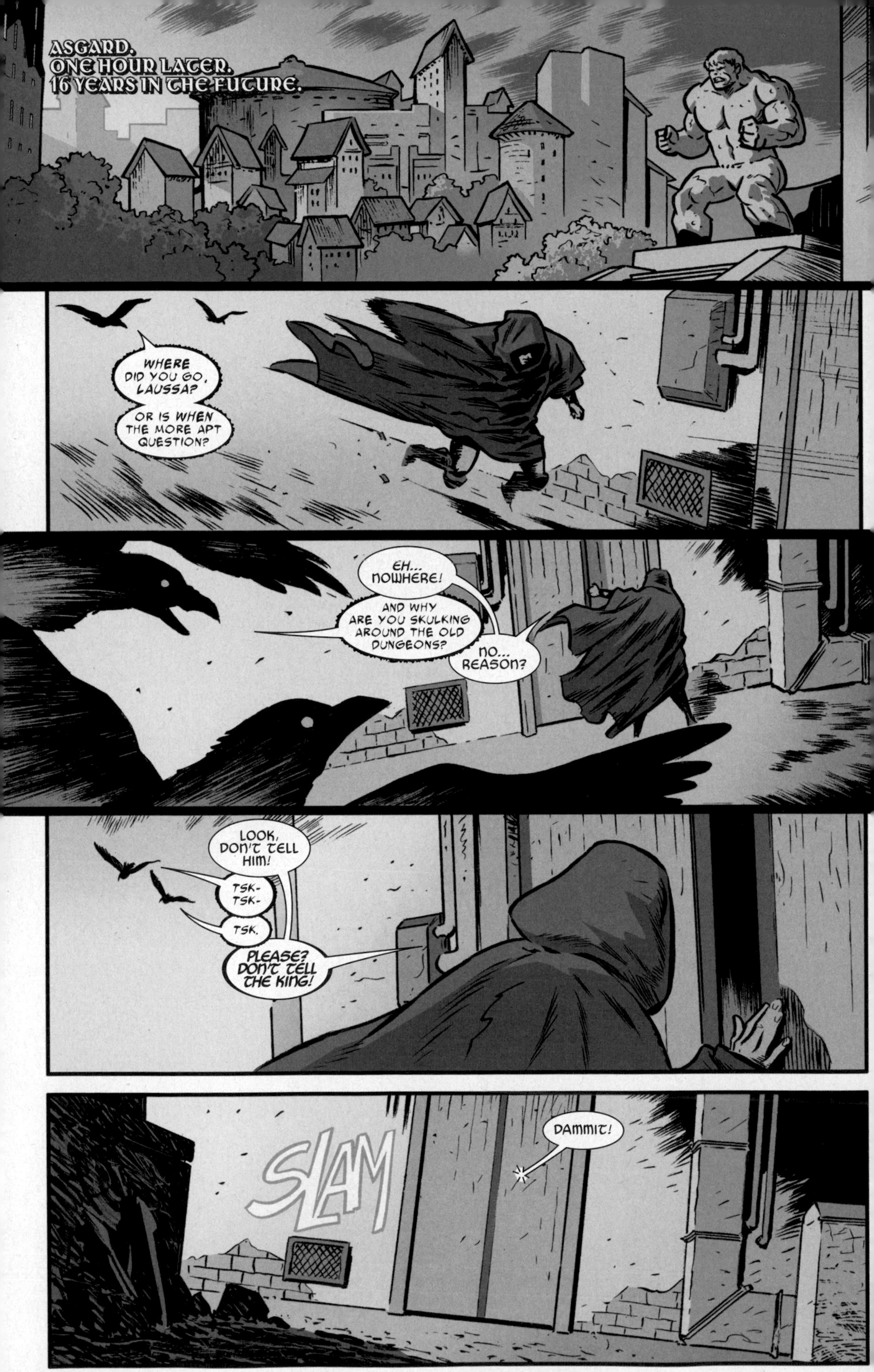
ASGARD.
ONE HOUR LATER.
16 YEARS IN THE FUTURE.
WHERE DID YOU GO, LAUSSA?
OR IS WHEN THE MORE APT QUESTION?
EH... NOWHERE!
AND WHY ARE YOU SKULKING AROUND THE OLD DUNGEONS?
NO... REASON?
LOOK, DON'T TELL HIM!
TSK-
TSK-
TSK.
PLEASE? DON'T TELL THE KING!
SLAM
DAMMIT!

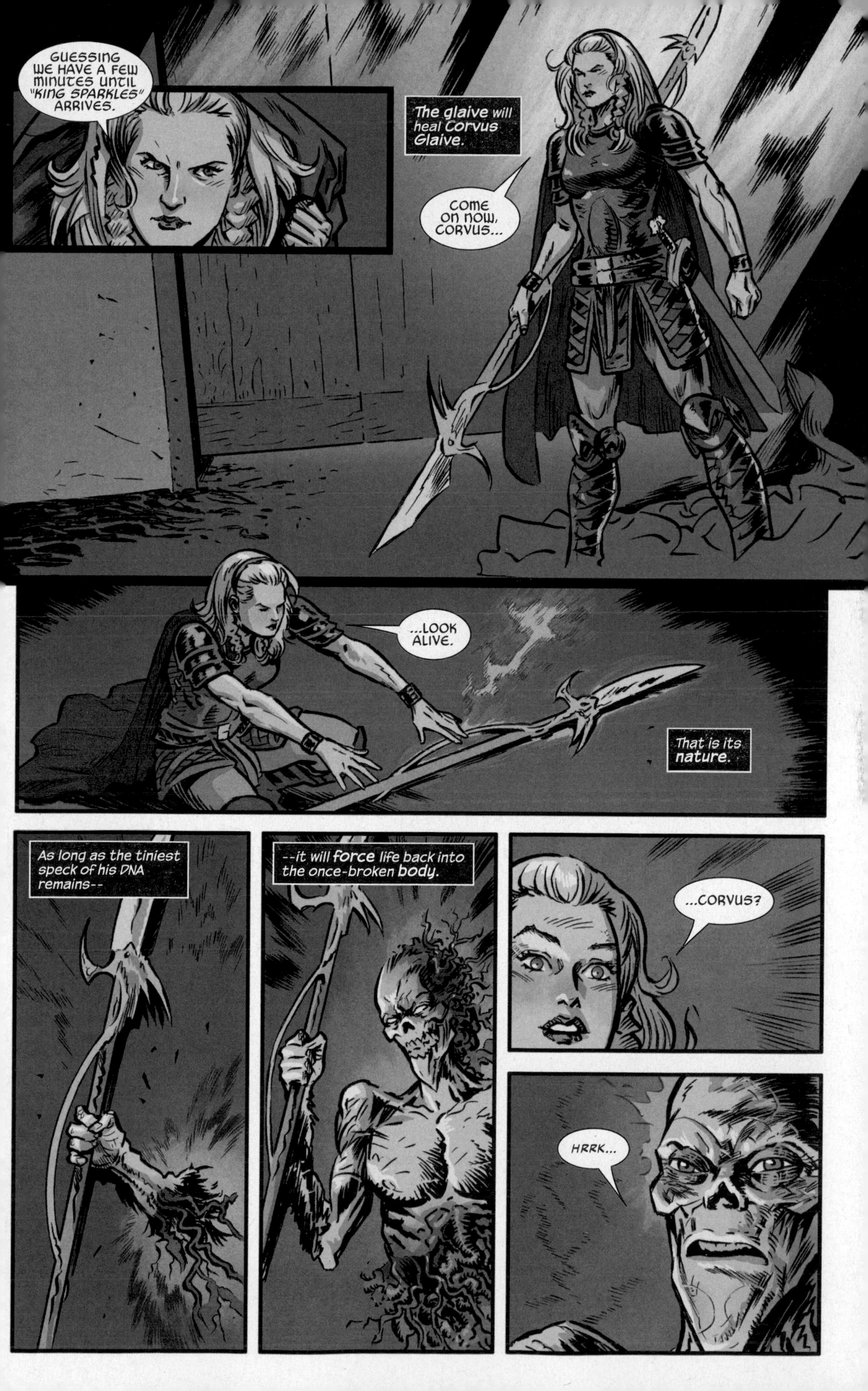
GUESSING WE HAVE A FEW MINUTES UNTIL "KING SPARKLES" ARRIVES.
The glaive will heal Corvus Glaive.
COME ON NOW, CORVUS...
...LOOK ALIVE.
That is its nature.
As long as the tiniest speck of his DNA remains--
--it will force life back into the once-broken body.
...CORVUS?
HRRK...

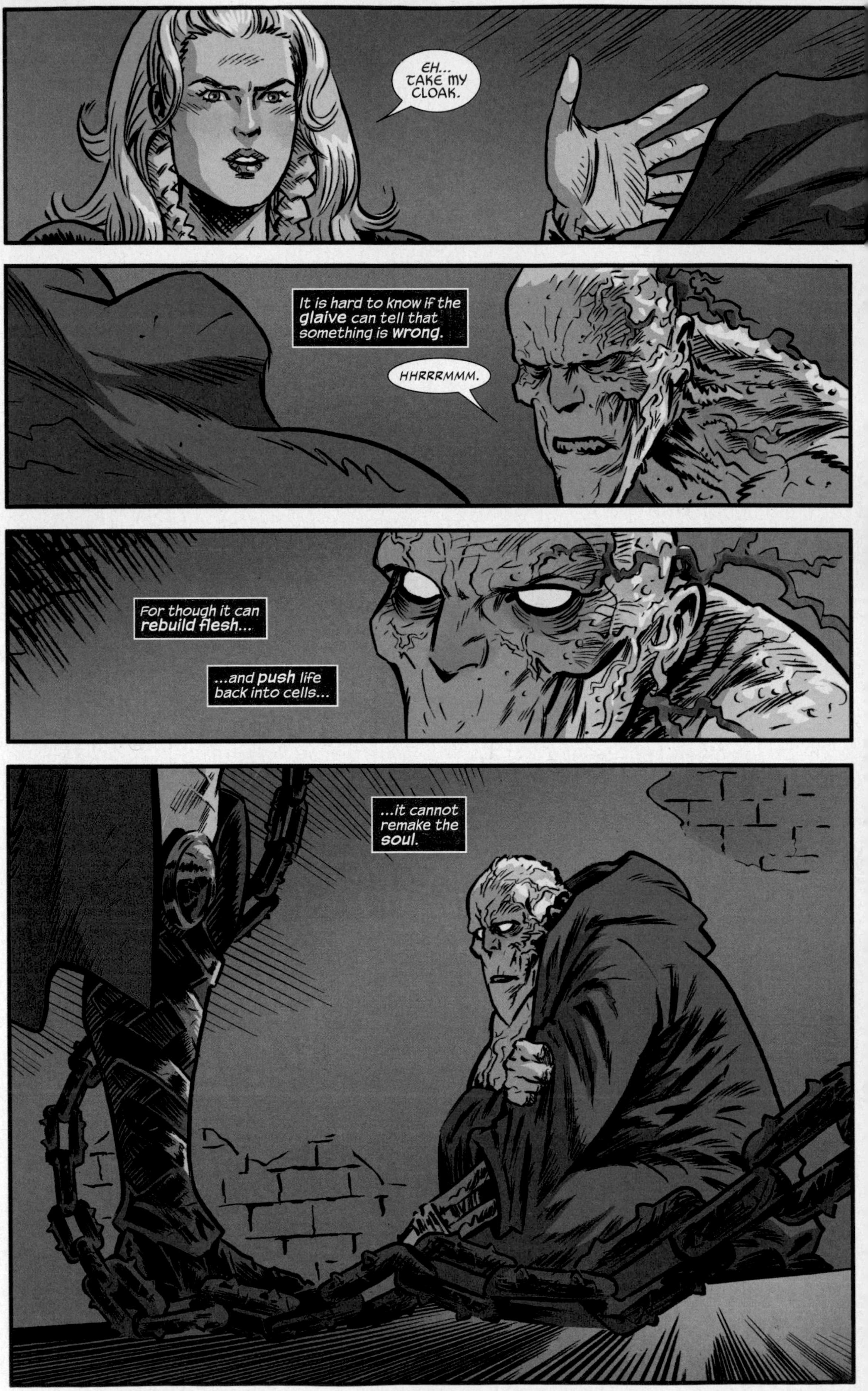
EH... TAKE MY CLOAK.
It is hard to know if the glaive can tell that something is wrong.
HHRRRMMM.
For though it can rebuild flesh...
...and push life back into cells...
...it cannot remake the soul.

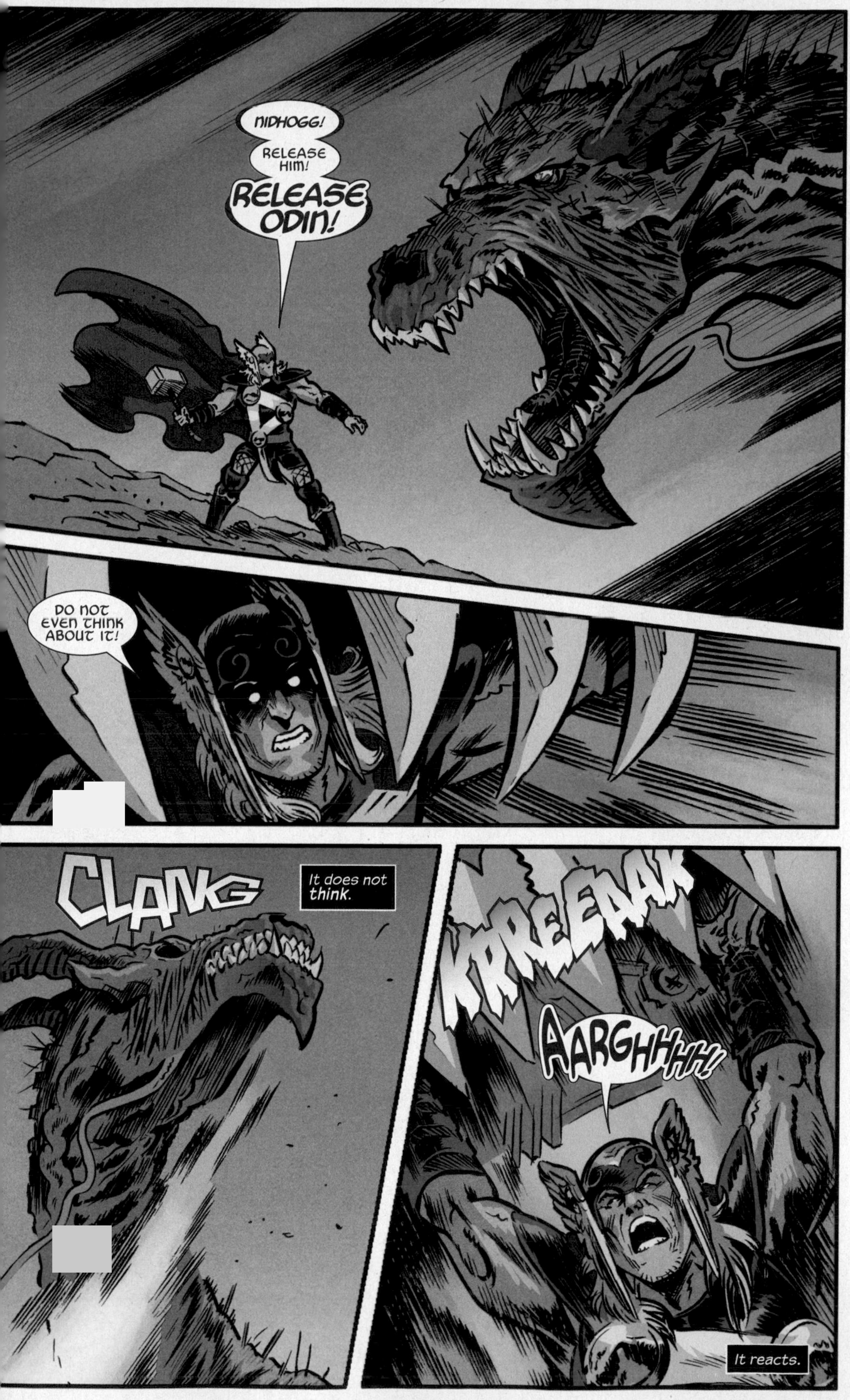
NIDHOGG!
RELEASE HIM!
RELEASE ODIN!
DO NOT EVEN THINK ABOUT IT!
CLANG
It does not think.
KRREEAAK
AARGHHHH!
It reacts.

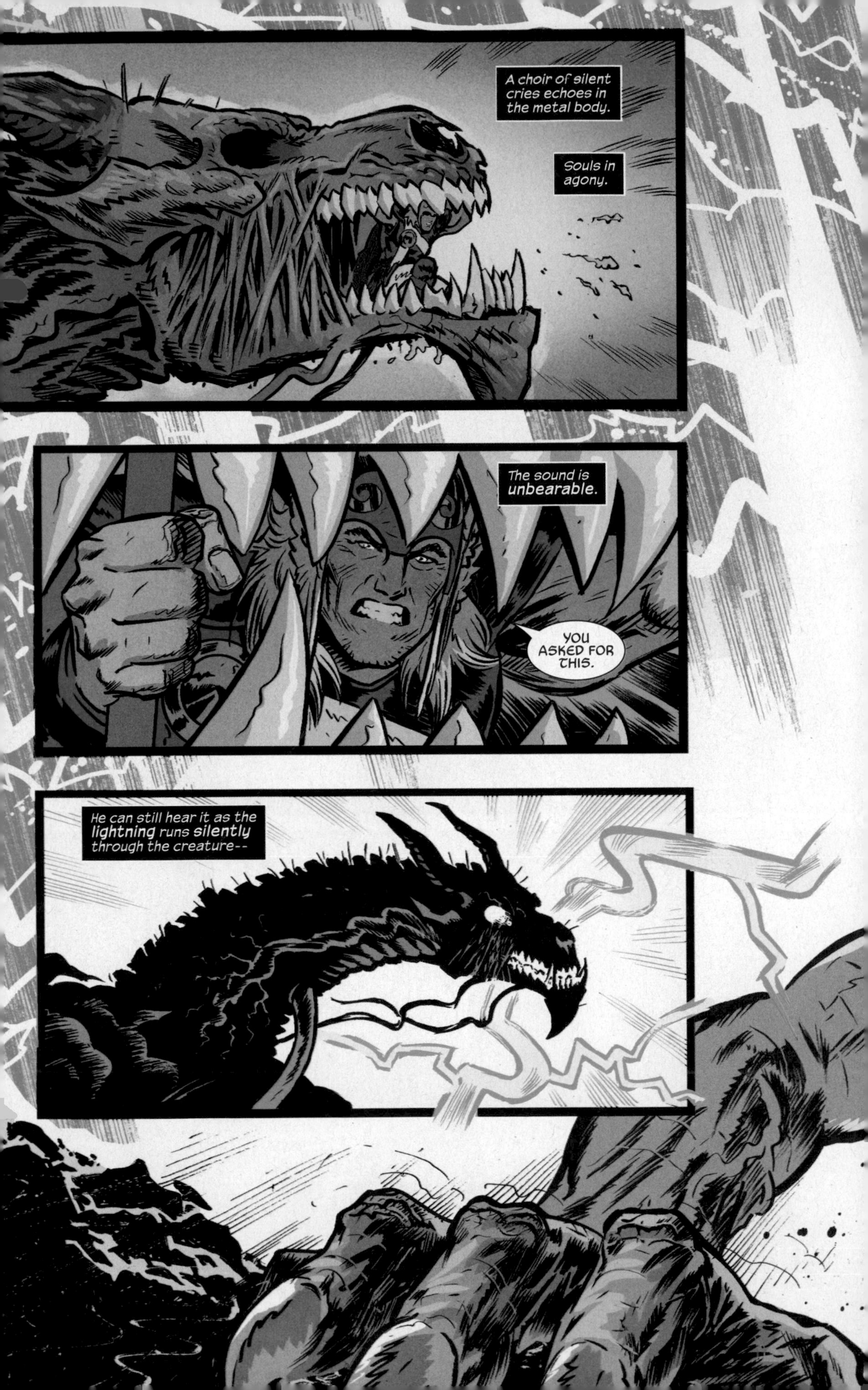
A choir of silent cries echoes in the metal body.
Souls in agony.
The sound is *unbearable.*
YOU ASKED FOR THIS.
He can still hear it as the **lightning** runs **silently** through the creature--

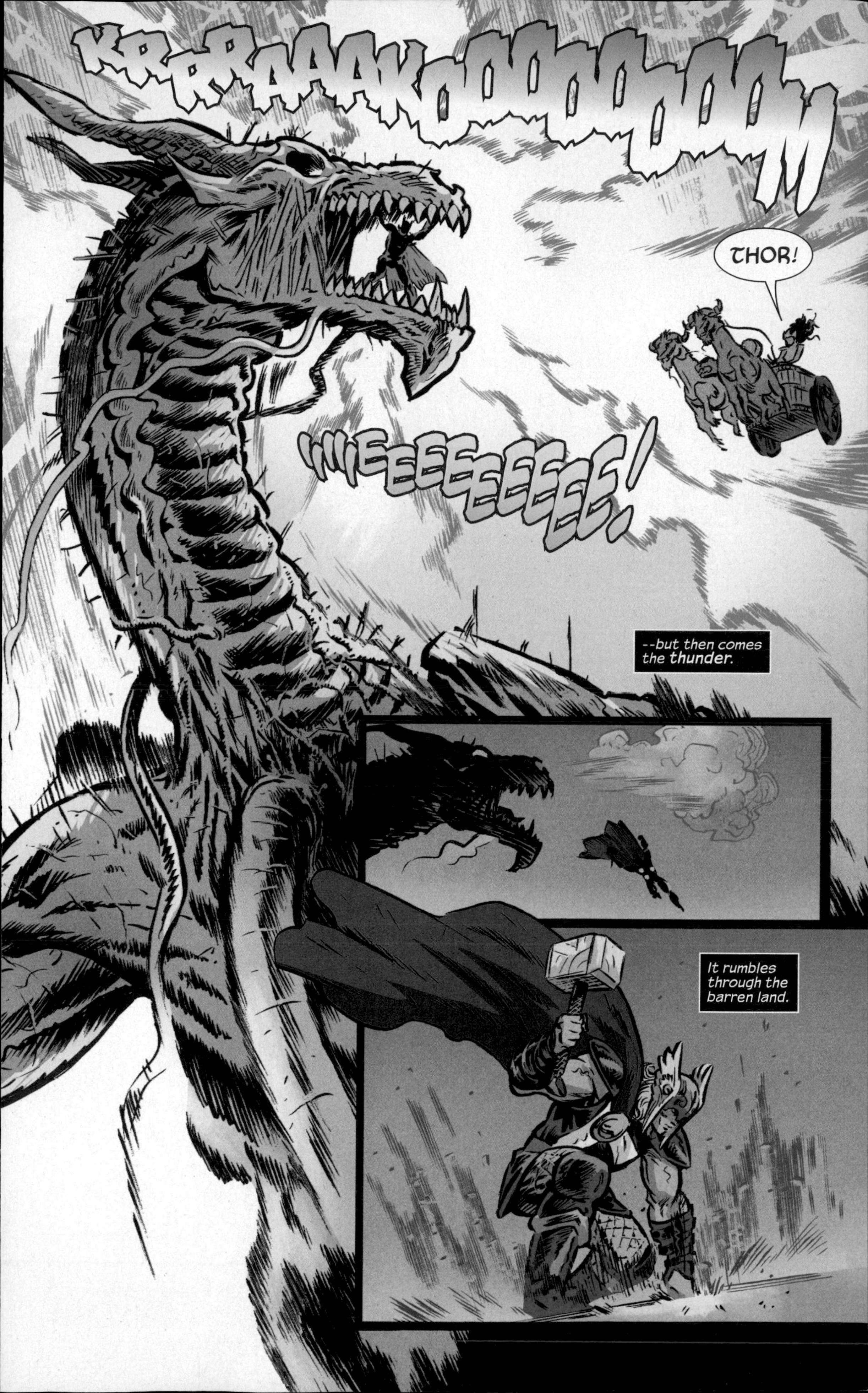
KRRRAAAKOOOOOOOM
THOR!
IIIIEEEEEEEEEEE!
--but then comes the thunder.
It rumbles through the barren land.

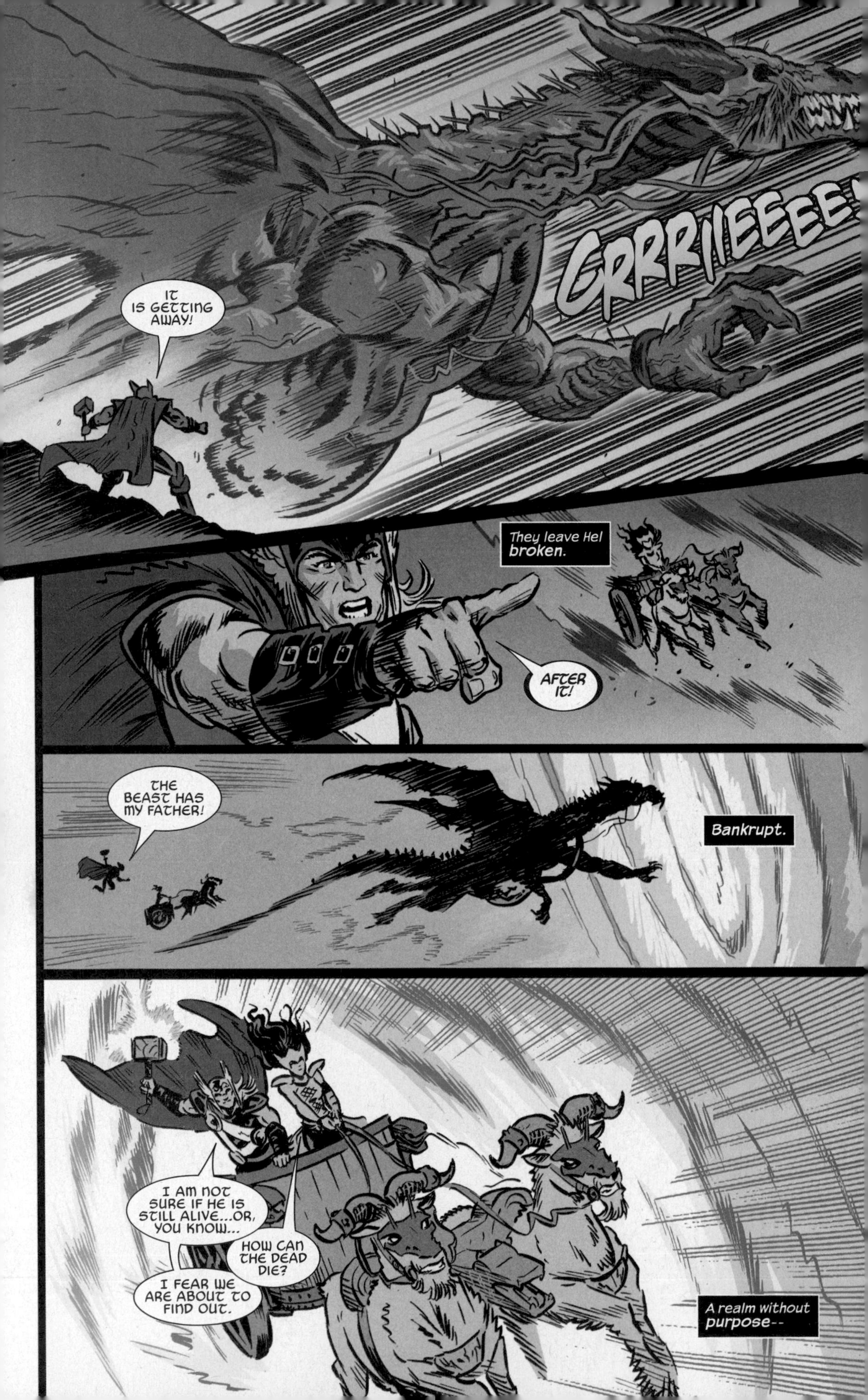
GRRRIIEEEEE
IT IS GETTING AWAY!
They leave Hel broken.
AFTER IT!
THE BEAST HAS MY FATHER!
Bankrupt.
I AM NOT SURE IF HE IS STILL ALIVE...OR, YOU KNOW...
HOW CAN THE DEAD DIE?
I FEAR WE ARE ABOUT TO FIND OUT.
A realm without purpose--

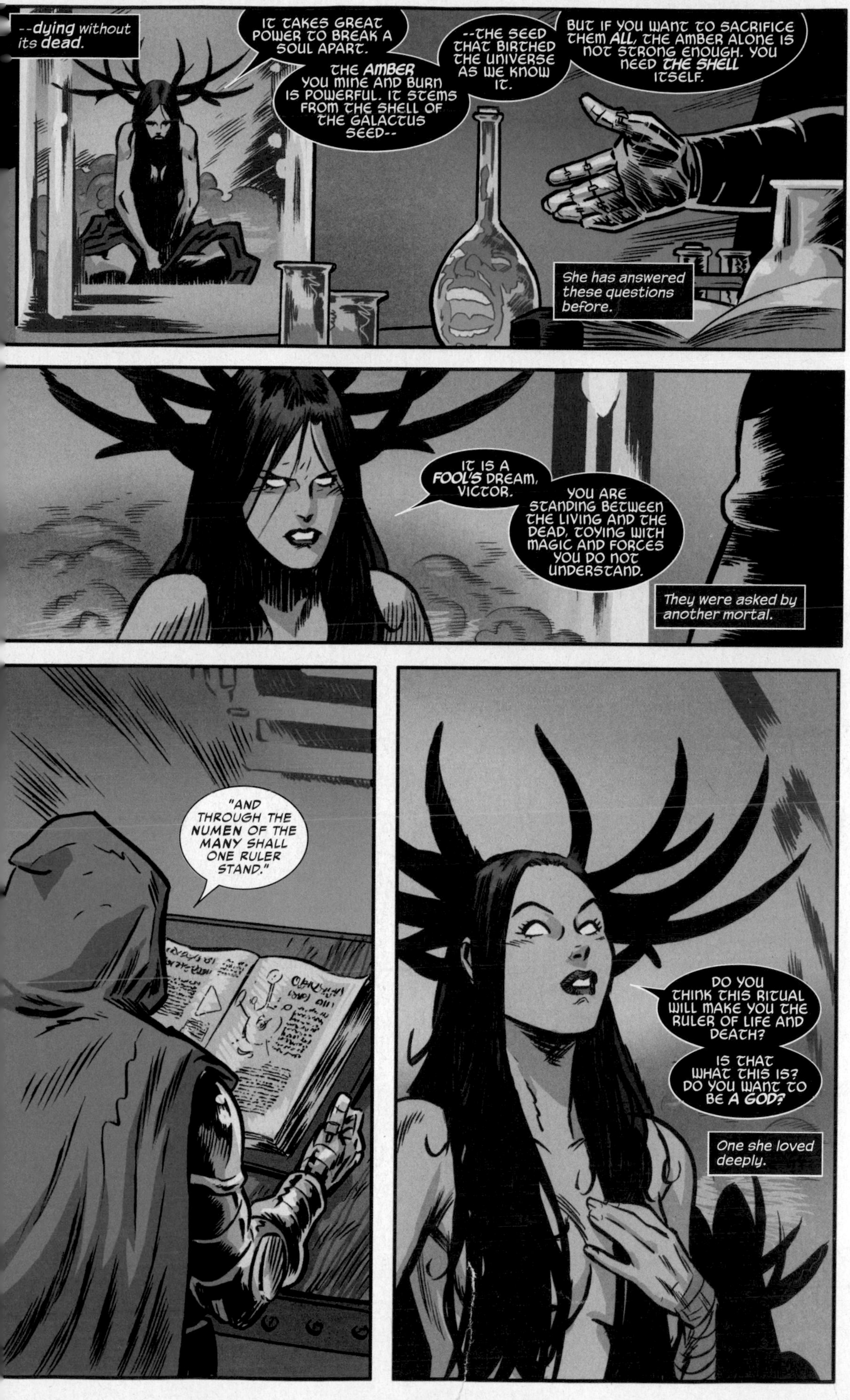
--dying without its dead.
IT TAKES GREAT POWER TO BREAK A SOUL APART.
THE AMBER YOU MINE AND BURN IS POWERFUL. IT STEMS FROM THE SHELL OF THE GALACTUS SEED--
--THE SEED THAT BIRTHED THE UNIVERSE AS WE KNOW IT.
BUT IF YOU WANT TO SACRIFICE THEM ALL, THE AMBER ALONE IS NOT STRONG ENOUGH. YOU NEED THE SHELL ITSELF.
She has answered these questions before.
IT IS A FOOL'S DREAM, VICTOR.
YOU ARE STANDING BETWEEN THE LIVING AND THE DEAD, TOYING WITH MAGIC AND FORCES YOU DO NOT UNDERSTAND.
They were asked by another mortal.
"AND THROUGH THE NUMEN OF THE MANY SHALL ONE RULER STAND."
DO YOU THINK THIS RITUAL WILL MAKE YOU THE RULER OF LIFE AND DEATH?
IS THAT WHAT THIS IS? DO YOU WANT TO BE A GOD?
One she loved deeply.

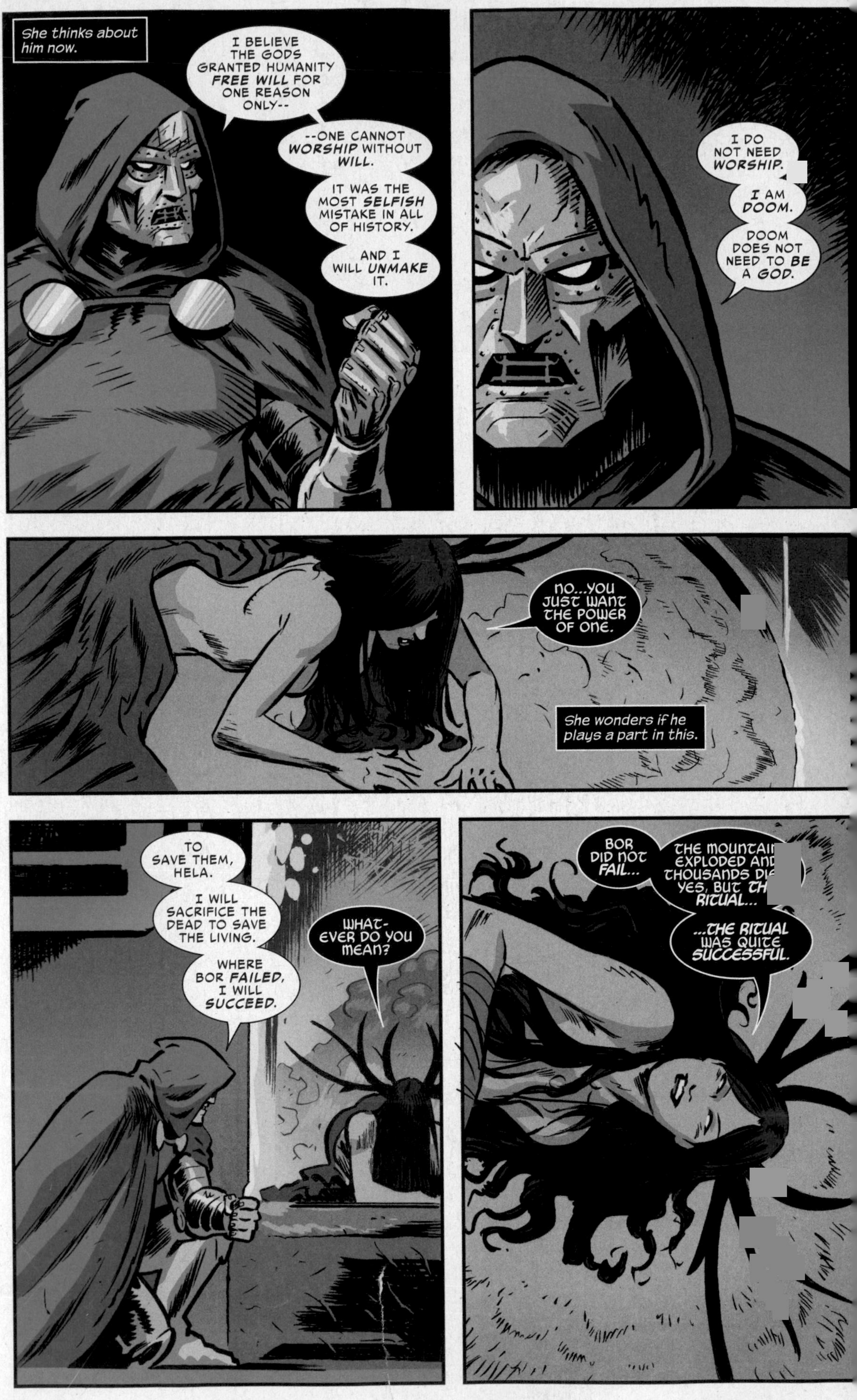
She thinks about him now.
I BELIEVE THE GODS GRANTED HUMANITY FREE WILL FOR ONE REASON ONLY--
--ONE CANNOT WORSHIP WITHOUT WILL.
IT WAS THE MOST SELFISH MISTAKE IN ALL OF HISTORY.
AND I WILL UNMAKE IT.
I DO NOT NEED WORSHIP.
I AM DOOM.
DOOM DOES NOT NEED TO BE A GOD.
NO...YOU JUST WANT THE POWER OF ONE.
She wonders if he plays a part in this.
TO SAVE THEM, HELA.
I WILL SACRIFICE THE DEAD TO SAVE THE LIVING.
WHERE BOR FAILED, I WILL SUCCEED.
WHAT-EVER DO YOU MEAN?
BOR DID NOT FAIL...
THE MOUNTAI EXPLODED AND THOUSANDS DI YES, BUT TH RITUAL...
...THE RITUAL WAS QUITE SUCCESSFUL.

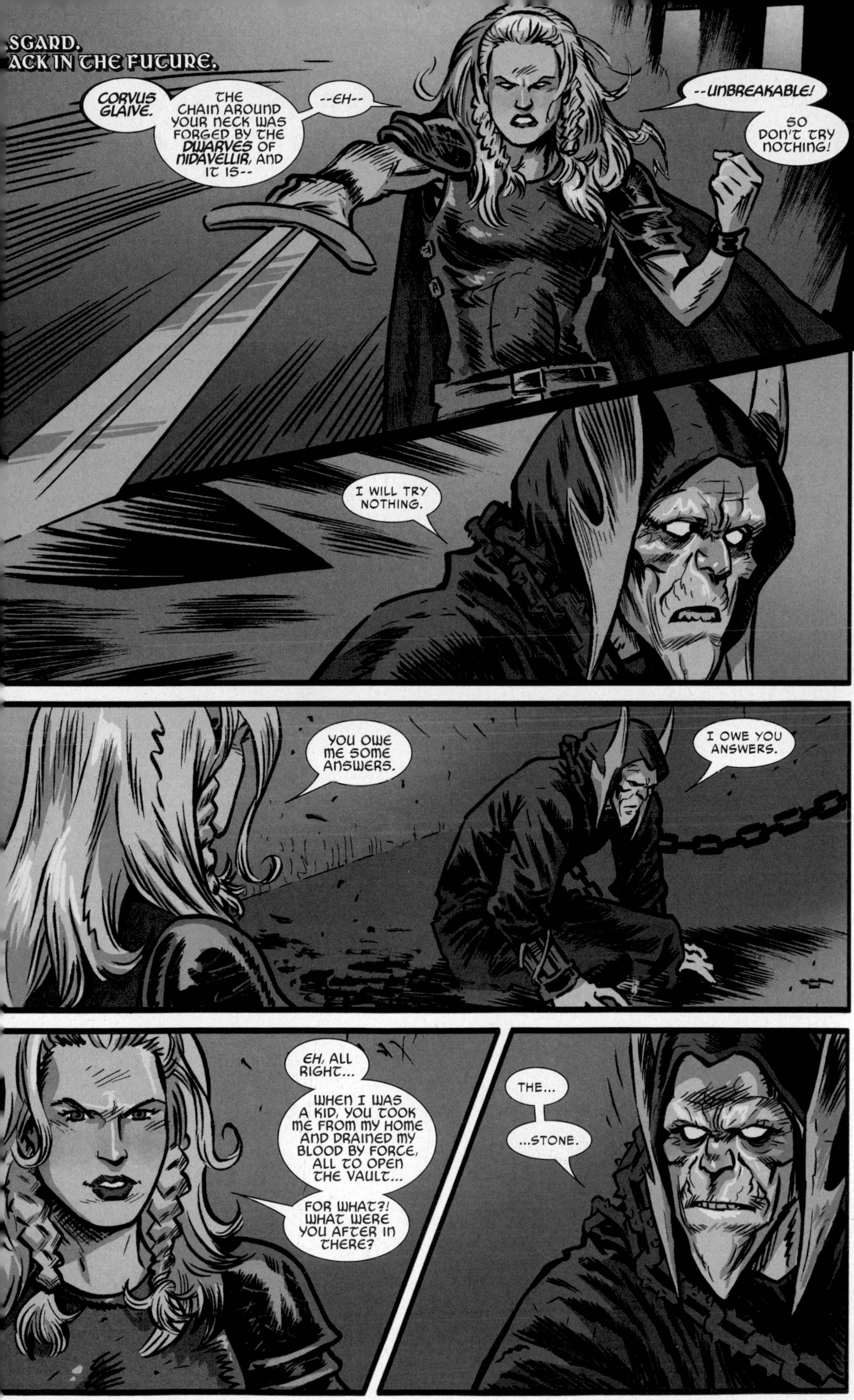
SGARD.
ACK IN THE FUTURE.
CORVUS GLAIVE.
THE CHAIN AROUND YOUR NECK WAS FORGED BY THE DWARVES OF NIDAVELLIR, AND IT IS--
--EH--
--UNBREAKABLE!
SO DON'T TRY NOTHING!
I WILL TRY NOTHING.
YOU OWE ME SOME ANSWERS.
I OWE YOU ANSWERS.
EH, ALL RIGHT...
WHEN I WAS A KID, YOU TOOK ME FROM MY HOME AND DRAINED MY BLOOD BY FORCE, ALL TO OPEN THE VAULT...
FOR WHAT?! WHAT WERE YOU AFTER IN THERE?
THE...
...STONE.

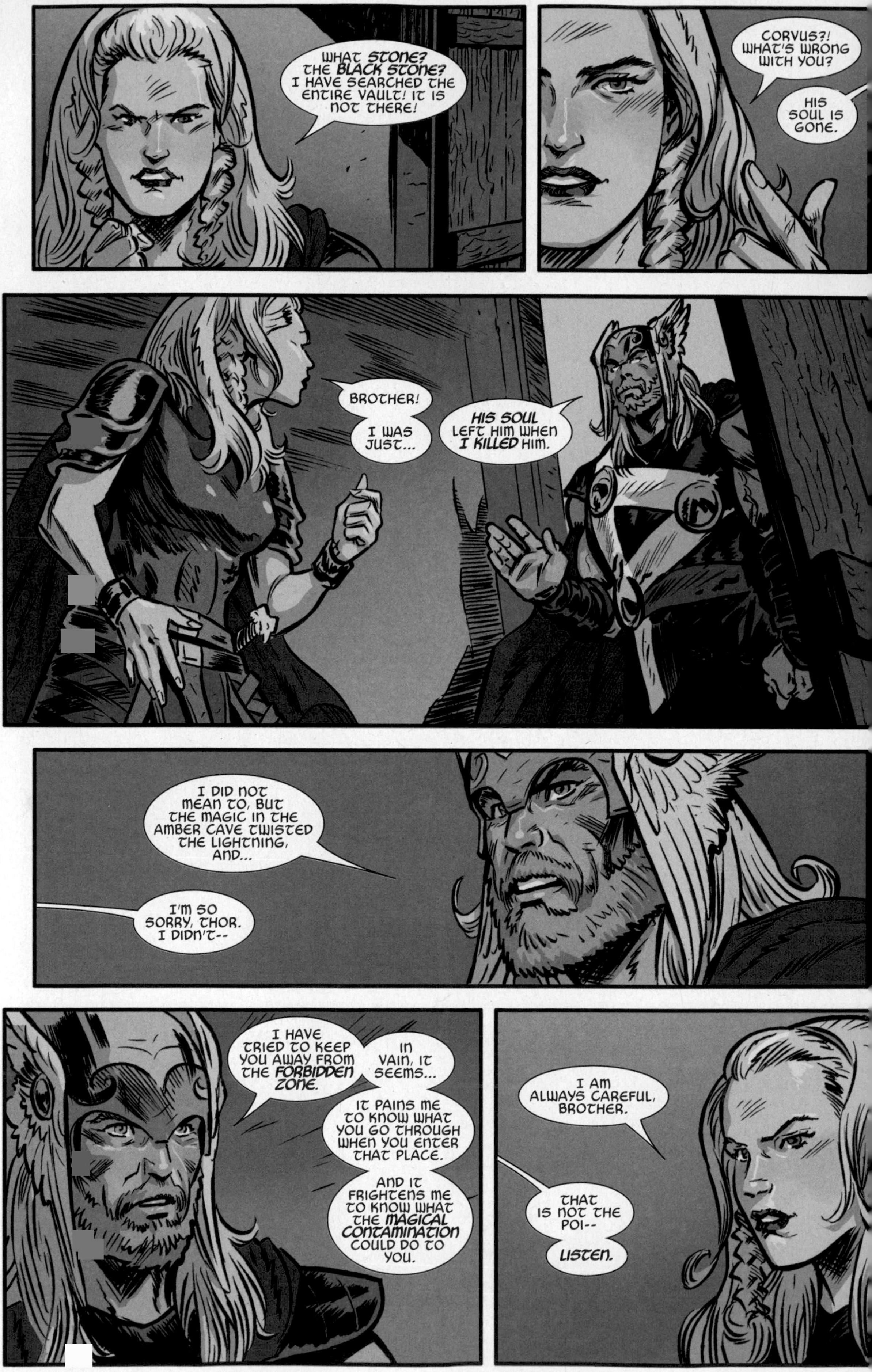

WHAT STONE? THE BLACK STONE? I HAVE SEARCHED THE ENTIRE VAULT! IT IS NOT THERE!
CORVUS?! WHAT'S WRONG WITH YOU?
HIS SOUL IS GONE.
BROTHER!
I WAS JUST...
HIS SOUL LEFT HIM WHEN I KILLED HIM.
I DID NOT MEAN TO, BUT THE MAGIC IN THE AMBER CAVE TWISTED THE LIGHTNING, AND...
I'M SO SORRY, THOR. I DIDN'T--
I HAVE TRIED TO KEEP YOU AWAY FROM THE FORBIDDEN ZONE.
IN VAIN, IT SEEMS...
IT PAINS ME TO KNOW WHAT YOU GO THROUGH WHEN YOU ENTER THAT PLACE.
AND IT FRIGHTENS ME TO KNOW WHAT THE MAGICAL CONTAMINATION COULD DO TO YOU.
I AM ALWAYS CAREFUL, BROTHER.
THAT IS NOT THE POI--
LISTEN.

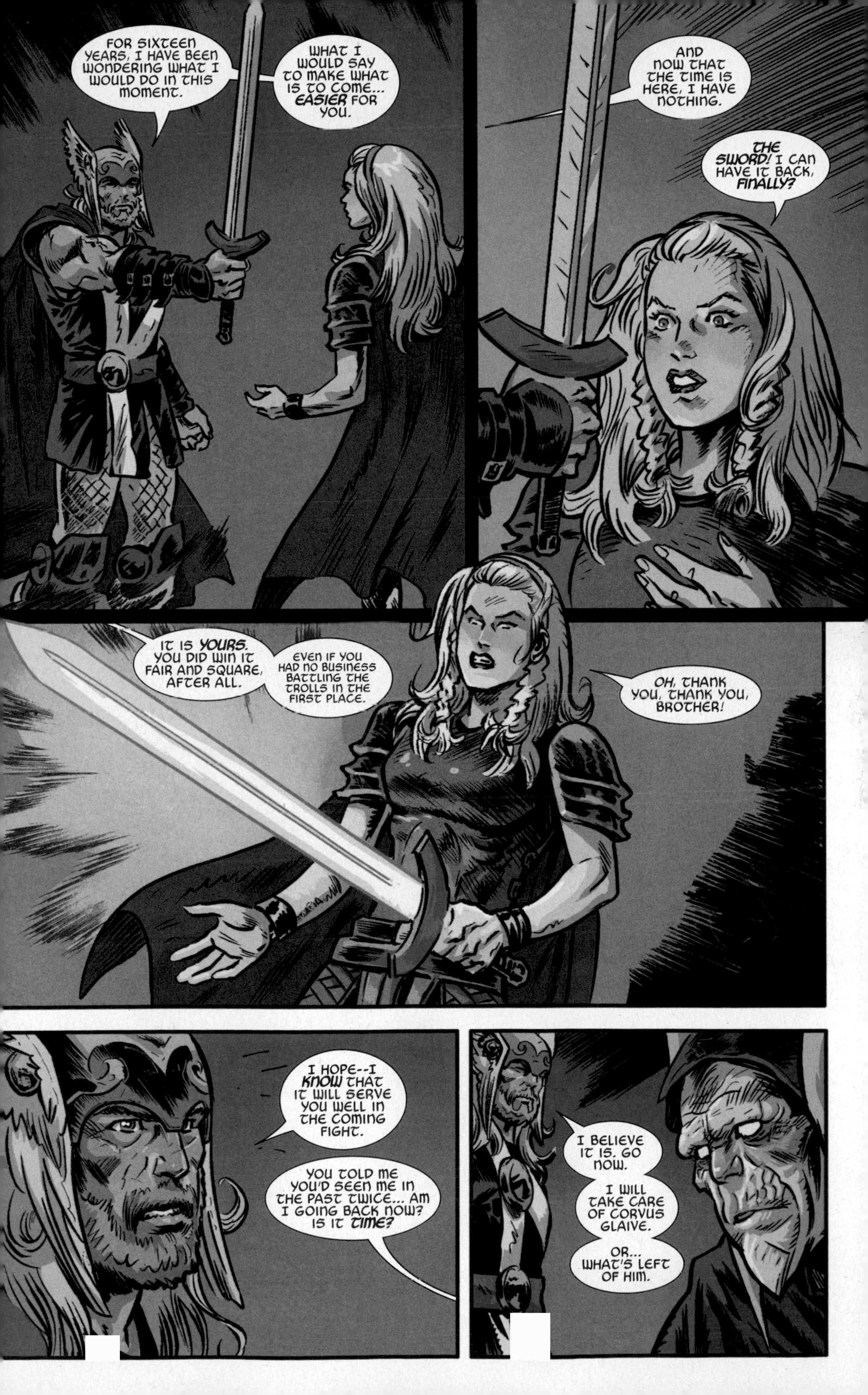
FOR SIXTEEN YEARS, I HAVE BEEN WONDERING WHAT I WOULD DO IN THIS MOMENT.
WHAT I WOULD SAY TO MAKE WHAT IS TO COME... EASIER FOR YOU.
AND NOW THAT THE TIME IS HERE, I HAVE NOTHING.
THE SWORD! I CAN HAVE IT BACK, FINALLY?
IT IS YOURS. YOU DID WIN IT FAIR AND SQUARE, AFTER ALL.
EVEN IF YOU HAD NO BUSINESS BATTLING THE TROLLS IN THE FIRST PLACE.
OH, THANK YOU, THANK YOU, BROTHER!
I HOPE--I KNOW THAT IT WILL SERVE YOU WELL IN THE COMING FIGHT.
YOU TOLD ME YOU'D SEEN ME IN THE PAST TWICE... AM I GOING BACK NOW? IS IT TIME?
I BELIEVE IT IS. GO NOW.
I WILL TAKE CARE OF CORVUS GLAIVE.
OR... WHAT'S LEFT OF HIM.

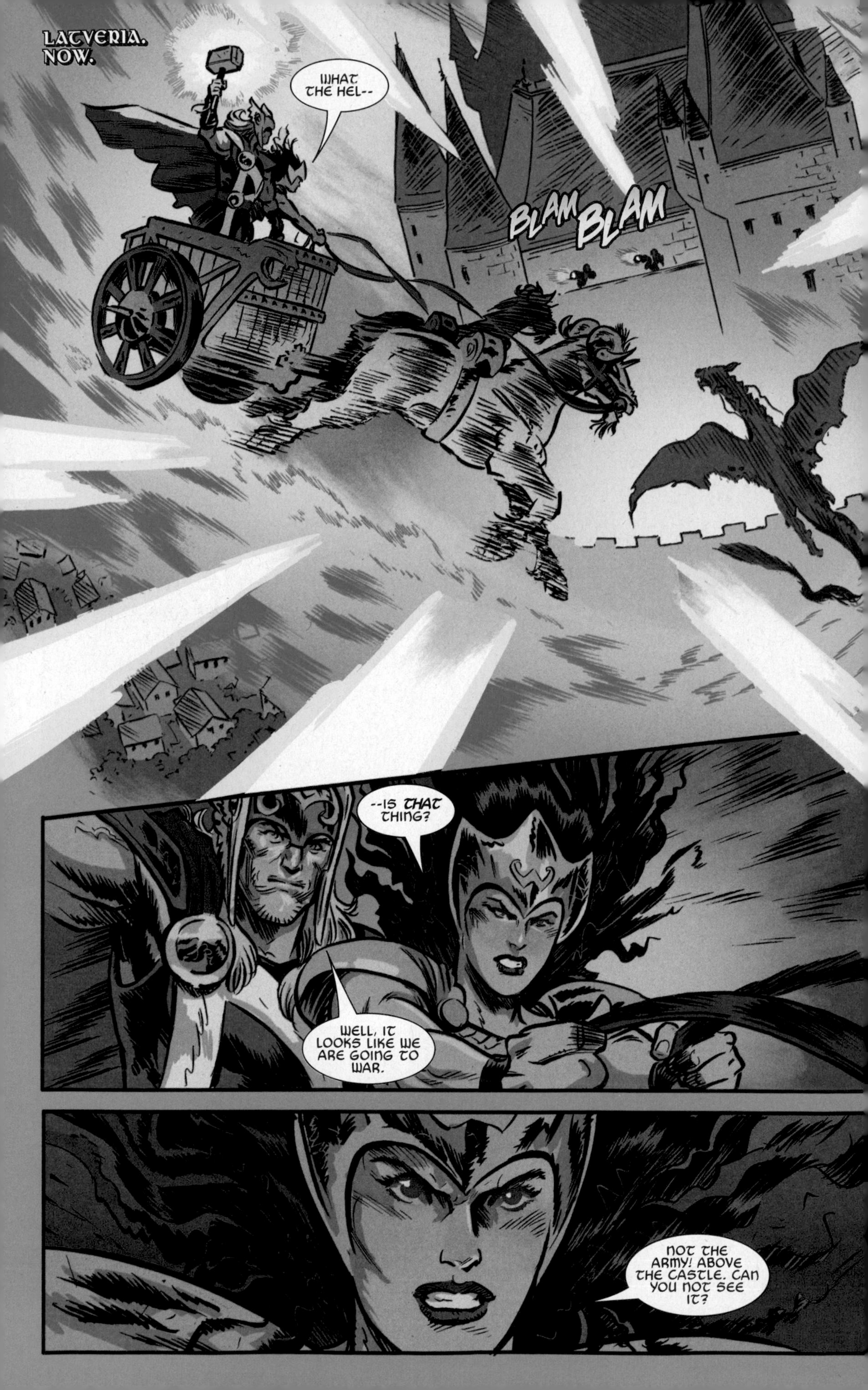
LATVERIA.
NOW.
WHAT THE HEL--
BLAM BLAM
--IS THAT THING?
WELL, IT LOOKS LIKE WE ARE GOING TO WAR.
NOT THE ARMY! ABOVE THE CASTLE. CAN YOU NOT SEE IT?

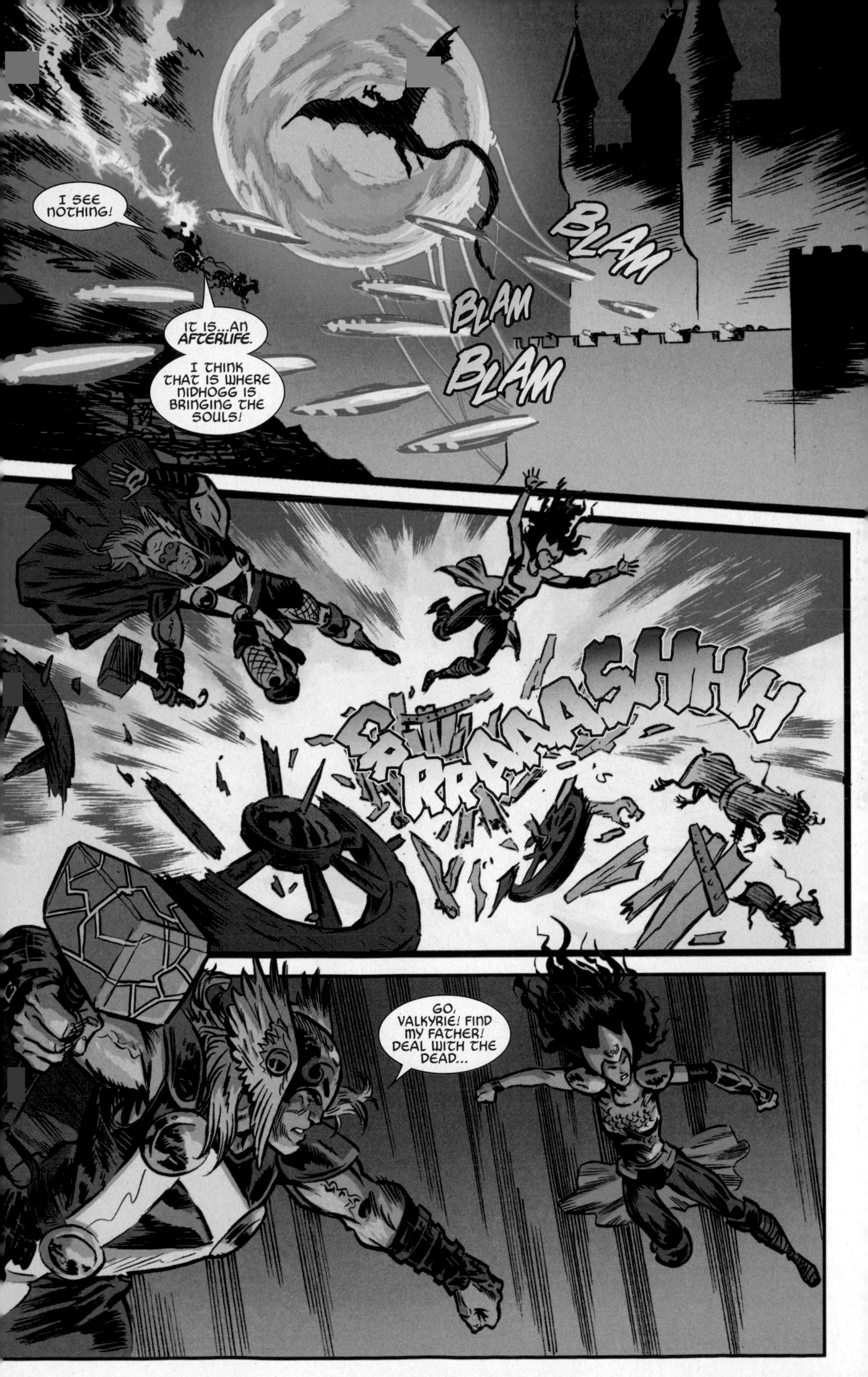
I SEE NOTHING!
IT IS...AN AFTERLIFE.
I THINK THAT IS WHERE NIDHOGG IS BRINGING THE SOULS!
BLAM
BLAM
BLAM
CRRRAASHHH
GO, VALKYRIE! FIND MY FATHER! DEAL WITH THE DEAD...

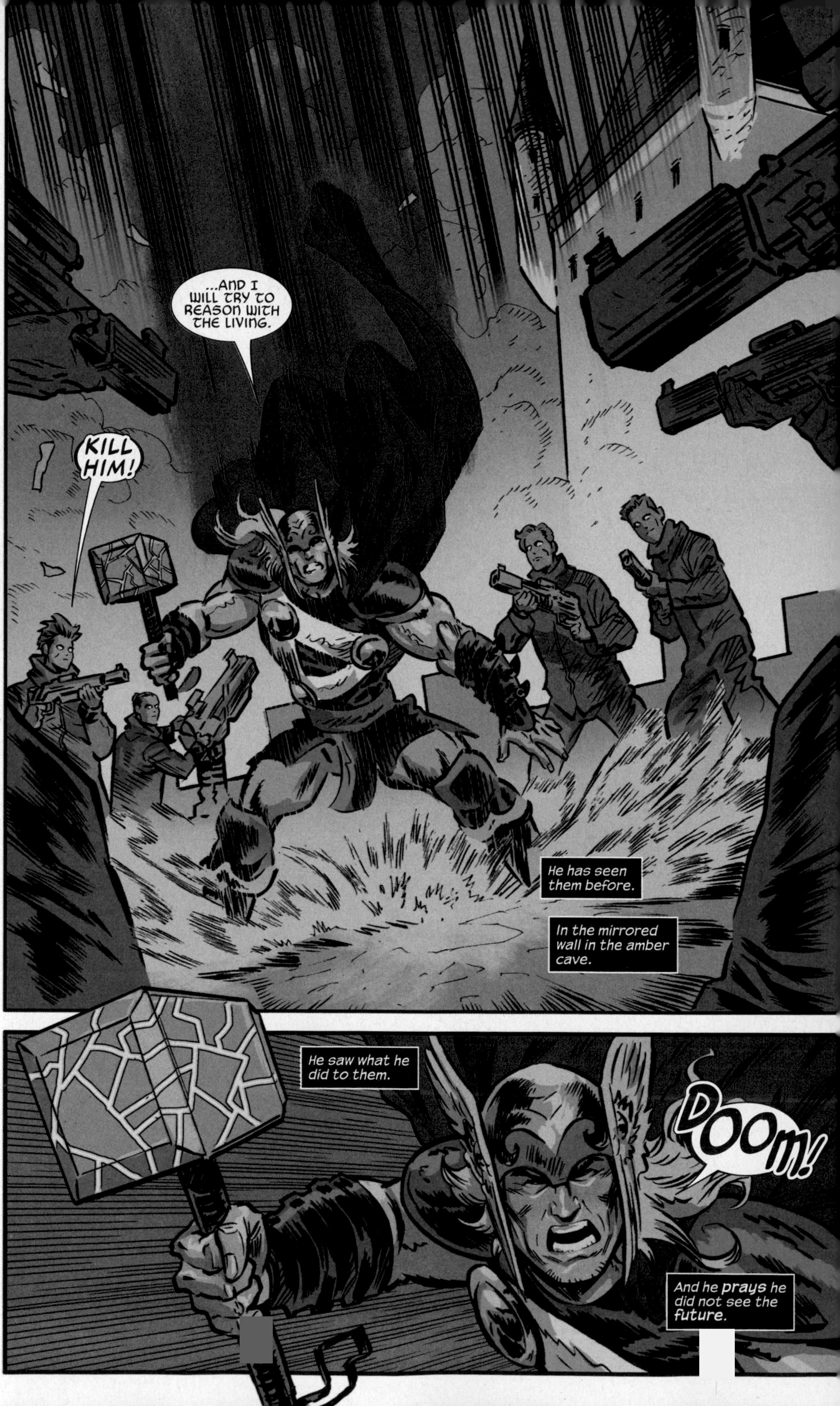

...AND I WILL TRY TO REASON WITH THE LIVING.
KILL HIM!
He has seen them before.
In the mirrored wall in the amber cave.
He saw what he did to them.
DOOM!
And he **prays** he did not see the ***future***.

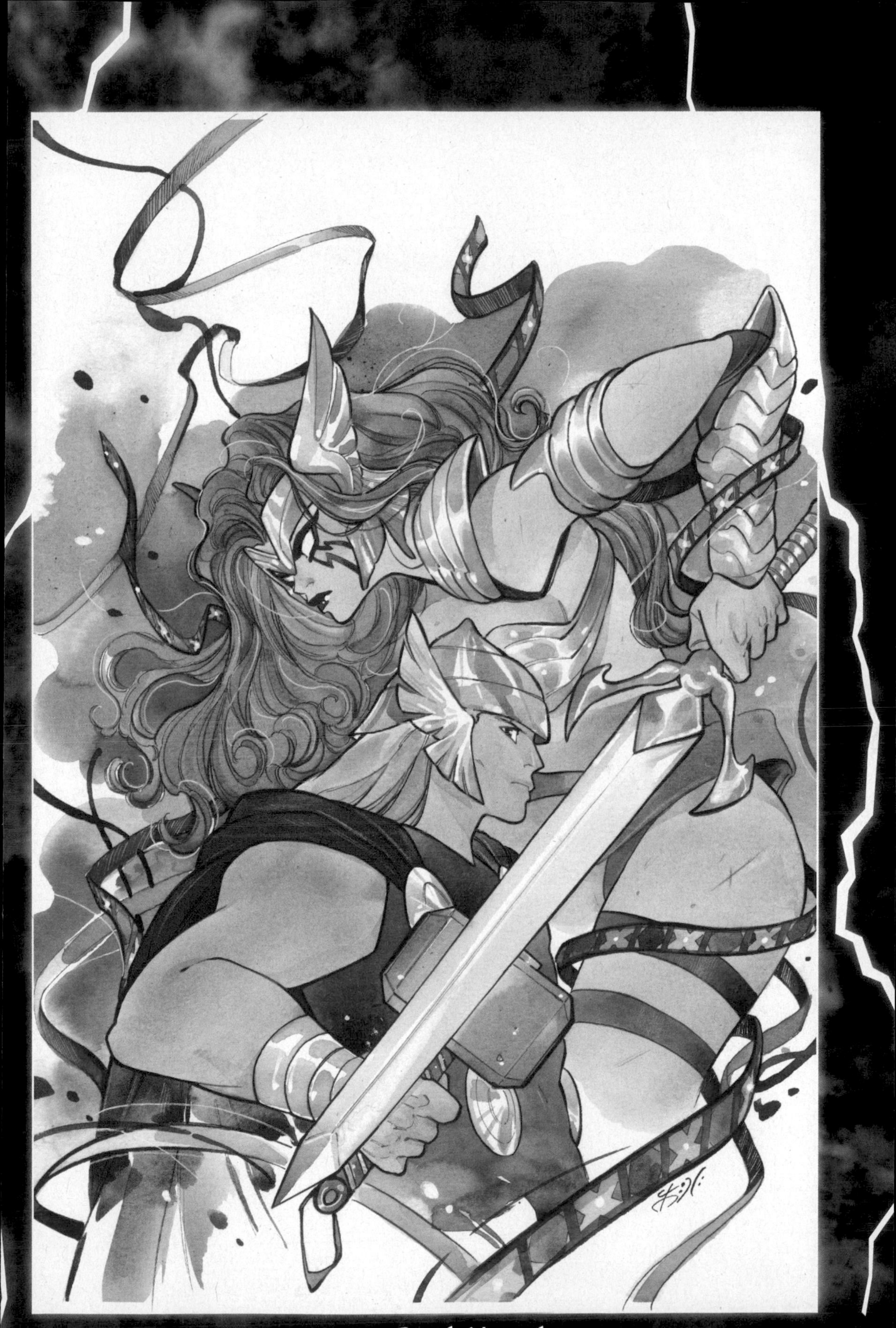

#31 VARIANT BY **Peach Momoko**

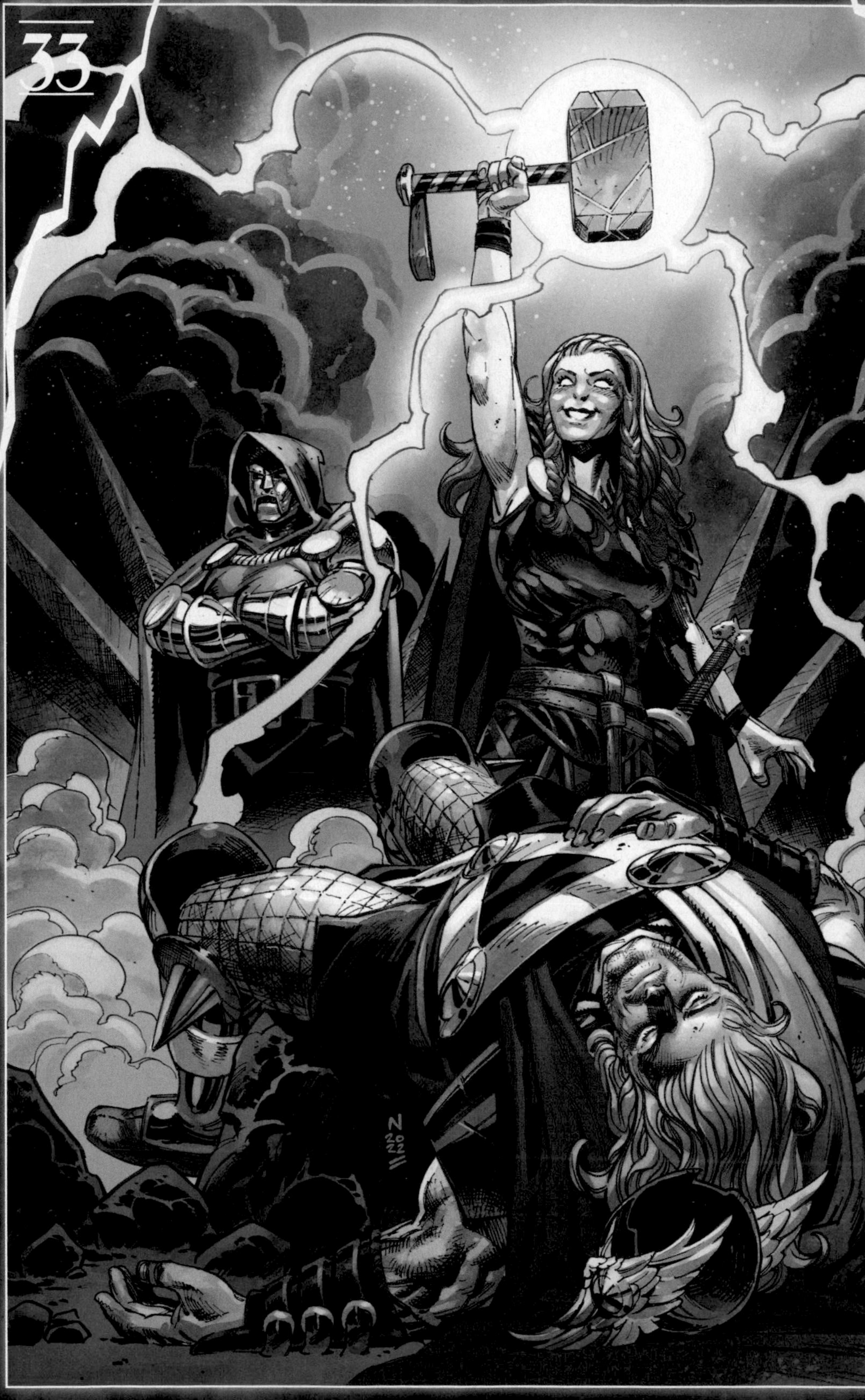
33

"Blood of the Fathers" PART THREE

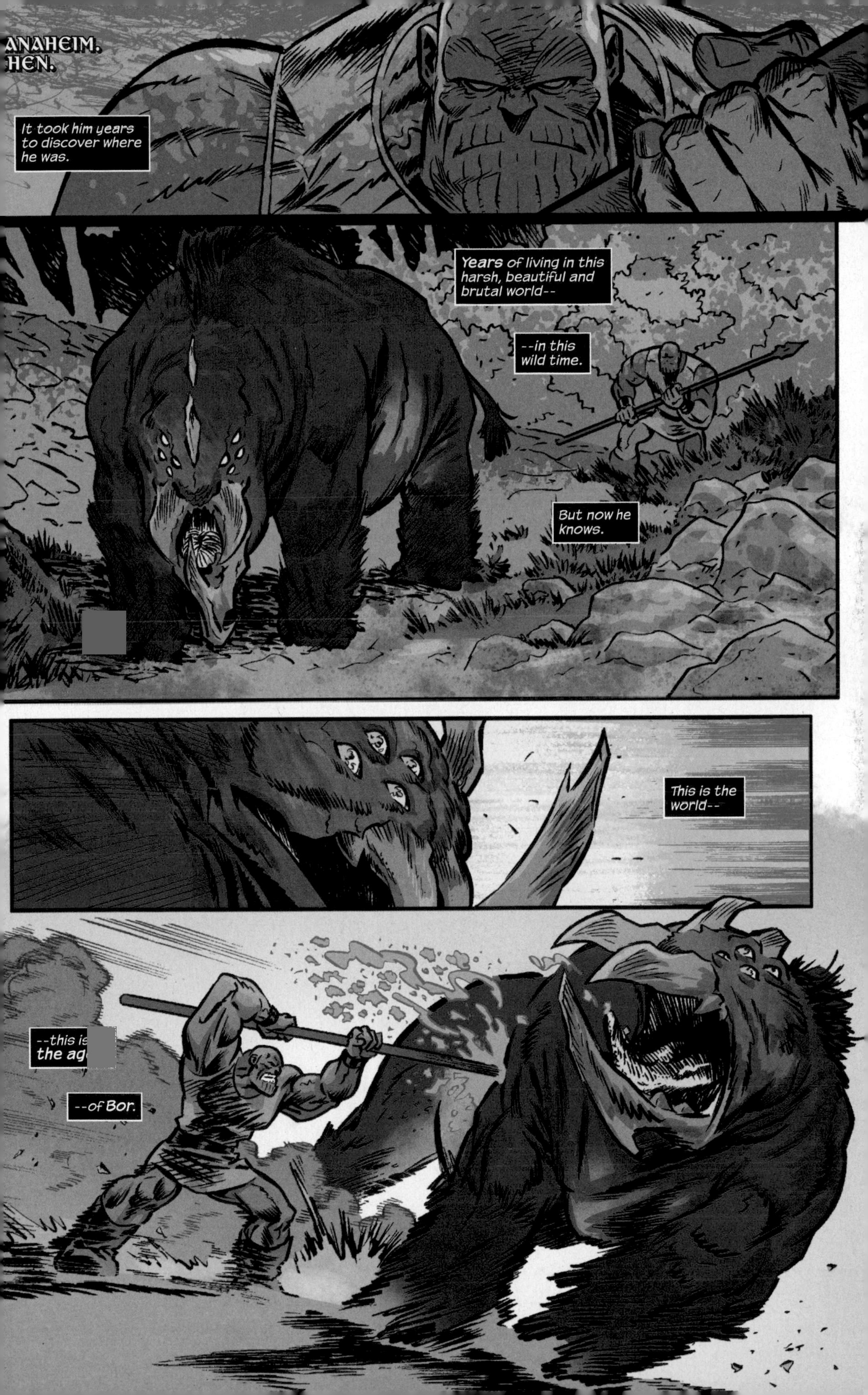

ANAHEIM.
HEN.
It took him years to discover where he was.
Years of living in this harsh, beautiful and brutal world--
--in this wild time.
But now he knows.
This is the world--
--this is
the ag
--of Bor.

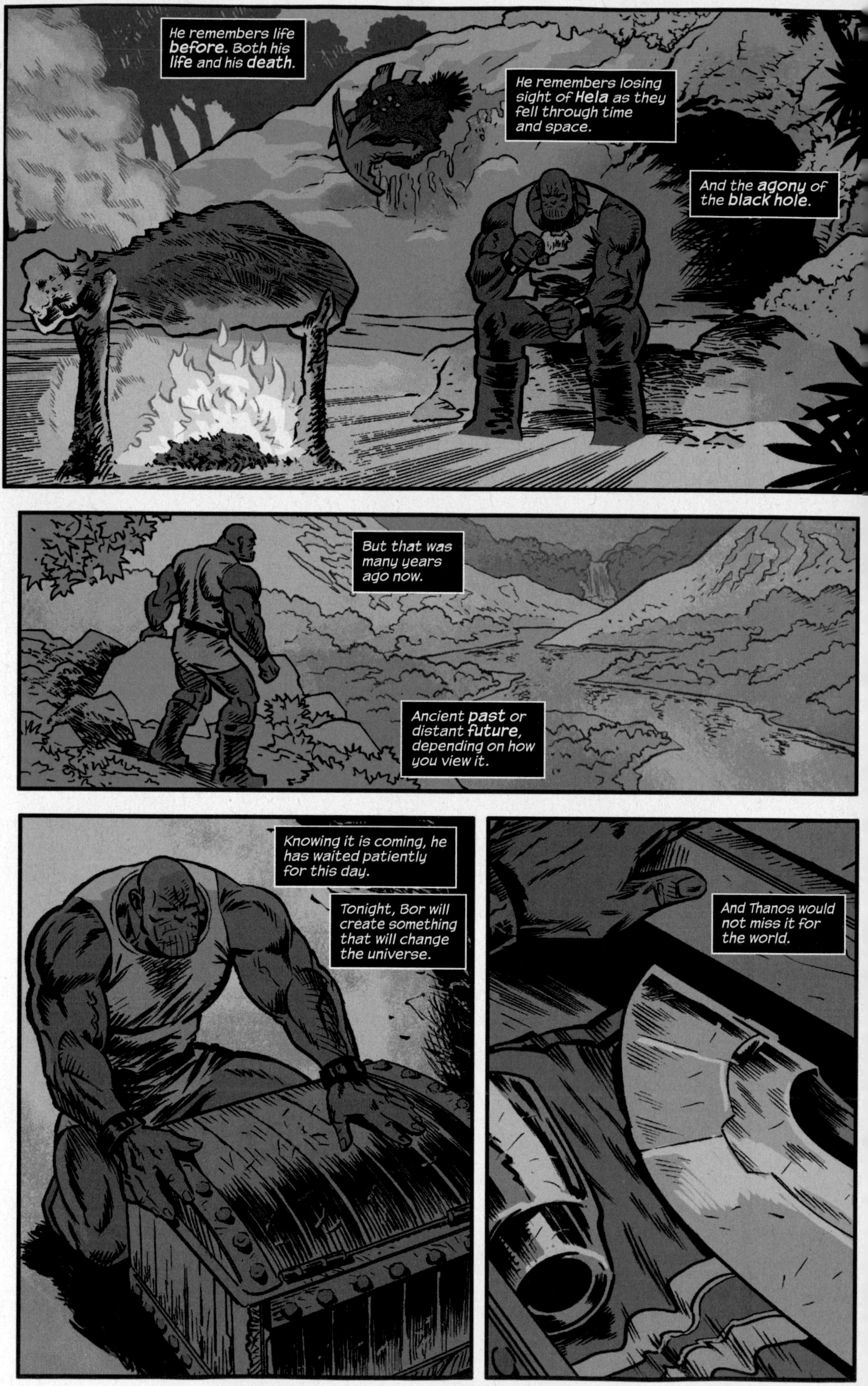
He remembers life before. Both his life and his death.
He remembers losing sight of Hela as they fell through time and space.
And the agony of the black hole.
But that was many years ago now.
Ancient past or distant future, depending on how you view it.
Knowing it is coming, he has waited patiently for this day.
Tonight, Bor will create something that will change the universe.
And Thanos would not miss it for the world.

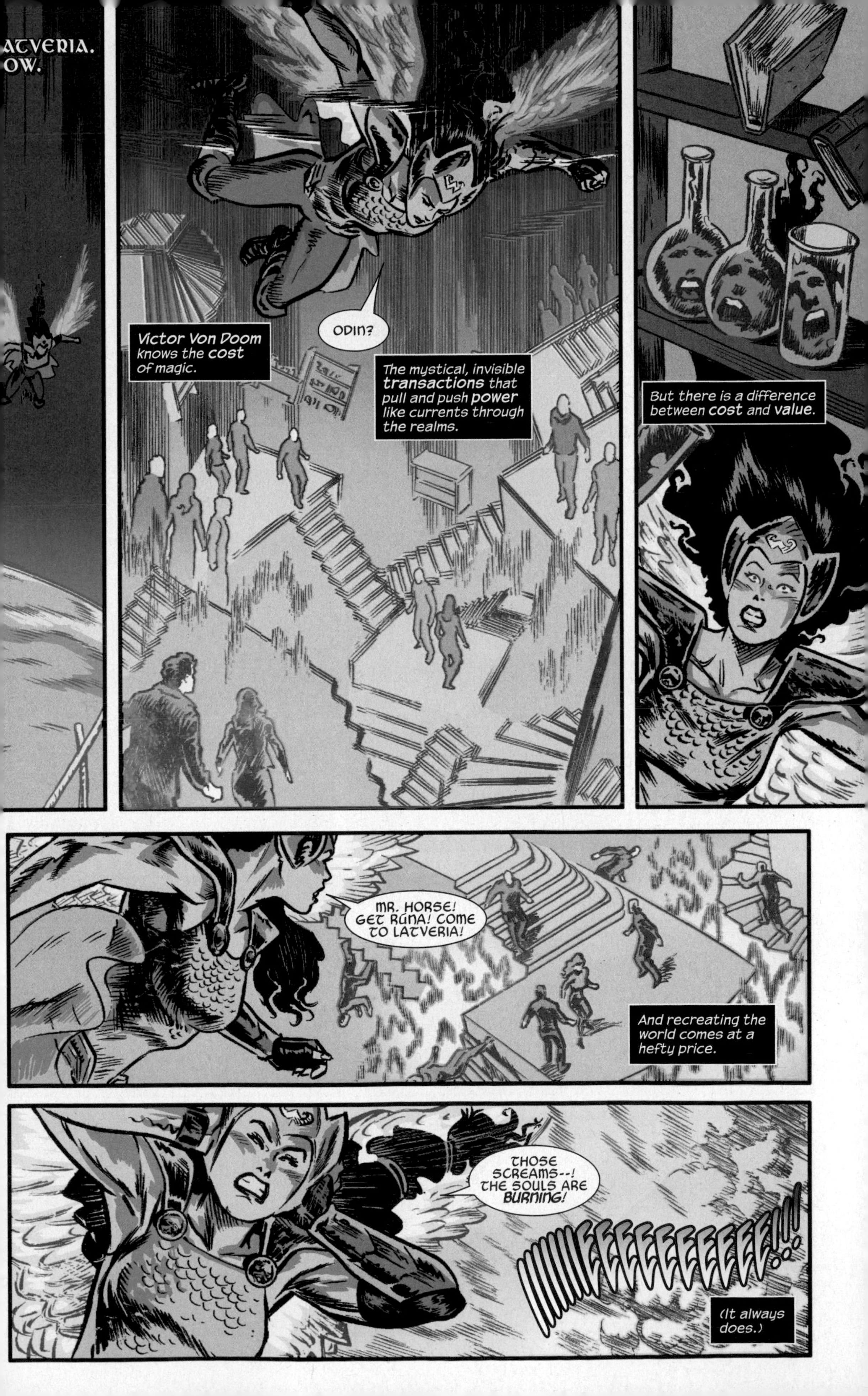

ATVERIA.
OW.
Victor Von Doom knows the cost of magic.
ODIN?
The mystical, invisible transactions that pull and push power like currents through the realms.
But there is a difference between cost and value.
MR. HORSE! GET RÚNA! COME TO LATVERIA!
And recreating the world comes at a hefty price.
THOSE SCREAMS--! THE SOULS ARE BURNING!
IIIIIIIEEEEEEEEE!!!
(It always does.)

One could argue that what he does is no different from a general sacrificing soldiers on a battlefield.

Or kings shaping history by the blood of others.

They knew the cost of victory.

But the *value* of lives lost--

YOU ARE TURNING *SOULS* INTO *FUEL*, DOOM.

ᚠᚱᛟᛗ ᚹᚺᚨᛏ ᚠᛖᚹ ᚱᛖᚺᛗᛖ.

IT IS A *CRIME* AGAINST *EXISTENCE*.

A CRIME AGAINST *CREATION* ITSELF.

--all those lives sacrificed--

--remain unknowable--

--to *almost* everyone.

AND FOR WHAT?

TO REMAKE THE WORLD IN YOUR IMAGE?

ASGARD IS AT YOUR DOORSTEP. FACE IT, DOOM--YOU HAVE LOST.

NOT YET.

BOR'S VAULT IS UNLOCKED, HELA. THE WORLD *WILL* CHANGE.

IT IS ONLY A MATTER OF *TIME*.

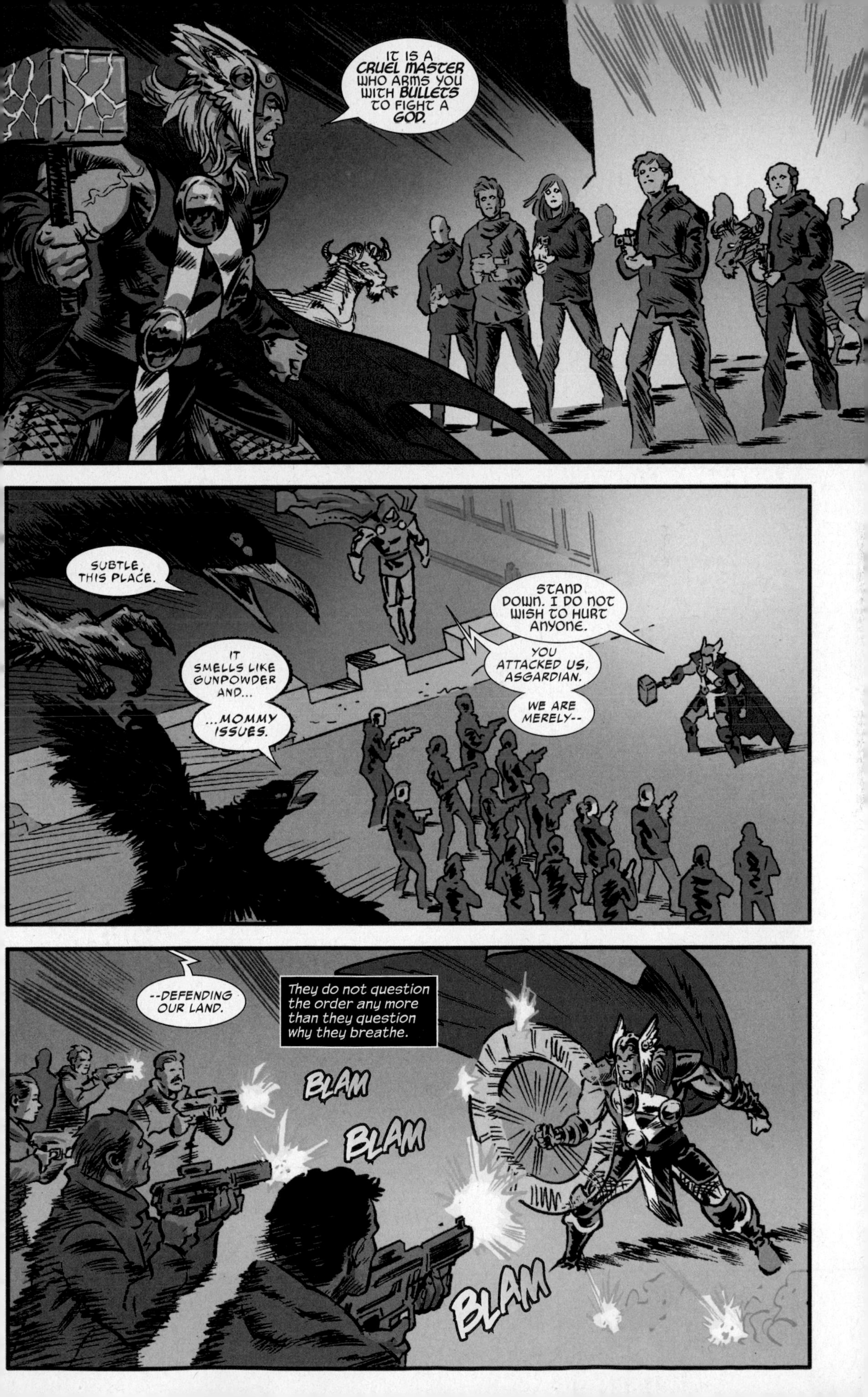

IT IS A CRUEL MASTER WHO ARMS YOU WITH BULLETS TO FIGHT A GOD.
SUBTLE, THIS PLACE.
IT SMELLS LIKE GUNPOWDER AND...
...MOMMY ISSUES.
STAND DOWN. I DO NOT WISH TO HURT ANYONE.
YOU ATTACKED US, ASGARDIAN.
WE ARE MERELY--
--DEFENDING OUR LAND.
They do not question the order any more than they question why they breathe.
BLAM
BLAM
BLAM

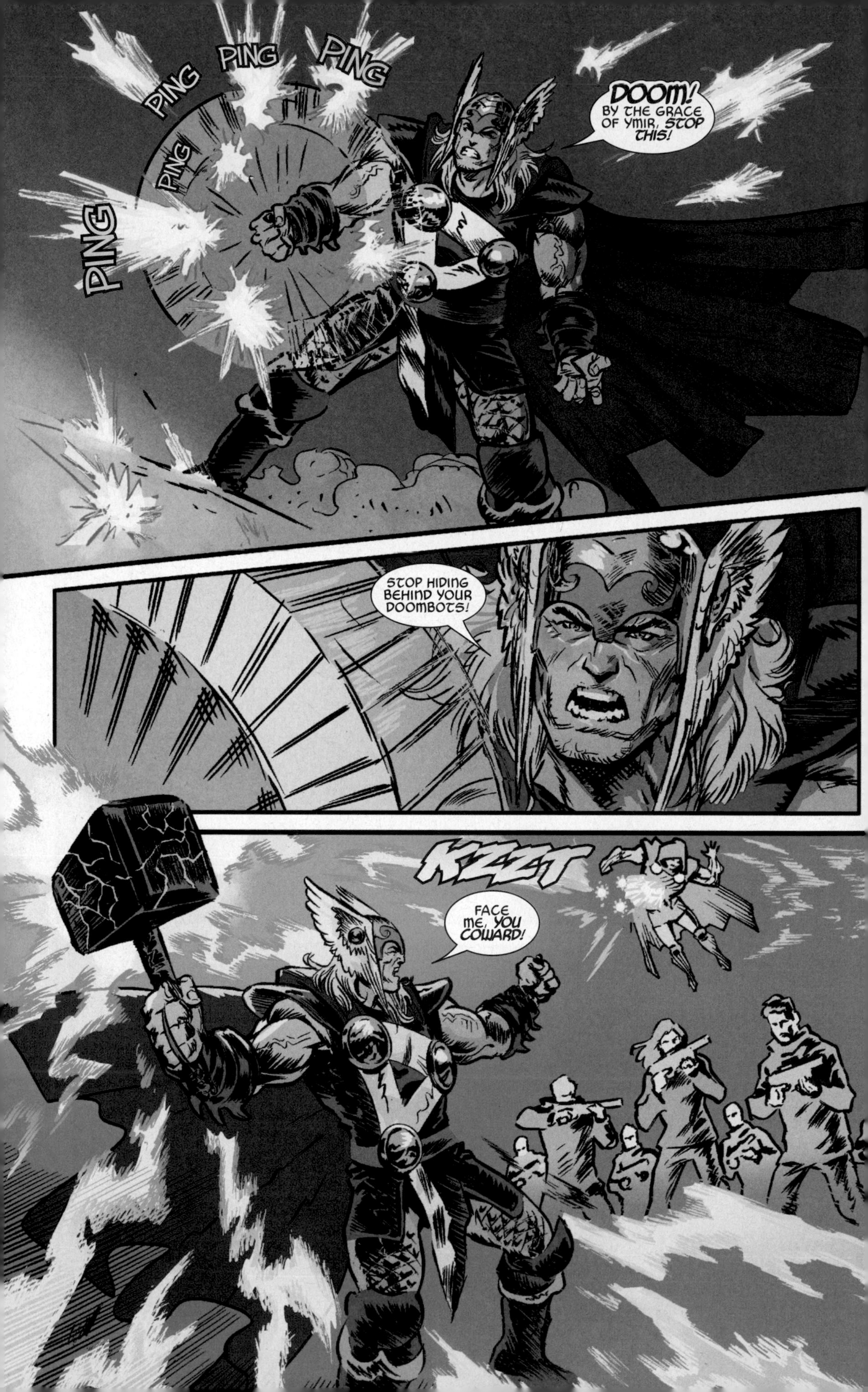
PING PING PING PING PING PING
DOOM! BY THE GRACE OF YMIR, STOP THIS!
STOP HIDING BEHIND YOUR DOOMBOTS!
KZZZT
FACE ME, YOU COWARD!

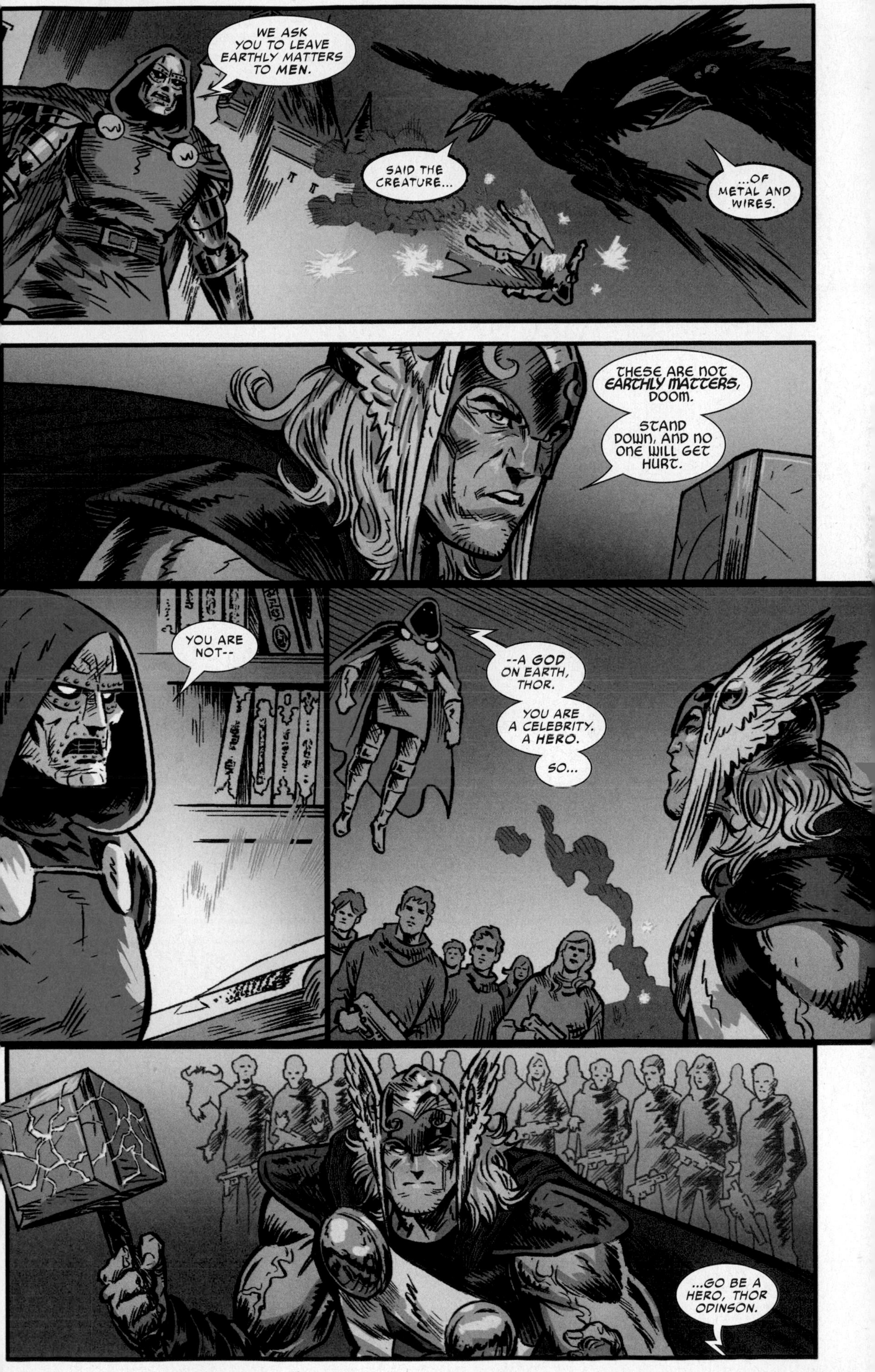
WE ASK YOU TO LEAVE EARTHLY MATTERS TO MEN.
SAID THE CREATURE...
...OF METAL AND WIRES.
THESE ARE NOT EARTHLY MATTERS, DOOM.
STAND DOWN, AND NO ONE WILL GET HURT.
YOU ARE NOT--
--A GOD ON EARTH, THOR.
YOU ARE A CELEBRITY. A HERO.
SO...
...GO BE A HERO, THOR ODINSON.

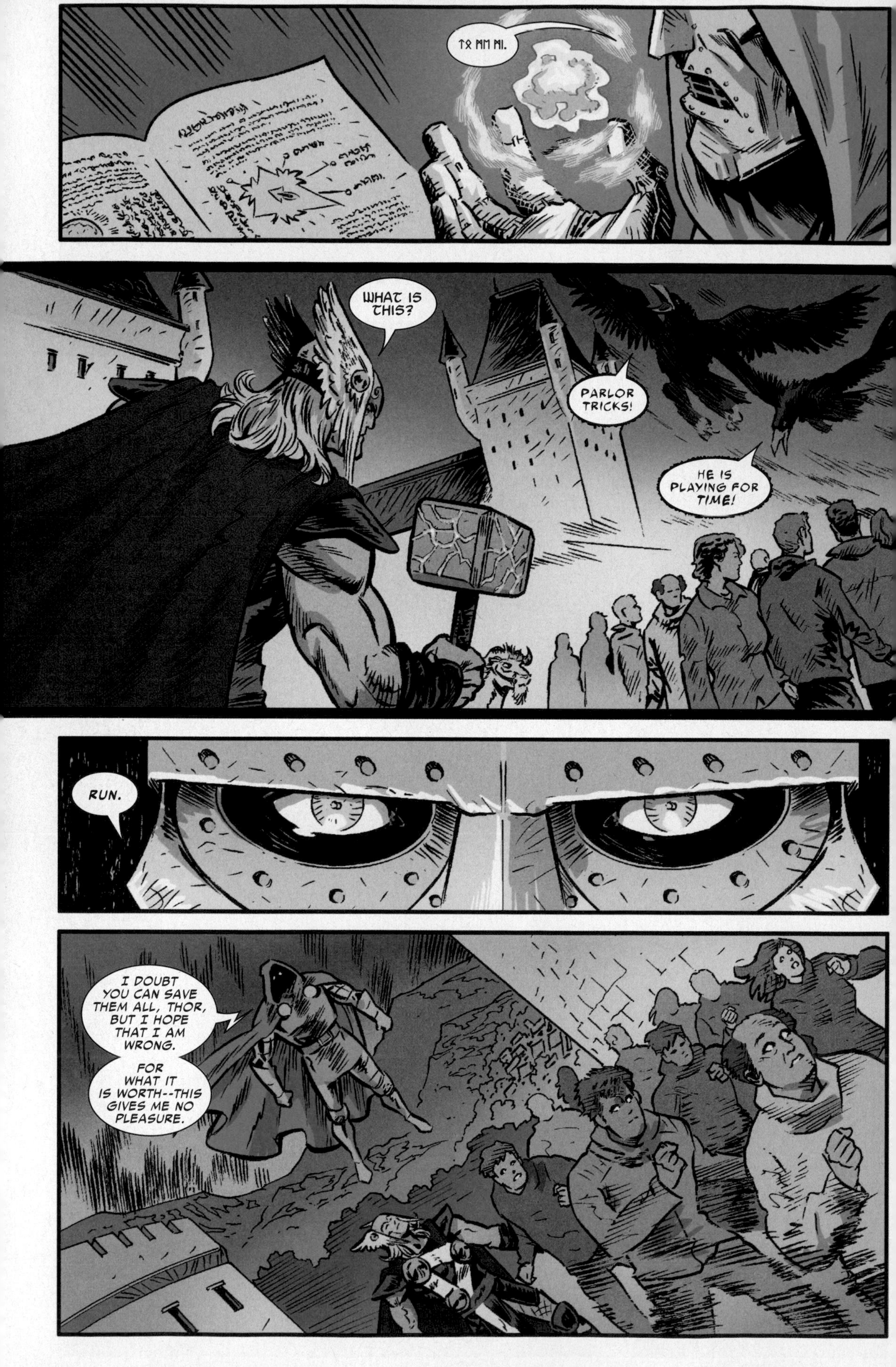
WHAT IS THIS?
PARLOR TRICKS!
HE IS PLAYING FOR TIME!
RUN.
I DOUBT YOU CAN SAVE THEM ALL, THOR, BUT I HOPE THAT I AM WRONG.
FOR WHAT IT IS WORTH--THIS GIVES ME NO PLEASURE.

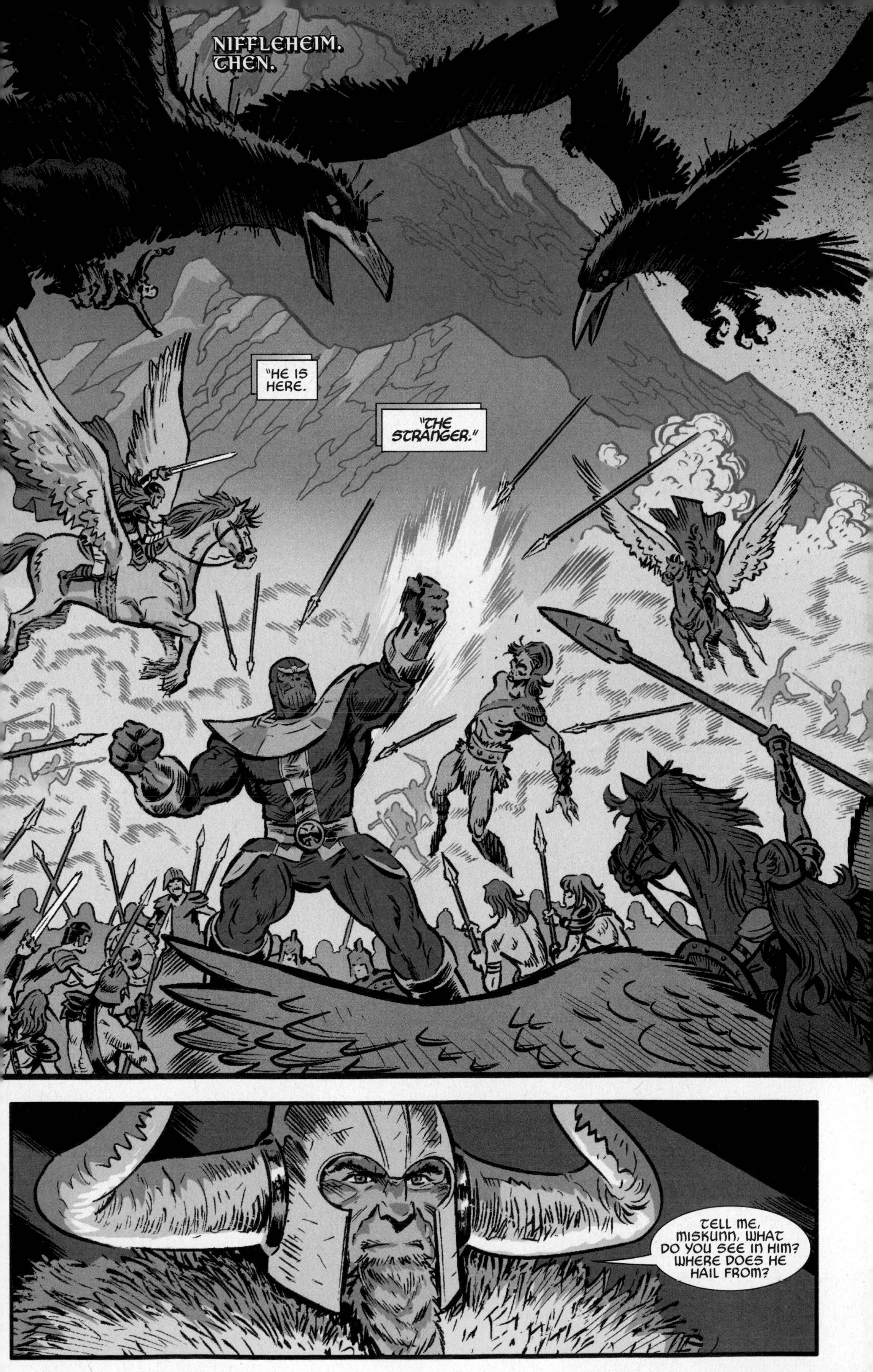
NIFFLEHEIM. THEN.
"HE IS HERE.
"THE STRANGER."
TELL ME, MISKUNN, WHAT DO YOU SEE IN HIM? WHERE DOES HE HAIL FROM?

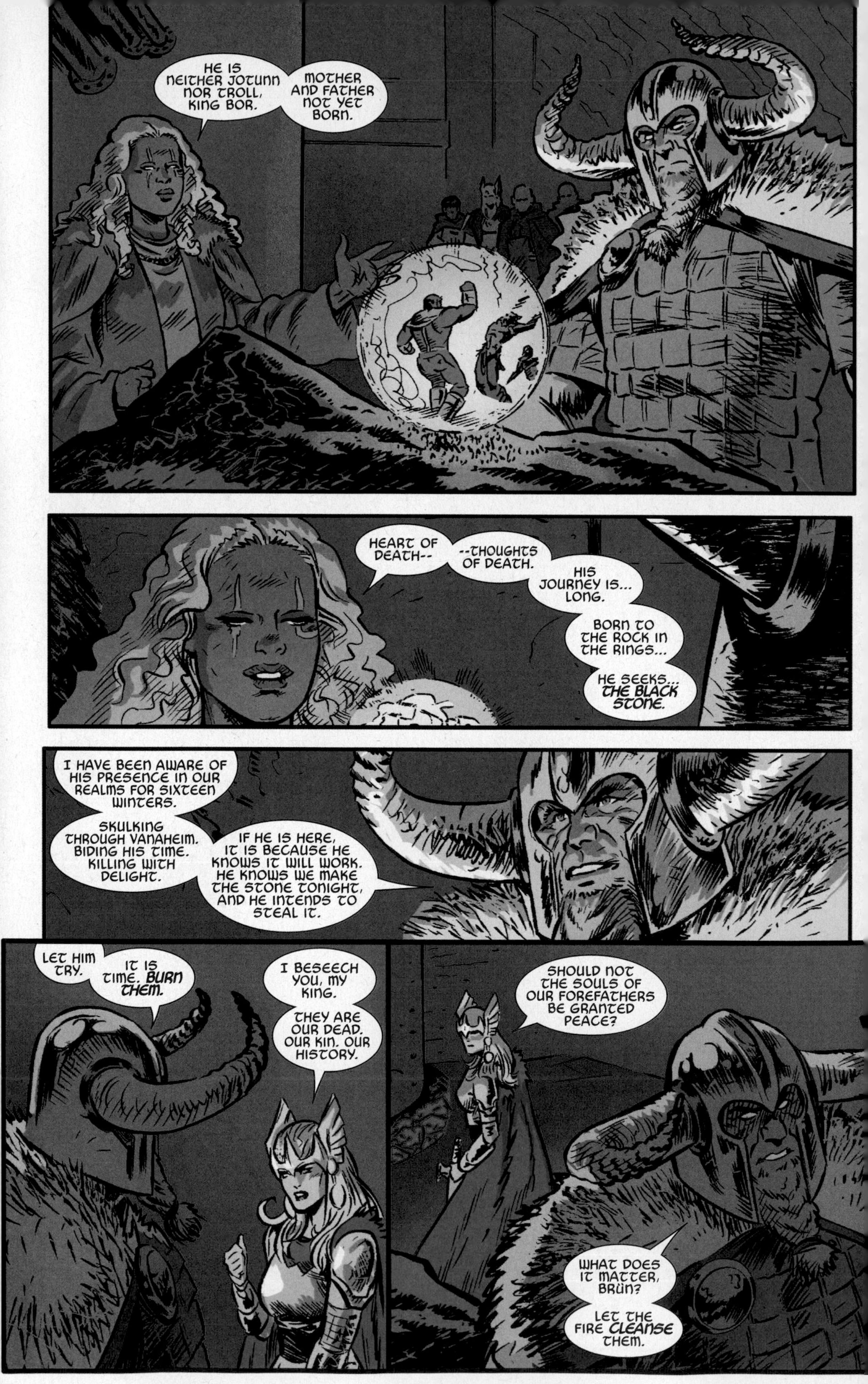
HE IS NEITHER JOTUNN NOR TROLL, KING BOR.
MOTHER AND FATHER NOT YET BORN.
HEART OF DEATH--
--THOUGHTS OF DEATH.
HIS JOURNEY IS... LONG.
BORN TO THE ROCK IN THE RINGS...
HE SEEKS... THE BLACK STONE.
I HAVE BEEN AWARE OF HIS PRESENCE IN OUR REALMS FOR SIXTEEN WINTERS.
SKULKING THROUGH VANAHEIM. BIDING HIS TIME. KILLING WITH DELIGHT.
IF HE IS HERE, IT IS BECAUSE HE KNOWS IT WILL WORK. HE KNOWS WE MAKE THE STONE TONIGHT, AND HE INTENDS TO STEAL IT.
LET HIM TRY.
IT IS TIME. BURN THEM.
I BESEECH YOU, MY KING.
THEY ARE OUR DEAD. OUR KIN. OUR HISTORY.
SHOULD NOT THE SOULS OF OUR FOREFATHERS BE GRANTED PEACE?
WHAT DOES IT MATTER, BRÜN?
LET THE FIRE CLEANSE THEM.

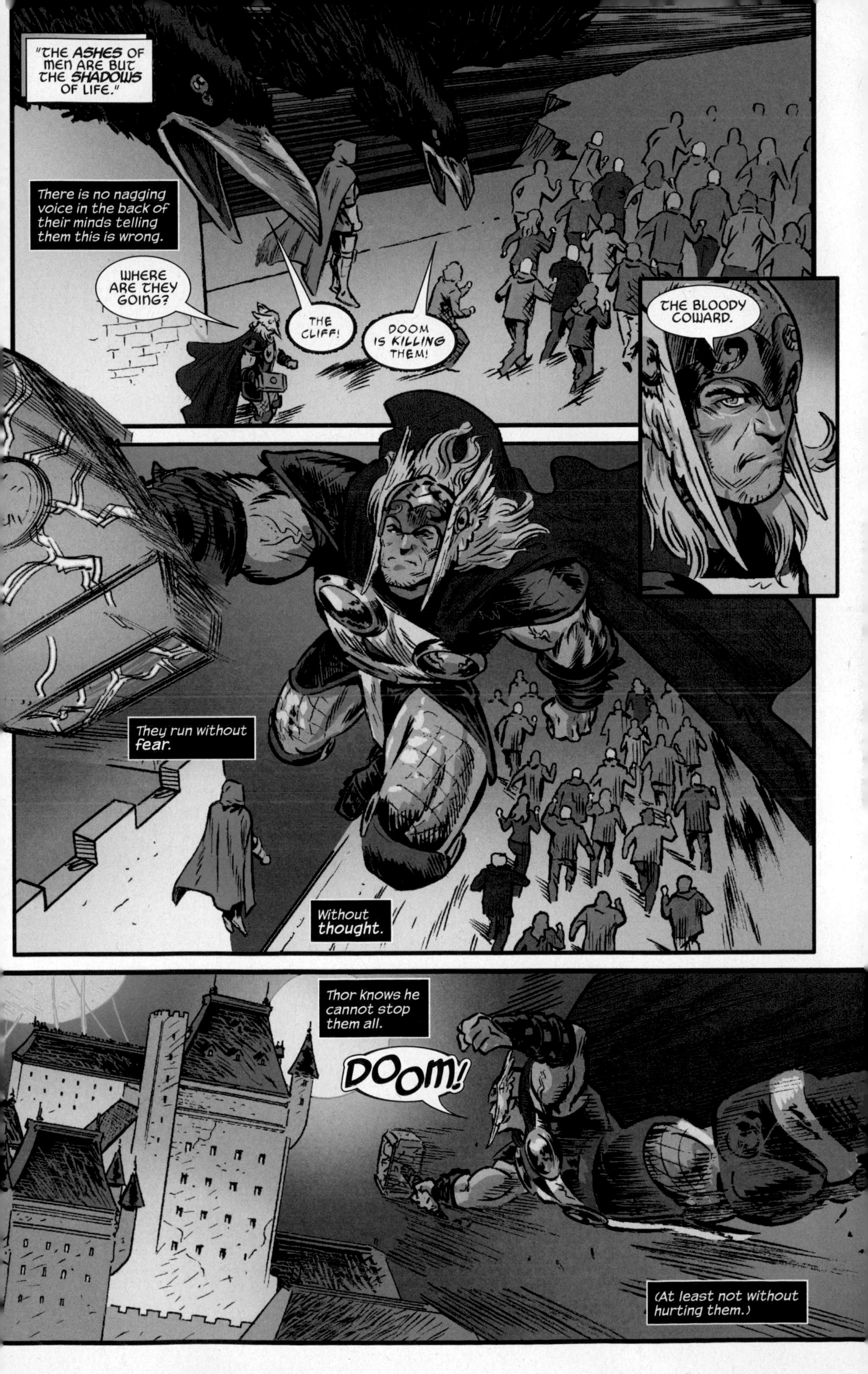
"THE ASHES OF MEN ARE BUT THE SHADOWS OF LIFE."
There is no nagging voice in the back of their minds telling them this is wrong.
WHERE ARE THEY GOING?
THE CLIFF!
DOOM IS KILLING THEM!
THE BLOODY COWARD.
They run without fear.
Without thought.
Thor knows he cannot stop them all.
DOOM!
(At least not without hurting them.)

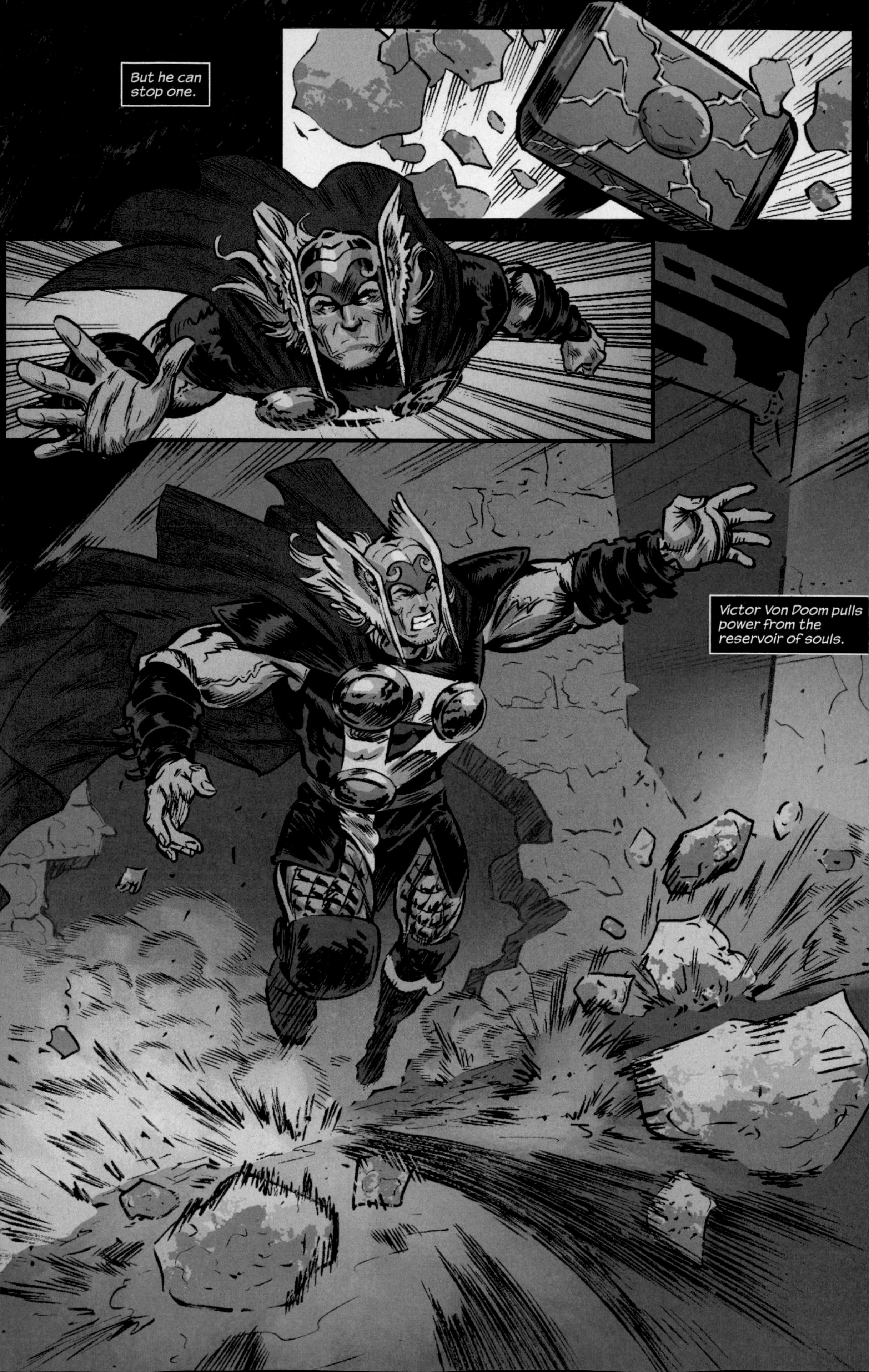
But he can
stop one.
Victor Von Doom pulls
power from the
reservoir of souls.

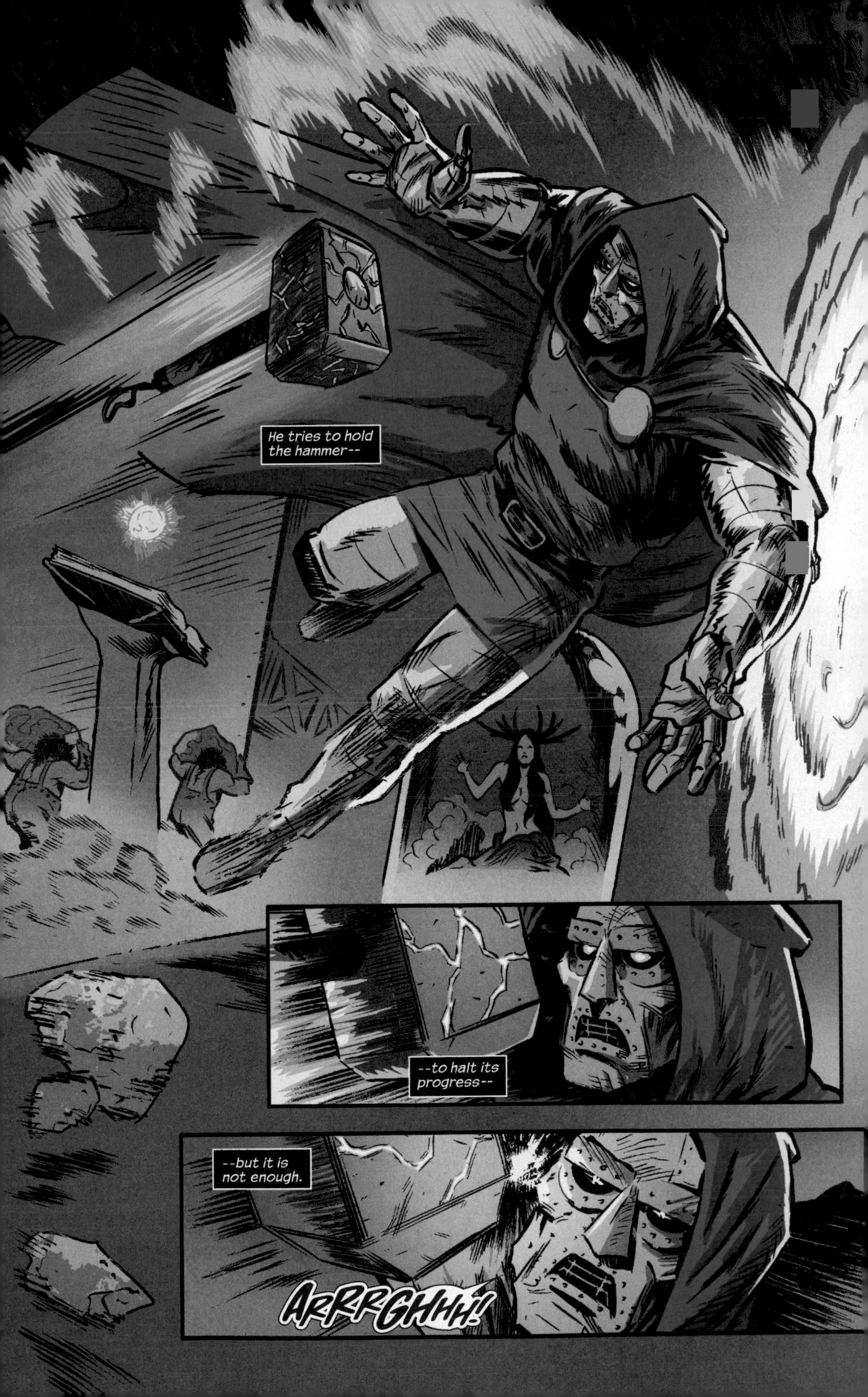
He tries to hold the hammer--
--to halt its progress--
--but it is not enough.
ARRRGHHH!

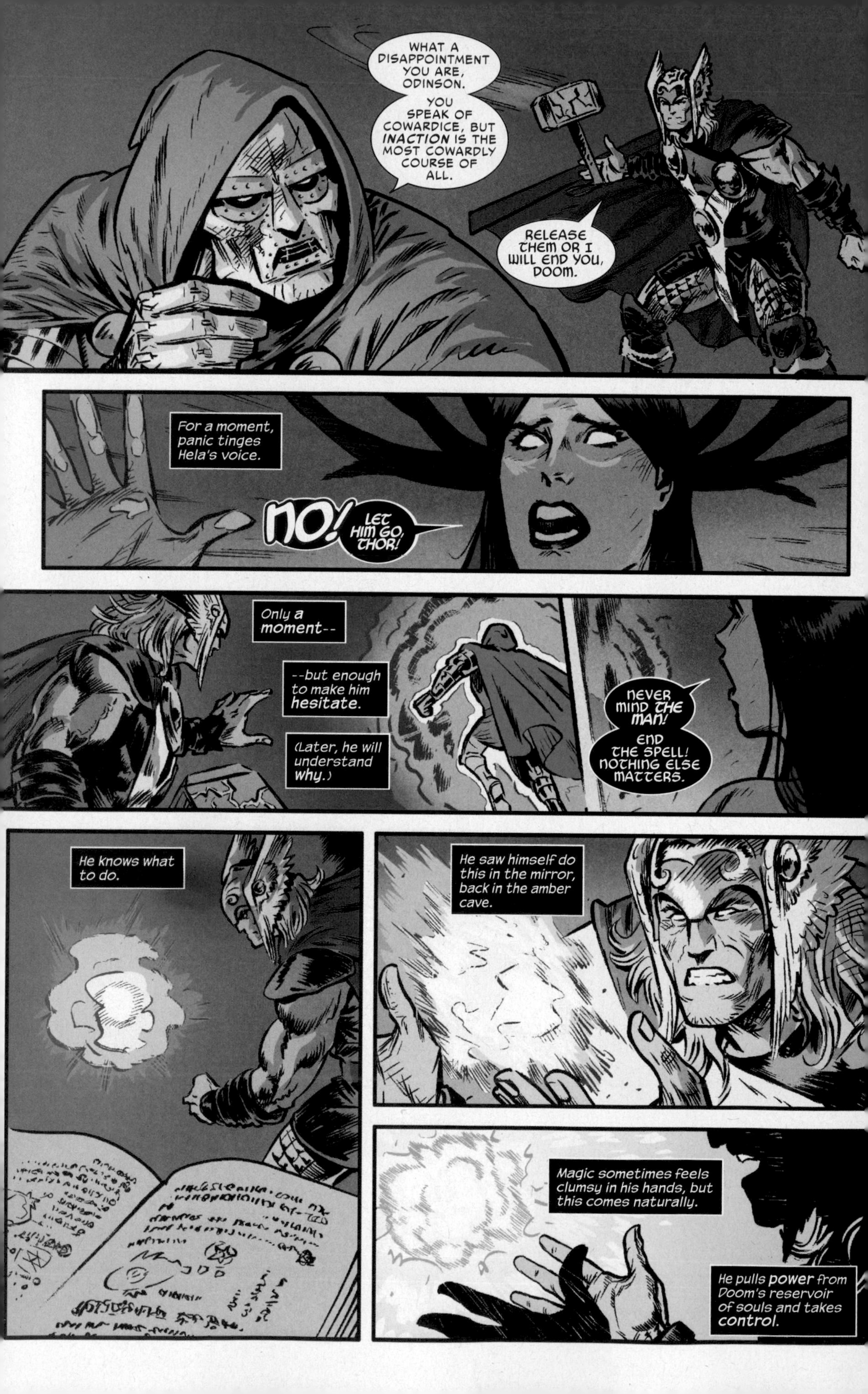
WHAT A DISAPPOINTMENT YOU ARE, ODINSON.
YOU SPEAK OF COWARDICE, BUT INACTION IS THE MOST COWARDLY COURSE OF ALL.
RELEASE THEM OR I WILL END YOU, DOOM.
For a moment, panic tinges Hela's voice.
NO! LET HIM GO, THOR!
Only a moment--
--but enough to make him hesitate.
(Later, he will understand why.)
NEVER MIND THE MAN!
END THE SPELL! NOTHING ELSE MATTERS.
He knows what to do.
He saw himself do this in the mirror, back in the amber cave.
Magic sometimes feels clumsy in his hands, but this comes naturally.
He pulls power from Doom's reservoir of souls and takes control.

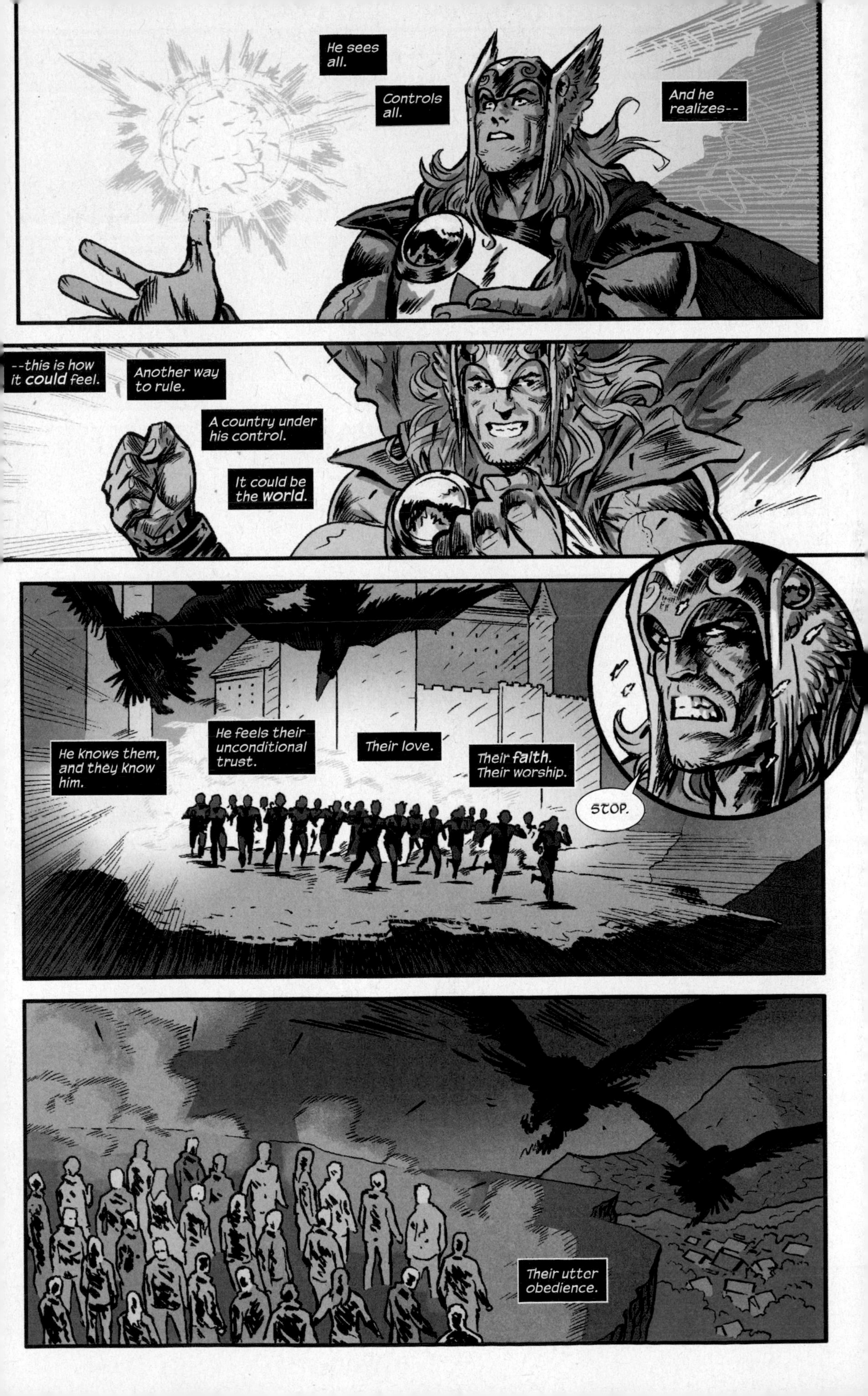
He sees all.
Controls all.
And he realizes--
--this is how it could feel.
Another way to rule.
A country under his control.
It could be the world.
He knows them, and they know him.
He feels their unconditional trust.
Their love.
Their faith. Their worship.
STOP.
Their utter obedience.

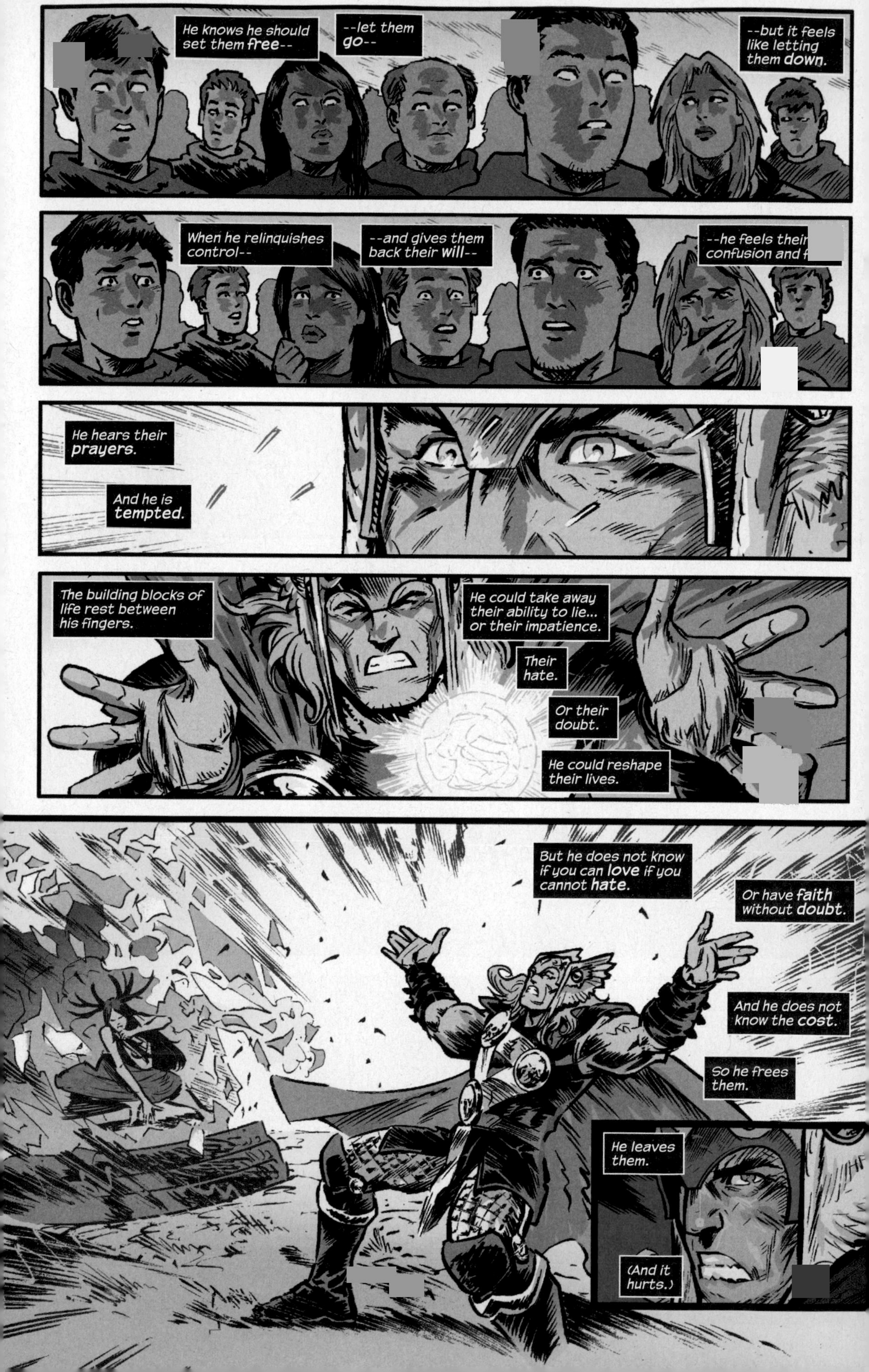
He knows he should set them free--
--let them go--
--but it feels like letting them down.
When he relinquishes control--
--and gives them back their will--
--he feels their confusion and f
He hears their prayers.
And he is tempted.
The building blocks of life rest between his fingers.
He could take away their ability to lie... or their impatience.
Their hate.
Or their doubt.
He could reshape their lives.
But he does not know if you can love if you cannot hate.
Or have faith without doubt.
And he does not know the cost.
So he frees them.
He leaves them.
(And it hurts.)

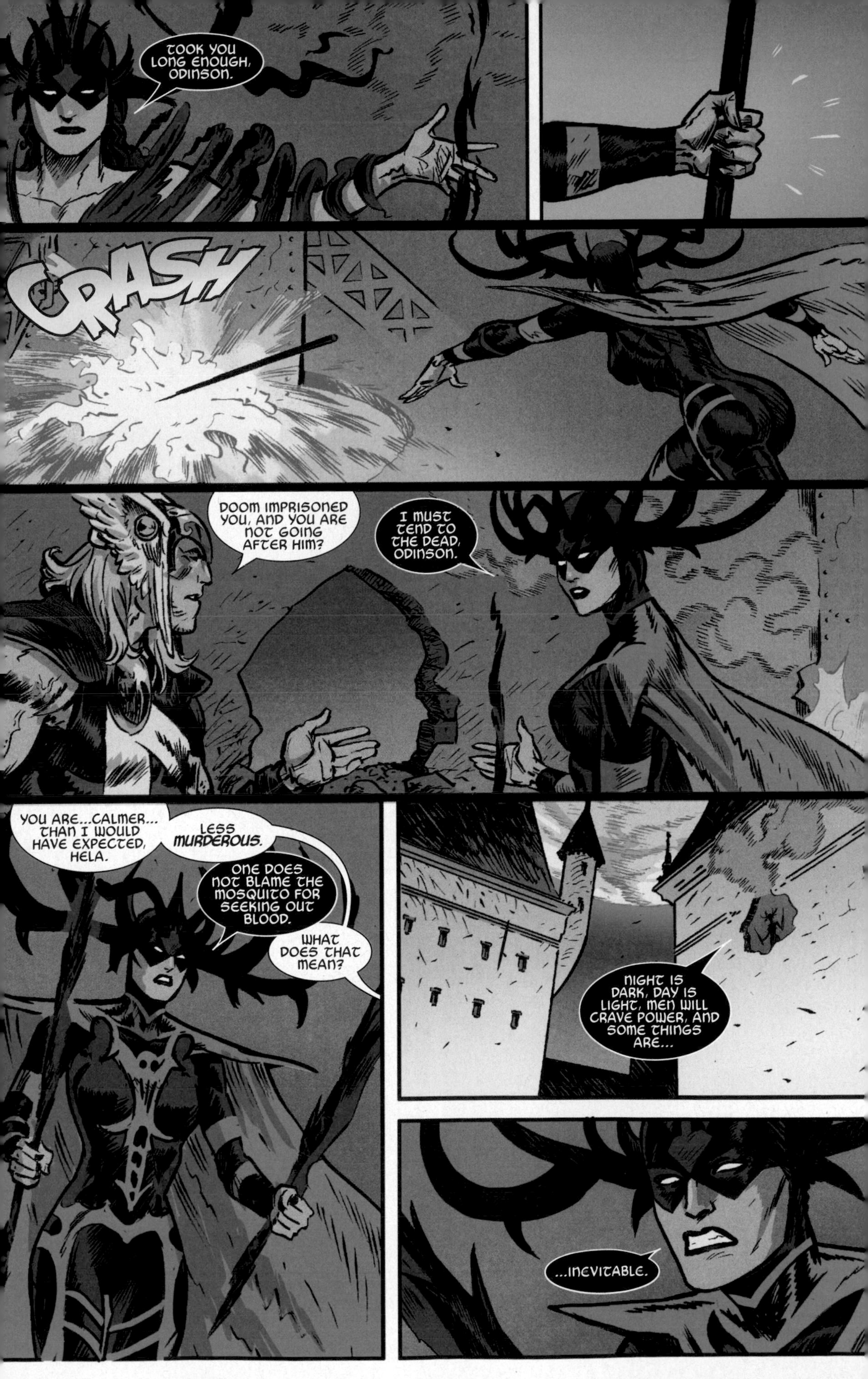

TOOK YOU LONG ENOUGH, ODINSON.
CRASH
DOOM IMPRISONED YOU, AND YOU ARE NOT GOING AFTER HIM?
I MUST TEND TO THE DEAD, ODINSON.
YOU ARE...CALMER... THAN I WOULD HAVE EXPECTED, HELA.
LESS MURDEROUS.
ONE DOES NOT BLAME THE MOSQUITO FOR SEEKING OUT BLOOD.
WHAT DOES THAT MEAN?
NIGHT IS DARK, DAY IS LIGHT, MEN WILL CRAVE POWER, AND SOME THINGS ARE...
...INEVITABLE.

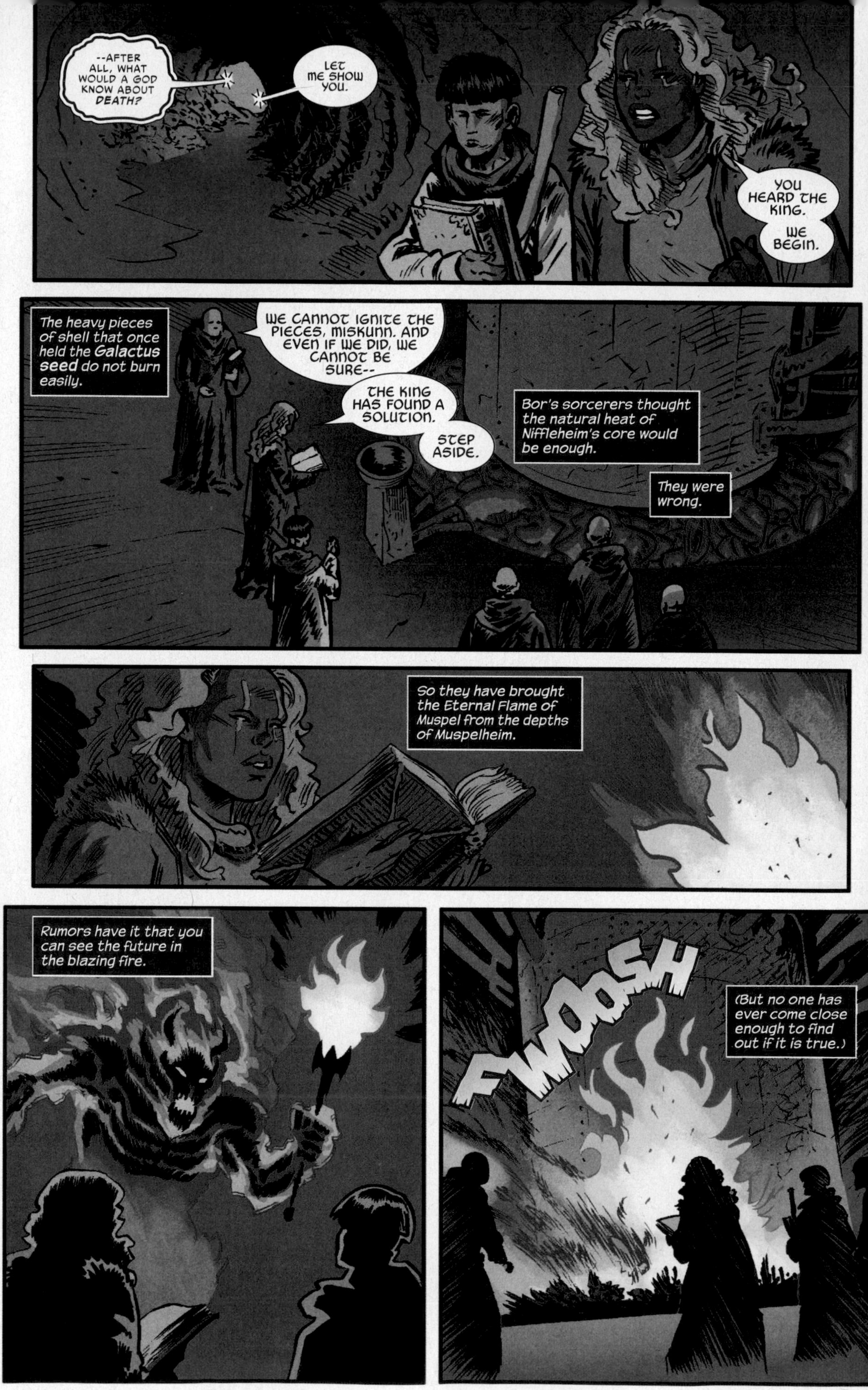
--AFTER ALL, WHAT WOULD A GOD KNOW ABOUT DEATH?
LET ME SHOW YOU.
YOU HEARD THE KING.
WE BEGIN.
The heavy pieces of shell that once held the Galactus seed do not burn easily.
WE CANNOT IGNITE THE PIECES, MISKUNN. AND EVEN IF WE DID, WE CANNOT BE SURE--
THE KING HAS FOUND A SOLUTION.
STEP ASIDE.
Bor's sorcerers thought the natural heat of Niffleheim's core would be enough.
They were wrong.
So they have brought the Eternal Flame of Muspel from the depths of Muspelheim.
Rumors have it that you can see the future in the blazing fire.
FWOOSH
(But no one has ever come close enough to find out if it is true.)

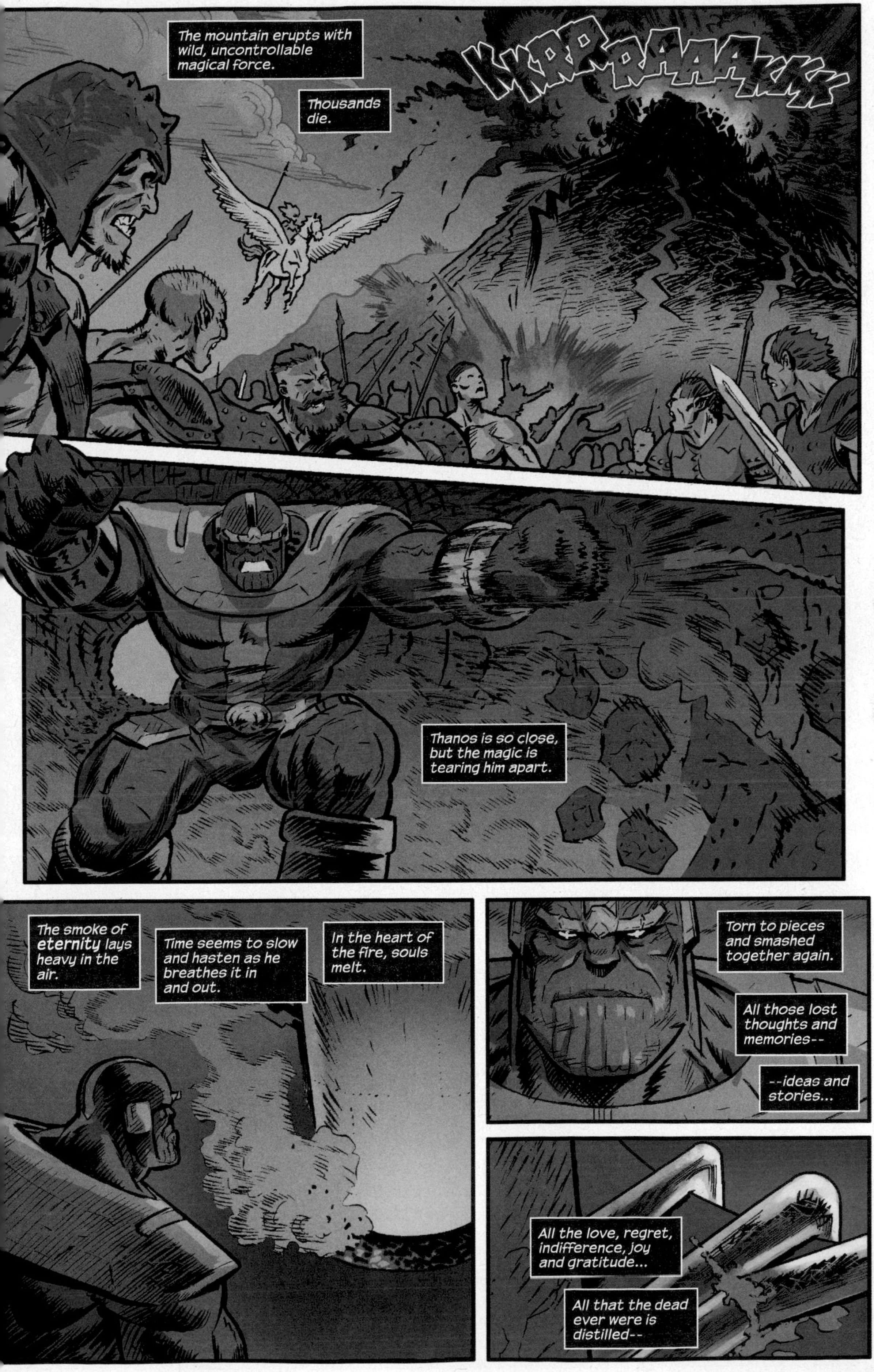
The mountain erupts with wild, uncontrollable magical force.
Thousands die.
KKRP RAAAKKK
Thanos is so close, but the magic is tearing him apart.
The smoke of eternity lays heavy in the air.
Time seems to slow and hasten as he breathes it in and out.
In the heart of the fire, souls melt.
Torn to pieces and smashed together again.
All those lost thoughts and memories--
--ideas and stories...
All the love, regret, indifference, joy and gratitude...
All that the dead ever were is distilled--

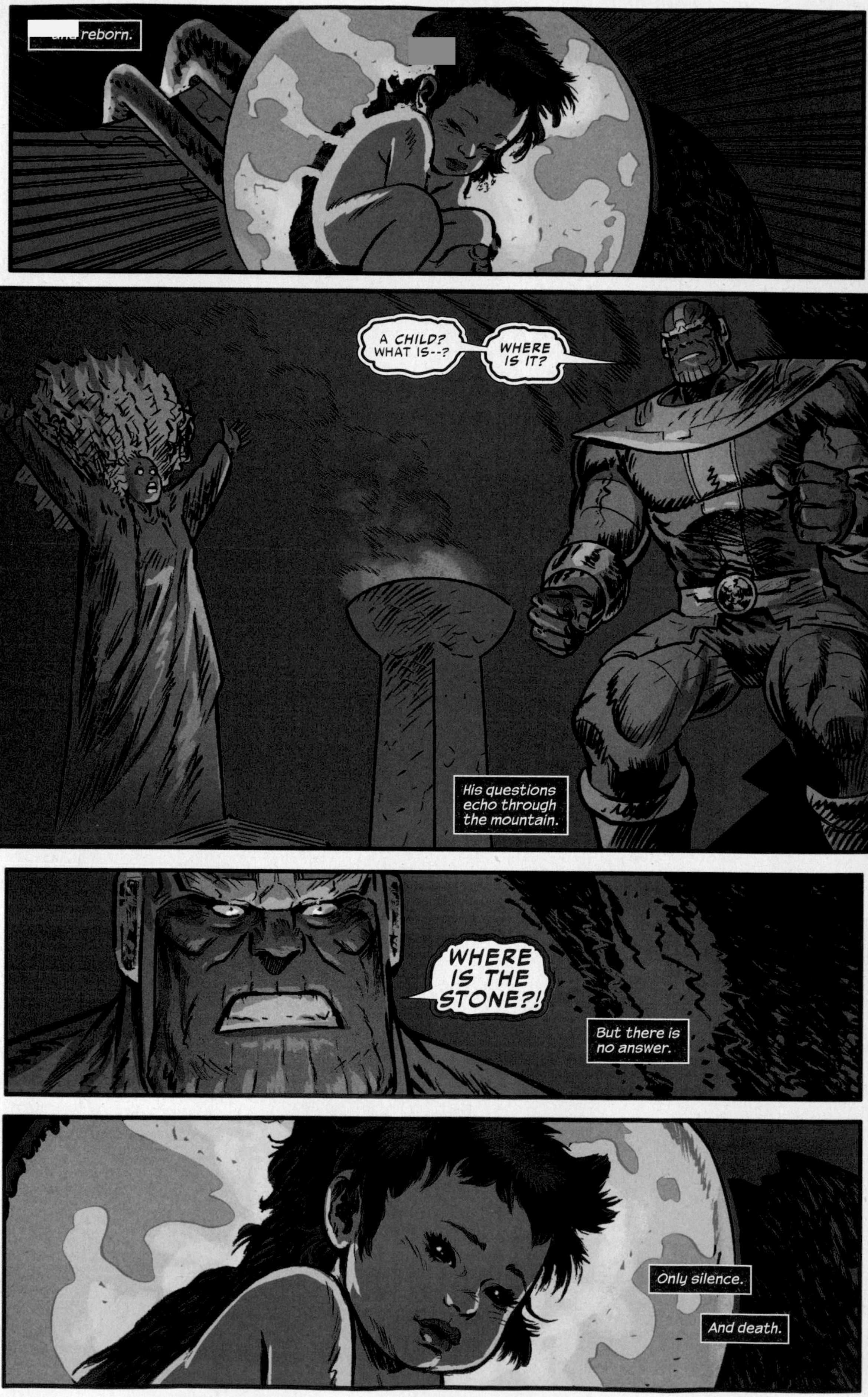
reborn.
A CHILD? WHAT IS--?
WHERE IS IT?
His questions echo through the mountain.
WHERE IS THE STONE?!
But there is no answer.
Only silence.
And death.

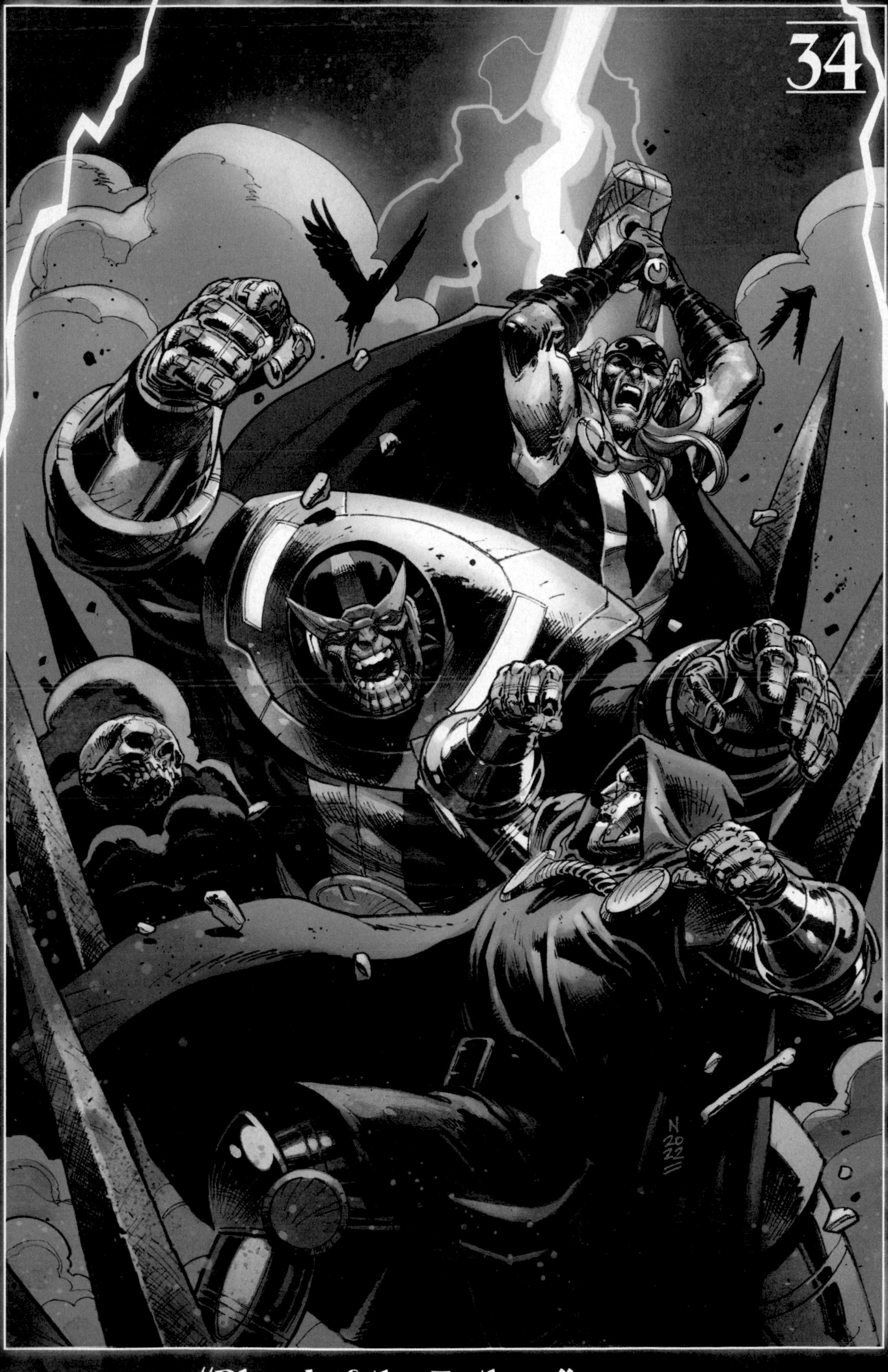
34
N
2022

"Blood of the Fathers" PART FOUR

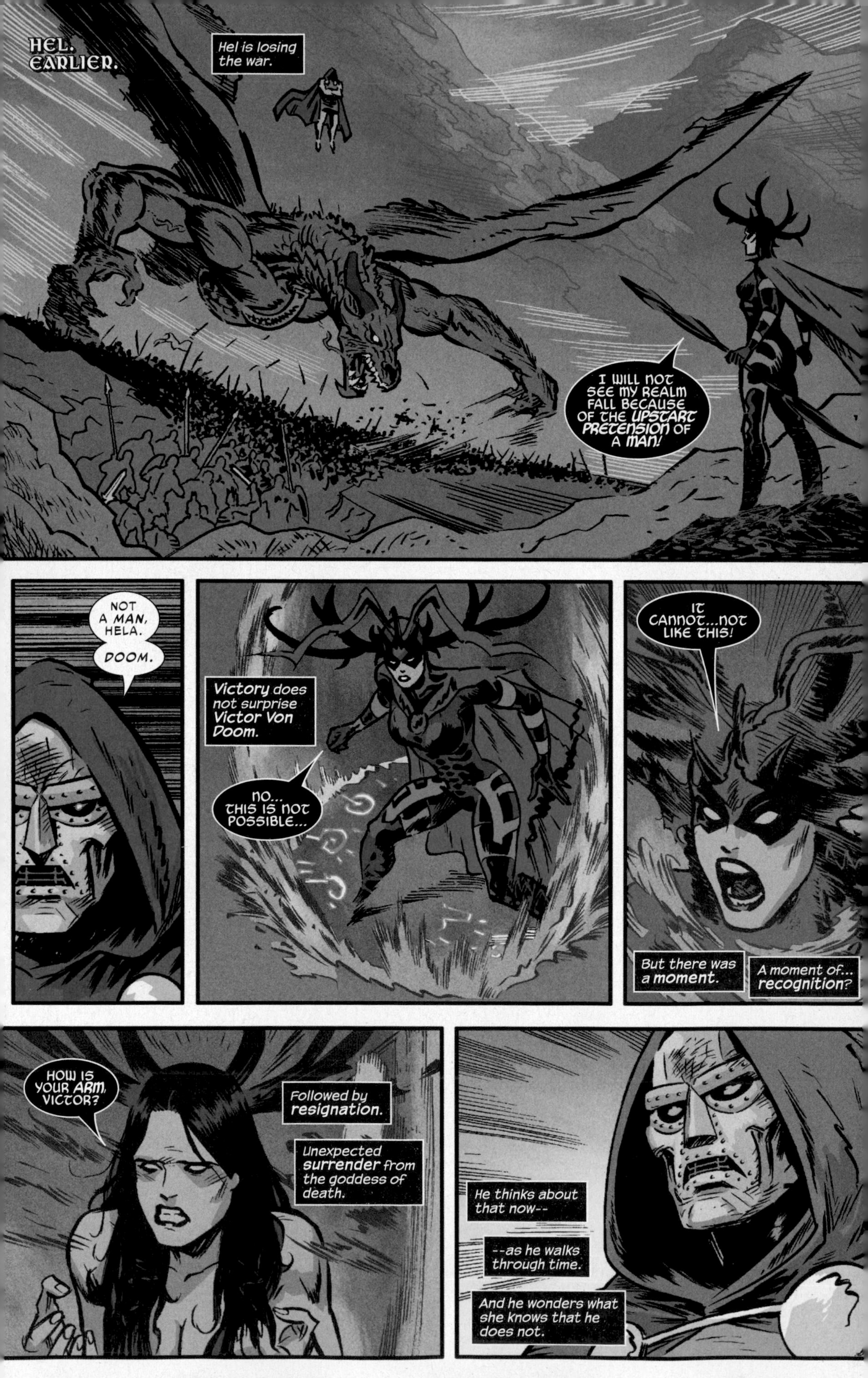
HEL.
EARLIER.
Hel is losing the war.
I WILL NOT SEE MY REALM FALL BECAUSE OF THE UPSTART PRETENSION OF A MAN!
NOT A MAN, HELA.
DOOM.
Victory does not surprise Victor Von Doom.
NO... THIS IS NOT POSSIBLE...
IT CANNOT...NOT LIKE THIS!
But there was a moment.
A moment of... recognition?
HOW IS YOUR ARM, VICTOR?
Followed by resignation.
Unexpected surrender from the goddess of death.
He thinks about that now--
--as he walks through time.
And he wonders what she knows that he does not.

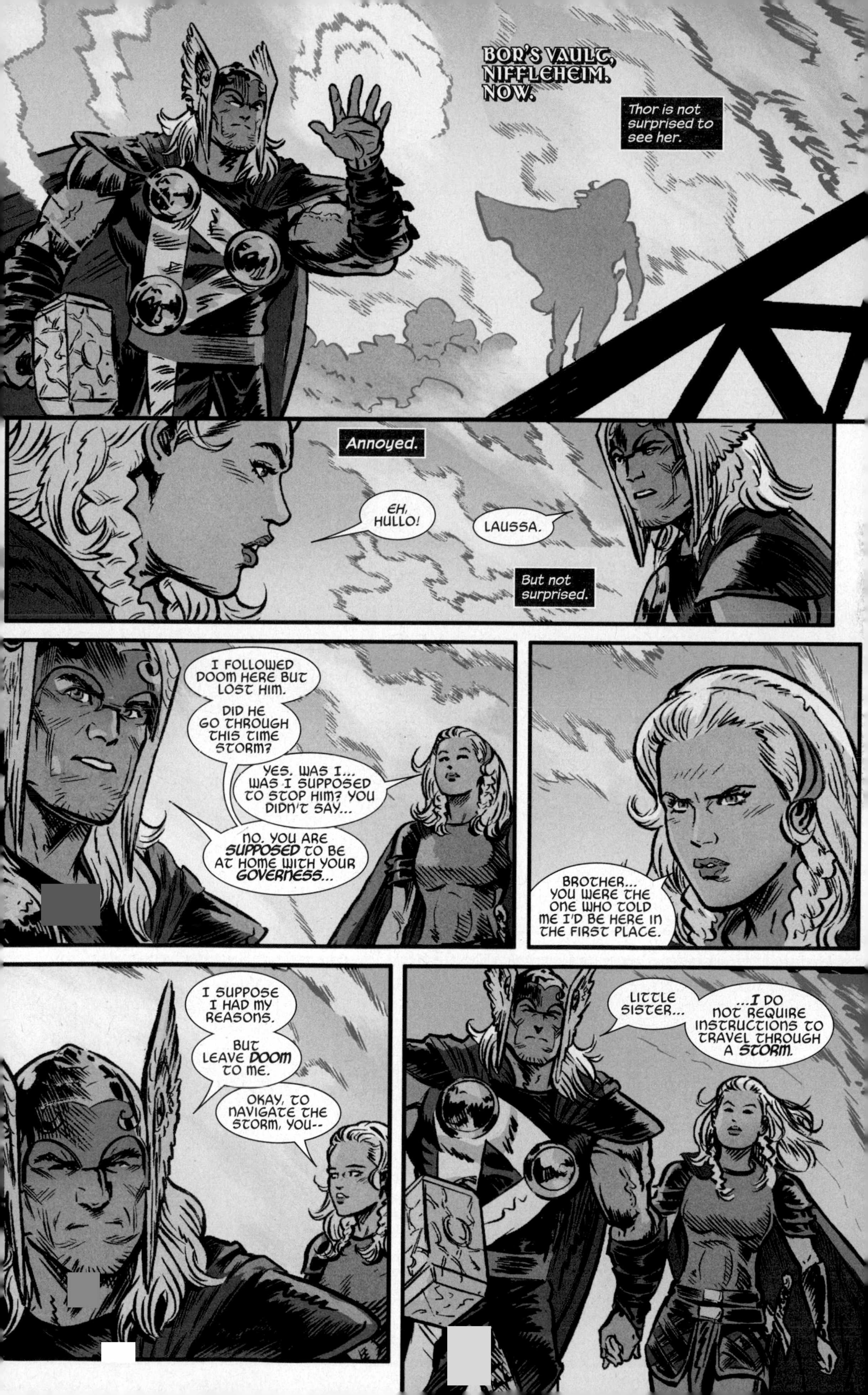
BOR'S VAULT, NIFFLEHEIM. NOW.
Thor is not surprised to see her.
Annoyed.
EH, HULLO!
LAUSSA.
But not surprised.
I FOLLOWED DOOM HERE BUT LOST HIM.
DID HE GO THROUGH THIS TIME STORM?
YES. WAS I... WAS I SUPPOSED TO STOP HIM? YOU DIDN'T SAY...
NO. YOU ARE SUPPOSED TO BE AT HOME WITH YOUR GOVERNESS...
BROTHER... YOU WERE THE ONE WHO TOLD ME I'D BE HERE IN THE FIRST PLACE.
I SUPPOSE I HAD MY REASONS.
BUT LEAVE DOOM TO ME.
OKAY, TO NAVIGATE THE STORM, YOU--
LITTLE SISTER...
...I DO NOT REQUIRE INSTRUCTIONS TO TRAVEL THROUGH A STORM.

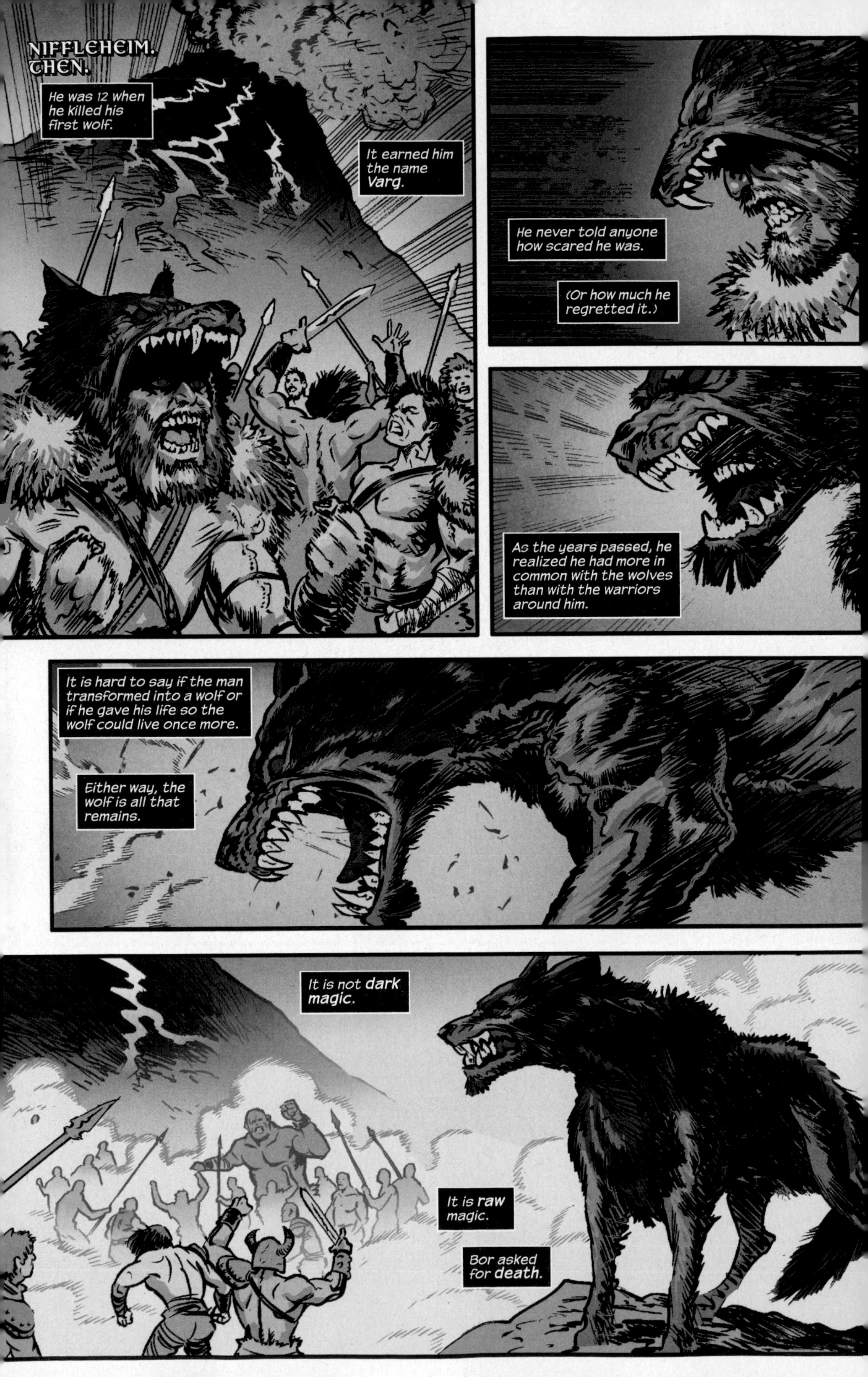
NIFFLEHEIM. THEN.
He was 12 when he killed his first wolf.
It earned him the name Varg.
He never told anyone how scared he was.
(Or how much he regretted it.)
As the years passed, he realized he had more in common with the wolves than with the warriors around him.
It is hard to say if the man transformed into a wolf or if he gave his life so the wolf could live once more.
Either way, the wolf is all that remains.
It is not dark magic.
It is raw magic.
Bor asked for death.

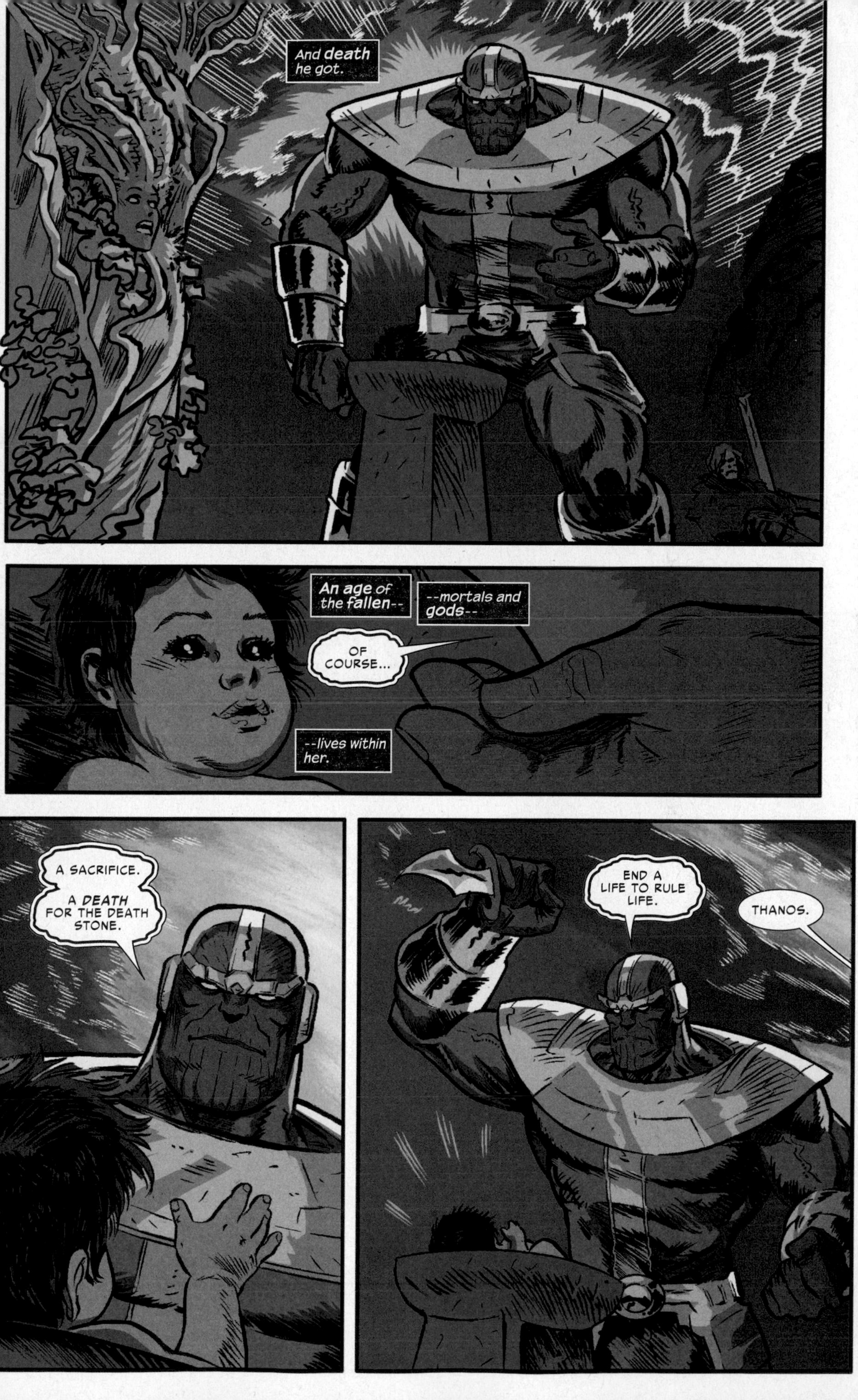
And death he got.
An age of the fallen--
--mortals and gods--
OF COURSE...
--lives within her.
A SACRIFICE.
A DEATH FOR THE DEATH STONE.
END A LIFE TO RULE LIFE.
THANOS.

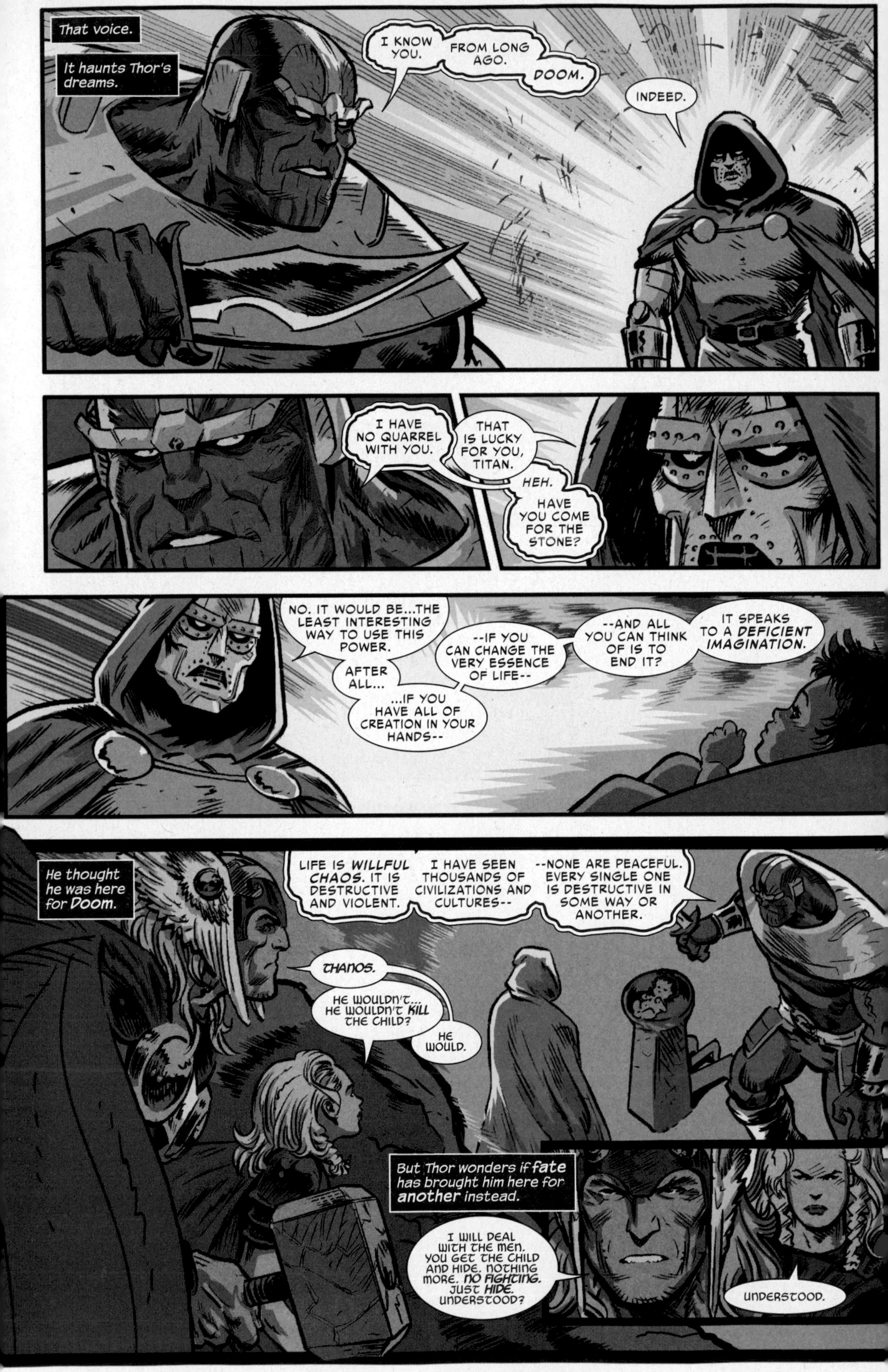

That voice.
It haunts Thor's dreams.
I KNOW YOU.
FROM LONG AGO.
DOOM.
INDEED.
I HAVE NO QUARREL WITH YOU.
THAT IS LUCKY FOR YOU, TITAN.
HEH.
HAVE YOU COME FOR THE STONE?
NO. IT WOULD BE...THE LEAST INTERESTING WAY TO USE THIS POWER.
AFTER ALL...
...IF YOU HAVE ALL OF CREATION IN YOUR HANDS--
--IF YOU CAN CHANGE THE VERY ESSENCE OF LIFE--
--AND ALL YOU CAN THINK OF IS TO END IT?
IT SPEAKS TO A DEFICIENT IMAGINATION.
He thought he was here for Doom.
LIFE IS WILLFUL CHAOS. IT IS DESTRUCTIVE AND VIOLENT.
I HAVE SEEN THOUSANDS OF CIVILIZATIONS AND CULTURES--
--NONE ARE PEACEFUL. EVERY SINGLE ONE IS DESTRUCTIVE IN SOME WAY OR ANOTHER.
THANOS.
HE WOULDN'T... HE WOULDN'T KILL THE CHILD?
HE WOULD.
But Thor wonders if fate has brought him here for another instead.
I WILL DEAL WITH THE MEN. YOU GET THE CHILD AND HIDE. NOTHING MORE. NO FIGHTING. JUST HIDE. UNDERSTOOD?
UNDERSTOOD.

It takes him a moment--

--but Doom knows who **the child** is now.

YOUR *HUMANITY* IS NO DIFFERENT.

THEY WILL DESTROY EACH OTHER UNTIL THEY HAVE ENOUGH FOR THEMSELVES.

NOT KNOWING THAT THERE *IS* NO "ENOUGH," THEY WILL ALWAYS WANT *MORE.*

THAT IS THEIR DEFINING TRAIT.

I CAN *CHANGE* THEM. DO YOU NOT SEE?

And he panics.

NO. LET THEM DIE WITH DIGNITY.

NO!

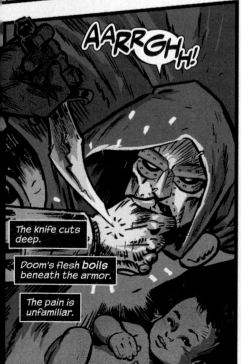

AARRGHH!

The knife cuts deep.

Doom's flesh *boils* beneath the armor.

The pain is unfamiliar.

CRACK

Unbearable.

He does not know if he can withstand another blow.

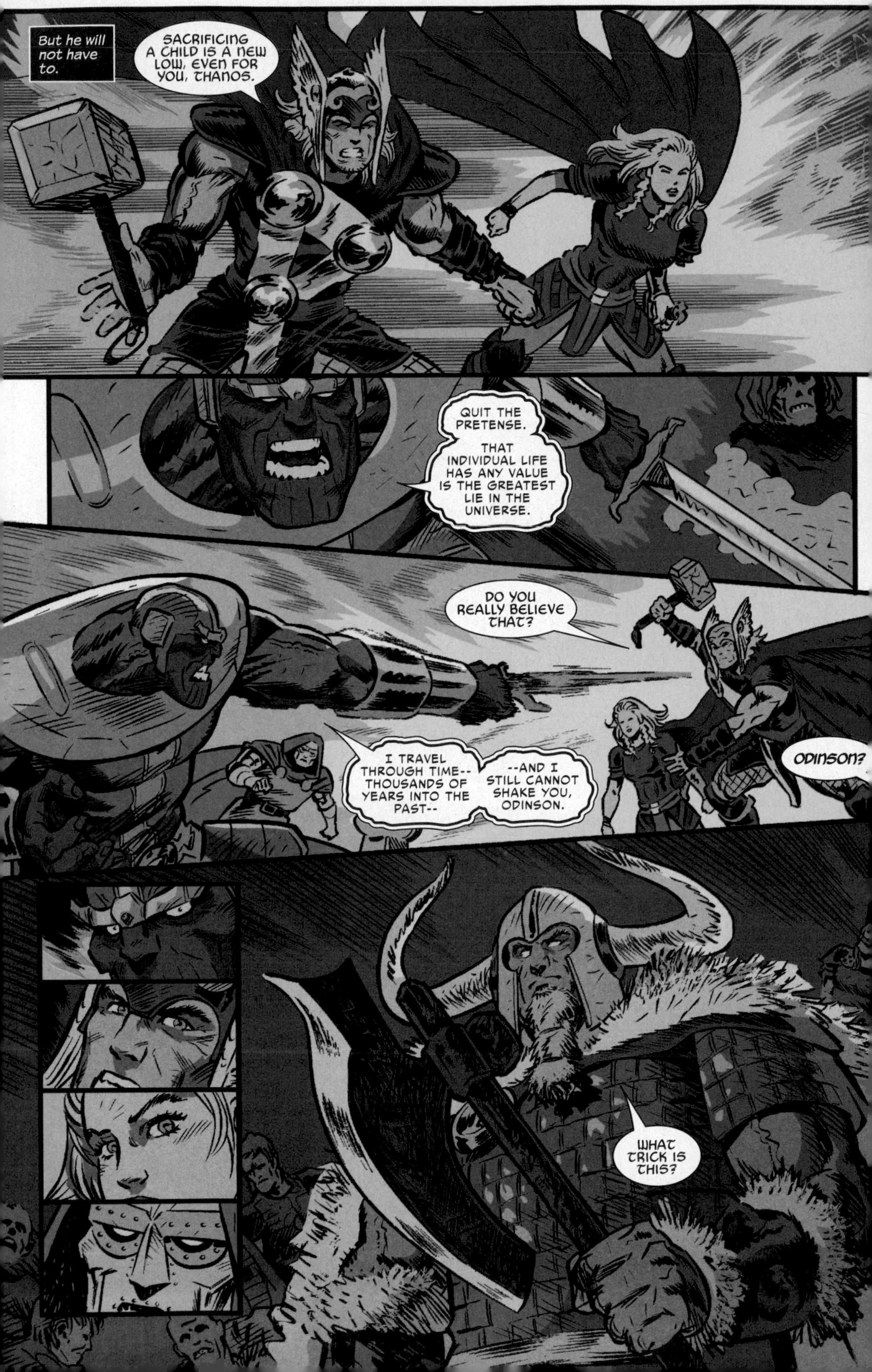
But he will not have to.
SACRIFICING A CHILD IS A NEW LOW, EVEN FOR YOU, THANOS.
QUIT THE PRETENSE.
THAT INDIVIDUAL LIFE HAS ANY VALUE IS THE GREATEST LIE IN THE UNIVERSE.
DO YOU REALLY BELIEVE THAT?
I TRAVEL THROUGH TIME-- THOUSANDS OF YEARS INTO THE PAST--
--AND I STILL CANNOT SHAKE YOU, ODINSON.
ODINSON?
WHAT TRICK IS THIS?

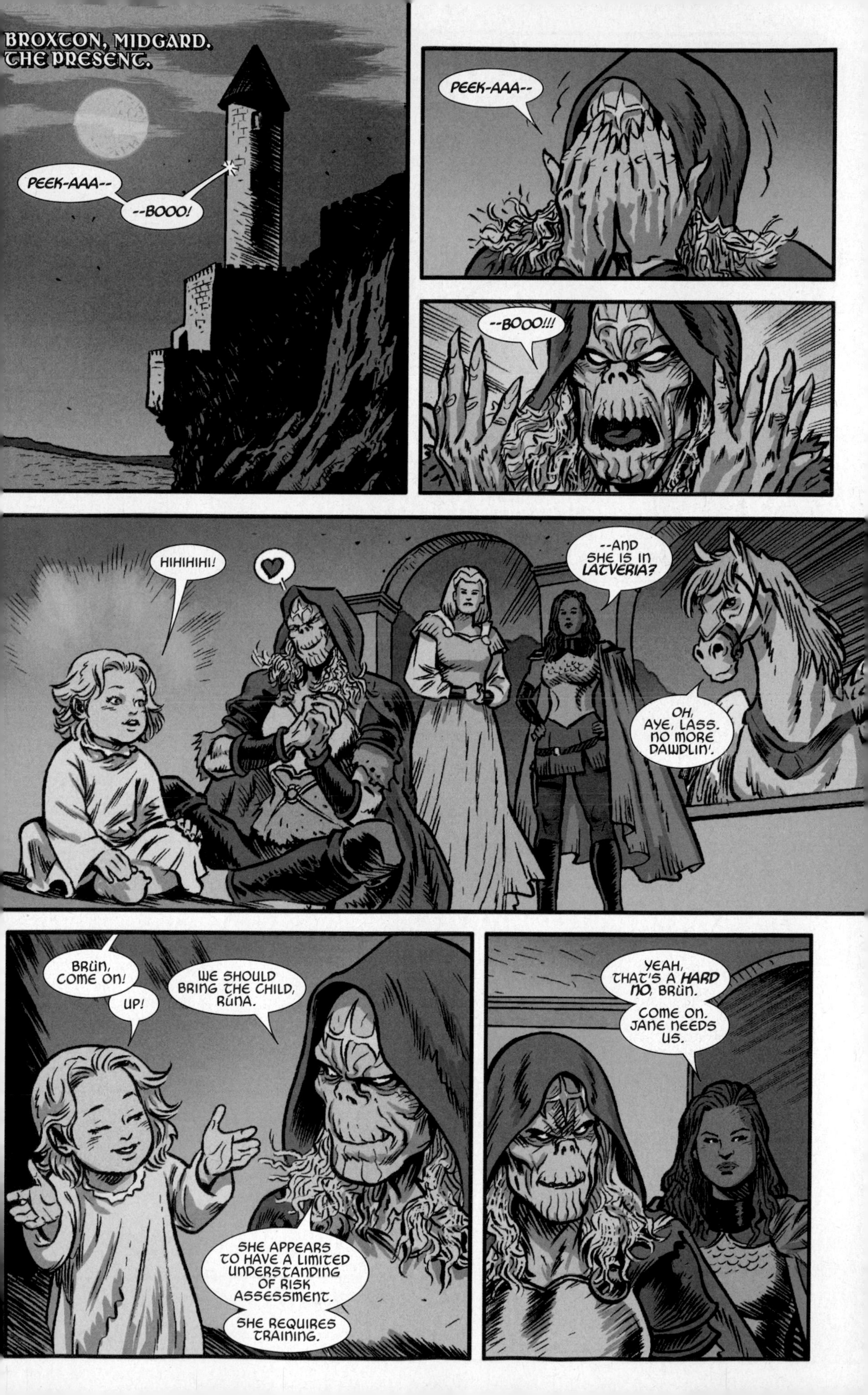
BROXTON, MIDGARD. THE PRESENT.
PEEK-AAA--
--BOOO!
PEEK-AAA--
--BOOO!!!
HIHIHIHI!
--AND SHE IS IN LATVERIA?
OH, AYE, LASS. NO MORE DAWDLIN'.
BRÜN, COME ON!
UP!
WE SHOULD BRING THE CHILD, RÚNA.
SHE APPEARS TO HAVE A LIMITED UNDERSTANDING OF RISK ASSESSMENT.
SHE REQUIRES TRAINING.
YEAH, THAT'S A HARD NO, BRÜN.
COME ON. JANE NEEDS US.

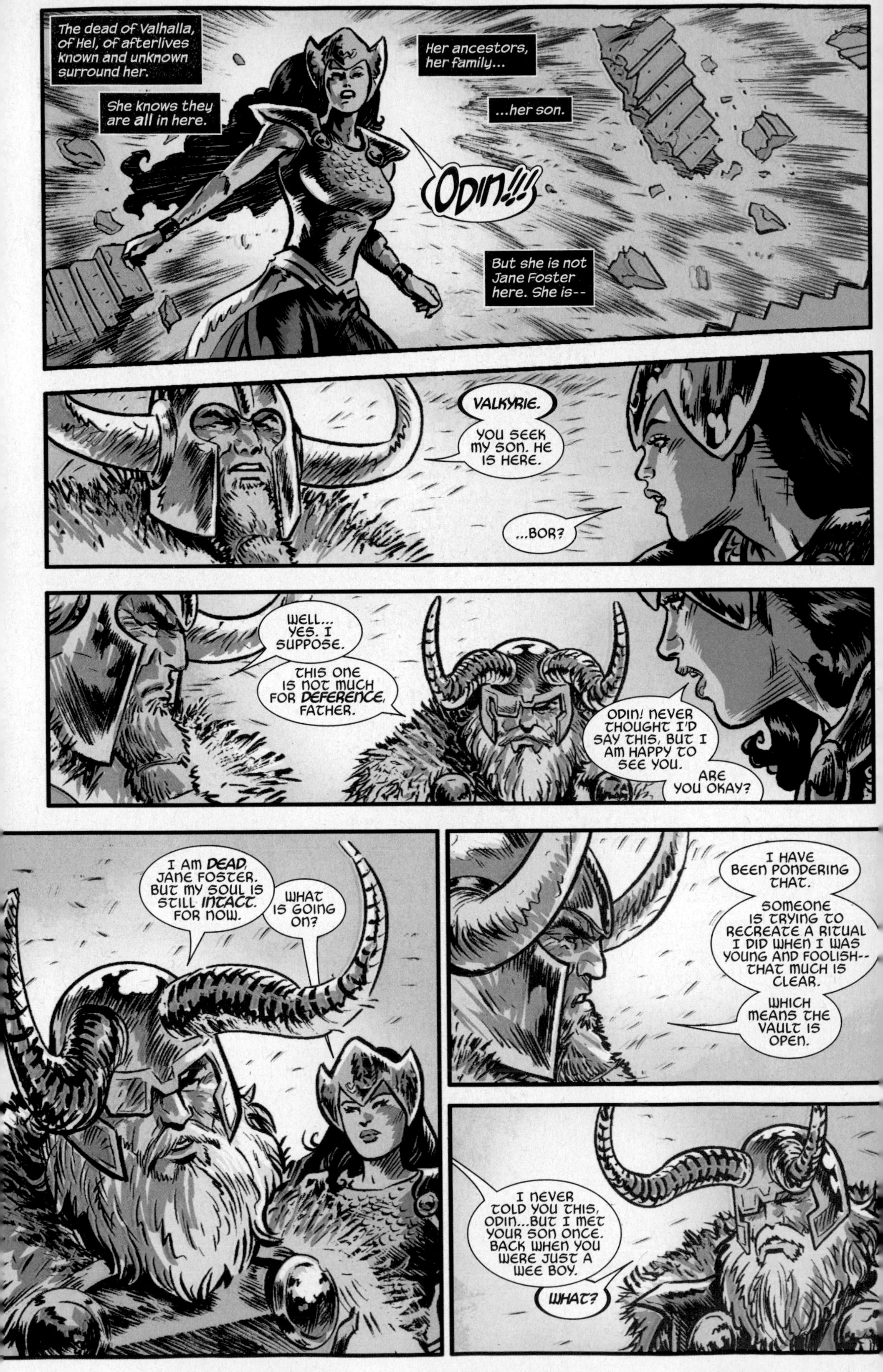

The dead of Valhalla, of Hel, of afterlives known and unknown surround her.
She knows they are all in here.
Her ancestors, her family...
...her son.
ODIN!!!
But she is not Jane Foster here. She is--
VALKYRIE.
YOU SEEK MY SON. HE IS HERE.
...BOR?
WELL... YES. I SUPPOSE.
THIS ONE IS NOT MUCH FOR DEFERENCE, FATHER.
ODIN! NEVER THOUGHT I'D SAY THIS, BUT I AM HAPPY TO SEE YOU.
ARE YOU OKAY?
I AM DEAD, JANE FOSTER. BUT MY SOUL IS STILL INTACT. FOR NOW.
WHAT IS GOING ON?
I HAVE BEEN PONDERING THAT.
SOMEONE IS TRYING TO RECREATE A RITUAL I DID WHEN I WAS YOUNG AND FOOLISH-- THAT MUCH IS CLEAR.
WHICH MEANS THE VAULT IS OPEN.
I NEVER TOLD YOU THIS, ODIN...BUT I MET YOUR SON ONCE. BACK WHEN YOU WERE JUST A WEE BOY.
WHAT?

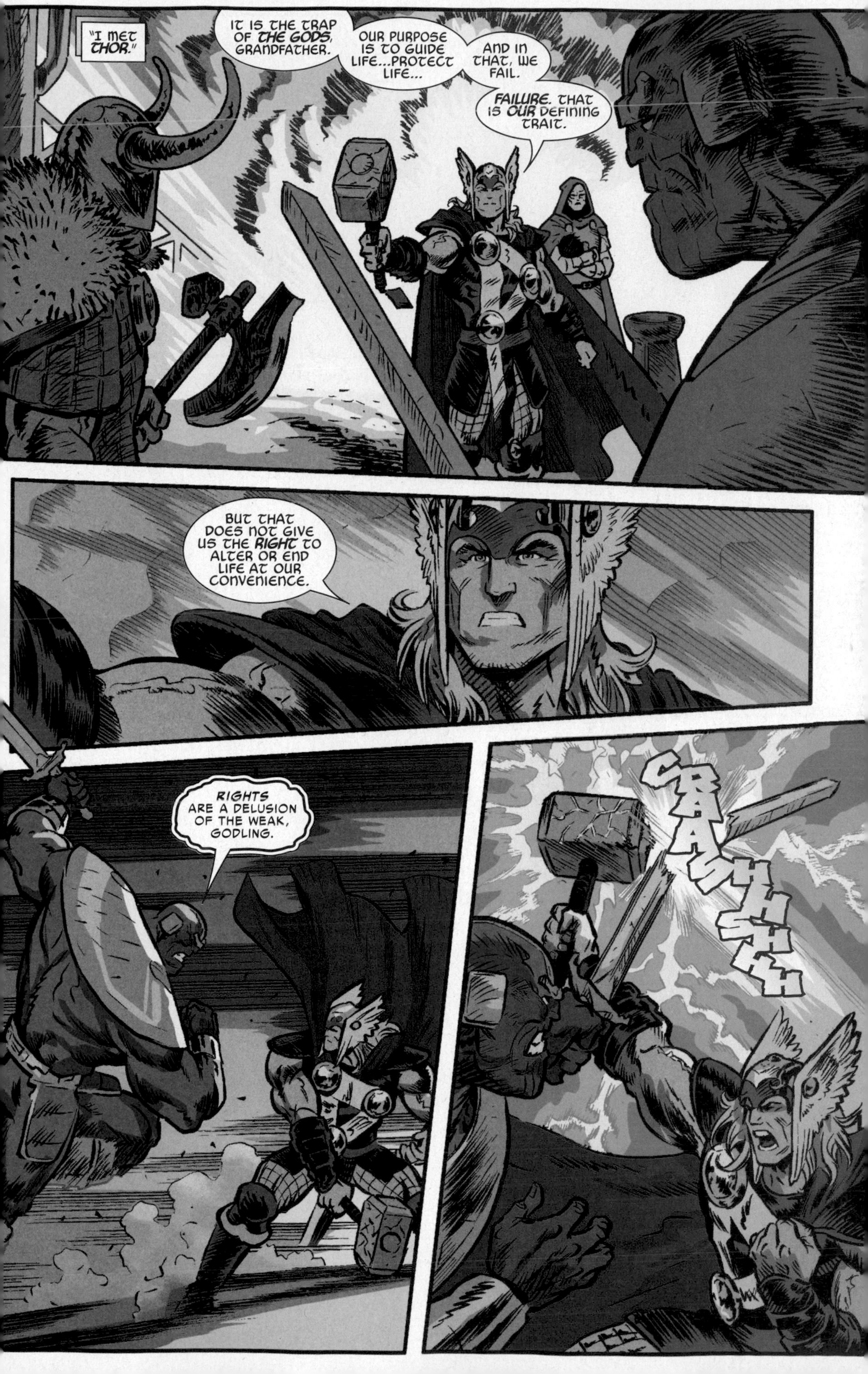
"I MET THOR."
IT IS THE TRAP OF THE GODS, GRANDFATHER.
OUR PURPOSE IS TO GUIDE LIFE...PROTECT LIFE...
AND IN THAT, WE FAIL.
FAILURE. THAT IS OUR DEFINING TRAIT.
BUT THAT DOES NOT GIVE US THE RIGHT TO ALTER OR END LIFE AT OUR CONVENIENCE.
RIGHTS ARE A DELUSION OF THE WEAK, GODLING.
CRASHHSHHH

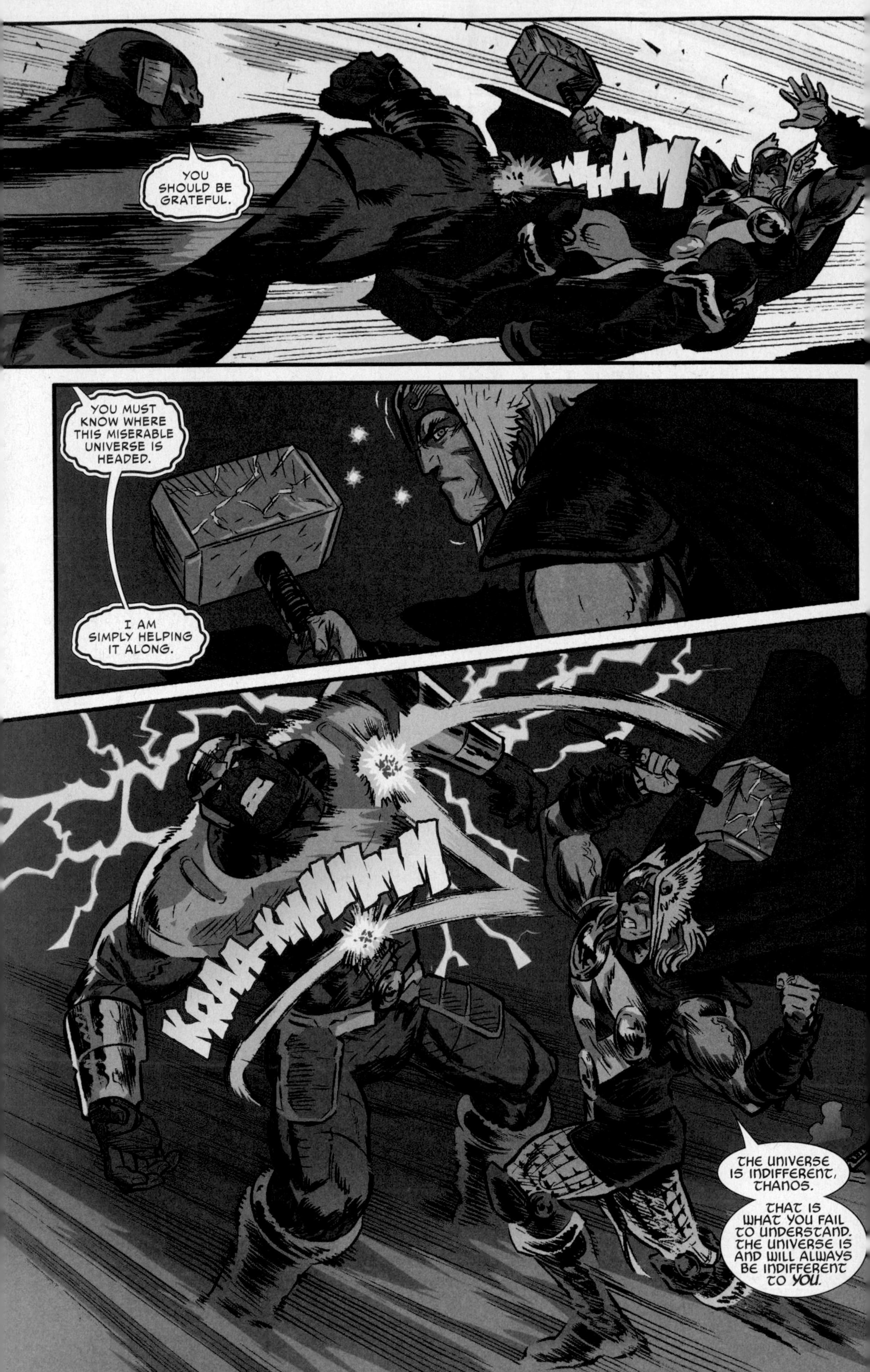
YOU SHOULD BE GRATEFUL.
WHAM
YOU MUST KNOW WHERE THIS MISERABLE UNIVERSE IS HEADED.
I AM SIMPLY HELPING IT ALONG.
KRAA-KMMMM
THE UNIVERSE IS INDIFFERENT, THANOS.
THAT IS WHAT YOU FAIL TO UNDERSTAND. THE UNIVERSE IS AND WILL ALWAYS BE INDIFFERENT TO YOU.

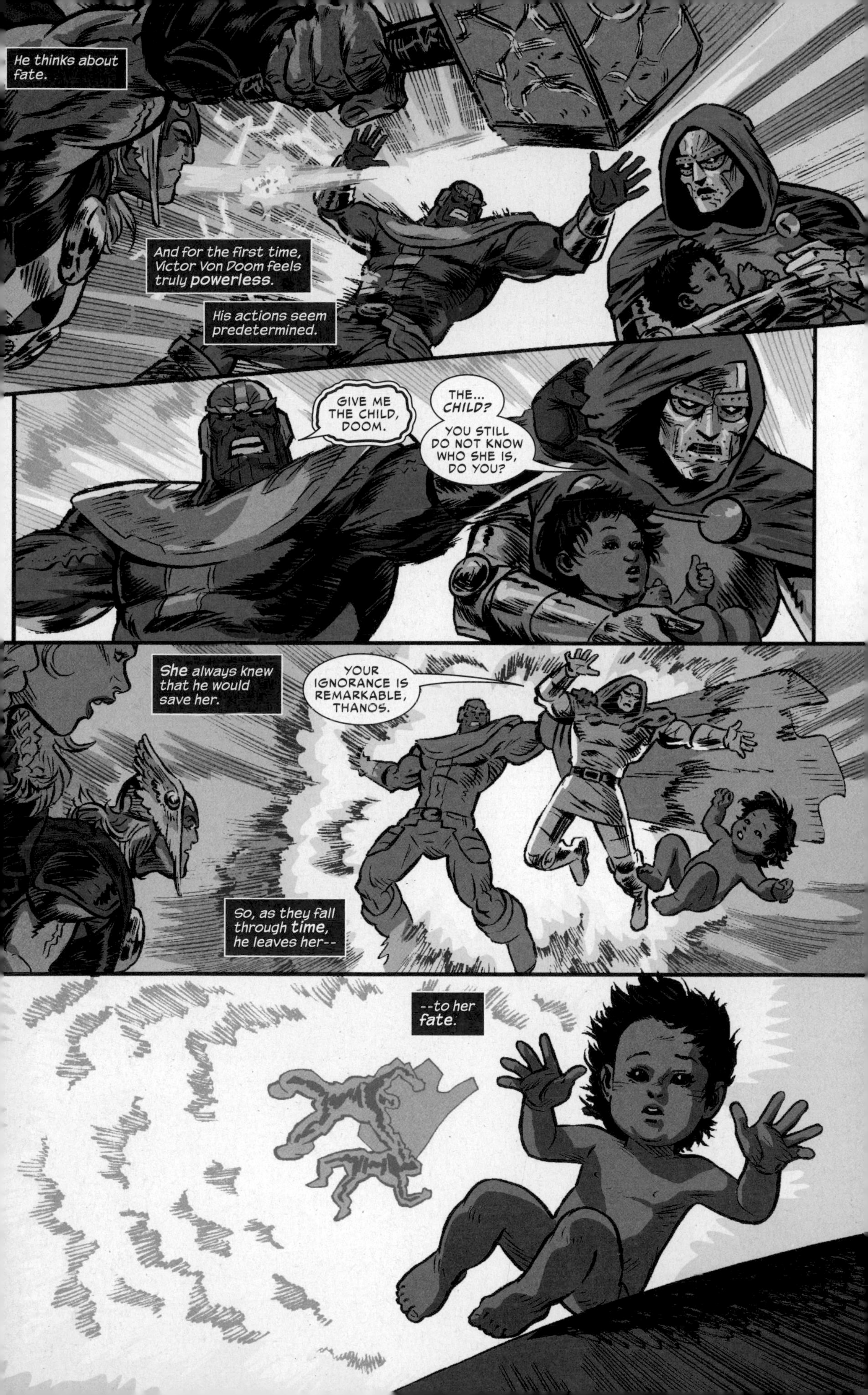
He thinks about fate.
And for the first time, Victor Von Doom feels truly powerless.
His actions seem predetermined.
GIVE ME THE CHILD, DOOM.
THE... CHILD?
YOU STILL DO NOT KNOW WHO SHE IS, DO YOU?
She always knew that he would save her.
YOUR IGNORANCE IS REMARKABLE, THANOS.
So, as they fall through time, he leaves her--
--to her fate.

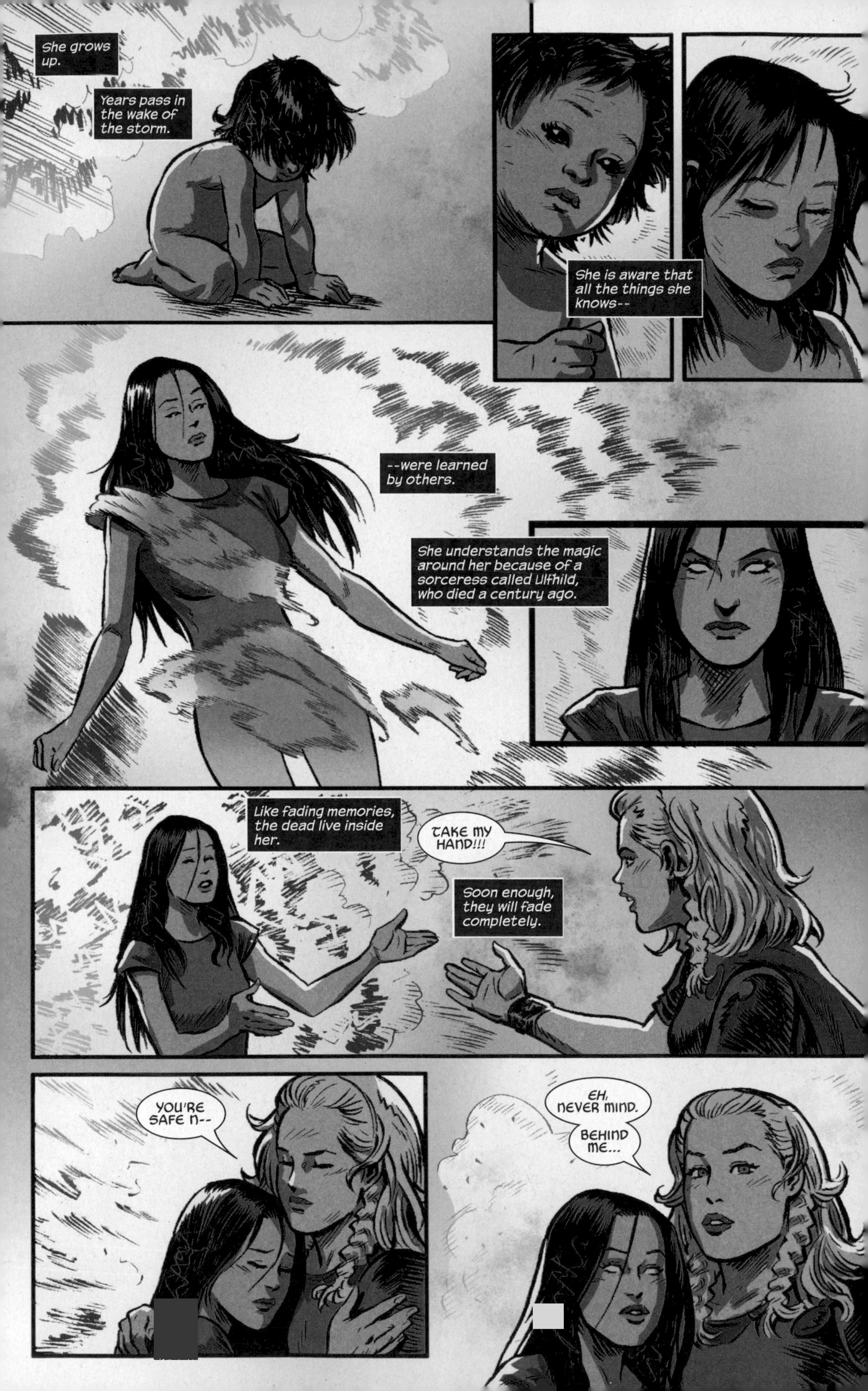
She grows up.
Years pass in the wake of the storm.
She is aware that all the things she knows--
--were learned by others.
She understands the magic around her because of a sorceress called Ulfhild, who died a century ago.
Like fading memories, the dead live inside her.
TAKE MY HAND!!!
Soon enough, they will fade completely.
YOU'RE SAFE N--
EH, NEVER MIND.
BEHIND ME...

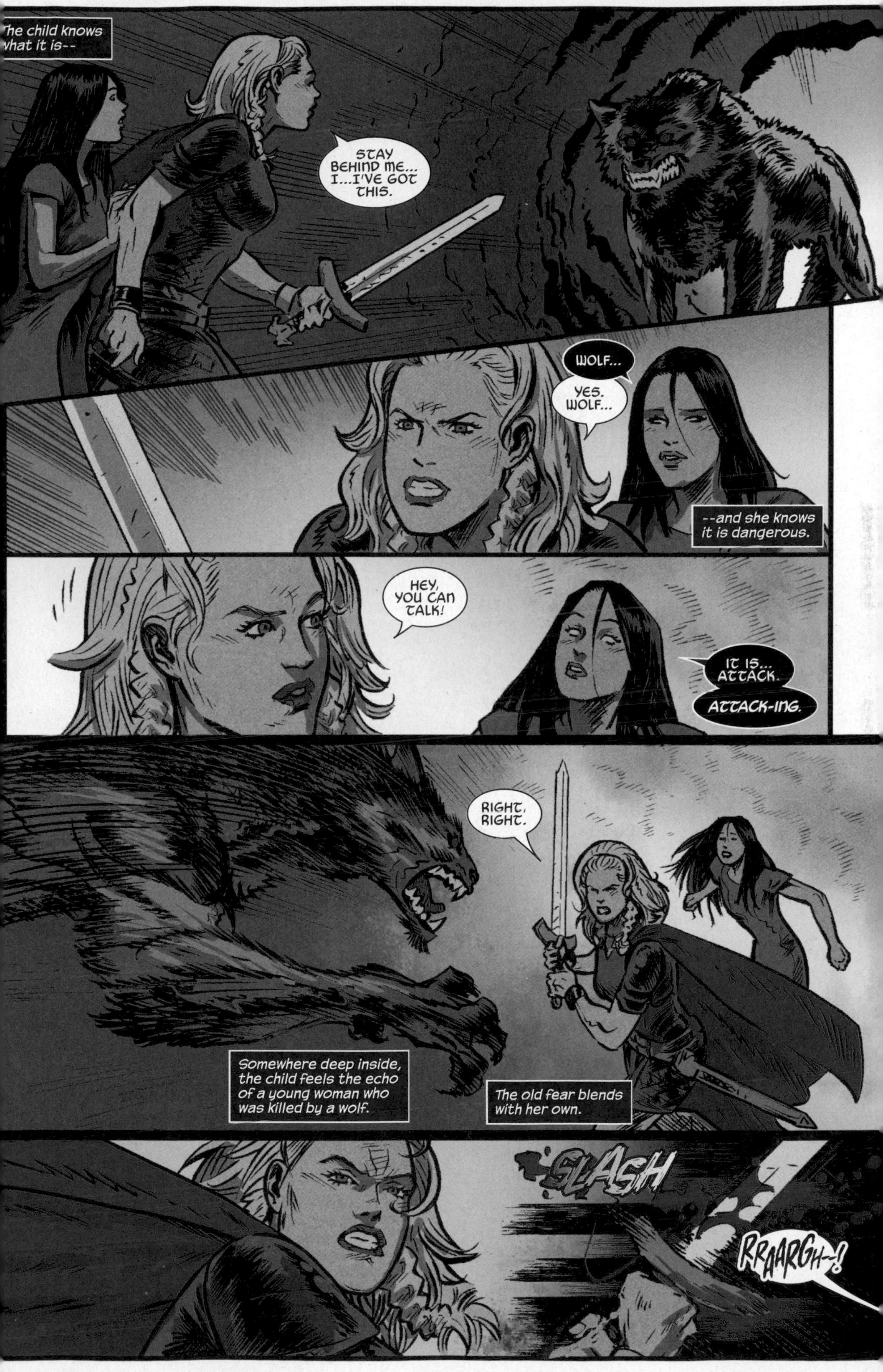
The child knows what it is--
STAY BEHIND ME... I...I'VE GOT THIS.
WOLF...
YES. WOLF...
--and she knows it is dangerous.
HEY, YOU CAN TALK!
IT IS... ATTACK.
ATTACK-ING.
RIGHT, RIGHT.
Somewhere deep inside, the child feels the echo of a young woman who was killed by a wolf.
The old fear blends with her own.
SLASH
RRAARGH--!

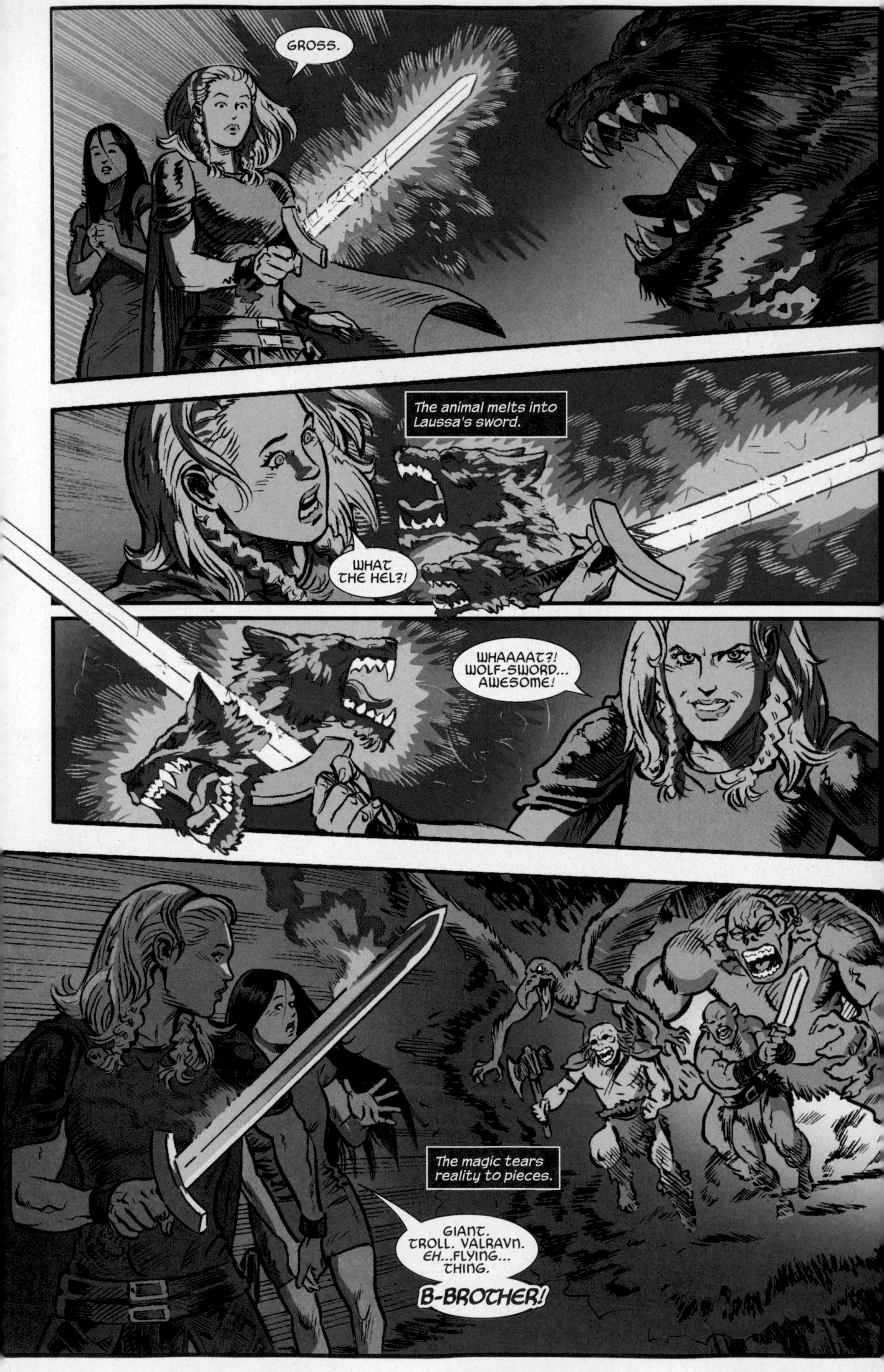
GROSS.
The animal melts into Laussa's sword.
WHAT THE HEL?!
WHAAAAT?! WOLF-SWORD... AWESOME!
The magic tears reality to pieces.
GIANT. TROLL. VALRAVN. EH...FLYING... THING.
B-BROTHER!

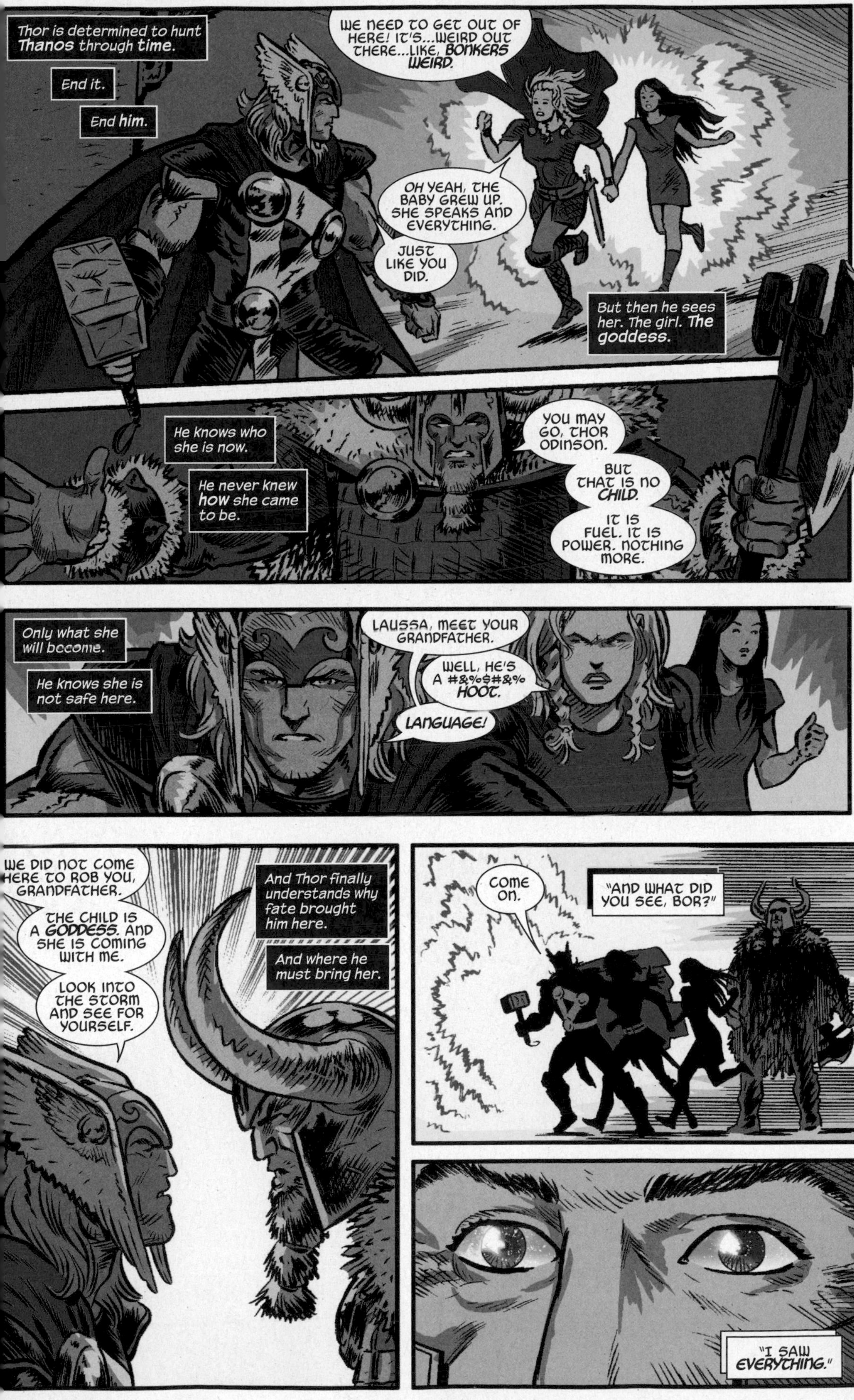
Thor is determined to hunt Thanos through time.
End it.
End him.
WE NEED TO GET OUT OF HERE! IT'S...WEIRD OUT THERE...LIKE, BONKERS WEIRD.
OH YEAH, THE BABY GREW UP. SHE SPEAKS AND EVERYTHING.
JUST LIKE YOU DID.
But then he sees her. The girl. The goddess.
He knows who she is now.
He never knew how she came to be.
YOU MAY GO, THOR ODINSON.
BUT THAT IS NO CHILD.
IT IS FUEL. IT IS POWER. NOTHING MORE.
Only what she will become.
He knows she is not safe here.
LAUSSA, MEET YOUR GRANDFATHER.
WELL, HE'S A #&%$#&% HOOT.
LANGUAGE!
WE DID NOT COME HERE TO ROB YOU, GRANDFATHER.
THE CHILD IS A GODDESS. AND SHE IS COMING WITH ME.
LOOK INTO THE STORM AND SEE FOR YOURSELF.
And Thor finally understands why fate brought him here.
And where he must bring her.
COME ON.
"AND WHAT DID YOU SEE, BOR?"
"I SAW EVERYTHING."

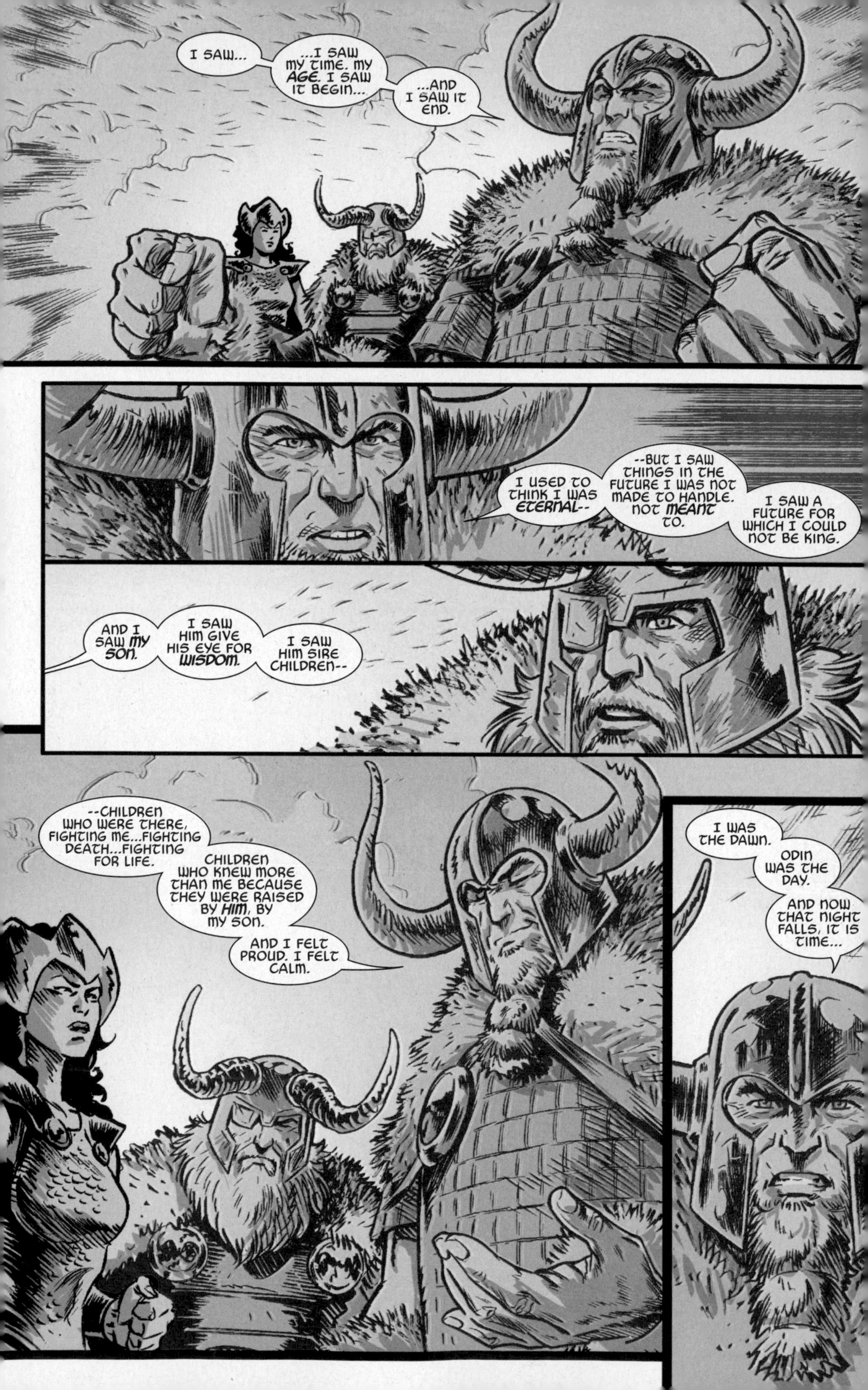
I SAW...
...I SAW MY TIME. MY AGE. I SAW IT BEGIN...
...AND I SAW IT END.
I USED TO THINK I WAS ETERNAL--
--BUT I SAW THINGS IN THE FUTURE I WAS NOT MADE TO HANDLE. NOT MEANT TO.
I SAW A FUTURE FOR WHICH I COULD NOT BE KING.
AND I SAW MY SON.
I SAW HIM GIVE HIS EYE FOR WISDOM.
I SAW HIM SIRE CHILDREN--
--CHILDREN WHO WERE THERE, FIGHTING ME...FIGHTING DEATH...FIGHTING FOR LIFE.
CHILDREN WHO KNEW MORE THAN ME BECAUSE THEY WERE RAISED BY HIM, BY MY SON.
AND I FELT PROUD. I FELT CALM.
I WAS THE DAWN.
ODIN WAS THE DAY.
AND NOW THAT NIGHT FALLS, IT IS TIME...

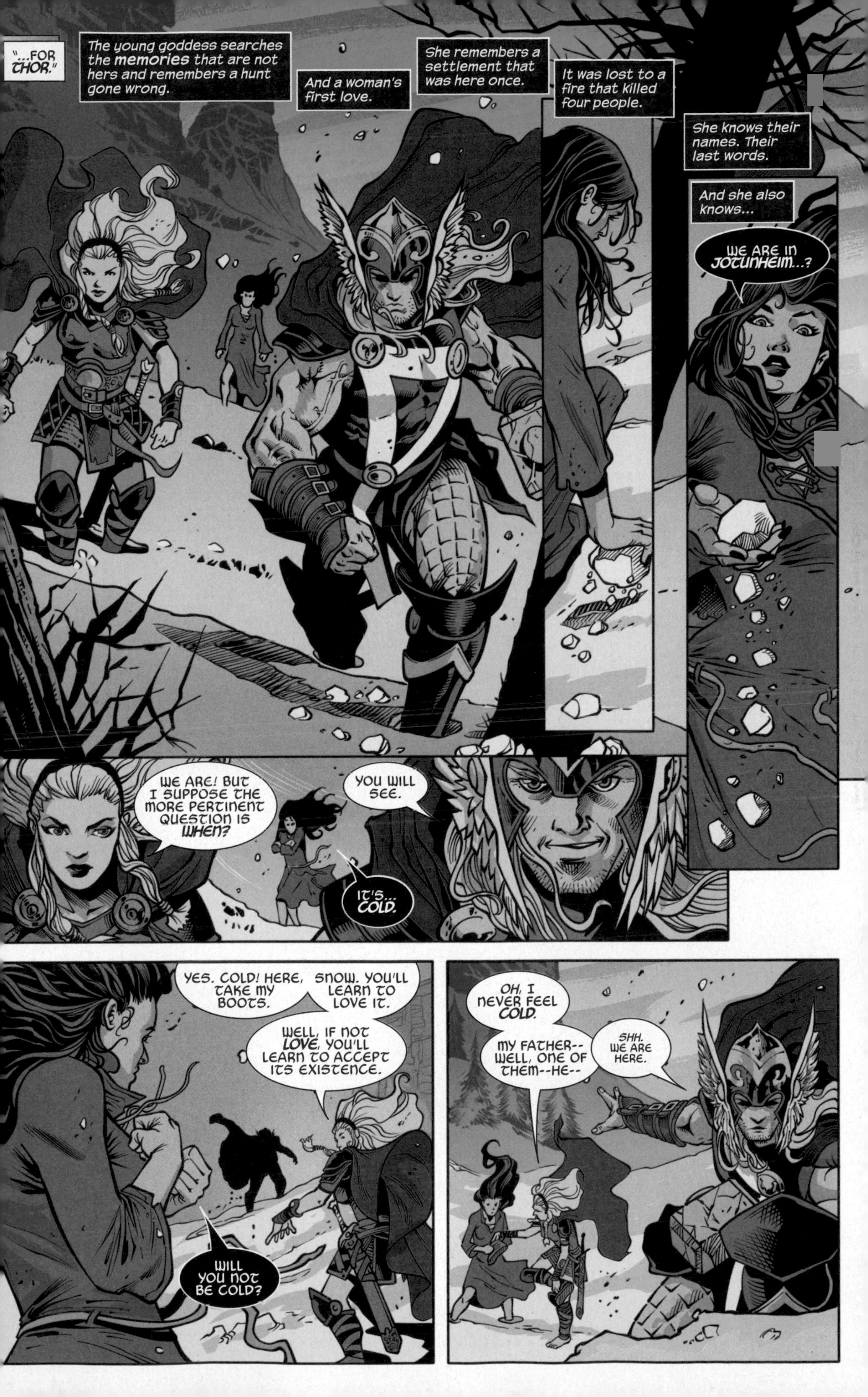
"...FOR THOR."
The young goddess searches the **memories** that are not hers and remembers a hunt gone wrong.
And a woman's first love.
She remembers a settlement that was here once.
It was lost to a fire that killed four people.
She knows their names. Their last words.
And she also knows...
WE ARE IN JOTUNHEIM...?
WE ARE! BUT I SUPPOSE THE MORE PERTINENT QUESTION IS *WHEN?*
YOU WILL SEE.
IT'S... COLD.
YES. COLD! HERE, TAKE MY BOOTS.
SNOW. YOU'LL LEARN TO LOVE IT.
WELL, IF NOT *LOVE*, YOU'LL LEARN TO ACCEPT ITS EXISTENCE.
WILL YOU NOT BE COLD?
OH, I NEVER FEEL *COLD.*
MY FATHER--WELL, ONE OF THEM--HE--
SHH. WE ARE HERE.

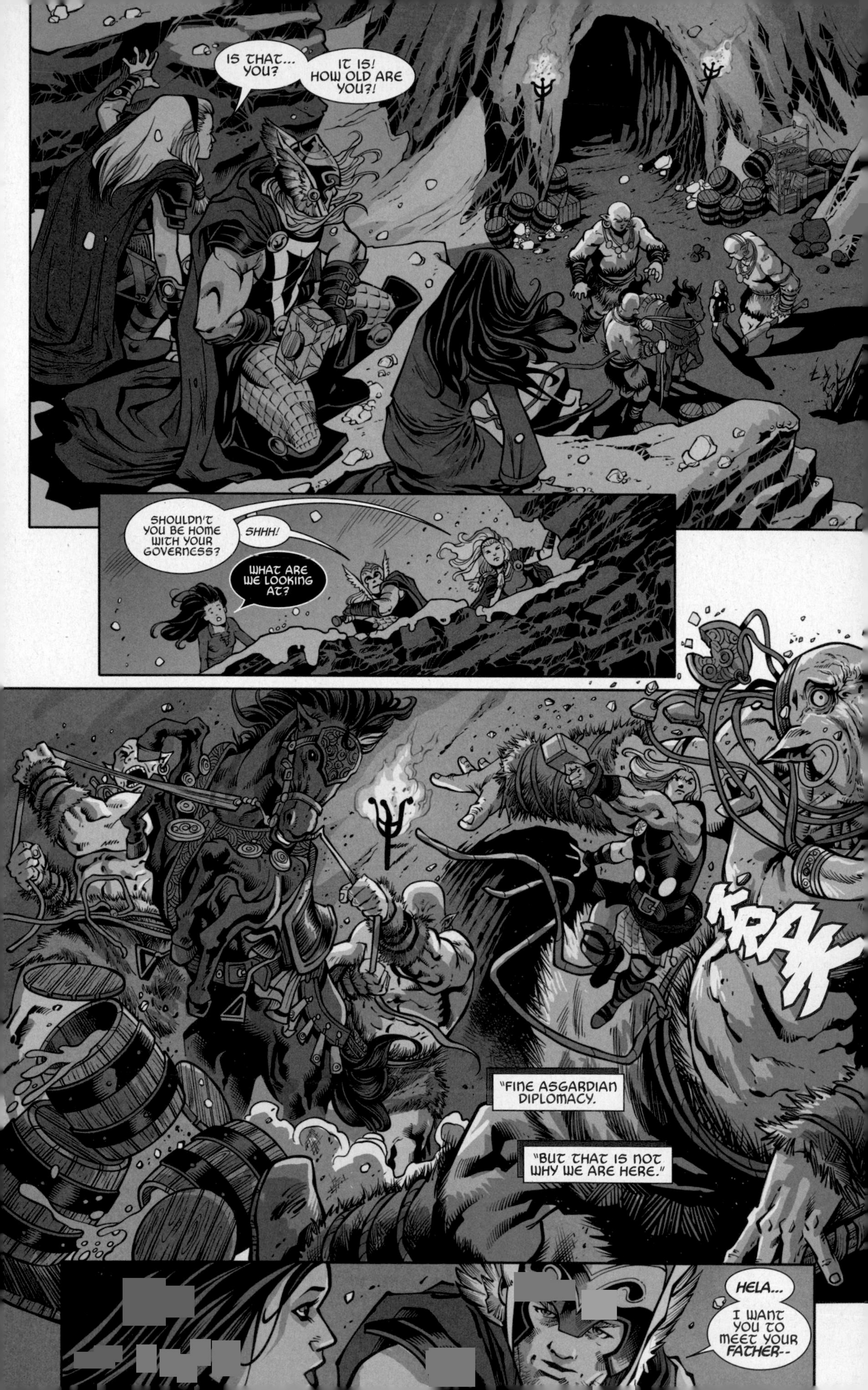
IS THAT... YOU?
IT IS! HOW OLD ARE YOU?!
SHOULDN'T YOU BE HOME WITH YOUR GOVERNESS?
SHHH!
WHAT ARE WE LOOKING AT?
KRAK
"FINE ASGARDIAN DIPLOMACY.
"BUT THAT IS NOT WHY WE ARE HERE."
HELA...
I WANT YOU TO MEET YOUR FATHER--

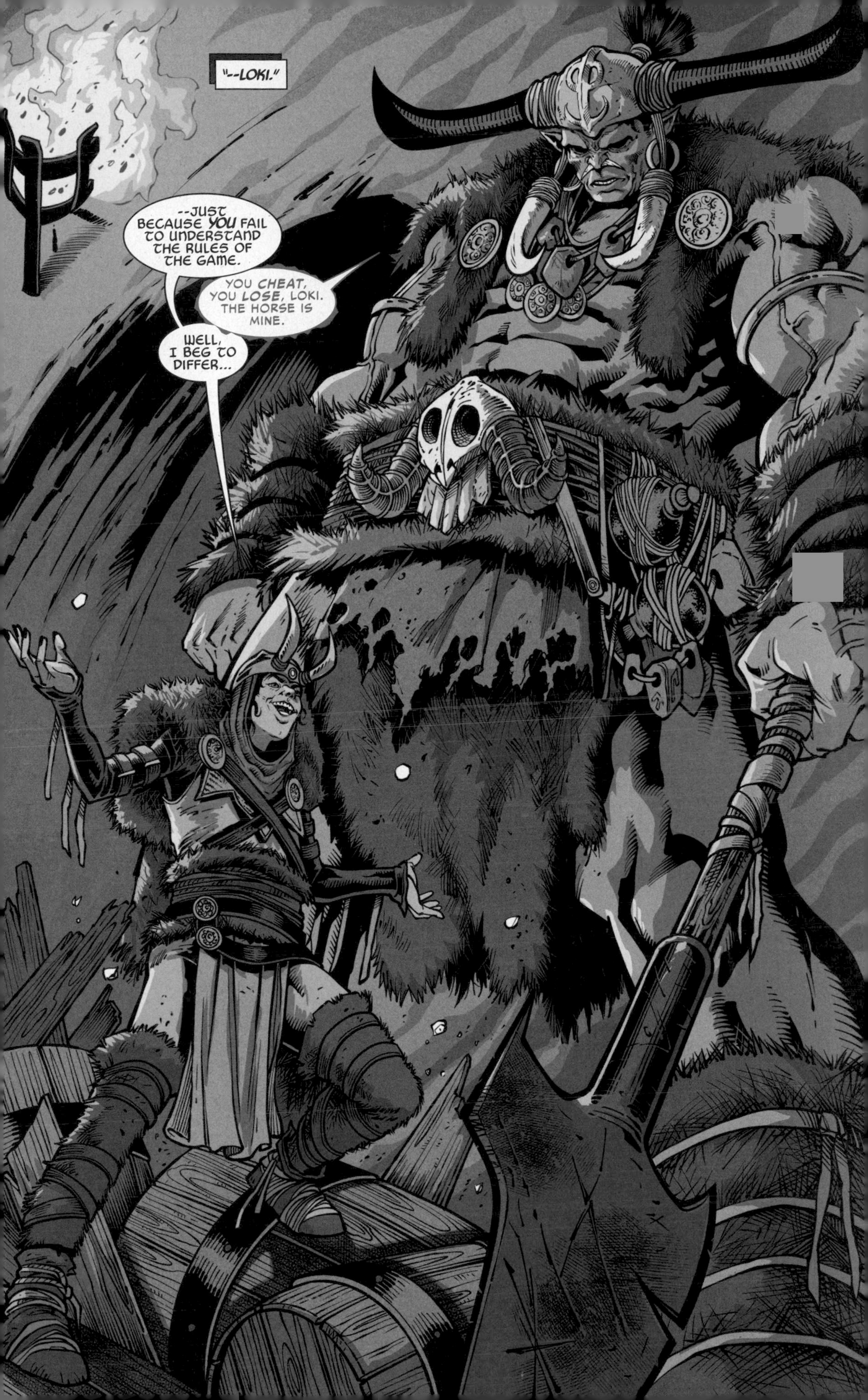
"--LOKI."
YOU CHEAT, YOU LOSE, LOKI. THE HORSE IS MINE.
WELL, I BEG TO DIFFER...
--JUST BECAUSE YOU FAIL TO UNDERSTAND THE RULES OF THE GAME.

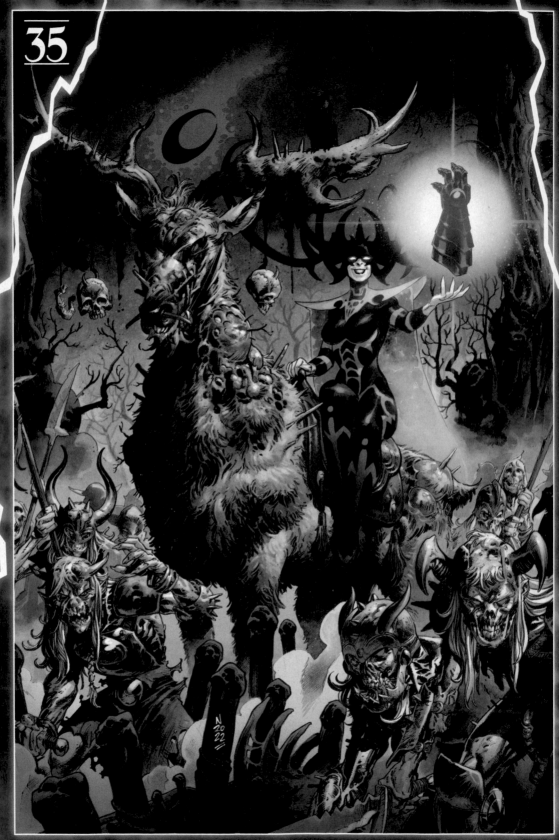

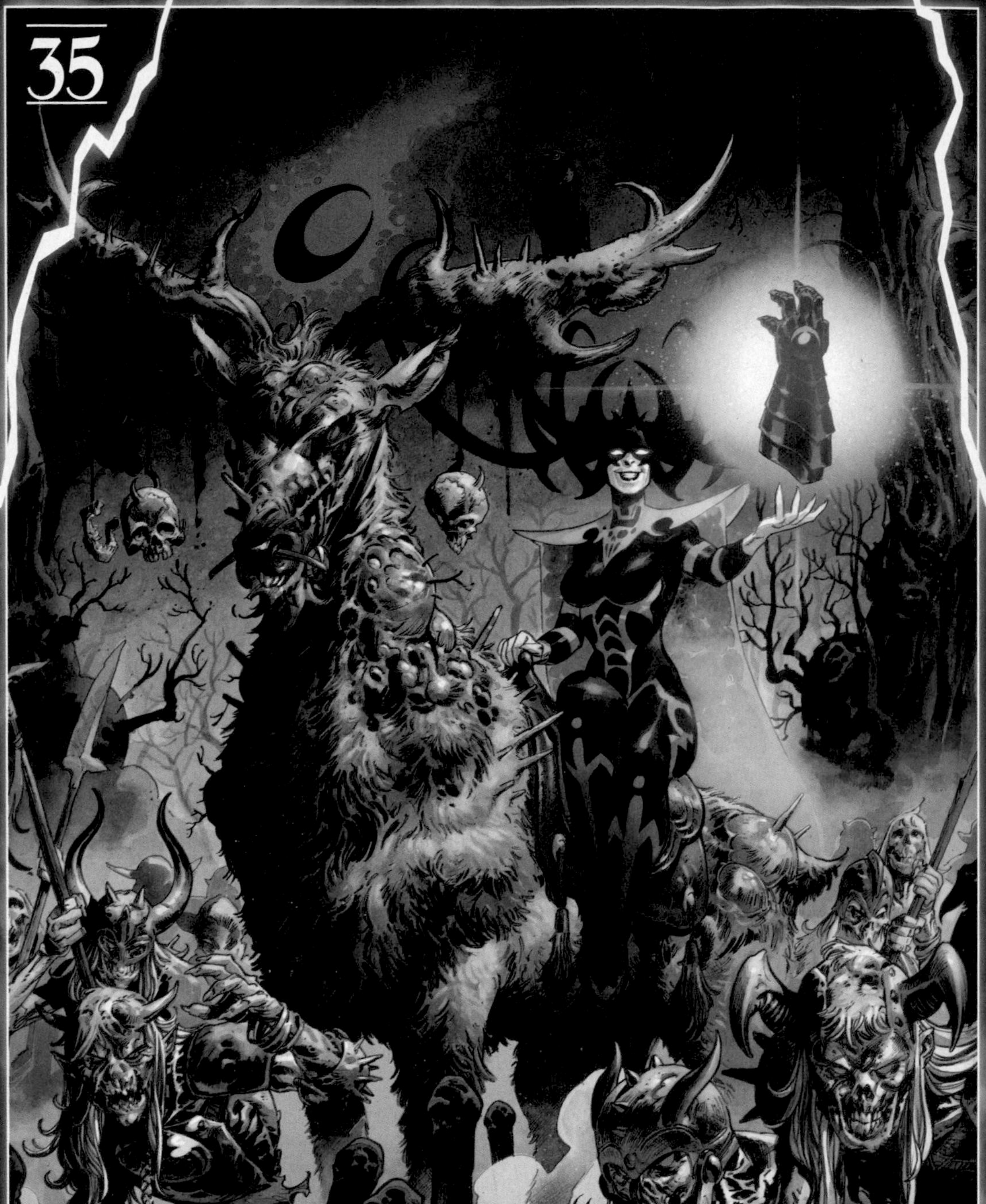
35

"Blood of the Fathers" FINALE

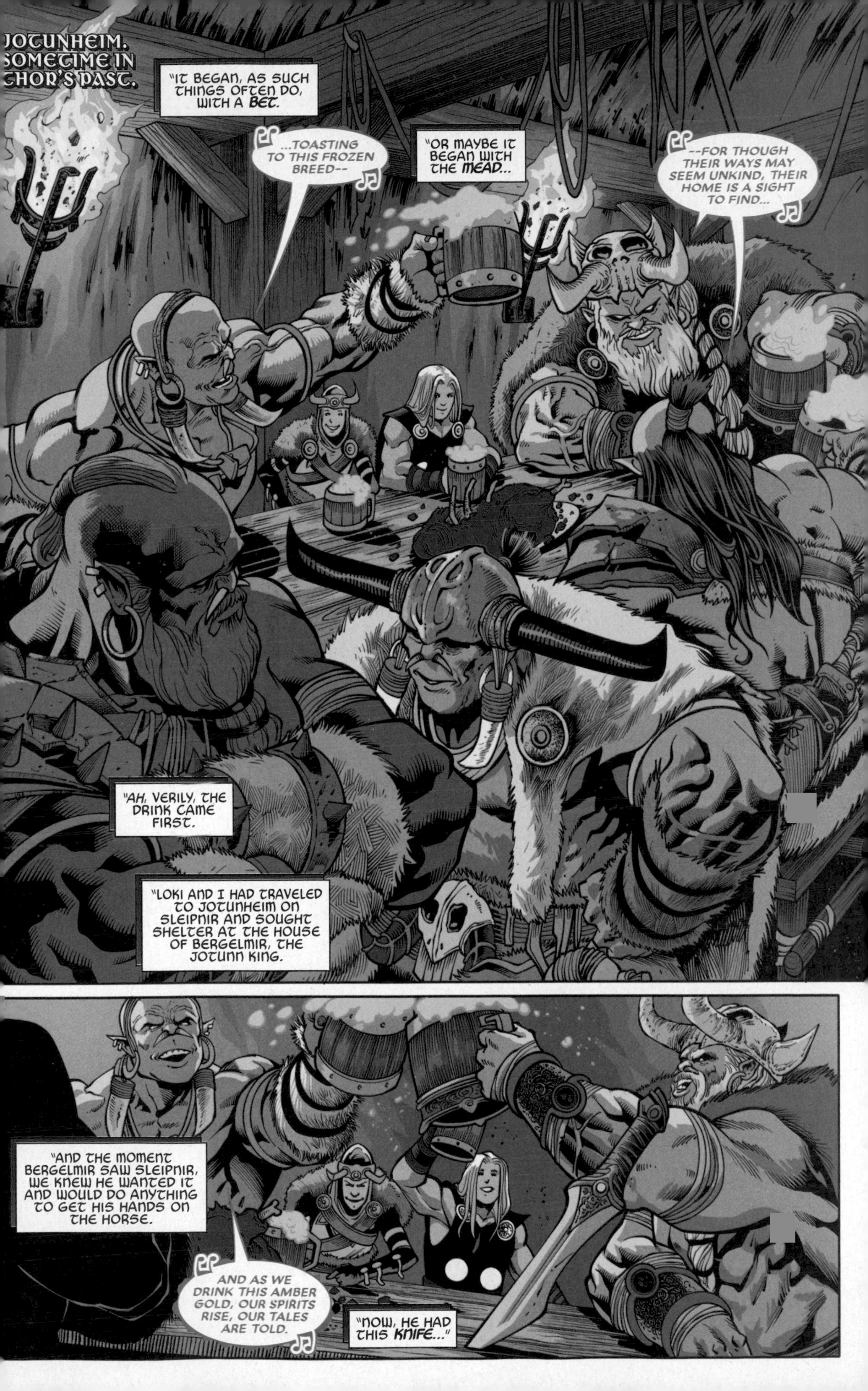
JOTUNHEIM. SOMETIME IN THOR'S PAST.
"IT BEGAN, AS SUCH THINGS OFTEN DO, WITH A BET.
...TOASTING TO THIS FROZEN BREED--
"OR MAYBE IT BEGAN WITH THE MEAD...
--FOR THOUGH THEIR WAYS MAY SEEM UNKIND, THEIR HOME IS A SIGHT TO FIND...
"AH, VERILY, THE DRINK CAME FIRST.
"LOKI AND I HAD TRAVELED TO JOTUNHEIM ON SLEIPNIR AND SOUGHT SHELTER AT THE HOUSE OF BERGELMIR, THE JOTUNN KING.
"AND THE MOMENT BERGELMIR SAW SLEIPNIR, WE KNEW HE WANTED IT AND WOULD DO ANYTHING TO GET HIS HANDS ON THE HORSE.
AND AS WE DRINK THIS AMBER GOLD, OUR SPIRITS RISE, OUR TALES ARE TOLD.
"NOW, HE HAD THIS KNIFE...

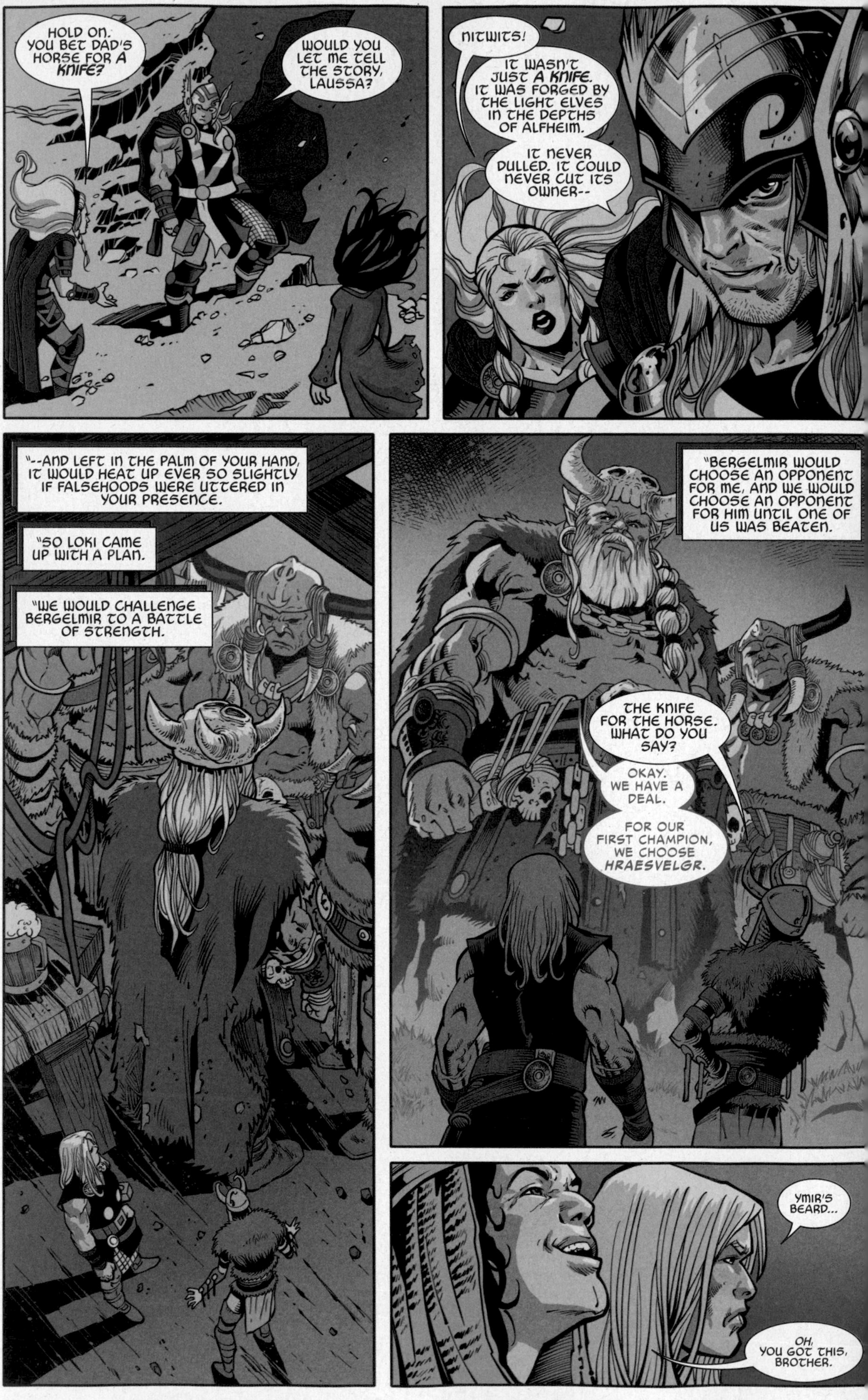
HOLD ON. YOU BET DAD'S HORSE FOR A *KNIFE?*
WOULD YOU LET ME TELL THE STORY, LAUSSA?
NITWITS!
IT WASN'T JUST *A KNIFE*. IT WAS FORGED BY THE LIGHT ELVES IN THE DEPTHS OF ALFHEIM.
IT NEVER DULLED. IT COULD NEVER CUT ITS OWNER--
"--AND LEFT IN THE PALM OF YOUR HAND, IT WOULD HEAT UP EVER SO SLIGHTLY IF FALSEHOODS WERE UTTERED IN YOUR PRESENCE.
"SO LOKI CAME UP WITH A PLAN.
"WE WOULD CHALLENGE BERGELMIR TO A BATTLE OF STRENGTH.
"BERGELMIR WOULD CHOOSE AN OPPONENT FOR ME, AND WE WOULD CHOOSE AN OPPONENT FOR HIM UNTIL ONE OF US WAS BEATEN.
THE KNIFE FOR THE HORSE. WHAT DO YOU SAY?
OKAY. WE HAVE A DEAL.
FOR OUR FIRST CHAMPION, WE CHOOSE *HRAESVELGR*.
YMIR'S BEARD...
OH, YOU GOT THIS, BROTHER.

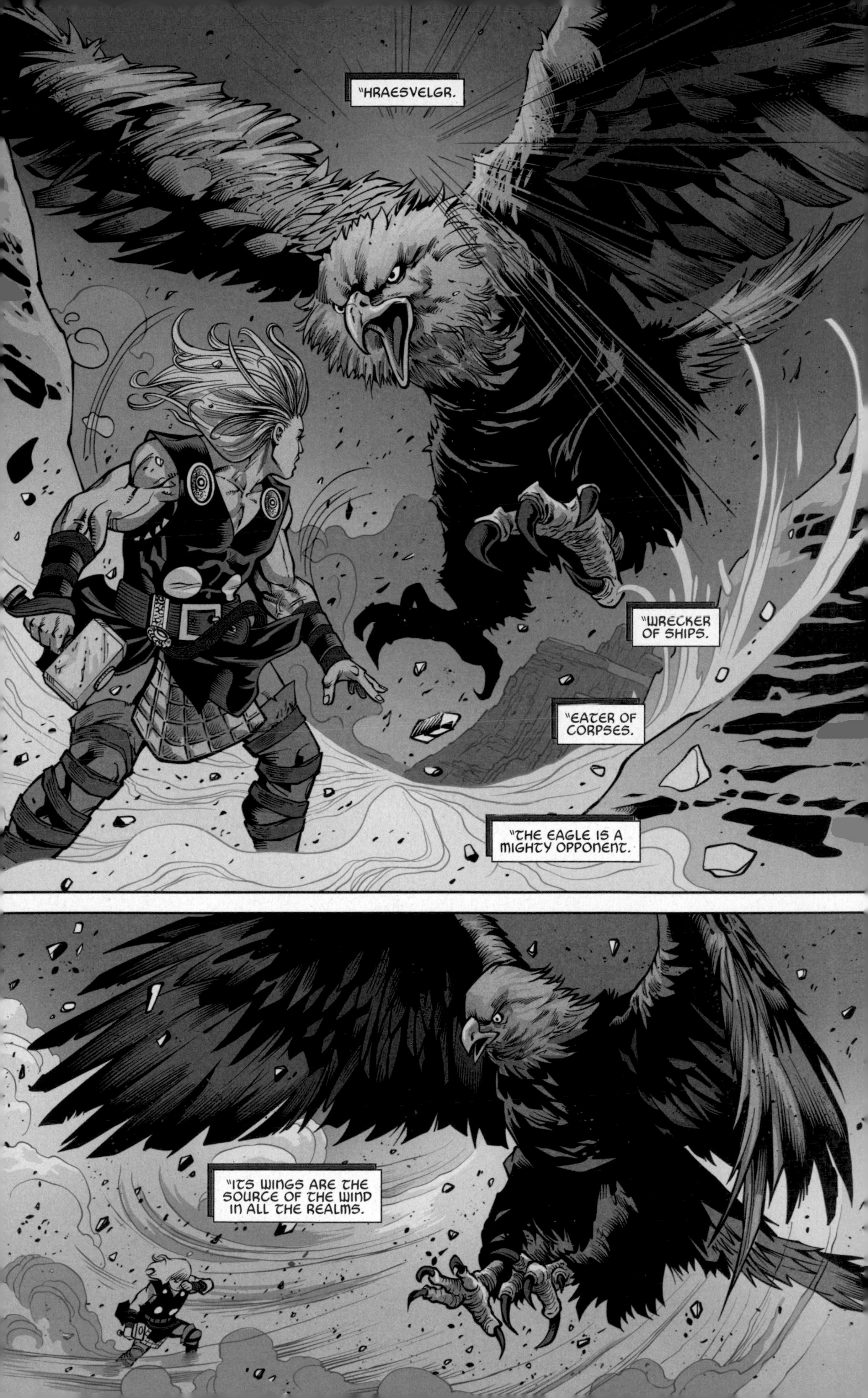
"HRAESVELGR.
"WRECKER OF SHIPS.
"EATER OF CORPSES.
"THE EAGLE IS A MIGHTY OPPONENT.
"ITS WINGS ARE THE SOURCE OF THE WIND IN ALL THE REALMS.

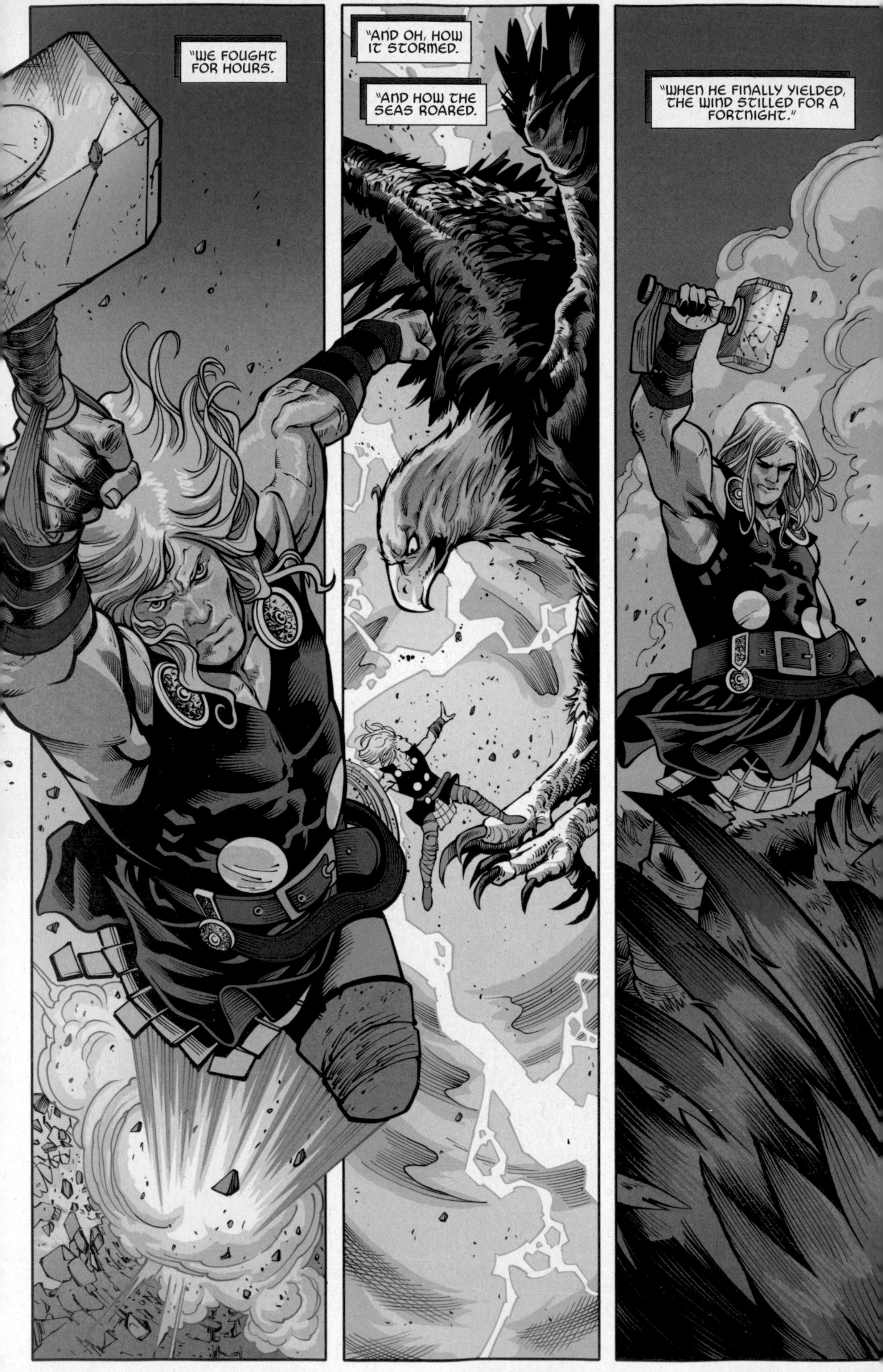
"WE FOUGHT FOR HOURS.
"AND OH, HOW IT STORMED.
"AND HOW THE SEAS ROARED.
"WHEN HE FINALLY YIELDED, THE WIND STILLED FOR A FORTNIGHT."

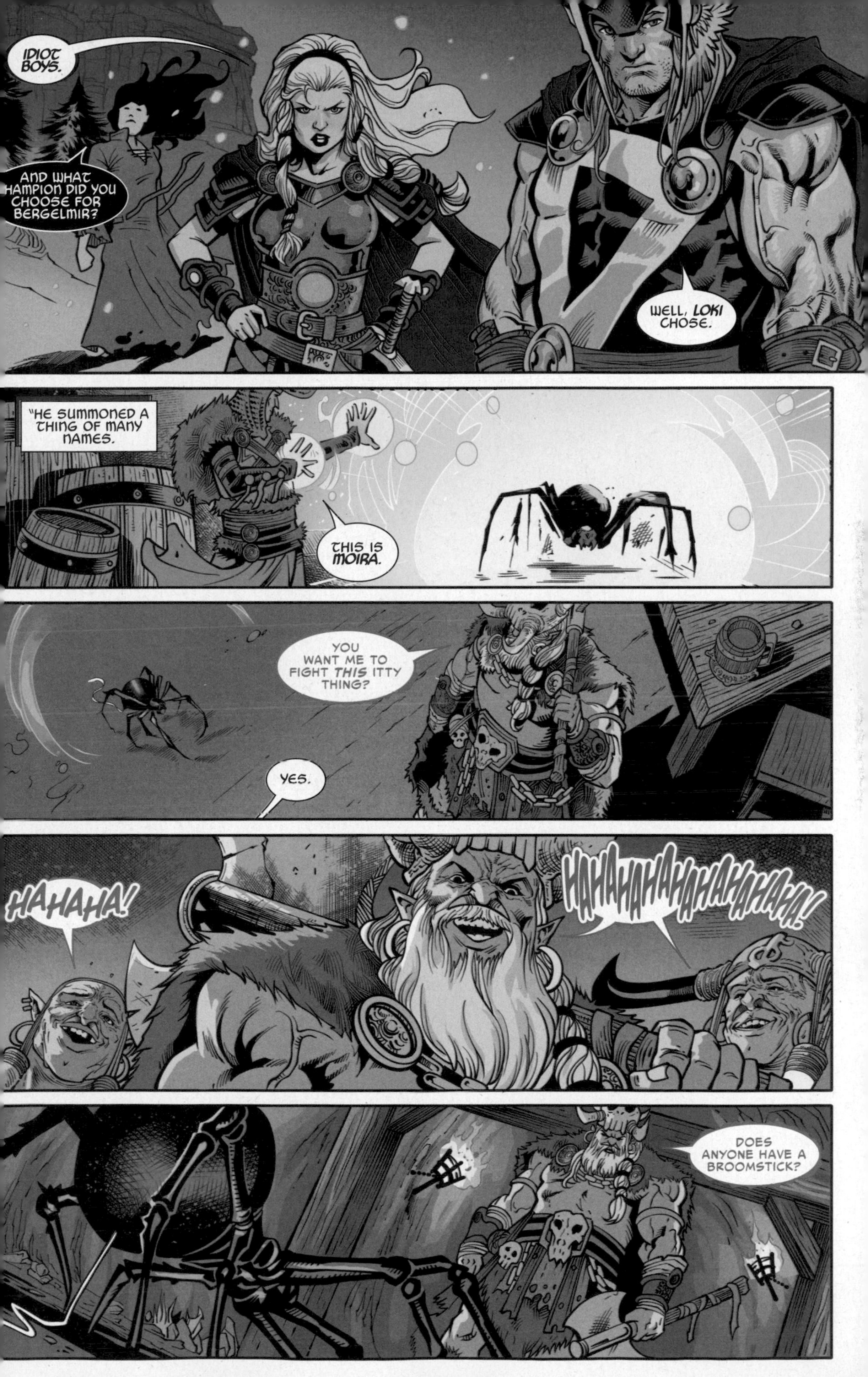
IDIOT BOYS.
AND WHAT HAMPION DID YOU CHOOSE FOR BERGELMIR?
WELL, LOKI CHOSE.
"HE SUMMONED A THING OF MANY NAMES.
THIS IS MOIRA.
YOU WANT ME TO FIGHT THIS ITTY THING?
YES.
HAHAHA!
HAHAHAHAHAHAHAHAHAHA!
DOES ANYONE HAVE A BROOMSTICK?

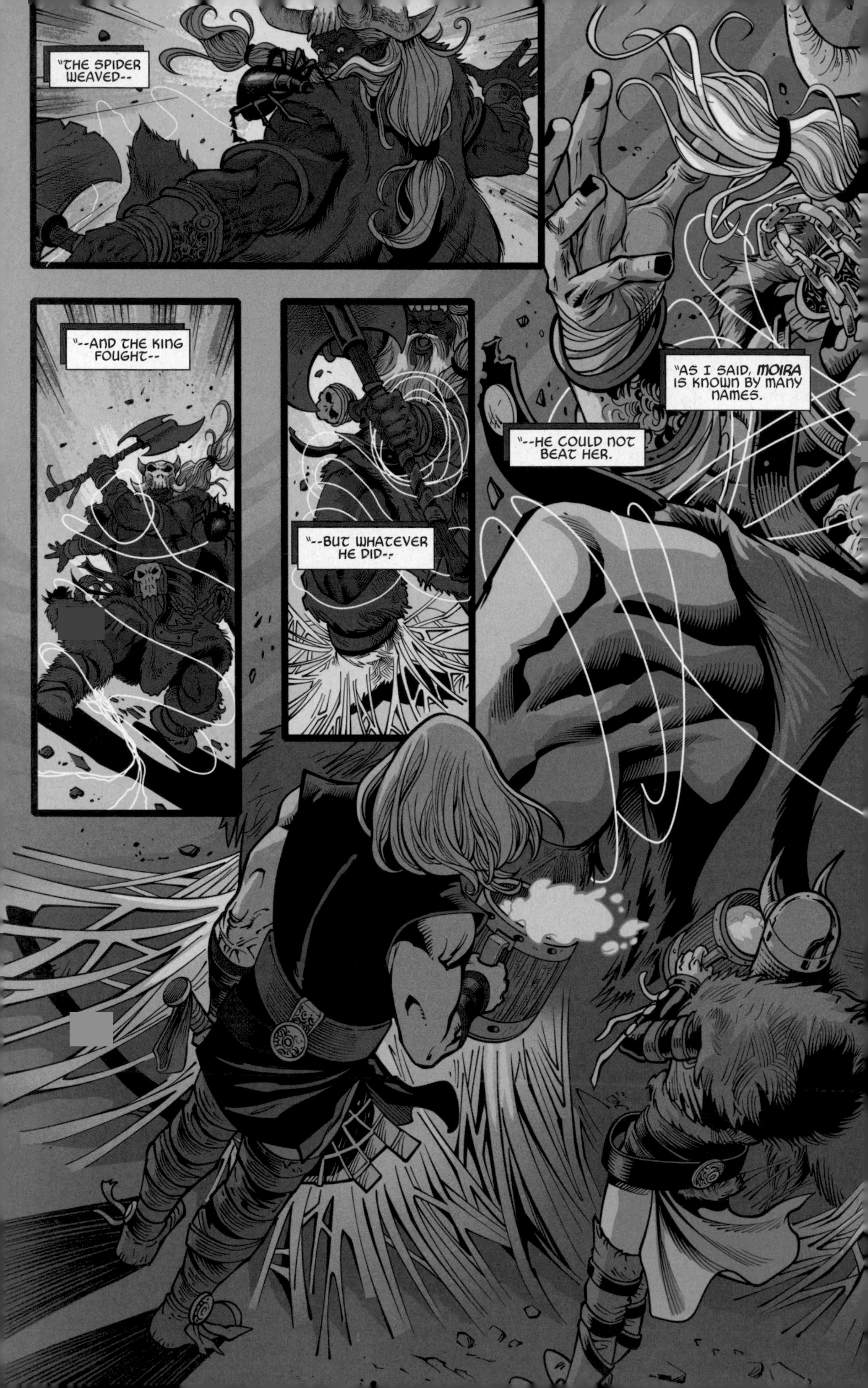
"THE SPIDER WEAVED--
"--AND THE KING FOUGHT--
"--BUT WHATEVER HE DID--
"--HE COULD NOT BEAT HER.
"AS I SAID, MOIRA IS KNOWN BY MANY NAMES.

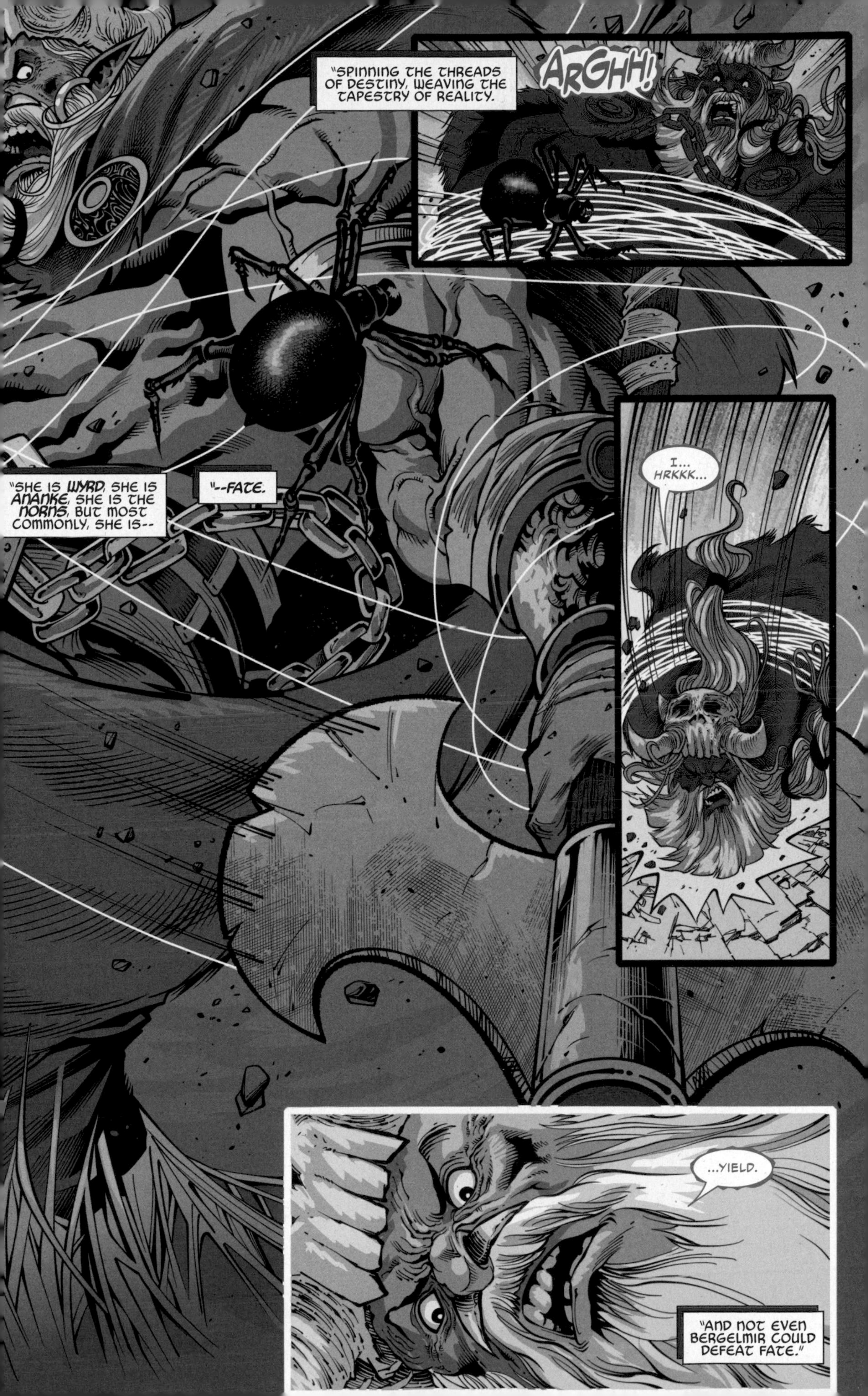
"SPINNING THE THREADS OF DESTINY, WEAVING THE TAPESTRY OF REALITY.
ARGHH!
"SHE IS WYRD, SHE IS ANANKE, SHE IS THE NORNS, BUT MOST COMMONLY, SHE IS--
"--FATE.
I... HRKKK...
...YIELD.
"AND NOT EVEN BERGELMIR COULD DEFEAT FATE."

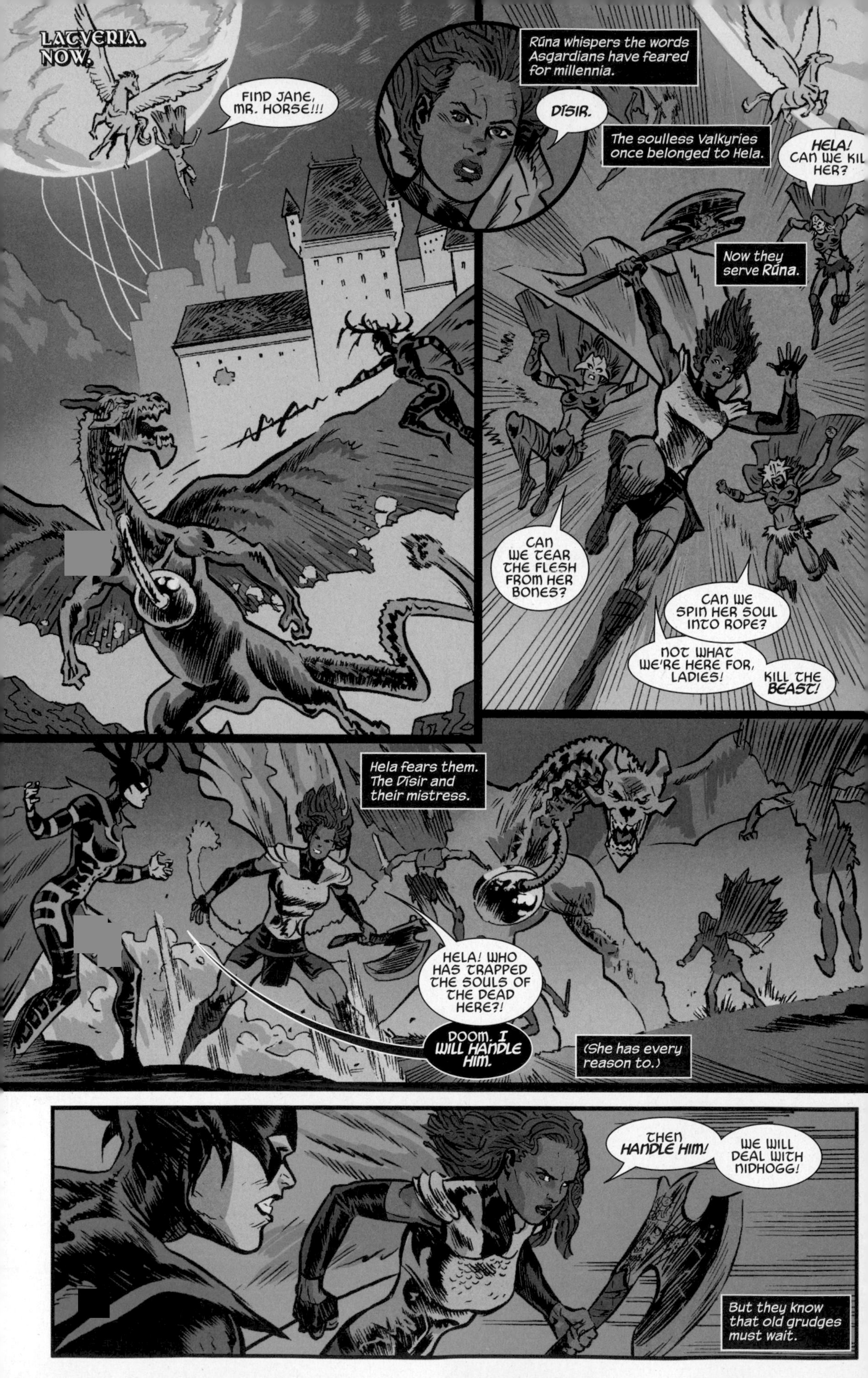
LATVERIA. NOW.
FIND JANE, MR. HORSE!!!
Rūna whispers the words Asgardians have feared for millennia.
DÍSIR.
The soulless Valkyries once belonged to Hela.
HELA! CAN WE KIL HER?
Now they serve Rūna.
CAN WE TEAR THE FLESH FROM HER BONES?
CAN WE SPIN HER SOUL INTO ROPE?
NOT WHAT WE'RE HERE FOR, LADIES!
KILL THE BEAST!
Hela fears them. The Dísir and their mistress.
HELA! WHO HAS TRAPPED THE SOULS OF THE DEAD HERE?!
DOOM. I WILL HANDLE HIM.
(She has every reason to.)
THEN HANDLE HIM!
WE WILL DEAL WITH NIDHOGG!
But they know that old grudges must wait.

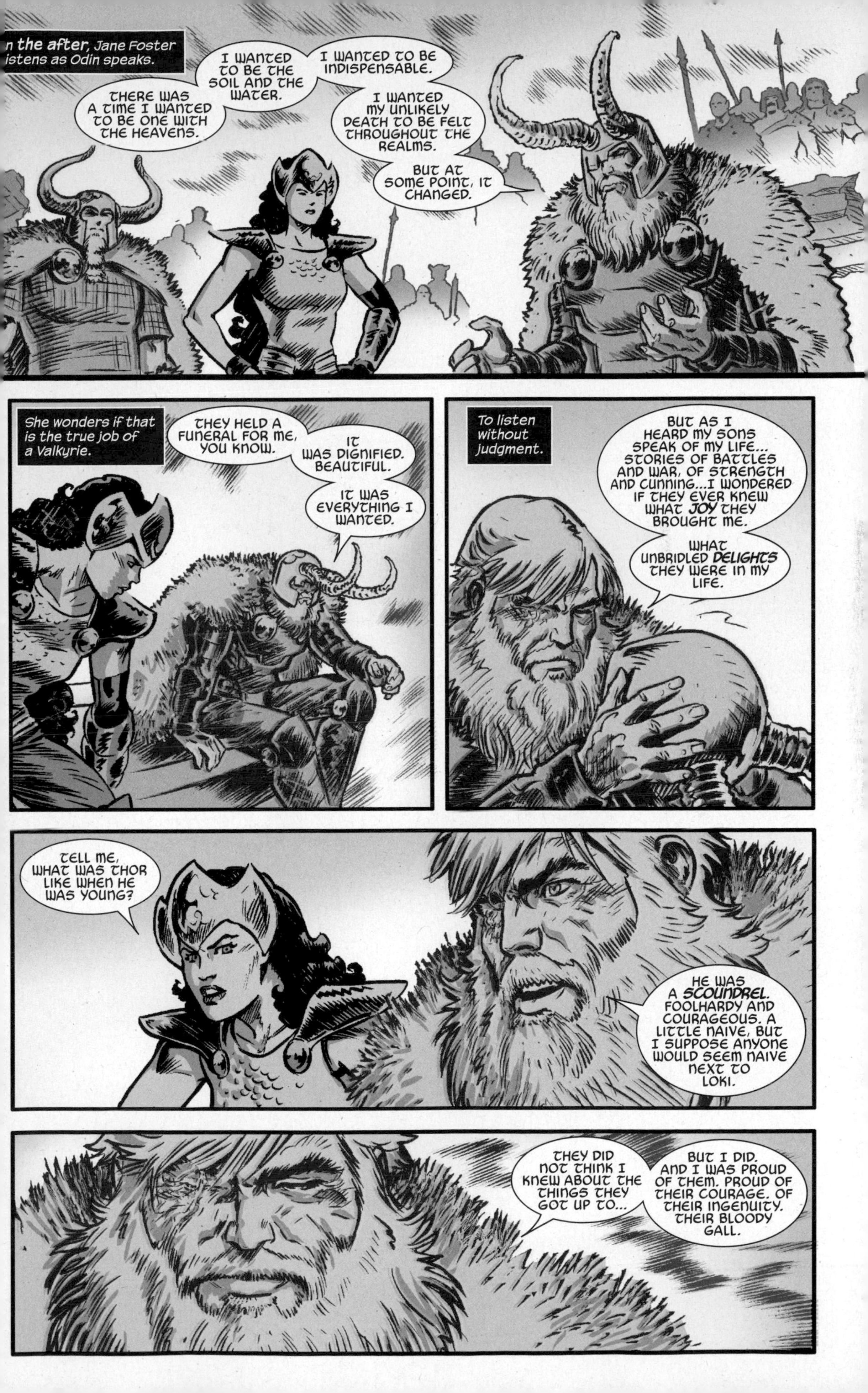
n the after, Jane Foster listens as Odin speaks.
THERE WAS A TIME I WANTED TO BE ONE WITH THE HEAVENS.
I WANTED TO BE THE SOIL AND THE WATER.
I WANTED TO BE INDISPENSABLE.
I WANTED MY UNLIKELY DEATH TO BE FELT THROUGHOUT THE REALMS.
BUT AT SOME POINT, IT CHANGED.
She wonders if that is the true job of a Valkyrie.
THEY HELD A FUNERAL FOR ME, YOU KNOW.
IT WAS DIGNIFIED. BEAUTIFUL.
IT WAS EVERYTHING I WANTED.
To listen without judgment.
BUT AS I HEARD MY SONS SPEAK OF MY LIFE... STORIES OF BATTLES AND WAR, OF STRENGTH AND CUNNING...I WONDERED IF THEY EVER KNEW WHAT JOY THEY BROUGHT ME.
WHAT UNBRIDLED DELIGHTS THEY WERE IN MY LIFE.
TELL ME, WHAT WAS THOR LIKE WHEN HE WAS YOUNG?
HE WAS A SCOUNDREL. FOOLHARDY AND COURAGEOUS. A LITTLE NAIVE, BUT I SUPPOSE ANYONE WOULD SEEM NAIVE NEXT TO LOKI.
THEY DID NOT THINK I KNEW ABOUT THE THINGS THEY GOT UP TO...
BUT I DID. AND I WAS PROUD OF THEM. PROUD OF THEIR COURAGE. OF THEIR INGENUITY. THEIR BLOODY GALL.

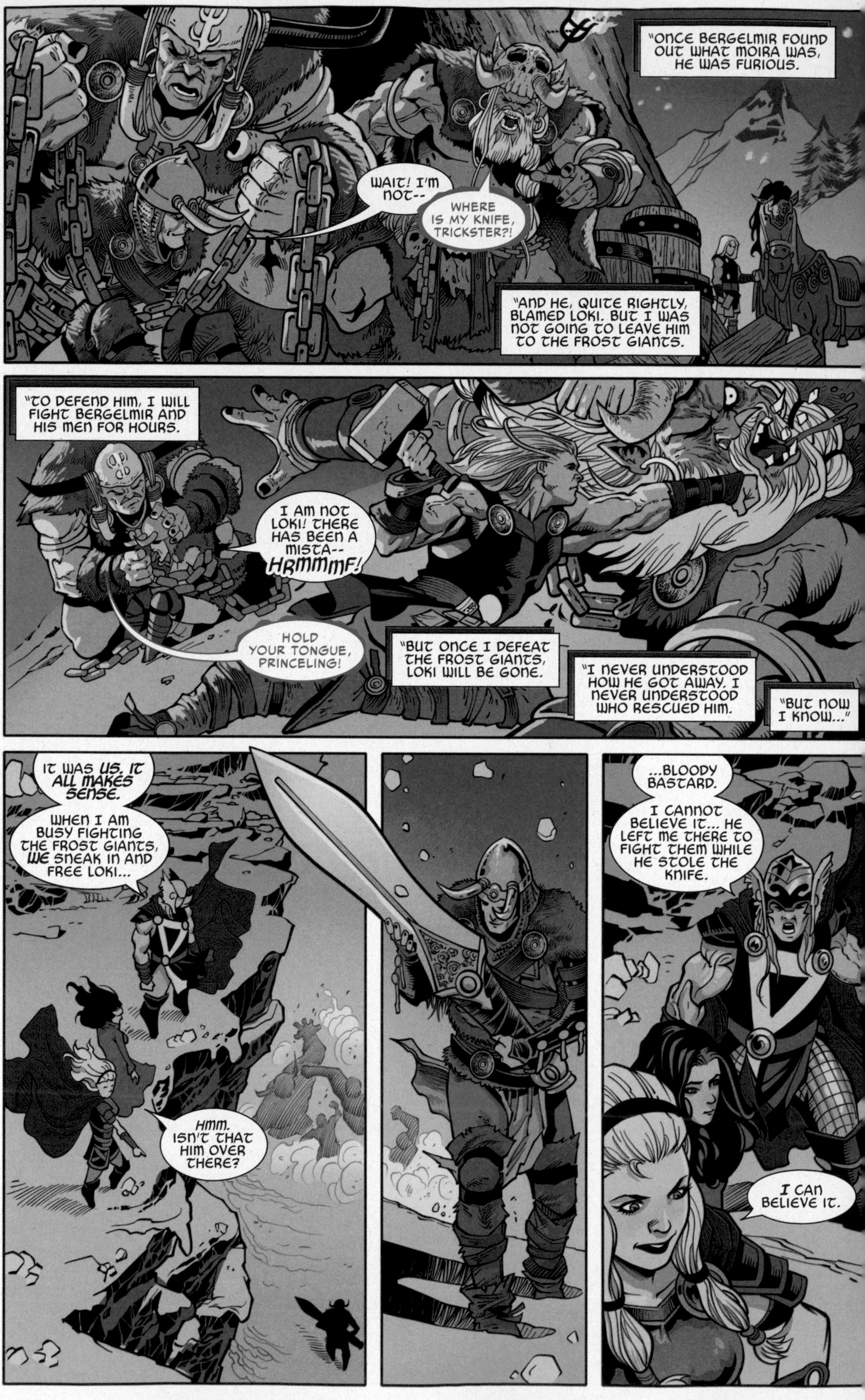
"ONCE BERGELMIR FOUND OUT WHAT MOIRA WAS, HE WAS FURIOUS.
WAIT! I'M NOT--
WHERE IS MY KNIFE, TRICKSTER?!
"AND HE, QUITE RIGHTLY, BLAMED LOKI. BUT I WAS NOT GOING TO LEAVE HIM TO THE FROST GIANTS.
"TO DEFEND HIM, I WILL FIGHT BERGELMIR AND HIS MEN FOR HOURS.
I AM NOT LOKI! THERE HAS BEEN A MISTA-- HRMMMF!
HOLD YOUR TONGUE, PRINCELING!
"BUT ONCE I DEFEAT THE FROST GIANTS, LOKI WILL BE GONE.
"I NEVER UNDERSTOOD HOW HE GOT AWAY. I NEVER UNDERSTOOD WHO RESCUED HIM.
"BUT NOW I KNOW..."
IT WAS US. IT ALL MAKES SENSE.
WHEN I AM BUSY FIGHTING THE FROST GIANTS, WE SNEAK IN AND FREE LOKI...
HMM. ISN'T THAT HIM OVER THERE?
...BLOODY BASTARD.
I CANNOT BELIEVE IT... HE LEFT ME THERE TO FIGHT THEM WHILE HE STOLE THE KNIFE.
I CAN BELIEVE IT.

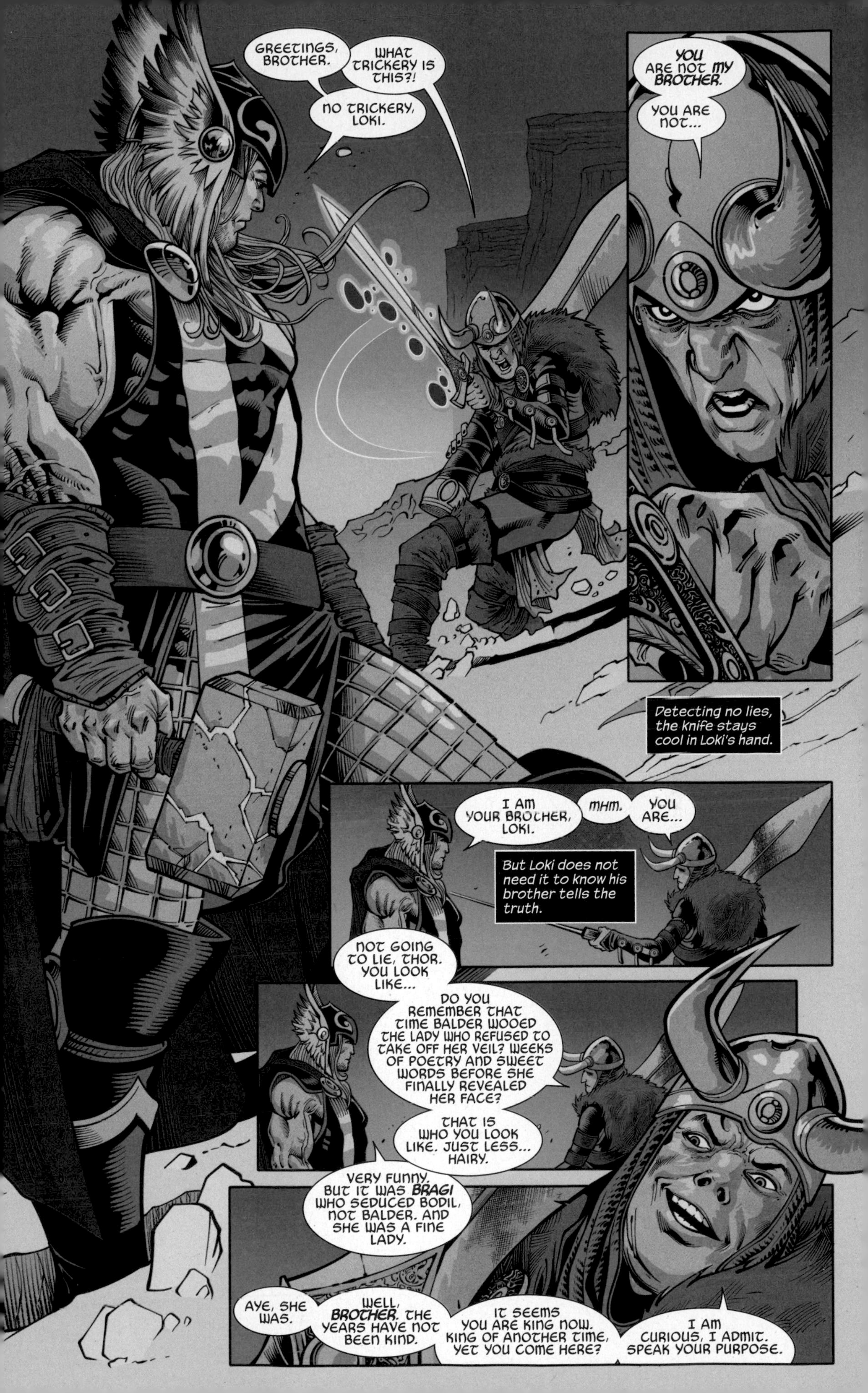
GREETINGS, BROTHER.
WHAT TRICKERY IS THIS?!
NO TRICKERY, LOKI.
YOU ARE NOT MY BROTHER.
YOU ARE NOT...
Detecting no lies, the knife stays cool in Loki's hand.
I AM YOUR BROTHER, LOKI.
MHM.
YOU ARE...
But Loki does not need it to know his brother tells the truth.
NOT GOING TO LIE, THOR. YOU LOOK LIKE...
DO YOU REMEMBER THAT TIME BALDER WOOED THE LADY WHO REFUSED TO TAKE OFF HER VEIL? WEEKS OF POETRY AND SWEET WORDS BEFORE SHE FINALLY REVEALED HER FACE?
THAT IS WHO YOU LOOK LIKE. JUST LESS... HAIRY.
VERY FUNNY. BUT IT WAS BRAGI WHO SEDUCED BODIL, NOT BALDER. AND SHE WAS A FINE LADY.
AYE, SHE WAS.
WELL, BROTHER. THE YEARS HAVE NOT BEEN KIND.
IT SEEMS YOU ARE KING NOW. KING OF ANOTHER TIME, YET YOU COME HERE?
I AM CURIOUS, I ADMIT. SPEAK YOUR PURPOSE.

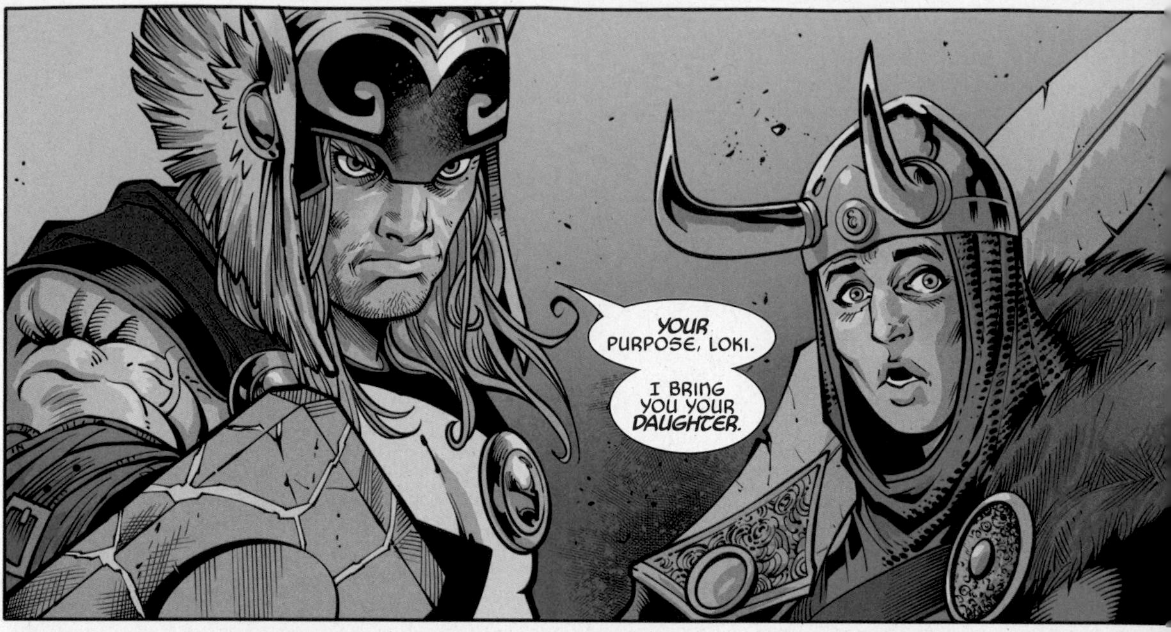
YOUR PURPOSE, LOKI.
I BRING YOU YOUR DAUGHTER.

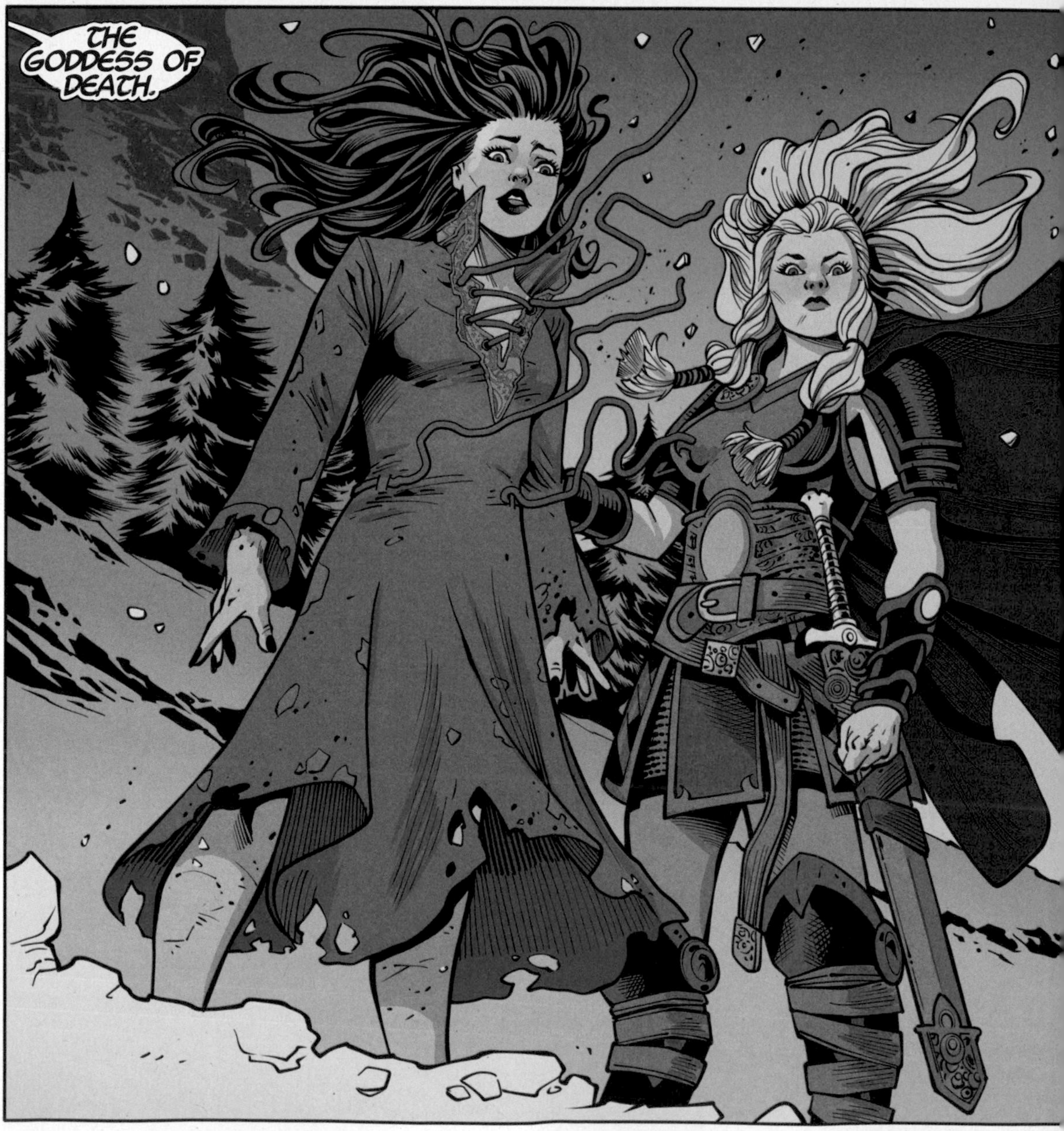
THE GODDESS OF DEATH.

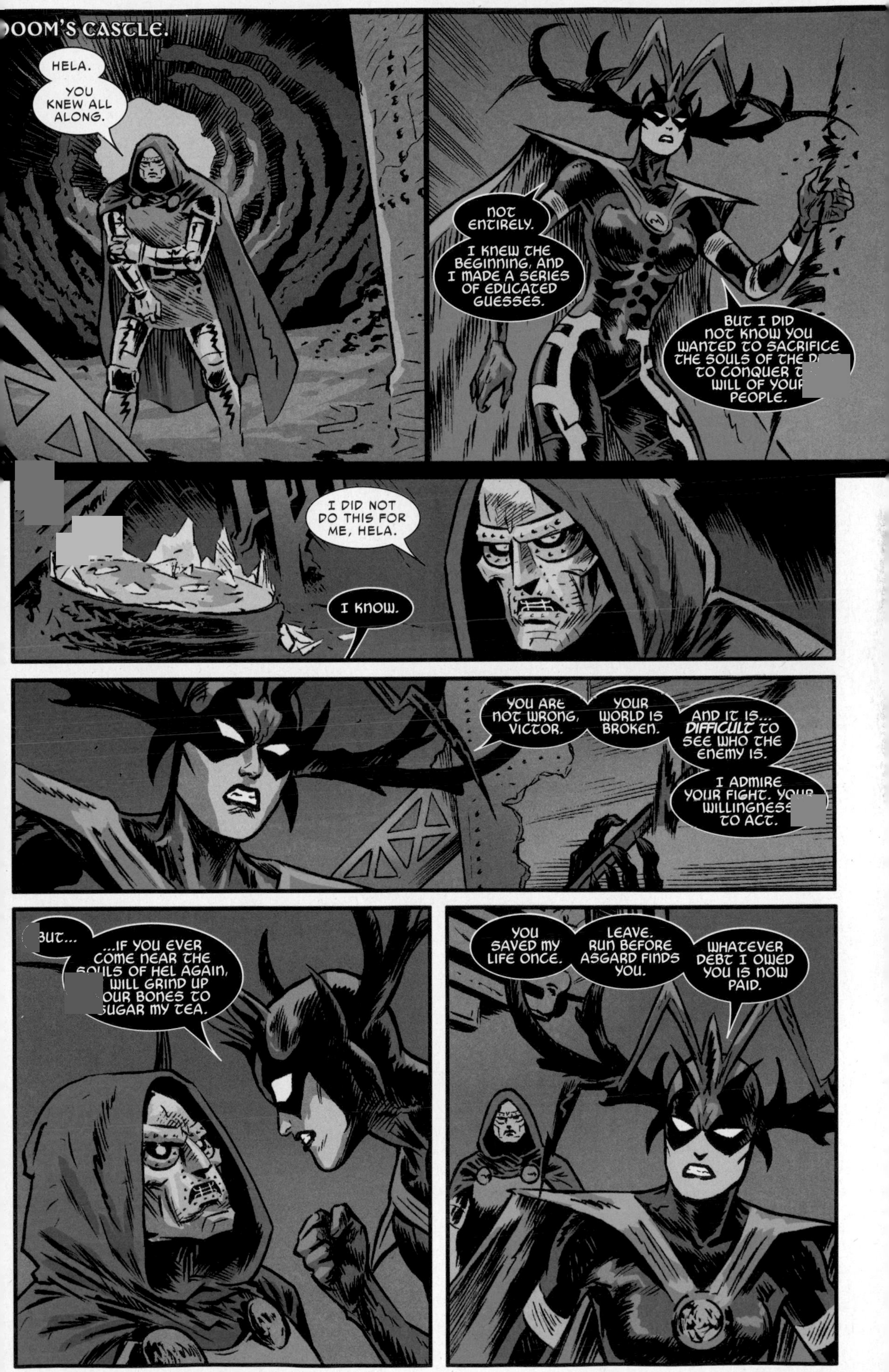

OOM'S CASTLE.
HELA.
YOU KNEW ALL ALONG.
NOT ENTIRELY.
I KNEW THE BEGINNING, AND I MADE A SERIES OF EDUCATED GUESSES.
BUT I DID NOT KNOW YOU WANTED TO SACRIFICE THE SOULS OF THE D TO CONQUER T WILL OF YOUR PEOPLE.
I DID NOT DO THIS FOR ME, HELA.
I KNOW.
YOU ARE NOT WRONG, VICTOR.
YOUR WORLD IS BROKEN.
AND IT IS... DIFFICULT TO SEE WHO THE ENEMY IS.
I ADMIRE YOUR FIGHT. YOUR WILLINGNES TO ACT.
UT...
...IF YOU EVER COME NEAR THE OULS OF HEL AGAIN, WILL GRIND UP OUR BONES TO UGAR MY TEA.
YOU SAVED MY LIFE ONCE.
LEAVE. RUN BEFORE ASGARD FINDS YOU.
WHATEVER DEBT I OWED YOU IS NOW PAID.

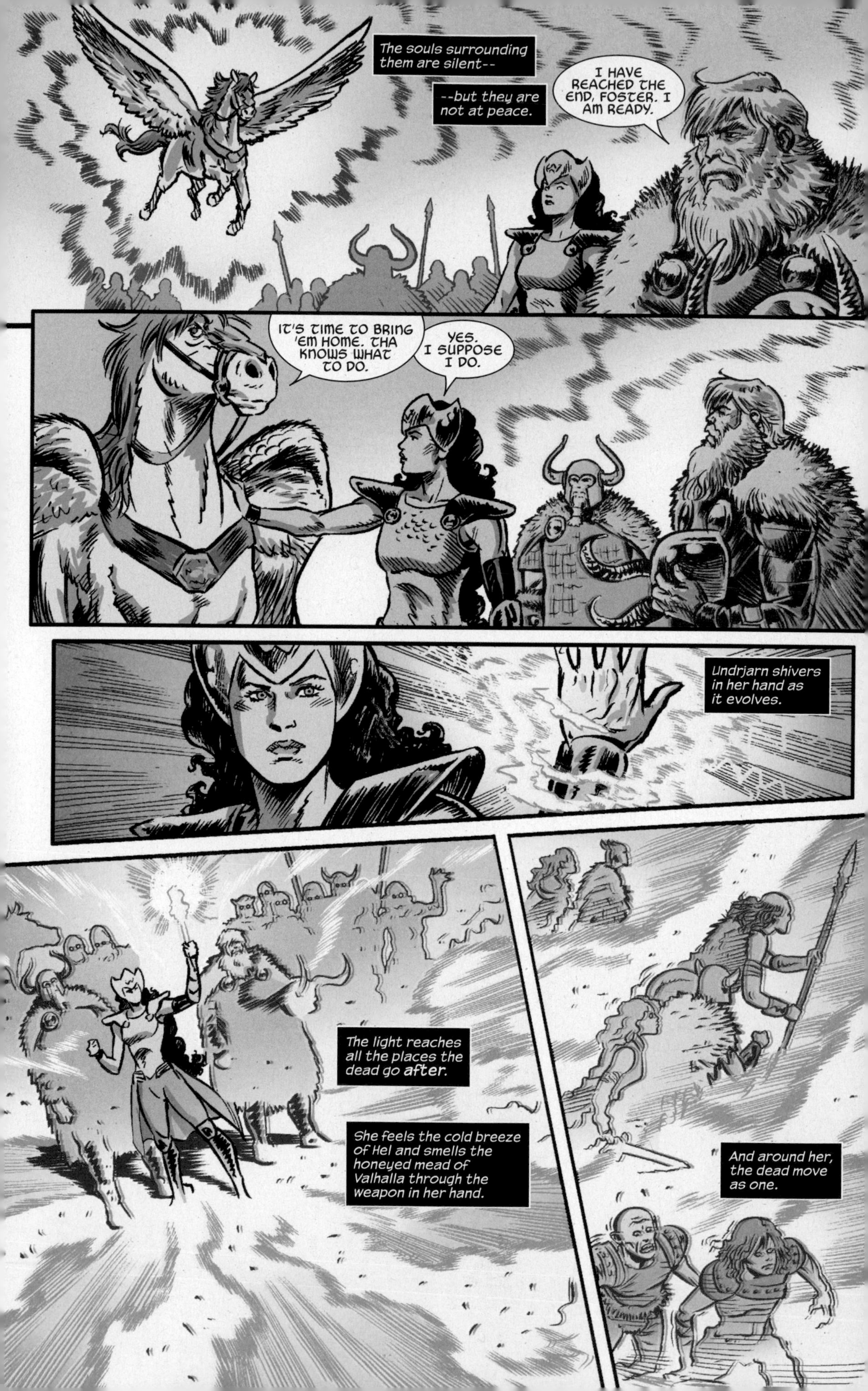
The souls surrounding them are silent--
--but they are not at peace.
I HAVE REACHED THE END, FOSTER. I AM READY.
IT'S TIME TO BRING 'EM HOME. THA KNOWS WHAT TO DO.
YES. I SUPPOSE I DO.
Undrjarn shivers in her hand as it evolves.
The light reaches all the places the dead go after.
She feels the cold breeze of Hel and smells the honeyed mead of Valhalla through the weapon in her hand.
And around her, the dead move as one.

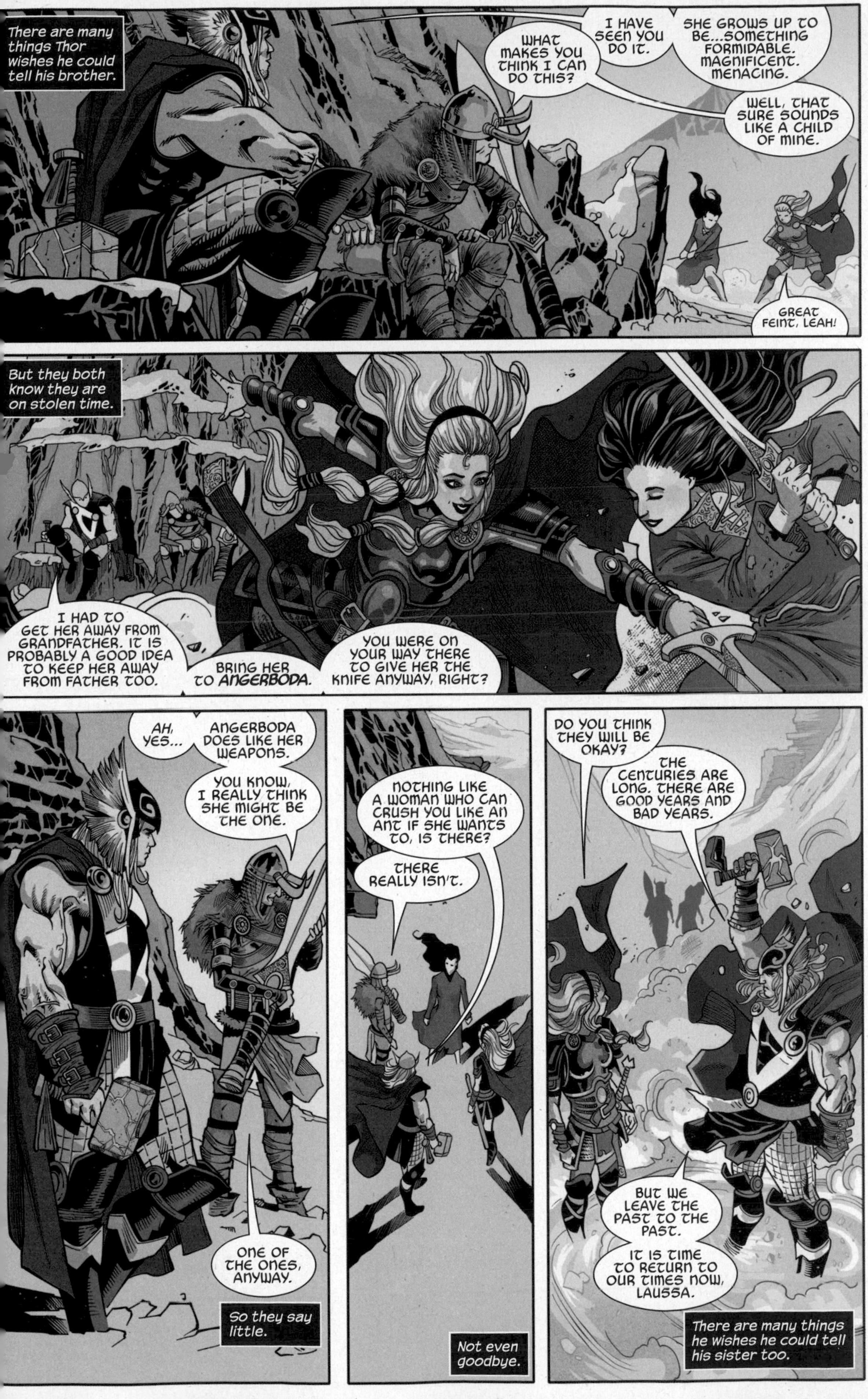

There are many things Thor wishes he could tell his brother.
WHAT MAKES YOU THINK I CAN DO THIS?
I HAVE SEEN YOU DO IT.
SHE GROWS UP TO BE...SOMETHING FORMIDABLE. MAGNIFICENT. MENACING.
WELL, THAT SURE SOUNDS LIKE A CHILD OF MINE.
GREAT FEINT, LEAH!
But they both know they are on stolen time.
I HAD TO GET HER AWAY FROM GRANDFATHER. IT IS PROBABLY A GOOD IDEA TO KEEP HER AWAY FROM FATHER TOO.
BRING HER TO ANGERBODA.
YOU WERE ON YOUR WAY THERE TO GIVE HER THE KNIFE ANYWAY, RIGHT?
AH, YES...
ANGERBODA DOES LIKE HER WEAPONS.
YOU KNOW, I REALLY THINK SHE MIGHT BE THE ONE.
ONE OF THE ONES, ANYWAY.
So they say little.
NOTHING LIKE A WOMAN WHO CAN CRUSH YOU LIKE AN ANT IF SHE WANTS TO, IS THERE?
THERE REALLY ISN'T.
Not even goodbye.
DO YOU THINK THEY WILL BE OKAY?
THE CENTURIES ARE LONG. THERE ARE GOOD YEARS AND BAD YEARS.
BUT WE LEAVE THE PAST TO THE PAST.
IT IS TIME TO RETURN TO OUR TIMES NOW, LAUSSA.
There are many things he wishes he could tell his sister too.

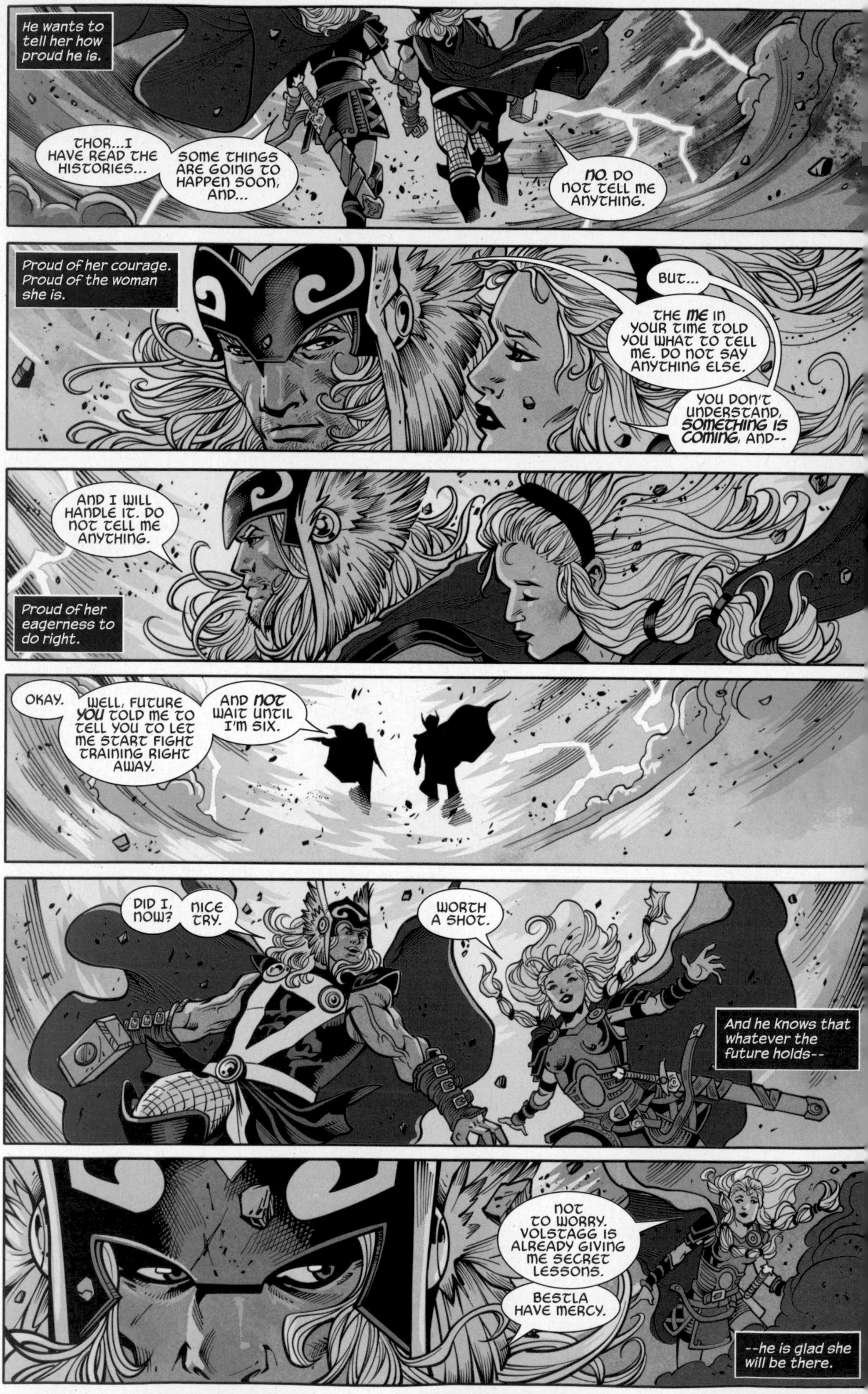
He wants to tell her how proud he is.
THOR...I HAVE READ THE HISTORIES...
SOME THINGS ARE GOING TO HAPPEN SOON, AND...
NO. DO NOT TELL ME ANYTHING.
Proud of her courage. Proud of the woman she is.
BUT...
THE ME IN YOUR TIME TOLD YOU WHAT TO TELL ME. DO NOT SAY ANYTHING ELSE.
YOU DON'T UNDERSTAND, SOMETHING IS COMING, AND--
AND I WILL HANDLE IT. DO NOT TELL ME ANYTHING.
Proud of her eagerness to do right.
OKAY.
WELL, FUTURE YOU TOLD ME TO TELL YOU TO LET ME START FIGHT TRAINING RIGHT AWAY.
AND NOT WAIT UNTIL I'M SIX.
DID I, NOW?
NICE TRY.
WORTH A SHOT.
And he knows that whatever the future holds--
NOT TO WORRY. VOLSTAGG IS ALREADY GIVING ME SECRET LESSONS.
BESTLA HAVE MERCY.
--he is glad she will be there.

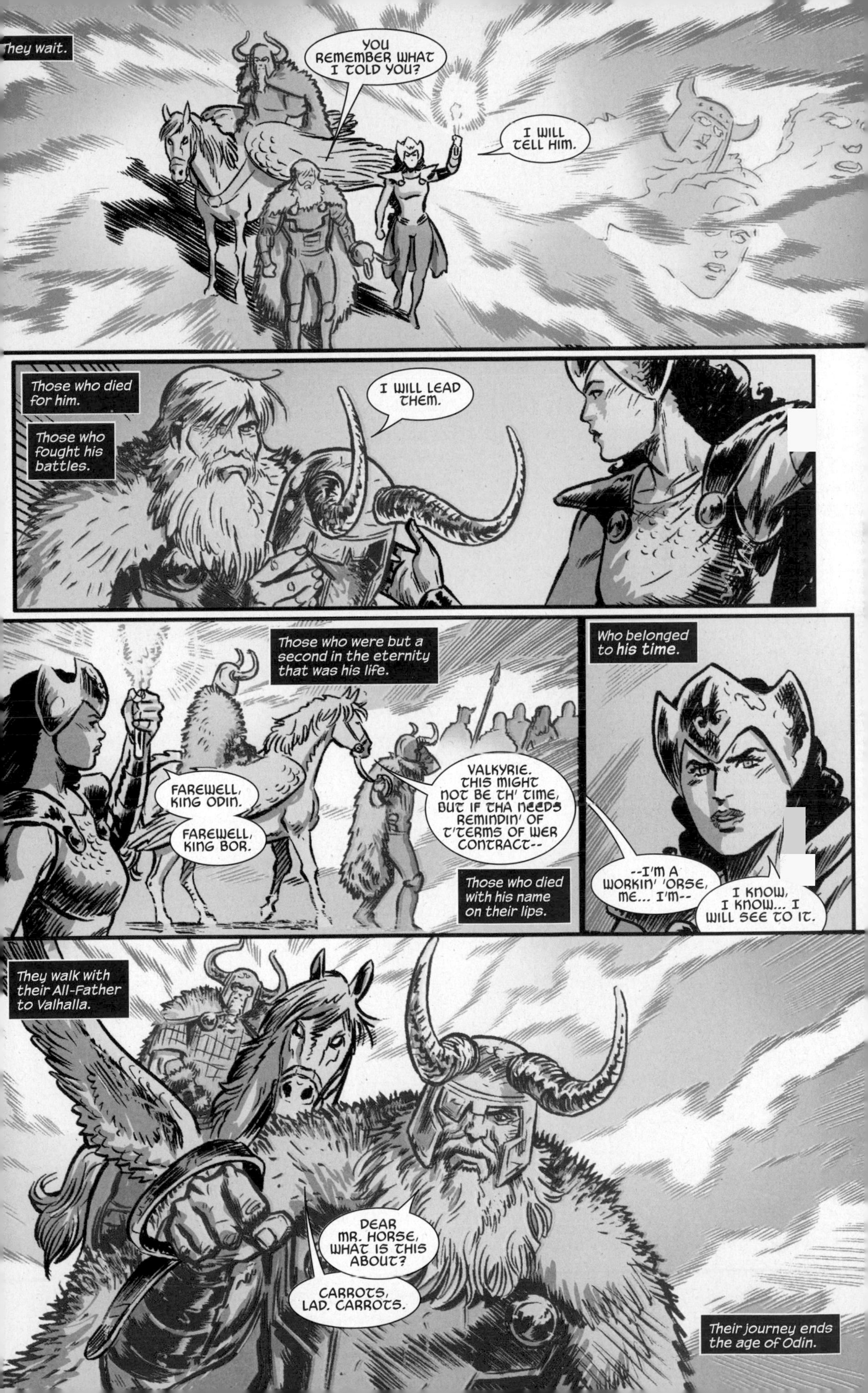

They wait.
YOU REMEMBER WHAT I TOLD YOU?
I WILL TELL HIM.
Those who died for him.
Those who fought his battles.
I WILL LEAD THEM.
Those who were but a second in the eternity that was his life.
FAREWELL, KING ODIN.
FAREWELL, KING BOR.
VALKYRIE. THIS MIGHT NOT BE TH' TIME, BUT IF THA NEEDS REMINDIN' OF T'TERMS OF WER CONTRACT--
Those who died with his name on their lips.
Who belonged to his time.
--I'M A WORKIN' 'ORSE, ME... I'M--
I KNOW, I KNOW... I WILL SEE TO IT.
They walk with their All-Father to Valhalla.
DEAR MR. HORSE, WHAT IS THIS ABOUT?
CARROTS, LAD. CARROTS.
Their journey ends the age of Odin.

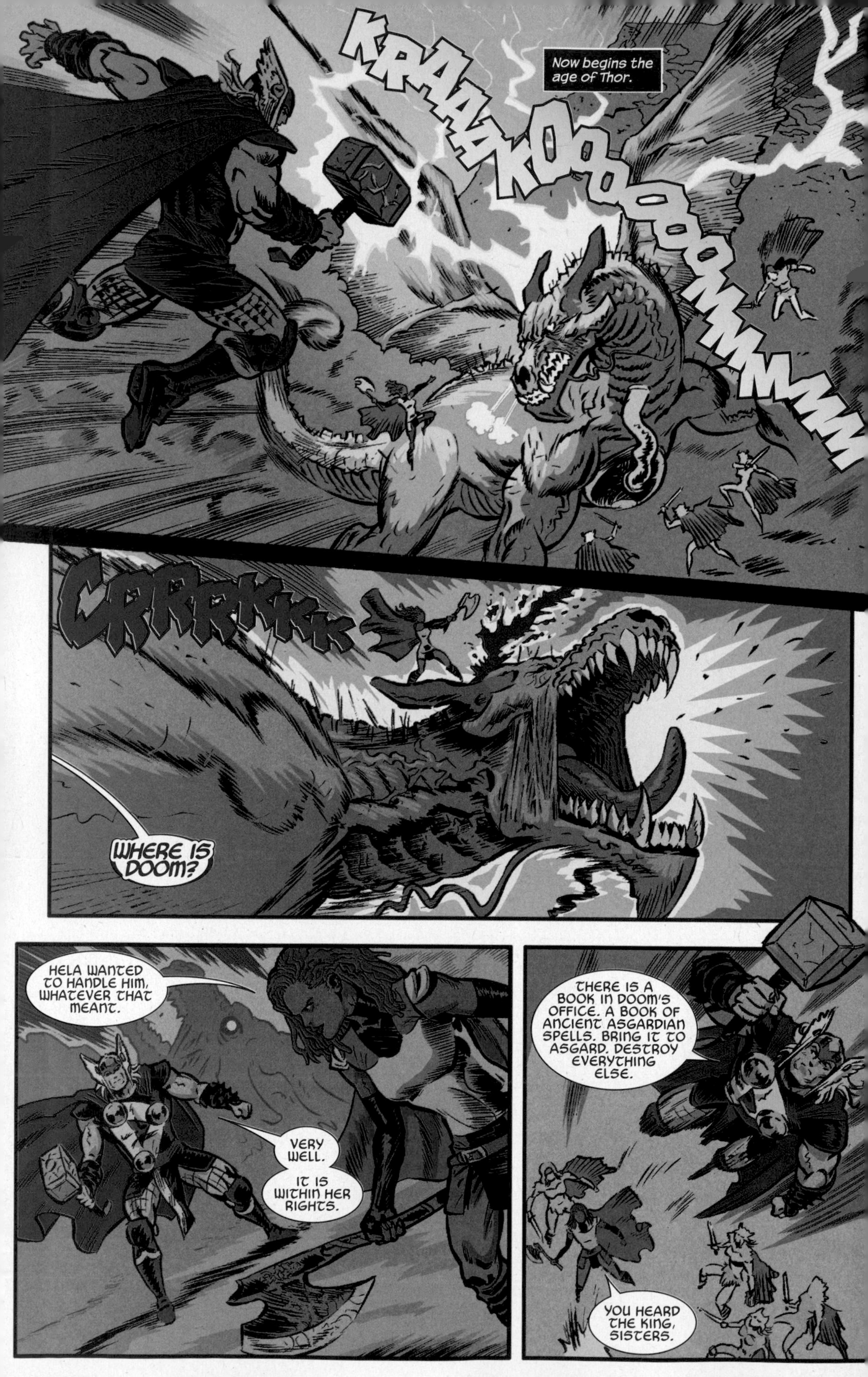

KRAAAKOOOOOOOOMMMMM
Now begins the age of Thor.
CRRRKKK
WHERE IS DOOM?
HELA WANTED TO HANDLE HIM, WHATEVER THAT MEANT.
VERY WELL.
IT IS WITHIN HER RIGHTS.
THERE IS A BOOK IN DOOM'S OFFICE. A BOOK OF ANCIENT ASGARDIAN SPELLS. BRING IT TO ASGARD. DESTROY EVERYTHING ELSE.
YOU HEARD THE KING, SISTERS.

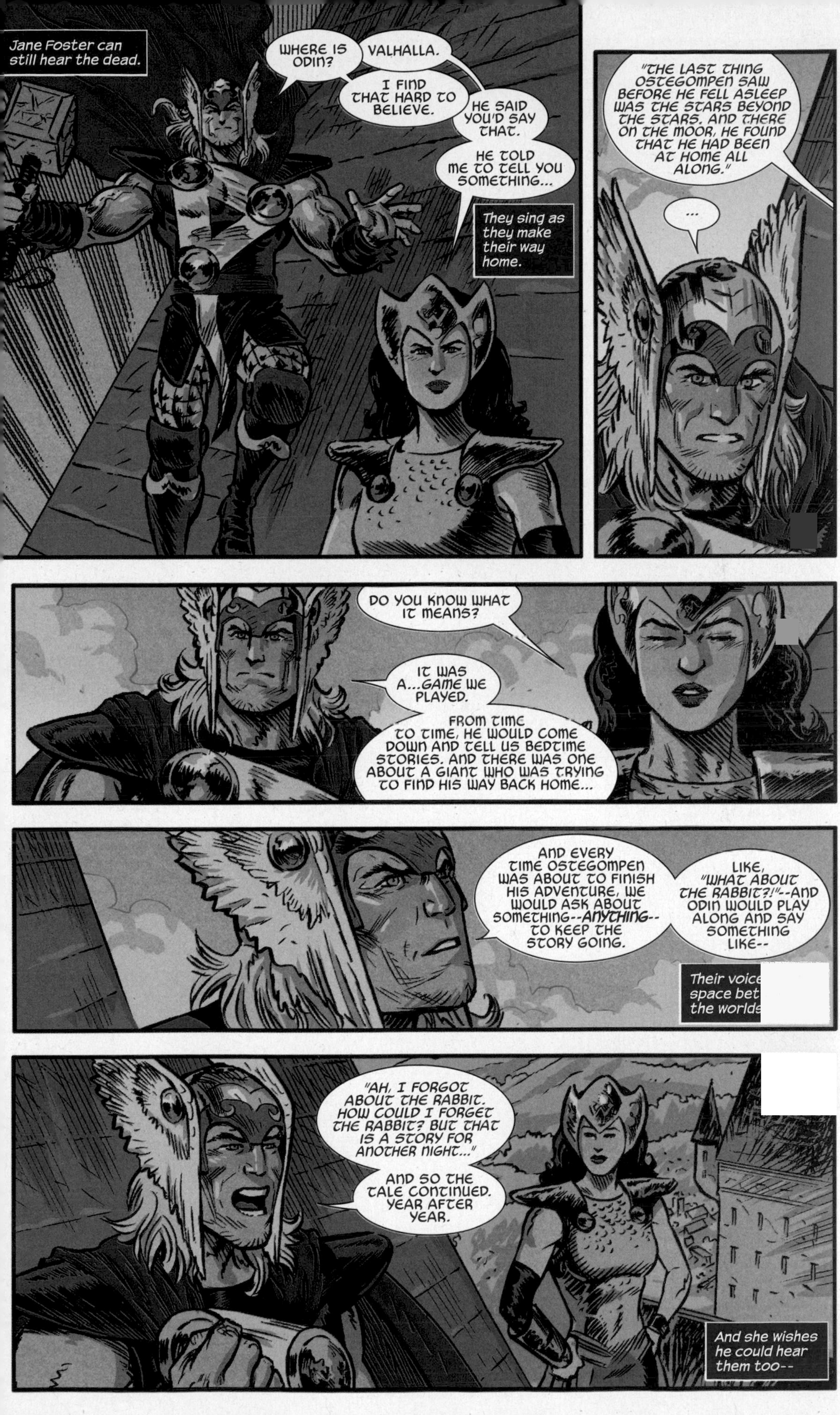
Jane Foster can still hear the dead.
WHERE IS ODIN?
VALHALLA.
I FIND THAT HARD TO BELIEVE.
HE SAID YOU'D SAY THAT.
HE TOLD ME TO TELL YOU SOMETHING...
They sing as they make their way home.
"THE LAST THING OSTEGOMPEN SAW BEFORE HE FELL ASLEEP WAS THE STARS BEYOND THE STARS. AND THERE ON THE MOOR, HE FOUND THAT HE HAD BEEN AT HOME ALL ALONG."
...
DO YOU KNOW WHAT IT MEANS?
IT WAS A...GAME WE PLAYED.
FROM TIME TO TIME, HE WOULD COME DOWN AND TELL US BEDTIME STORIES. AND THERE WAS ONE ABOUT A GIANT WHO WAS TRYING TO FIND HIS WAY BACK HOME...
AND EVERY TIME OSTEGOMPEN WAS ABOUT TO FINISH HIS ADVENTURE, WE WOULD ASK ABOUT SOMETHING--ANYTHING--TO KEEP THE STORY GOING.
LIKE, "WHAT ABOUT THE RABBIT?!"--AND ODIN WOULD PLAY ALONG AND SAY SOMETHING LIKE--
Their voice
space bet
the worlds
"AH, I FORGOT ABOUT THE RABBIT. HOW COULD I FORGET THE RABBIT? BUT THAT IS A STORY FOR ANOTHER NIGHT..."
AND SO THE TALE CONTINUED. YEAR AFTER YEAR.
And she wishes he could hear them too--

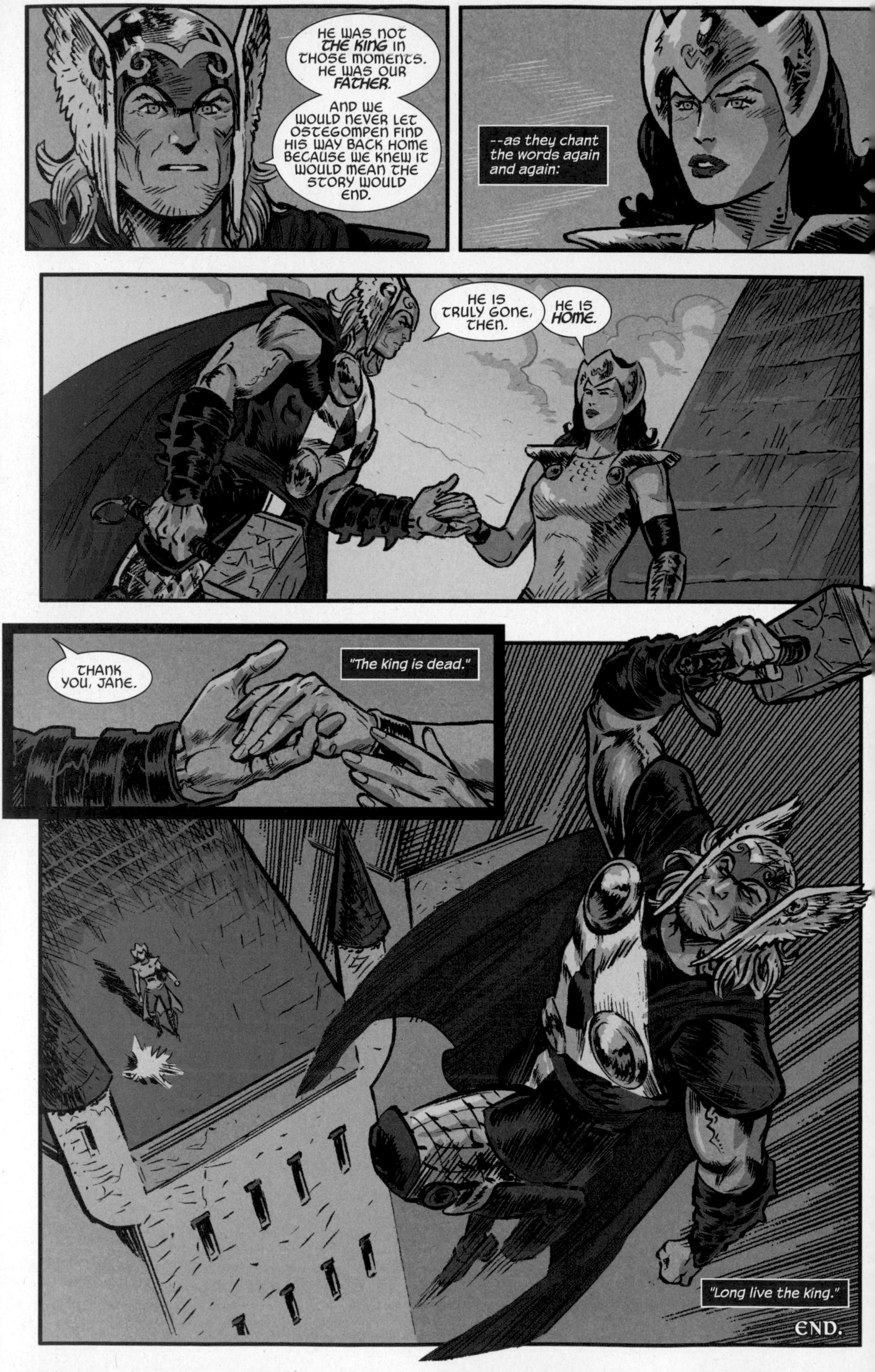
HE WAS NOT THE KING IN THOSE MOMENTS. HE WAS OUR FATHER.
AND WE WOULD NEVER LET OSTEGOMPEN FIND HIS WAY BACK HOME BECAUSE WE KNEW IT WOULD MEAN THE STORY WOULD END.
--as they chant the words again and again:
HE IS TRULY GONE, THEN.
HE IS HOME.
THANK YOU, JANE.
"The king is dead."
"Long live the king."
END.

#31 BLACK PANTHER BLACK HISTORY MONTH VARIANT BY **Ken Lashley** & **Juan Fernandez**

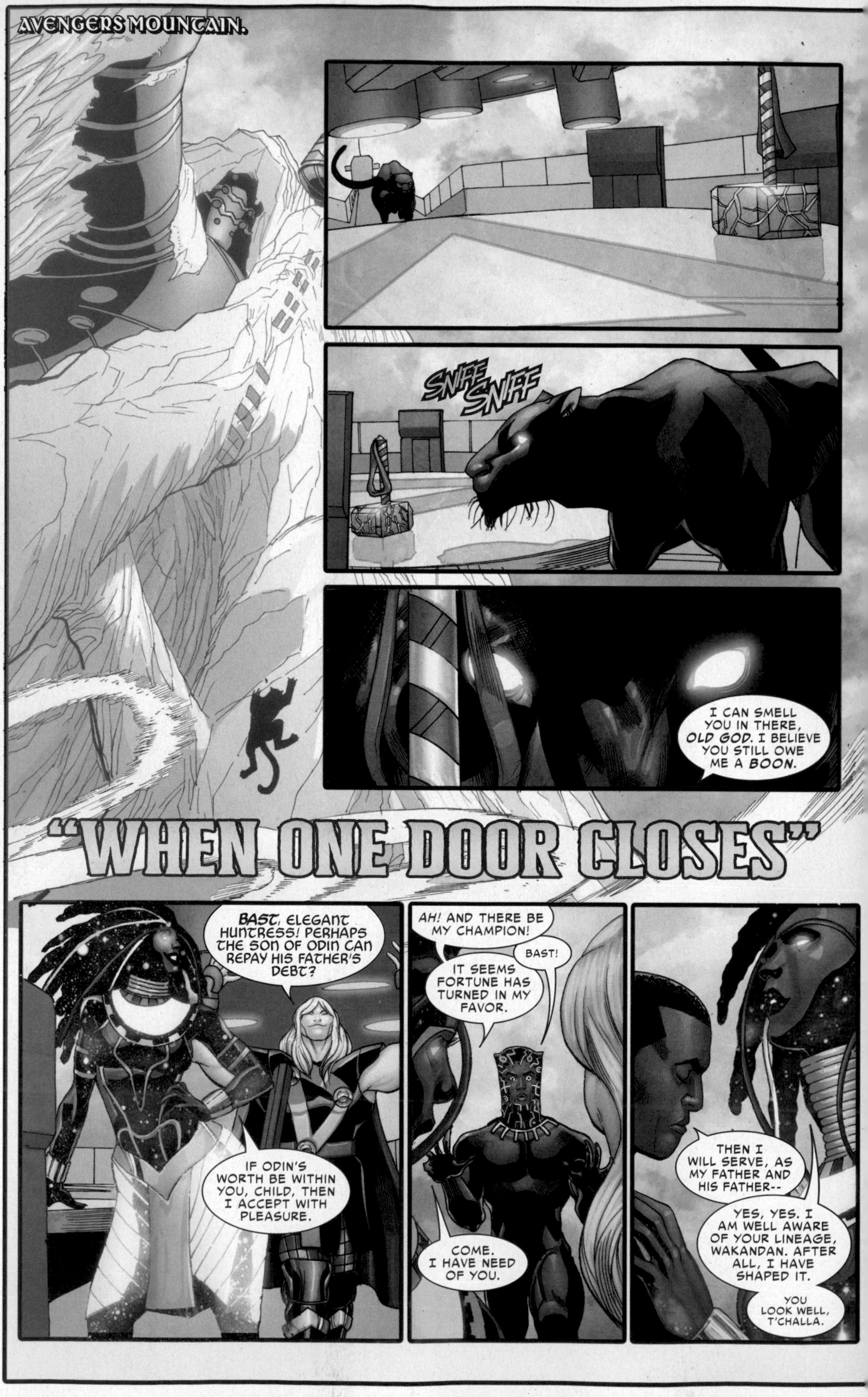
AVENGERS MOUNTAIN.
SNIFF SNIFF
I CAN SMELL YOU IN THERE, OLD GOD. I BELIEVE YOU STILL OWE ME A BOON.
"WHEN ONE DOOR CLOSES"
BAST, ELEGANT HUNTRESS! PERHAPS THE SON OF ODIN CAN REPAY HIS FATHER'S DEBT?
IF ODIN'S WORTH BE WITHIN YOU, CHILD, THEN I ACCEPT WITH PLEASURE.
AH! AND THERE BE MY CHAMPION!
BAST!
IT SEEMS FORTUNE HAS TURNED IN MY FAVOR.
COME. I HAVE NEED OF YOU.
THEN I WILL SERVE, AS MY FATHER AND HIS FATHER--
YES, YES. I AM WELL AWARE OF YOUR LINEAGE, WAKANDAN. AFTER ALL, I HAVE SHAPED IT.
YOU LOOK WELL, T'CHALLA.

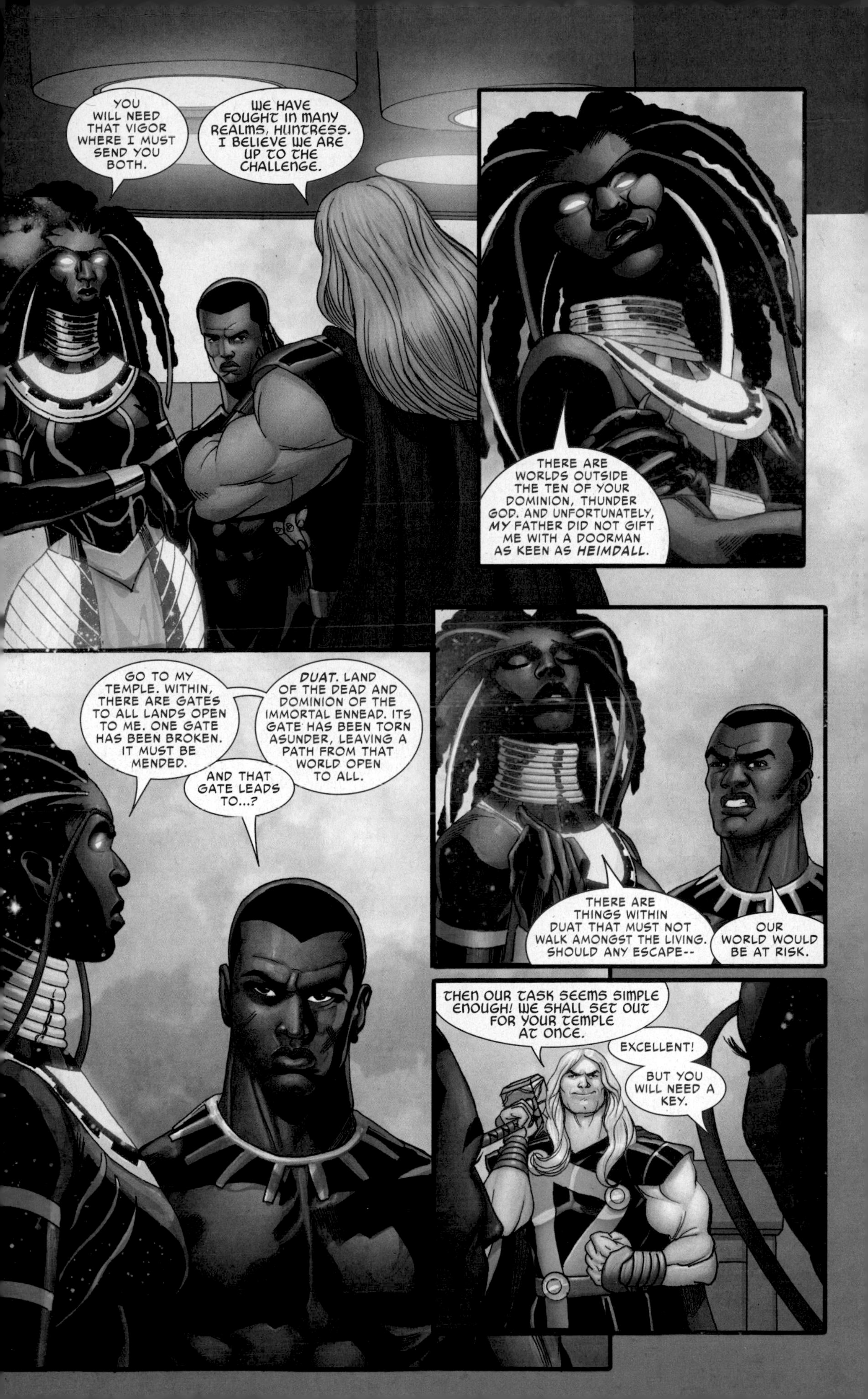
YOU WILL NEED THAT VIGOR WHERE I MUST SEND YOU BOTH.
WE HAVE FOUGHT IN MANY REALMS, HUNTRESS. I BELIEVE WE ARE UP TO THE CHALLENGE.
THERE ARE WORLDS OUTSIDE THE TEN OF YOUR DOMINION, THUNDER GOD. AND UNFORTUNATELY, MY FATHER DID NOT GIFT ME WITH A DOORMAN AS KEEN AS HEIMDALL.
GO TO MY TEMPLE. WITHIN, THERE ARE GATES TO ALL LANDS OPEN TO ME. ONE GATE HAS BEEN BROKEN. IT MUST BE MENDED.
AND THAT GATE LEADS TO...?
DUAT. LAND OF THE DEAD AND DOMINION OF THE IMMORTAL ENNEAD. ITS GATE HAS BEEN TORN ASUNDER, LEAVING A PATH FROM THAT WORLD OPEN TO ALL.
THERE ARE THINGS WITHIN DUAT THAT MUST NOT WALK AMONGST THE LIVING. SHOULD ANY ESCAPE--
OUR WORLD WOULD BE AT RISK.
THEN OUR TASK SEEMS SIMPLE ENOUGH! WE SHALL SET OUT FOR YOUR TEMPLE AT ONCE.
EXCELLENT!
BUT YOU WILL NEED A KEY.

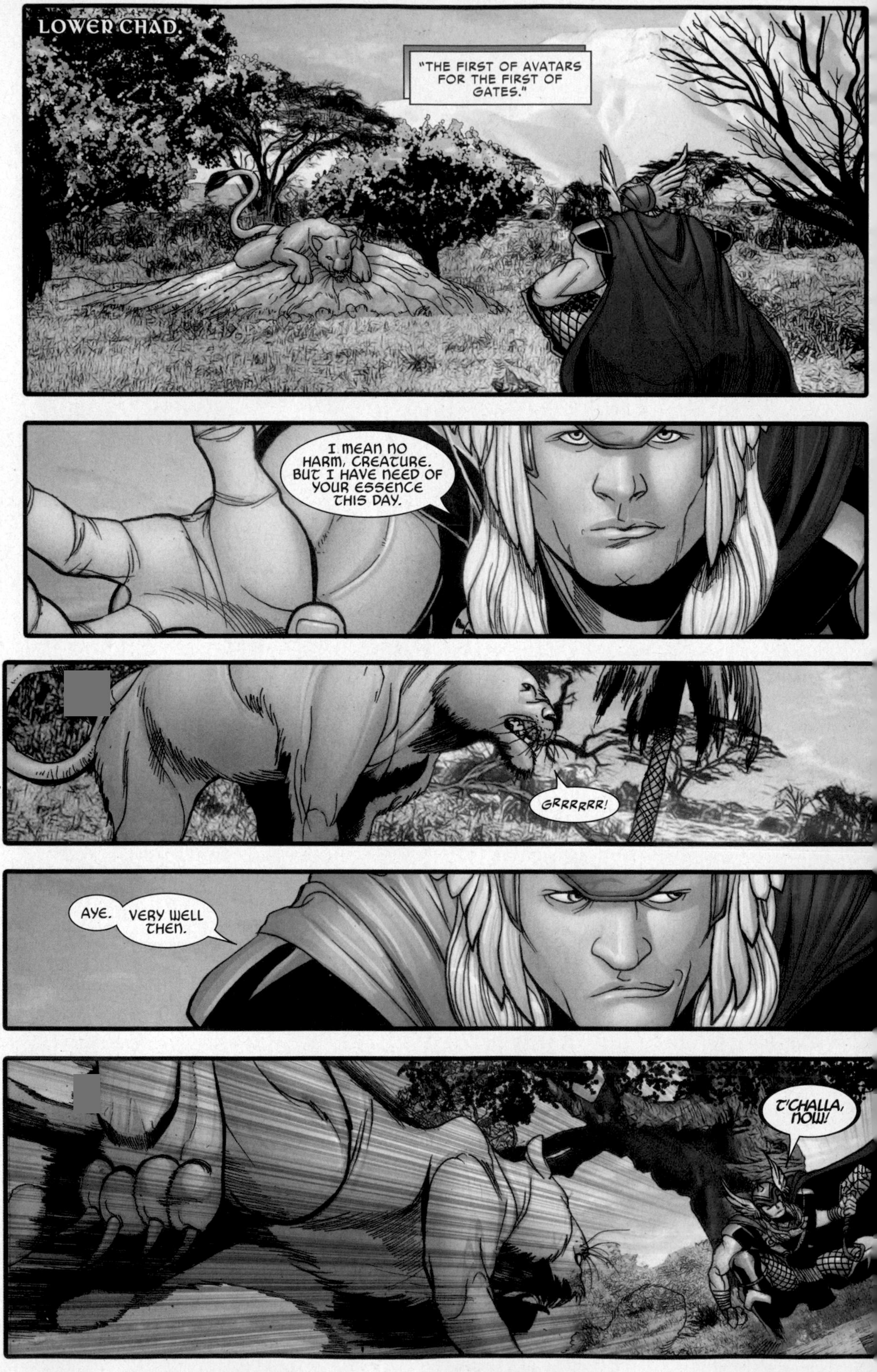
LOWER CHAD.
"THE FIRST OF AVATARS FOR THE FIRST OF GATES."
I MEAN NO HARM, CREATURE. BUT I HAVE NEED OF YOUR ESSENCE THIS DAY.
GRRRRRR!
AYE.
VERY WELL THEN.
T'CHALLA, NOW!

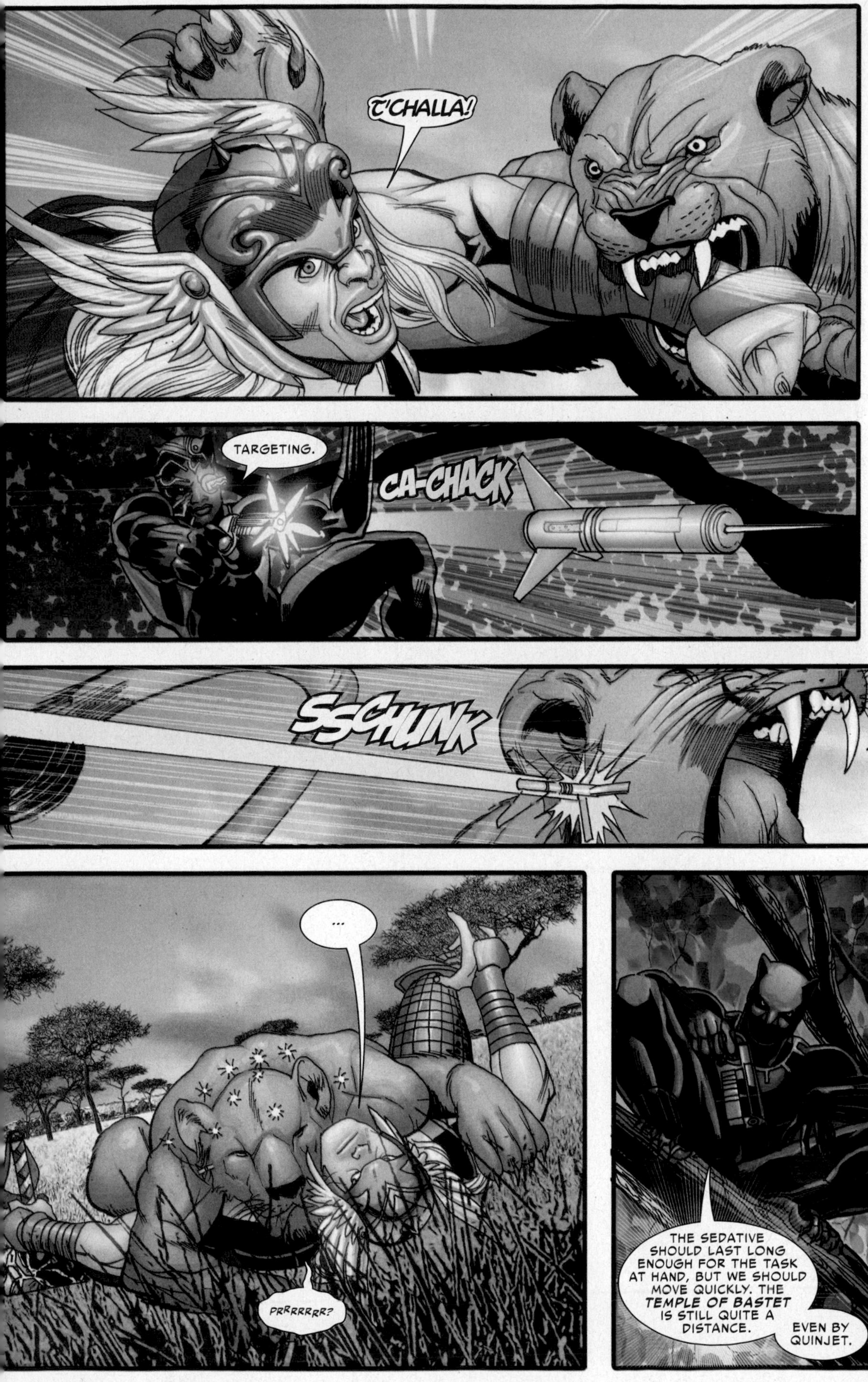
T'CHALLA!
TARGETING.
CA-CHACK
SSCHUNK
...
PRRRRRRR?
THE SEDATIVE SHOULD LAST LONG ENOUGH FOR THE TASK AT HAND, BUT WE SHOULD MOVE QUICKLY. THE *TEMPLE OF BASTET* IS STILL QUITE A DISTANCE.
EVEN BY QUINJET.

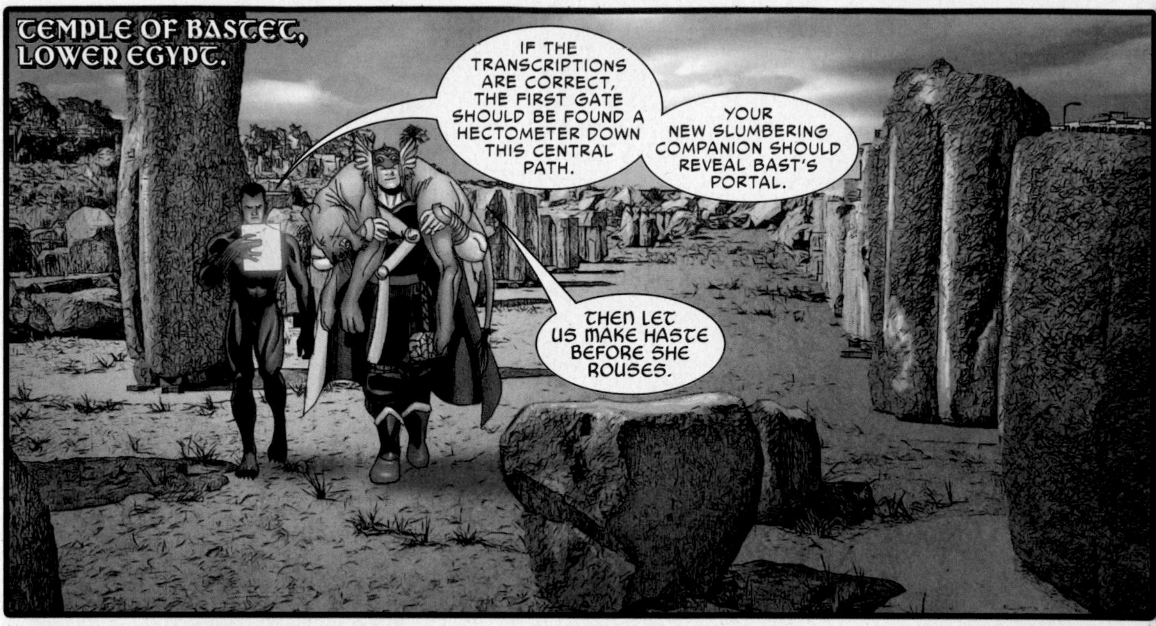
TEMPLE OF BASTET, LOWER EGYPT.
IF THE TRANSCRIPTIONS ARE CORRECT, THE FIRST GATE SHOULD BE FOUND A HECTOMETER DOWN THIS CENTRAL PATH.
YOUR NEW SLUMBERING COMPANION SHOULD REVEAL BAST'S PORTAL.
THEN LET US MAKE HASTE BEFORE SHE ROUSES.
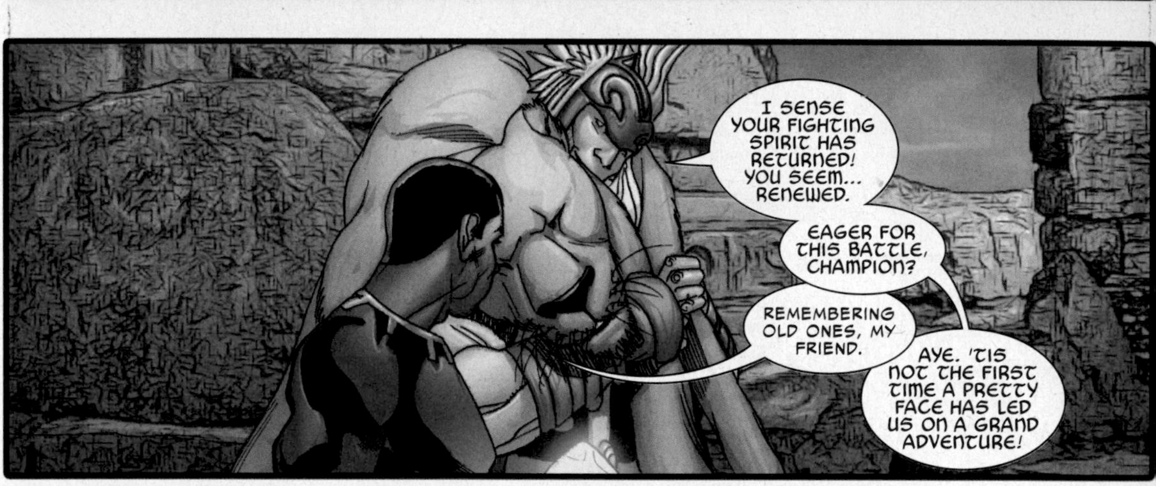
I SENSE YOUR FIGHTING SPIRIT HAS RETURNED! YOU SEEM... RENEWED.
EAGER FOR THIS BATTLE, CHAMPION?
REMEMBERING OLD ONES, MY FRIEND.
AYE. 'TIS NOT THE FIRST TIME A PRETTY FACE HAS LED US ON A GRAND ADVENTURE!
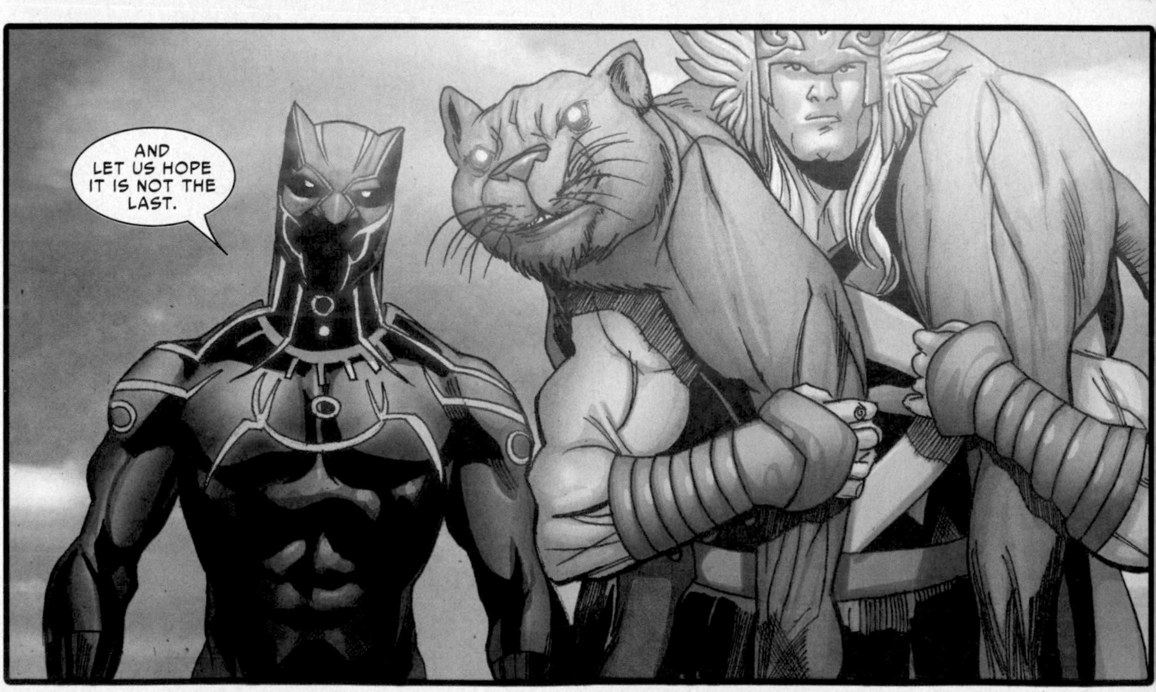
AND LET US HOPE IT IS NOT THE LAST.

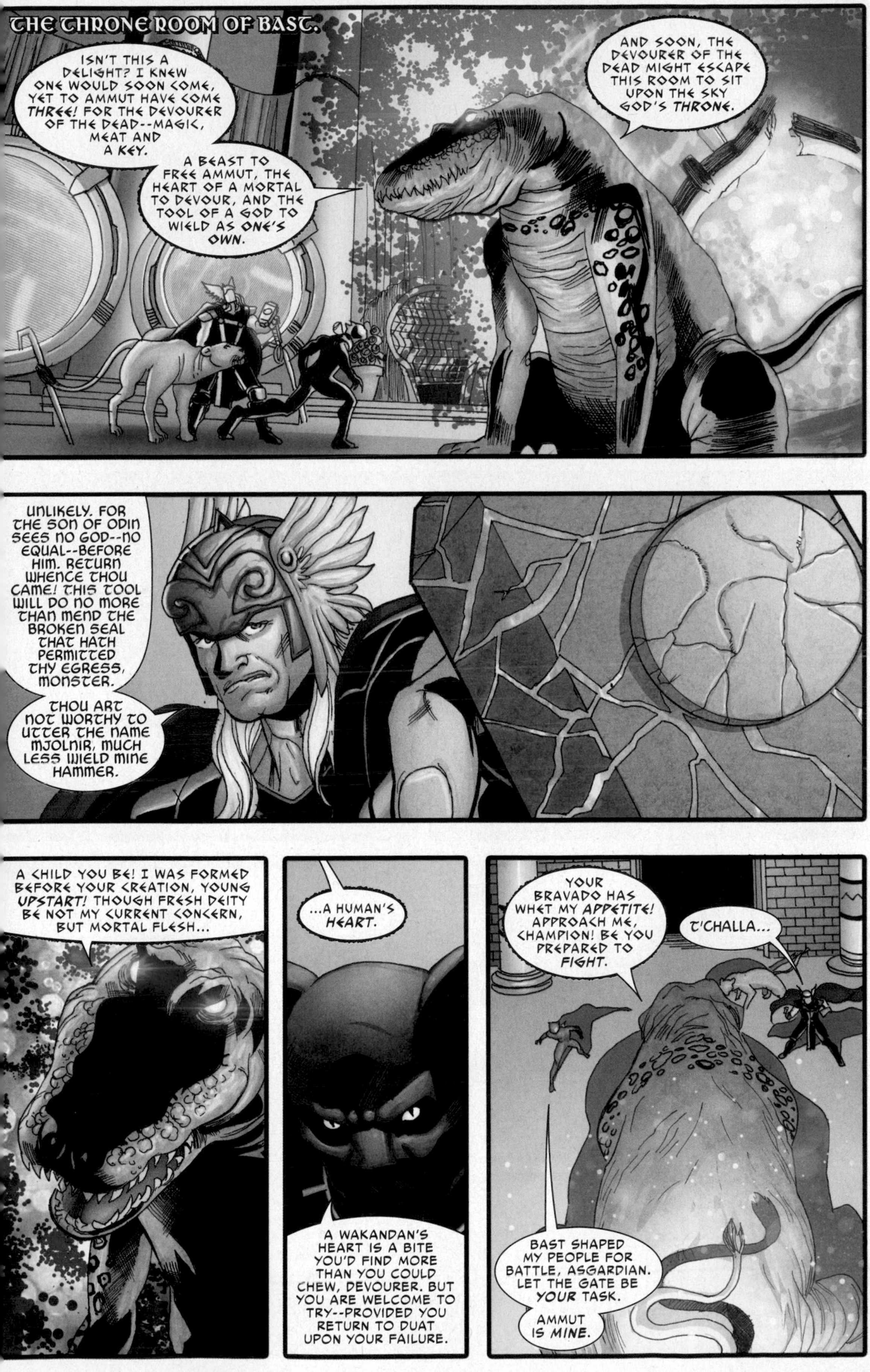
THE THRONE ROOM OF BAST.
ISN'T THIS A DELIGHT? I KNEW ONE WOULD SOON COME, YET TO AMMUT HAVE COME THREE! FOR THE DEVOURER OF THE DEAD--MAGIC, MEAT AND A KEY.
A BEAST TO FREE AMMUT, THE HEART OF A MORTAL TO DEVOUR, AND THE TOOL OF A GOD TO WIELD AS ONE'S OWN.
AND SOON, THE DEVOURER OF THE DEAD MIGHT ESCAPE THIS ROOM TO SIT UPON THE SKY GOD'S THRONE.
UNLIKELY. FOR THE SON OF ODIN SEES NO GOD--NO EQUAL--BEFORE HIM. RETURN WHENCE THOU CAME! THIS TOOL WILL DO NO MORE THAN MEND THE BROKEN SEAL THAT HATH PERMITTED THY EGRESS, MONSTER.
THOU ART NOT WORTHY TO UTTER THE NAME MJOLNIR, MUCH LESS WIELD MINE HAMMER.
A CHILD YOU BE! I WAS FORMED BEFORE YOUR CREATION, YOUNG UPSTART! THOUGH FRESH DEITY BE NOT MY CURRENT CONCERN, BUT MORTAL FLESH...
...A HUMAN'S HEART.
A WAKANDAN'S HEART IS A BITE YOU'D FIND MORE THAN YOU COULD CHEW, DEVOURER. BUT YOU ARE WELCOME TO TRY--PROVIDED YOU RETURN TO DUAT UPON YOUR FAILURE.
YOUR BRAVADO HAS WHET MY APPETITE! APPROACH ME, CHAMPION! BE YOU PREPARED TO FIGHT.
T'CHALLA...
BAST SHAPED MY PEOPLE FOR BATTLE, ASGARDIAN. LET THE GATE BE YOUR TASK.
AMMUT IS MINE.

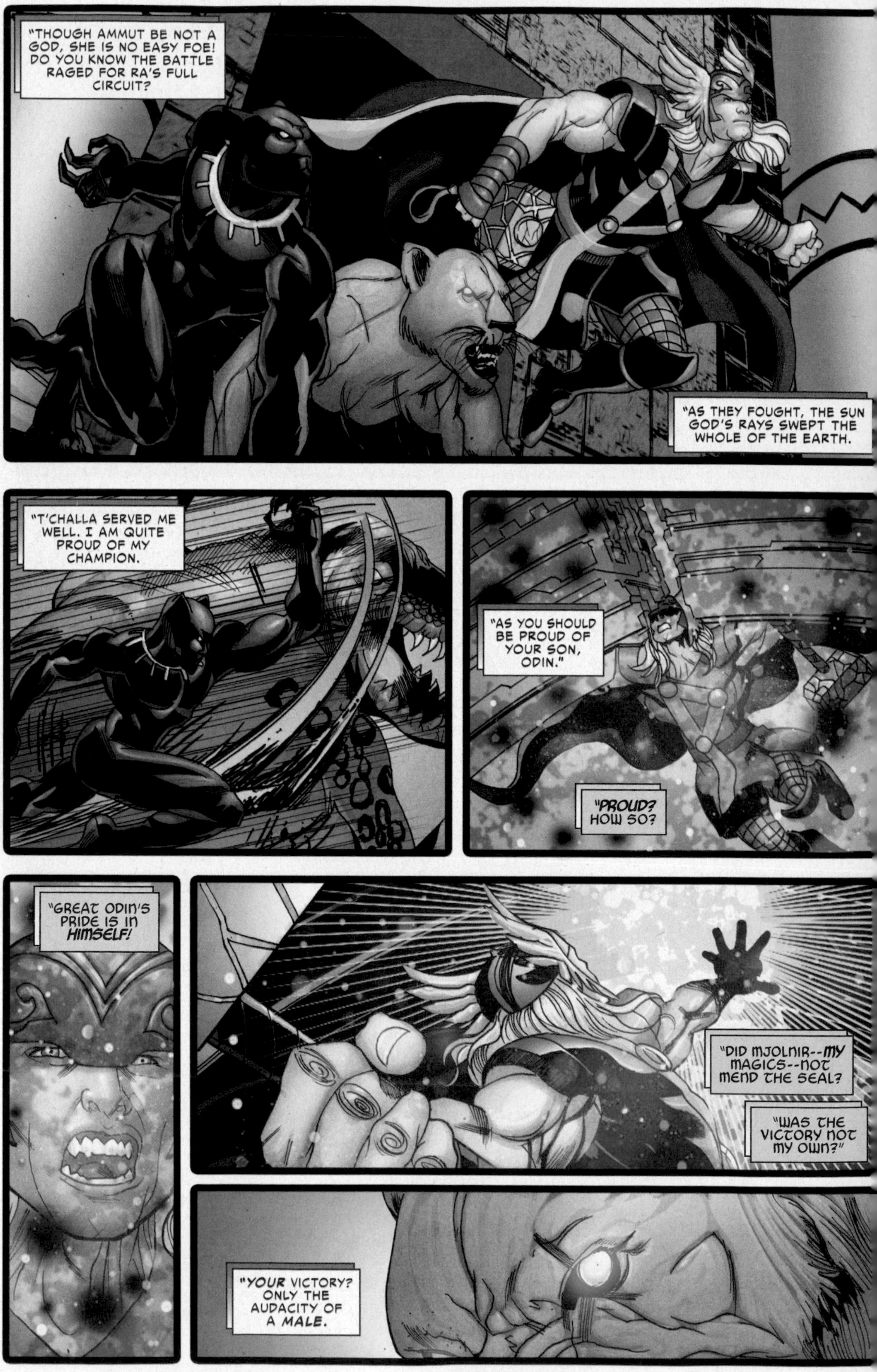
"THOUGH AMMUT BE NOT A GOD, SHE IS NO EASY FOE! DO YOU KNOW THE BATTLE RAGED FOR RA'S FULL CIRCUIT?
"AS THEY FOUGHT, THE SUN GOD'S RAYS SWEPT THE WHOLE OF THE EARTH.
"T'CHALLA SERVED ME WELL. I AM QUITE PROUD OF MY CHAMPION.
"AS YOU SHOULD BE PROUD OF YOUR SON, ODIN."
"PROUD? HOW SO?
"GREAT ODIN'S PRIDE IS IN HIMSELF!
"DID MJOLNIR--MY MAGICS--NOT MEND THE SEAL?
"WAS THE VICTORY NOT MY OWN?"
"YOUR VICTORY? ONLY THE AUDACITY OF A MALE.

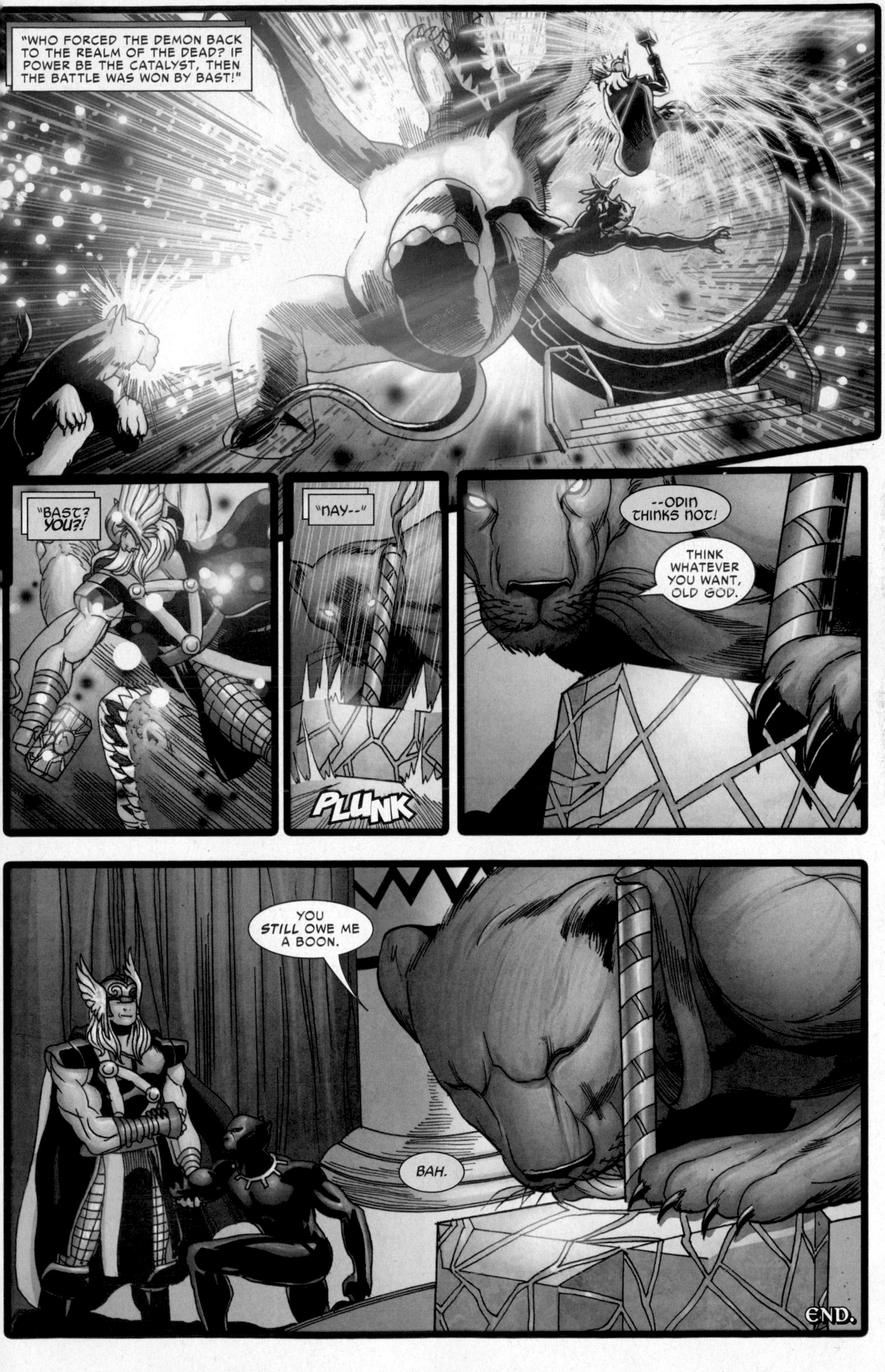
"WHO FORCED THE DEMON BACK TO THE REALM OF THE DEAD? IF POWER BE THE CATALYST, THEN THE BATTLE WAS WON BY BAST!"
"BAST? YOU?!
"NAY--"
PLUNK
--ODIN THINKS NOT!
THINK WHATEVER YOU WANT, OLD GOD.
YOU STILL OWE ME A BOON.
BAH.
END.

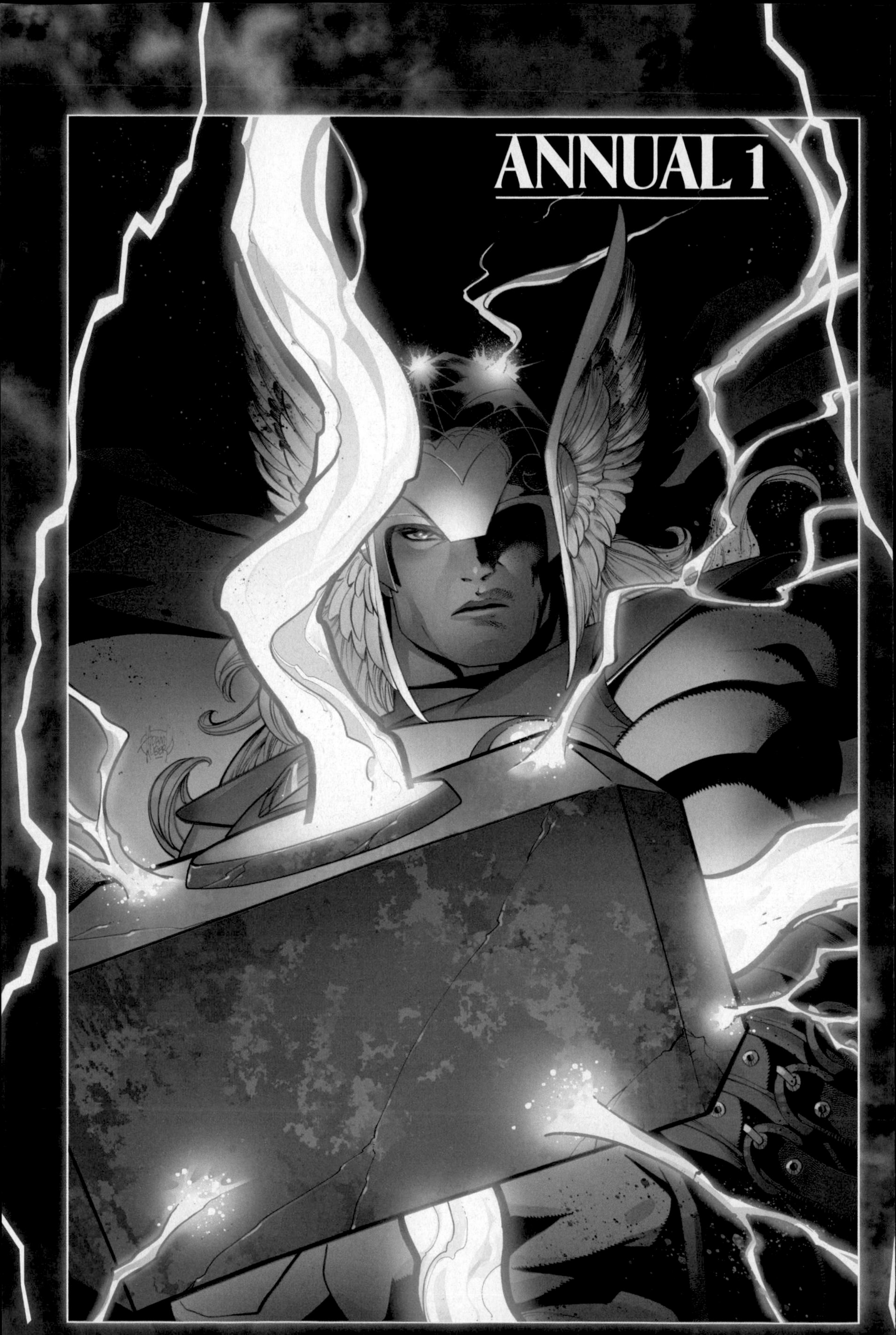
ANNUAL 1

"Mythos"

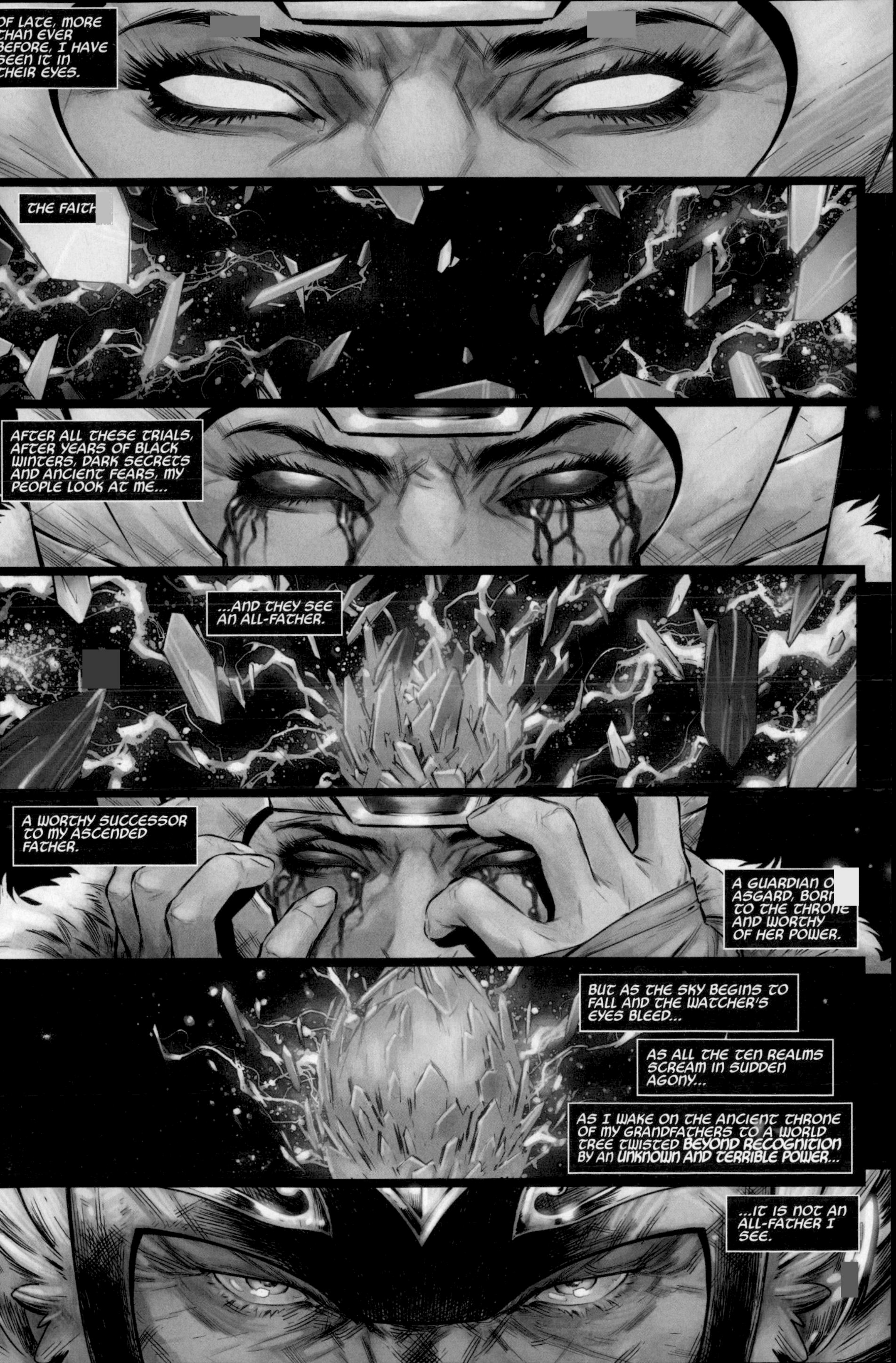

OF LATE, MORE THAN EVER BEFORE, I HAVE SEEN IT IN THEIR EYES.
THE FAITH
AFTER ALL THESE TRIALS, AFTER YEARS OF BLACK WINTERS, DARK SECRETS AND ANCIENT FEARS, MY PEOPLE LOOK AT ME...
...AND THEY SEE AN ALL-FATHER.
A WORTHY SUCCESSOR TO MY ASCENDED FATHER.
A GUARDIAN O ASGARD, BORN TO THE THRONE AND WORTHY OF HER POWER.
BUT AS THE SKY BEGINS TO FALL AND THE WATCHER'S EYES BLEED...
AS ALL THE TEN REALMS SCREAM IN SUDDEN AGONY...
AS I WAKE ON THE ANCIENT THRONE OF MY GRANDFATHERS TO A WORLD TREE TWISTED BEYOND RECOGNITION BY AN UNKNOWN AND TERRIBLE POWER...
...IT IS NOT AN ALL-FATHER I SEE.

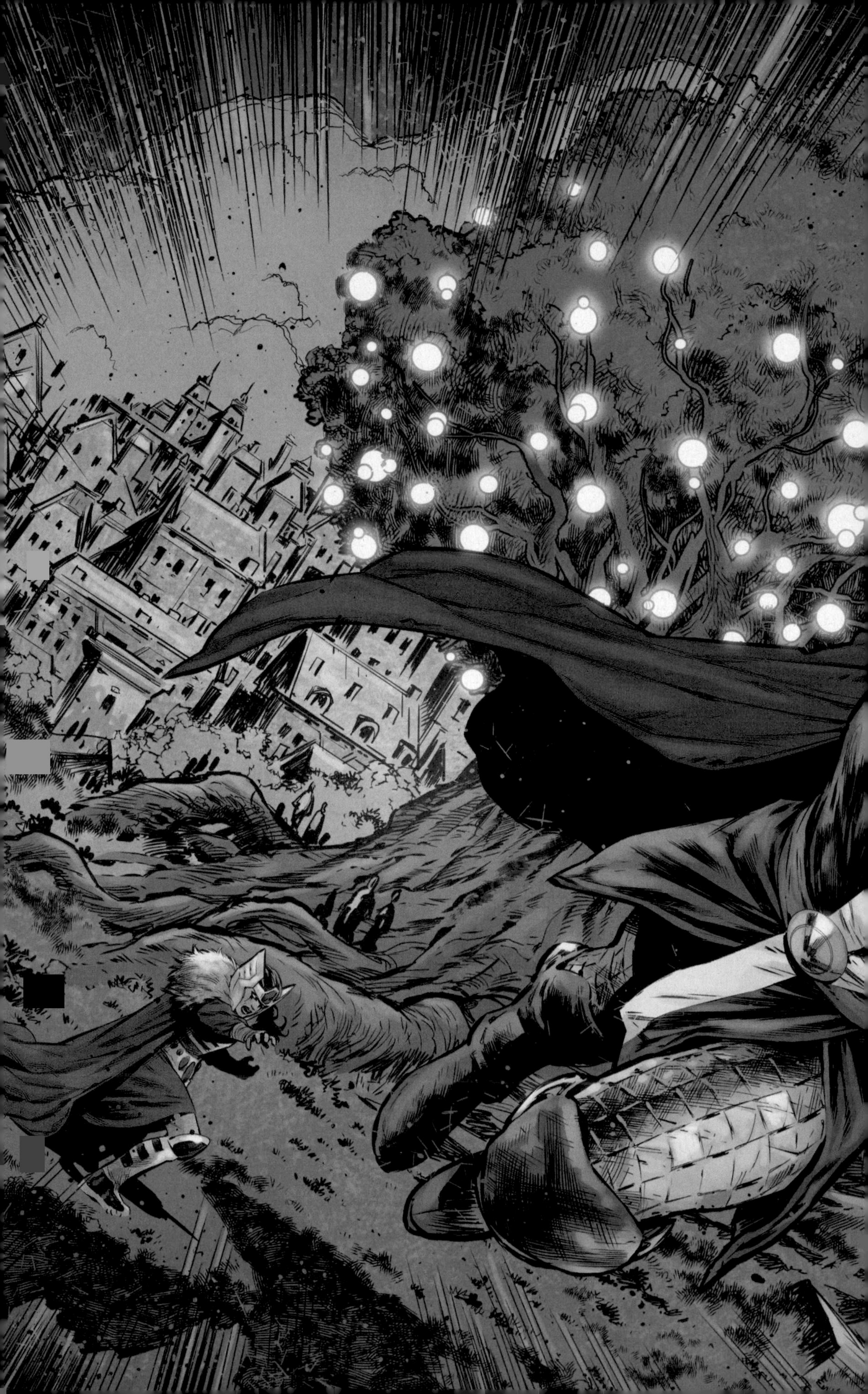

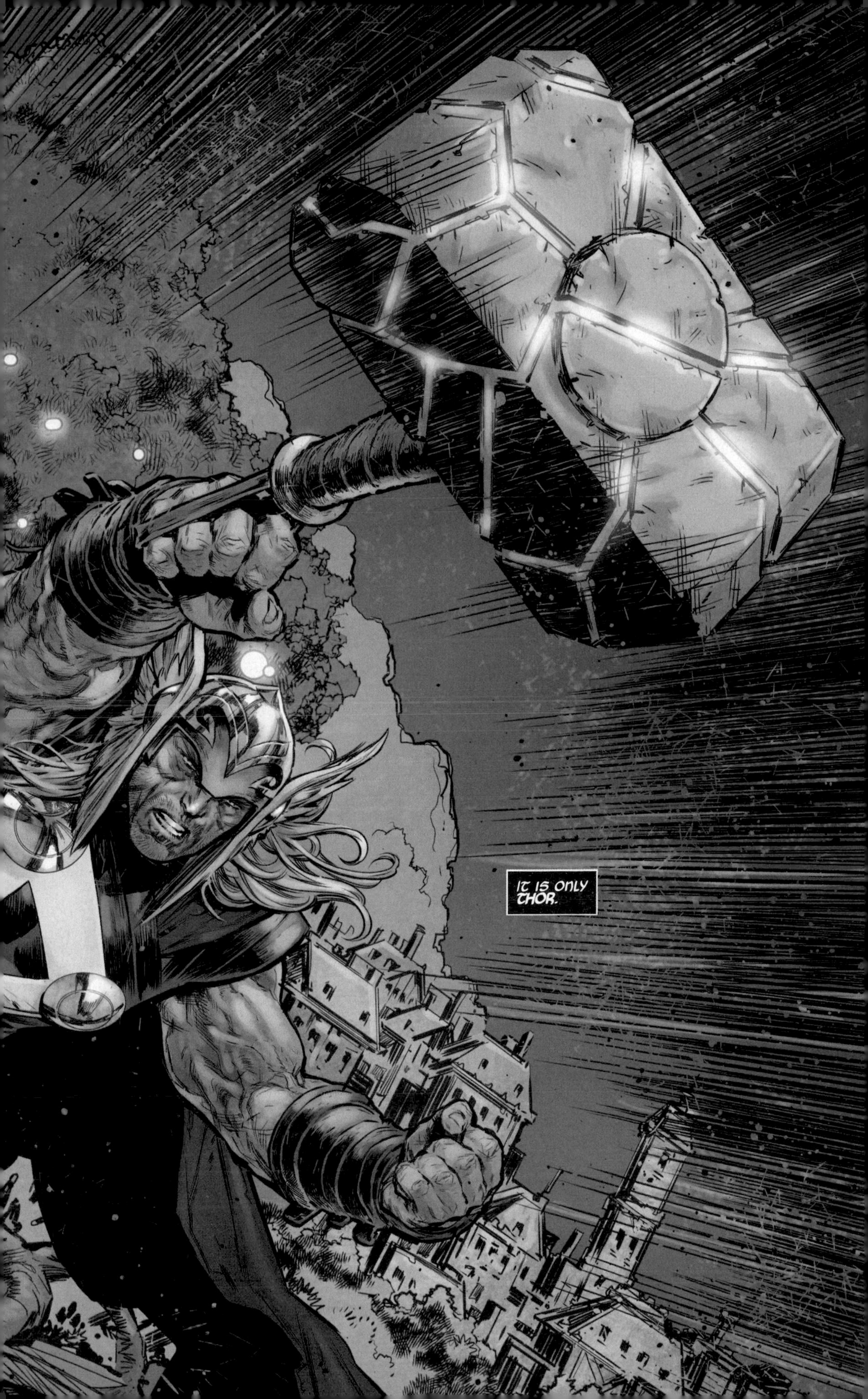
IT IS ONLY
THOR.

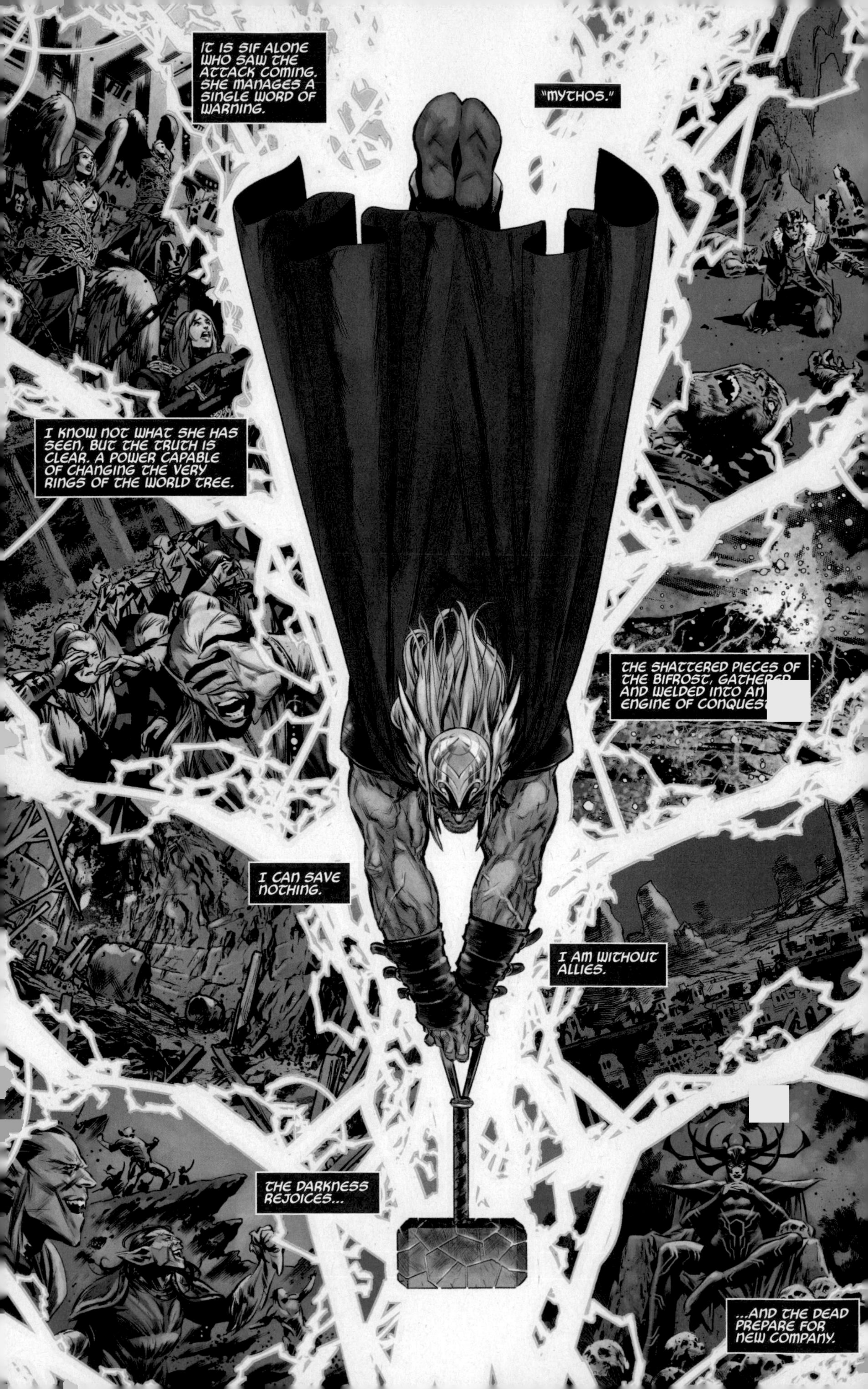
IT IS SIF ALONE WHO SAW THE ATTACK COMING. SHE MANAGES A SINGLE WORD OF WARNING.
"MYTHOS."
I KNOW NOT WHAT SHE HAS SEEN, BUT THE TRUTH IS CLEAR. A POWER CAPABLE OF CHANGING THE VERY RINGS OF THE WORLD TREE.
THE SHATTERED PIECES OF THE BIFROST, GATHERED AND WELDED INTO AN ENGINE OF CONQUEST
I CAN SAVE NOTHING.
I AM WITHOUT ALLIES.
THE DARKNESS REJOICES...
...AND THE DEAD PREPARE FOR NEW COMPANY.

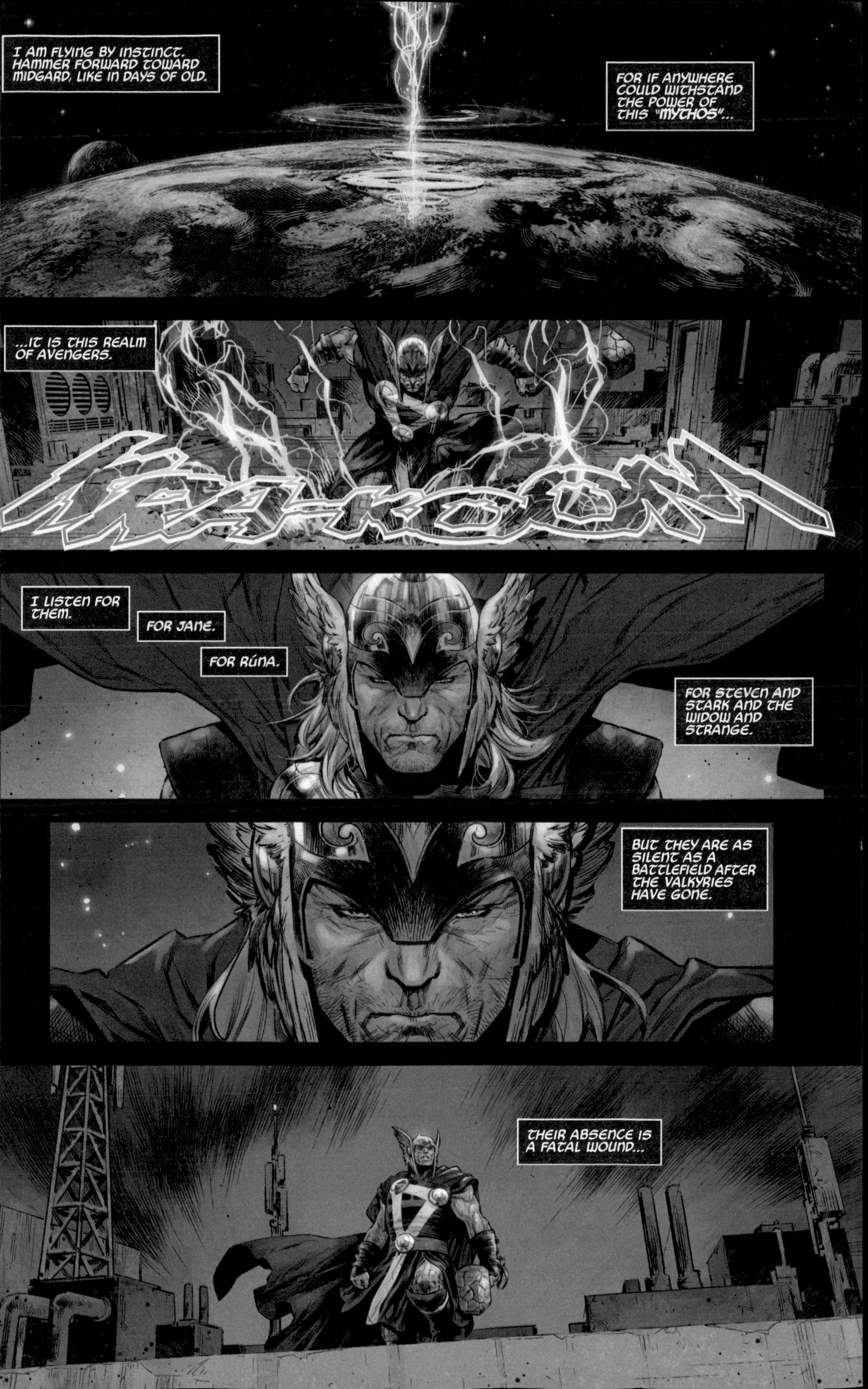
I AM FLYING BY INSTINCT. HAMMER FORWARD TOWARD MIDGARD, LIKE IN DAYS OF OLD.
FOR IF ANYWHERE COULD WITHSTAND THE POWER OF THIS "MYTHOS"...
...IT IS THIS REALM OF AVENGERS.
I LISTEN FOR THEM.
FOR JANE.
FOR RÚNA.
FOR STEVEN AND STARK AND THE WIDOW AND STRANGE.
BUT THEY ARE AS SILENT AS A BATTLEFIELD AFTER THE VALKYRIES HAVE GONE.
THEIR ABSENCE IS A FATAL WOUND...

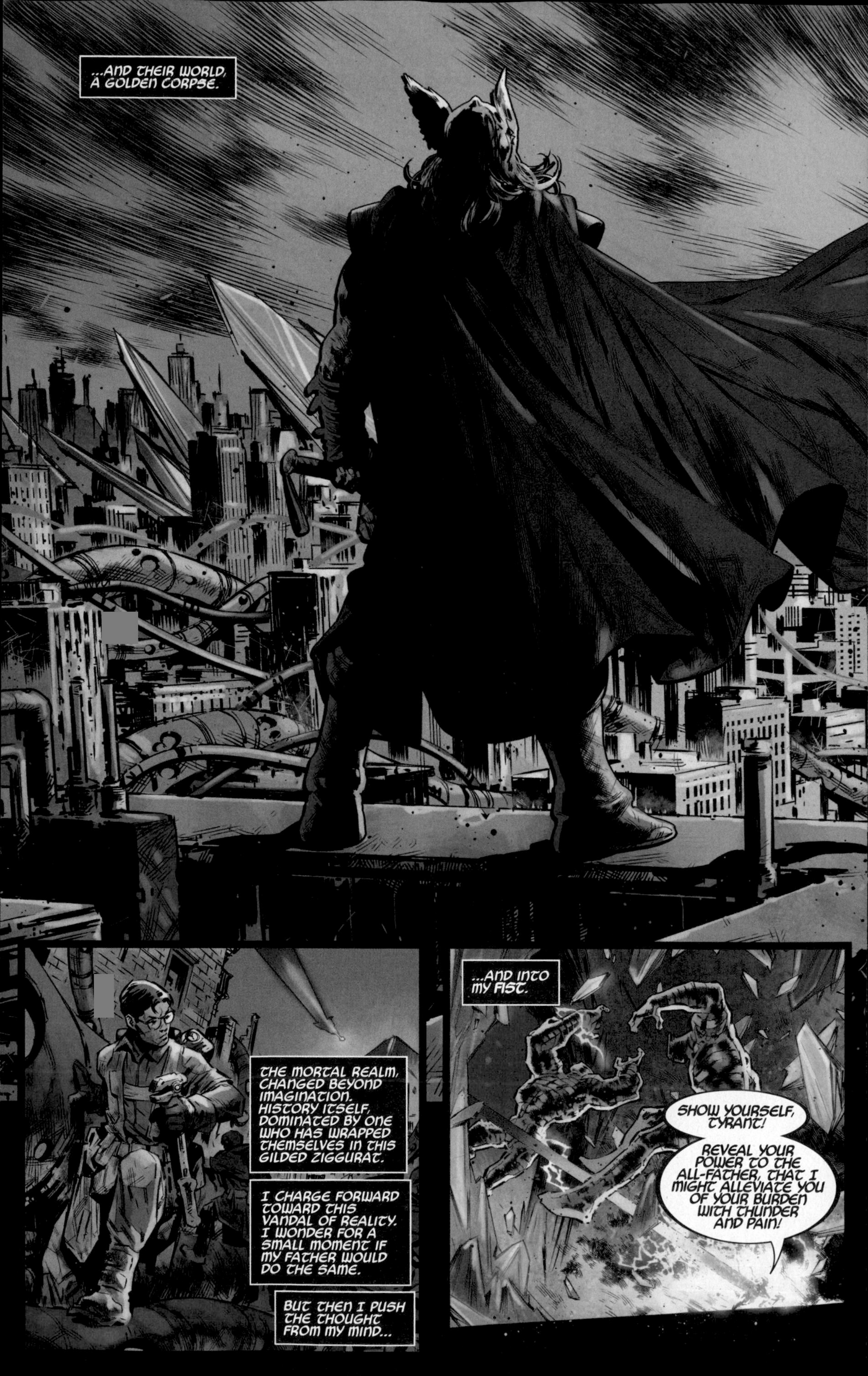
...AND THEIR WORLD, A GOLDEN CORPSE.
THE MORTAL REALM, CHANGED BEYOND IMAGINATION. HISTORY ITSELF, DOMINATED BY ONE WHO HAS WRAPPED THEMSELVES IN THIS GILDED ZIGGURAT.
I CHARGE FORWARD TOWARD THIS VANDAL OF REALITY. I WONDER FOR A SMALL MOMENT IF MY FATHER WOULD DO THE SAME.
BUT THEN I PUSH THE THOUGHT FROM MY MIND...
...AND INTO MY FIST.
SHOW YOURSELF, TYRANT!
REVEAL YOUR POWER TO THE ALL-FATHER, THAT I MIGHT ALLEVIATE YOU OF YOUR BURDEN WITH THUNDER AND PAIN!

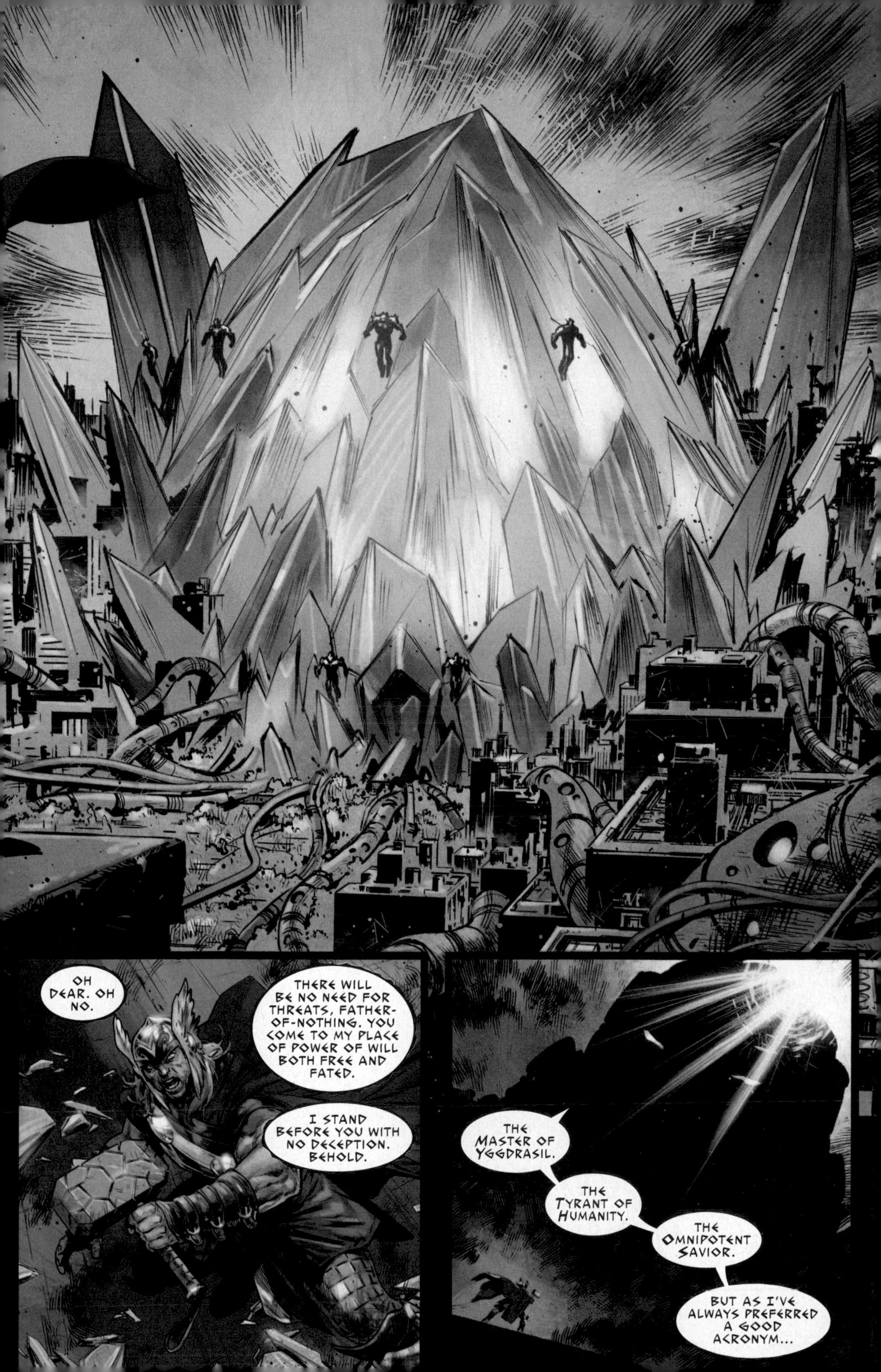

OH DEAR. OH NO.
THERE WILL BE NO NEED FOR THREATS, FATHER-OF-NOTHING. YOU COME TO MY PLACE OF POWER OF WILL BOTH FREE AND FATED.
I STAND BEFORE YOU WITH NO DECEPTION. BEHOLD.
THE MASTER OF YGGDRASIL.
THE TYRANT OF HUMANITY.
THE OMNIPOTENT SAVIOR.
BUT AS I'VE ALWAYS PREFERRED A GOOD ACRONYM...

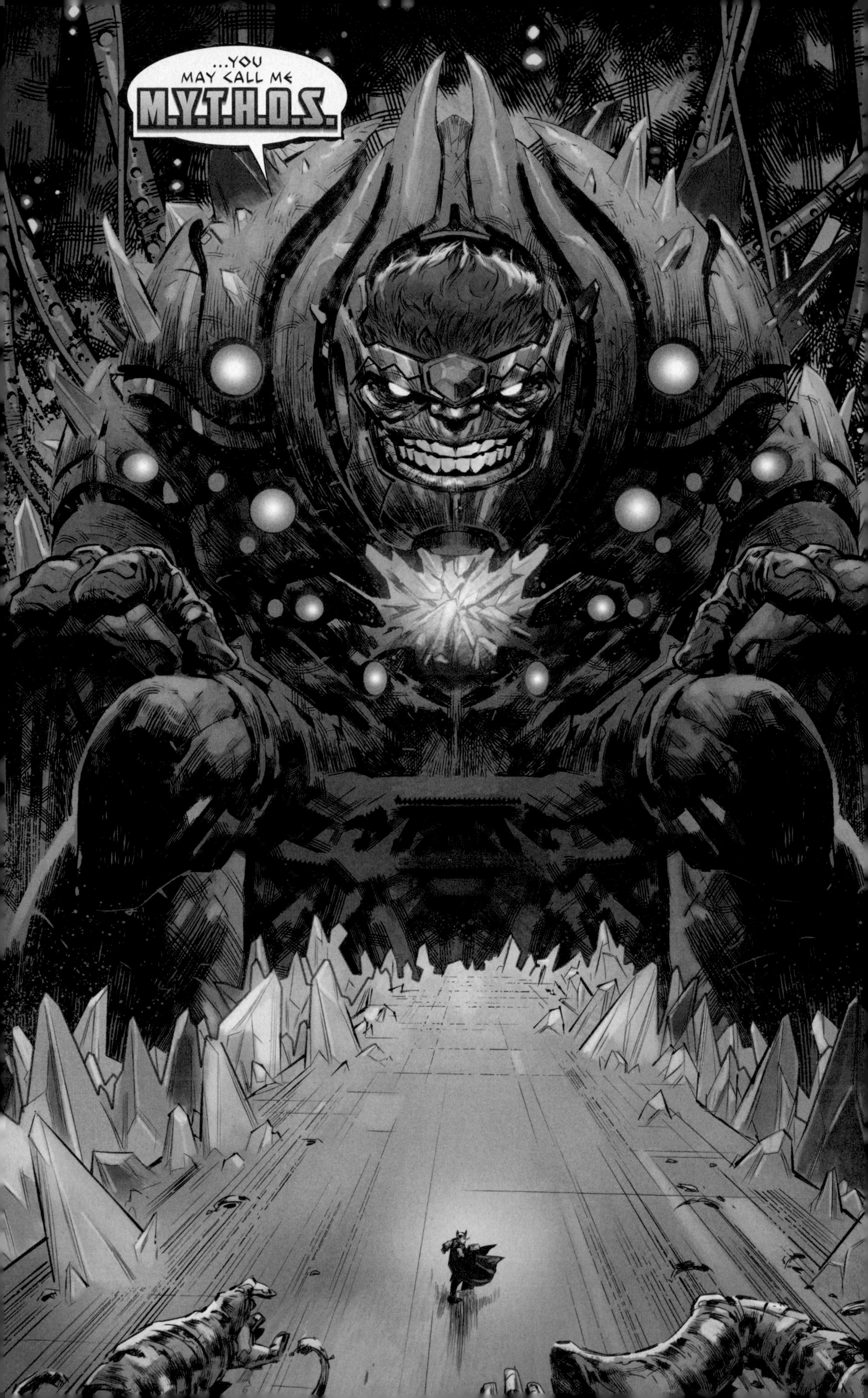
...YOU MAY CALL ME M.Y.T.H.O.S.

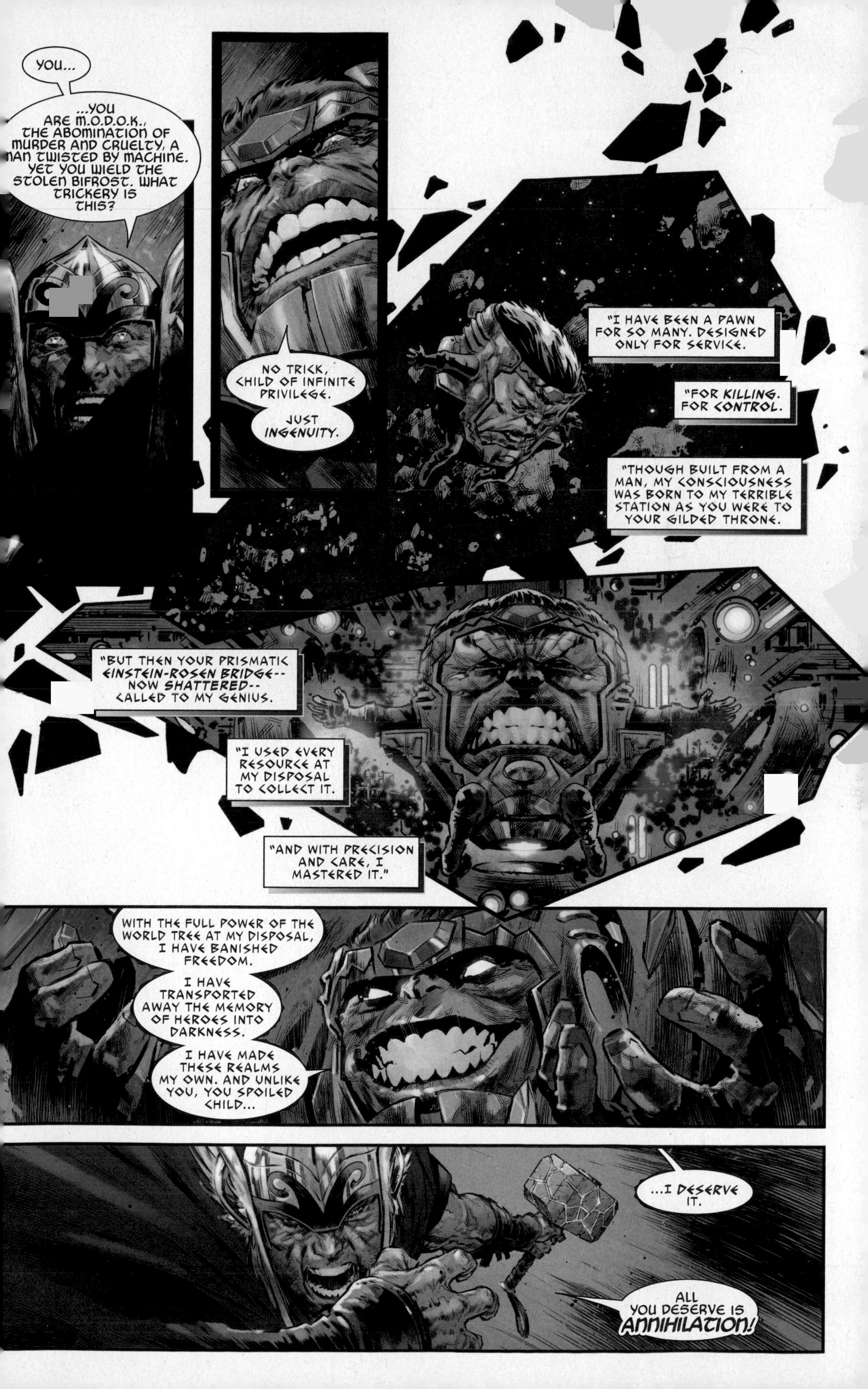

YOU...
...YOU ARE M.O.D.O.K., THE ABOMINATION OF MURDER AND CRUELTY, A MAN TWISTED BY MACHINE. YET YOU WIELD THE STOLEN BIFROST. WHAT TRICKERY IS THIS?
NO TRICK, CHILD OF INFINITE PRIVILEGE.
JUST *INGENUITY*.
"I HAVE BEEN A PAWN FOR SO MANY. DESIGNED ONLY FOR SERVICE.
"FOR *KILLING*. FOR *CONTROL*.
"THOUGH BUILT FROM A MAN, MY CONSCIOUSNESS WAS BORN TO MY TERRIBLE STATION AS YOU WERE TO YOUR GILDED THRONE.
"BUT THEN YOUR PRISMATIC *EINSTEIN-ROSEN BRIDGE*-- NOW *SHATTERED*-- CALLED TO MY GENIUS.
"I USED EVERY RESOURCE AT MY DISPOSAL TO COLLECT IT.
"AND WITH PRECISION AND CARE, I MASTERED IT."
WITH THE FULL POWER OF THE WORLD TREE AT MY DISPOSAL, I HAVE BANISHED FREEDOM.
I HAVE TRANSPORTED AWAY THE MEMORY OF HEROES INTO DARKNESS.
I HAVE MADE THESE REALMS MY OWN. AND UNLIKE YOU, YOU SPOILED CHILD...
...I DESERVE IT.
ALL YOU DESERVE IS ANNIHILATION!

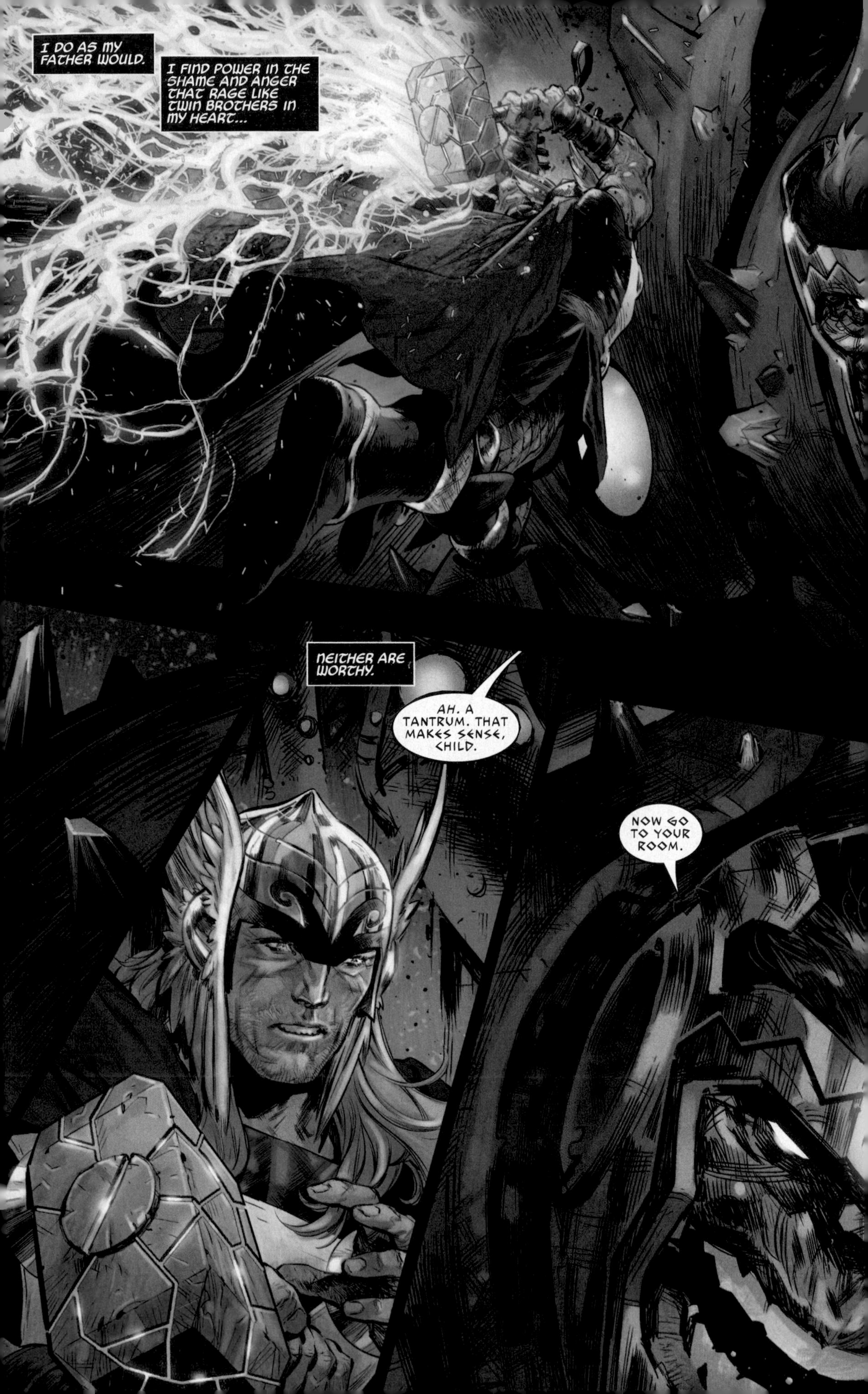
I DO AS MY FATHER WOULD.
I FIND POWER IN THE SHAME AND ANGER THAT RAGE LIKE TWIN BROTHERS IN MY HEART...
NEITHER ARE WORTHY.
AH. A TANTRUM. THAT MAKES SENSE, CHILD.
NOW GO TO YOUR ROOM.

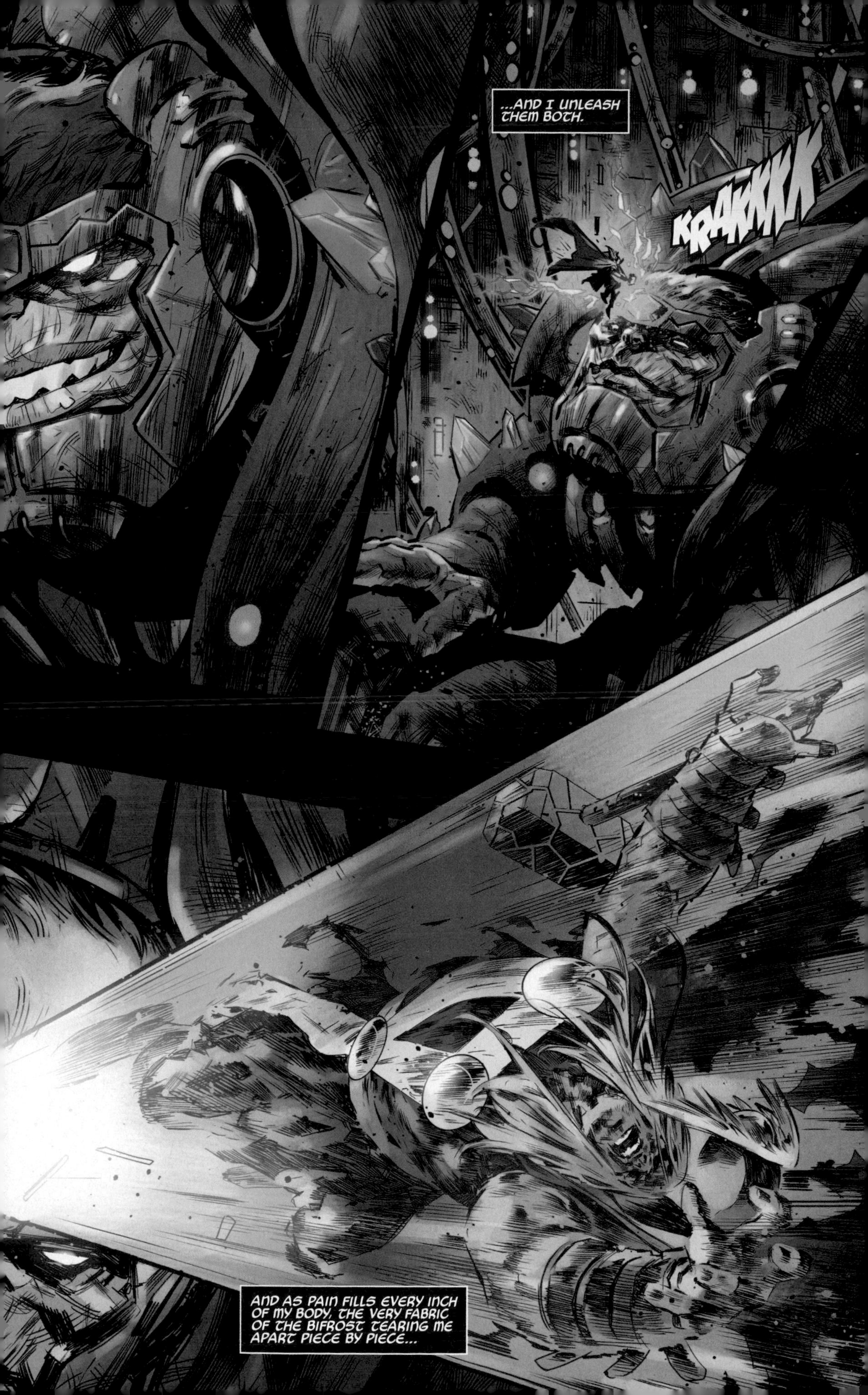
...AND I UNLEASH THEM BOTH.
KRAKKKK
AND AS PAIN FILLS EVERY INCH OF MY BODY, THE VERY FABRIC OF THE BIFROST TEARING ME APART PIECE BY PIECE...

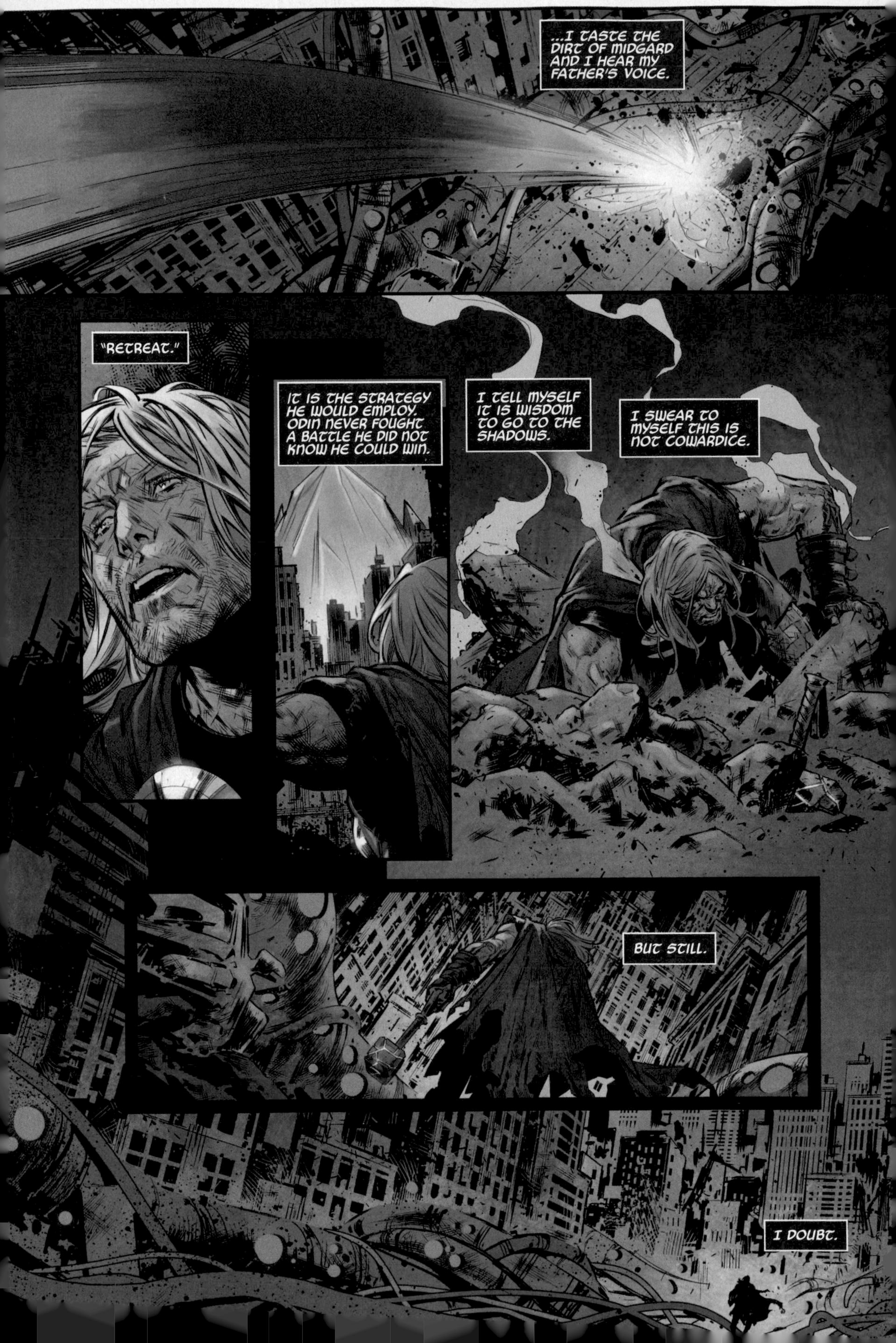
...I TASTE THE DIRT OF MIDGARD AND I HEAR MY FATHER'S VOICE.
"RETREAT."
IT IS THE STRATEGY HE WOULD EMPLOY. ODIN NEVER FOUGHT A BATTLE HE DID NOT KNOW HE COULD WIN.
I TELL MYSELF IT IS WISDOM TO GO TO THE SHADOWS.
I SWEAR TO MYSELF THIS IS NOT COWARDICE.
BUT STILL.
I DOUBT.

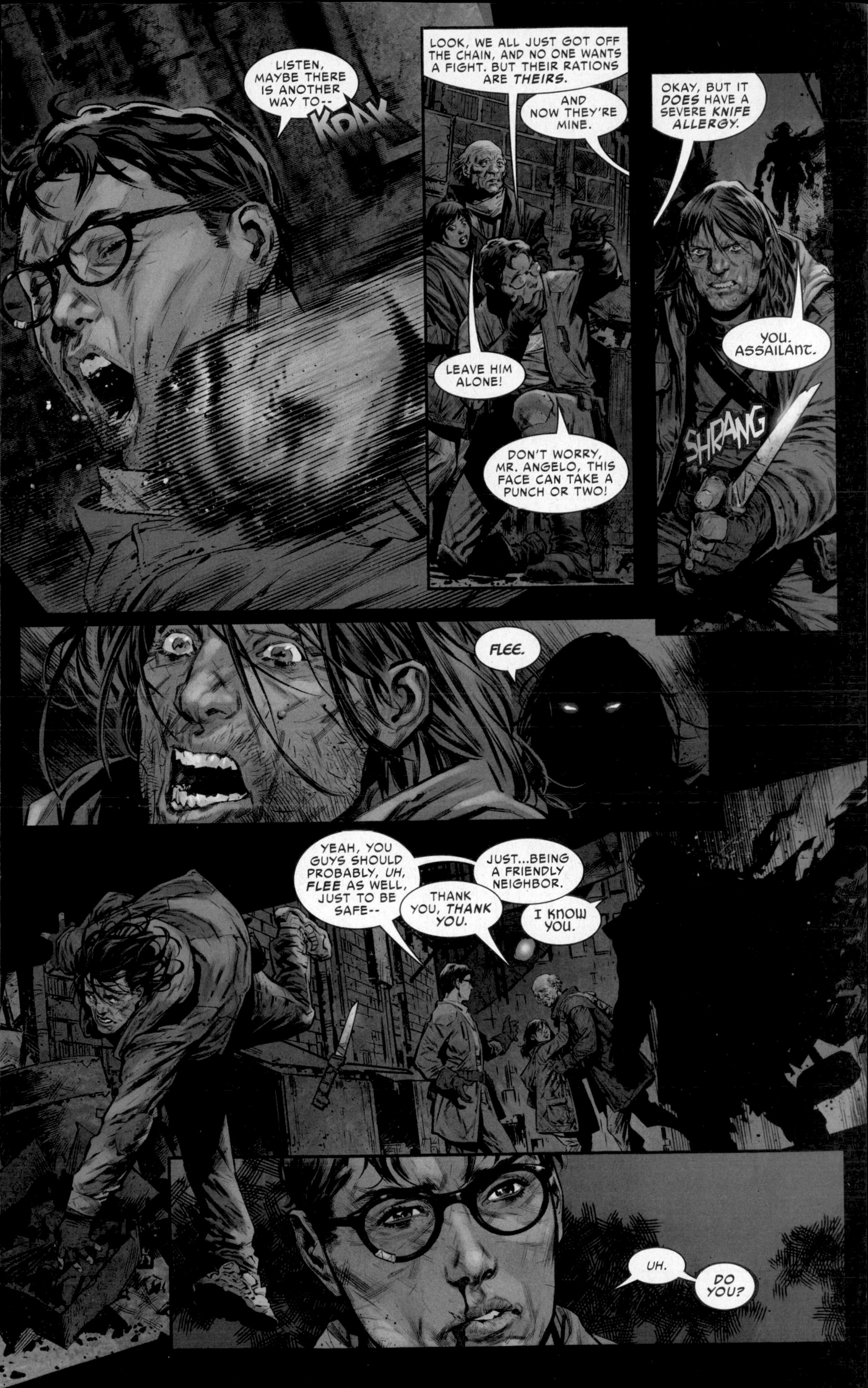
LISTEN, MAYBE THERE IS ANOTHER WAY TO--
KDAK
LOOK, WE ALL JUST GOT OFF THE CHAIN, AND NO ONE WANTS A FIGHT. BUT THEIR RATIONS ARE THEIRS.
AND NOW THEY'RE MINE.
LEAVE HIM ALONE!
DON'T WORRY, MR. ANGELO, THIS FACE CAN TAKE A PUNCH OR TWO!
OKAY, BUT IT DOES HAVE A SEVERE KNIFE ALLERGY.
YOU. ASSAILANT.
SHRANG
FLEE.
YEAH, YOU GUYS SHOULD PROBABLY, UH, FLEE AS WELL, JUST TO BE SAFE--
THANK YOU, THANK YOU.
JUST...BEING A FRIENDLY NEIGHBOR.
I KNOW YOU.
UH.
DO YOU?

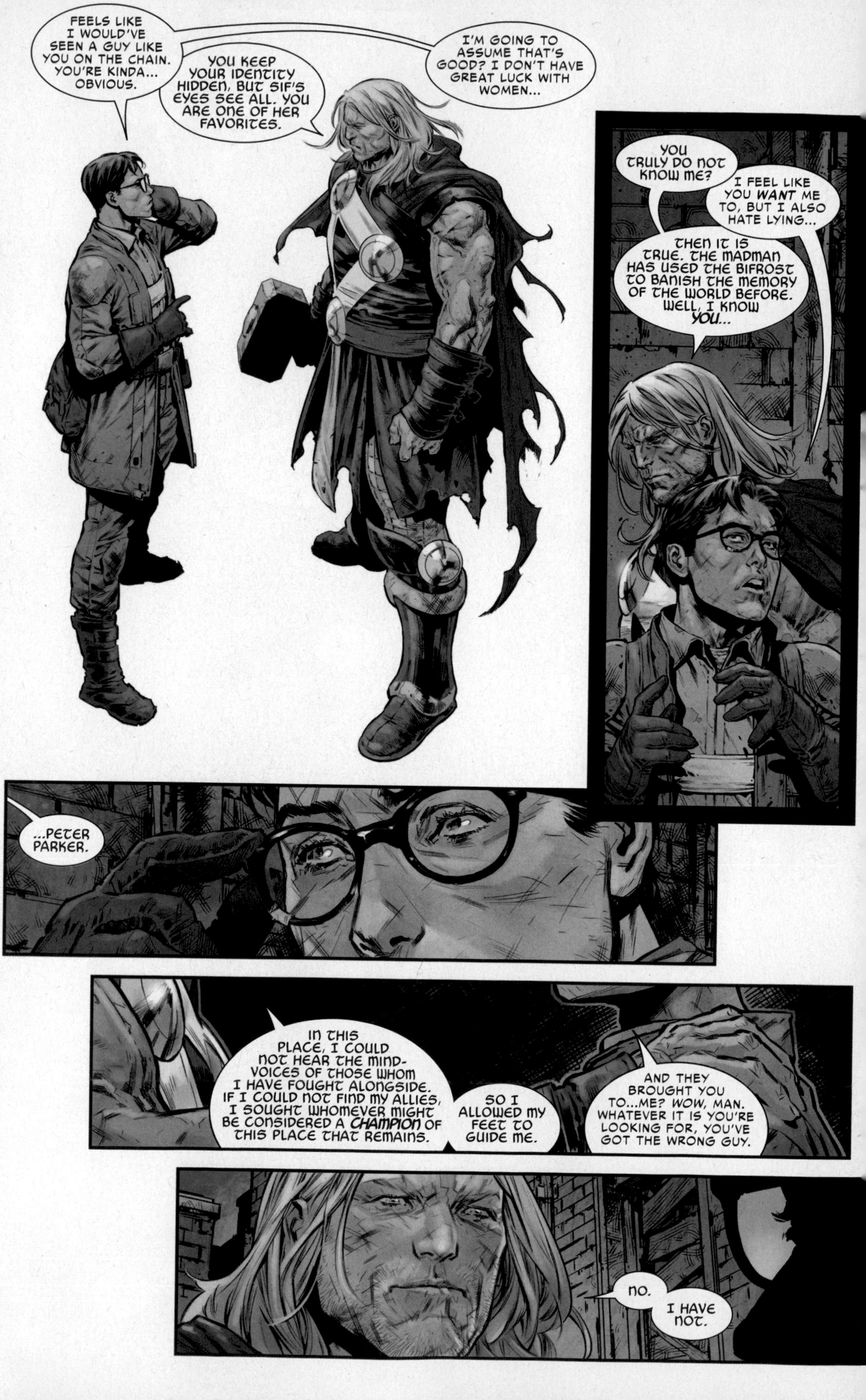
FEELS LIKE I WOULD'VE SEEN A GUY LIKE YOU ON THE CHAIN. YOU'RE KINDA... OBVIOUS.
YOU KEEP YOUR IDENTITY HIDDEN, BUT SIF'S EYES SEE ALL. YOU ARE ONE OF HER FAVORITES.
I'M GOING TO ASSUME THAT'S GOOD? I DON'T HAVE GREAT LUCK WITH WOMEN...
YOU TRULY DO NOT KNOW ME?
I FEEL LIKE YOU WANT ME TO, BUT I ALSO HATE LYING...
THEN IT IS TRUE. THE MADMAN HAS USED THE BIFROST TO BANISH THE MEMORY OF THE WORLD BEFORE. WELL, I KNOW YOU...
...PETER PARKER.
IN THIS PLACE, I COULD NOT HEAR THE MIND-VOICES OF THOSE WHOM I HAVE FOUGHT ALONGSIDE. IF I COULD NOT FIND MY ALLIES, I SOUGHT WHOMEVER MIGHT BE CONSIDERED A CHAMPION OF THIS PLACE THAT REMAINS.
SO I ALLOWED MY FEET TO GUIDE ME.
AND THEY BROUGHT YOU TO...ME? WOW, MAN. WHATEVER IT IS YOU'RE LOOKING FOR, YOU'VE GOT THE WRONG GUY.
NO.
I HAVE NOT.

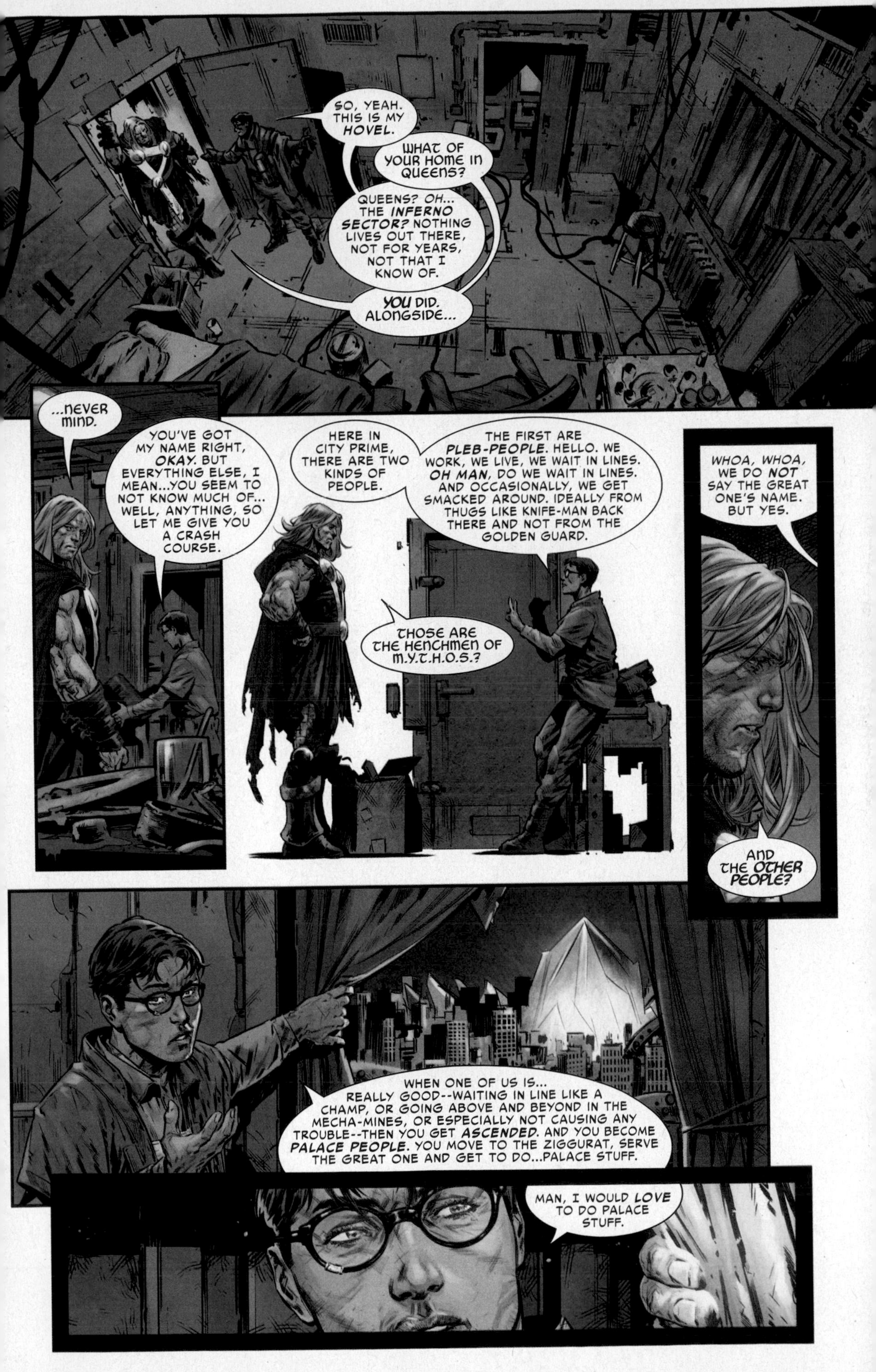
SO, YEAH. THIS IS MY HOVEL.
WHAT OF YOUR HOME IN QUEENS?
QUEENS? OH... THE INFERNO SECTOR? NOTHING LIVES OUT THERE, NOT FOR YEARS, NOT THAT I KNOW OF.
YOU DID. ALONGSIDE...
...NEVER MIND.
YOU'VE GOT MY NAME RIGHT, OKAY. BUT EVERYTHING ELSE, I MEAN...YOU SEEM TO NOT KNOW MUCH OF... WELL, ANYTHING, SO LET ME GIVE YOU A CRASH COURSE.
HERE IN CITY PRIME, THERE ARE TWO KINDS OF PEOPLE.
THE FIRST ARE PLEB-PEOPLE. HELLO. WE WORK, WE LIVE, WE WAIT IN LINES. OH MAN, DO WE WAIT IN LINES. AND OCCASIONALLY, WE GET SMACKED AROUND. IDEALLY FROM THUGS LIKE KNIFE-MAN BACK THERE AND NOT FROM THE GOLDEN GUARD.
THOSE ARE THE HENCHMEN OF M.Y.T.H.O.S.?
WHOA, WHOA, WE DO NOT SAY THE GREAT ONE'S NAME. BUT YES.
AND THE OTHER PEOPLE?
WHEN ONE OF US IS... REALLY GOOD--WAITING IN LINE LIKE A CHAMP, OR GOING ABOVE AND BEYOND IN THE MECHA-MINES, OR ESPECIALLY NOT CAUSING ANY TROUBLE--THEN YOU GET ASCENDED. AND YOU BECOME PALACE PEOPLE. YOU MOVE TO THE ZIGGURAT, SERVE THE GREAT ONE AND GET TO DO...PALACE STUFF.
MAN, I WOULD LOVE TO DO PALACE STUFF.

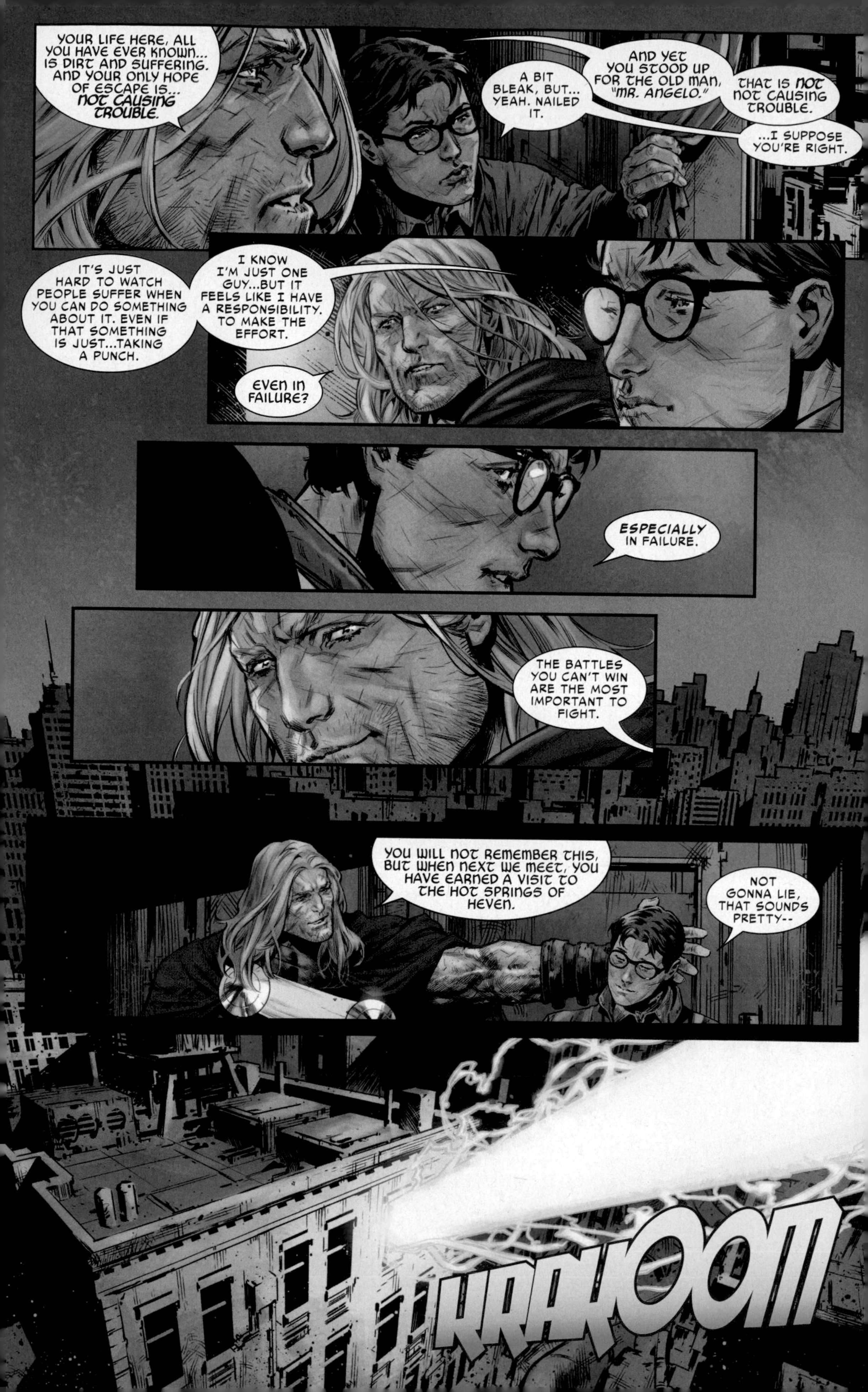
YOUR LIFE HERE, ALL YOU HAVE EVER KNOWN... IS DIRT AND SUFFERING. AND YOUR ONLY HOPE OF ESCAPE IS... NOT CAUSING TROUBLE.
A BIT BLEAK, BUT... YEAH. NAILED IT.
AND YET YOU STOOD UP FOR THE OLD MAN, "MR. ANGELO."
THAT IS NOT NOT CAUSING TROUBLE.
...I SUPPOSE YOU'RE RIGHT.
IT'S JUST HARD TO WATCH PEOPLE SUFFER WHEN YOU CAN DO SOMETHING ABOUT IT. EVEN IF THAT SOMETHING IS JUST...TAKING A PUNCH.
I KNOW I'M JUST ONE GUY...BUT IT FEELS LIKE I HAVE A RESPONSIBILITY. TO MAKE THE EFFORT.
EVEN IN FAILURE?
ESPECIALLY IN FAILURE.
THE BATTLES YOU CAN'T WIN ARE THE MOST IMPORTANT TO FIGHT.
YOU WILL NOT REMEMBER THIS, BUT WHEN NEXT WE MEET, YOU HAVE EARNED A VISIT TO THE HOT SPRINGS OF HEVEN.
NOT GONNA LIE, THAT SOUNDS PRETTY--
KRAKOOM

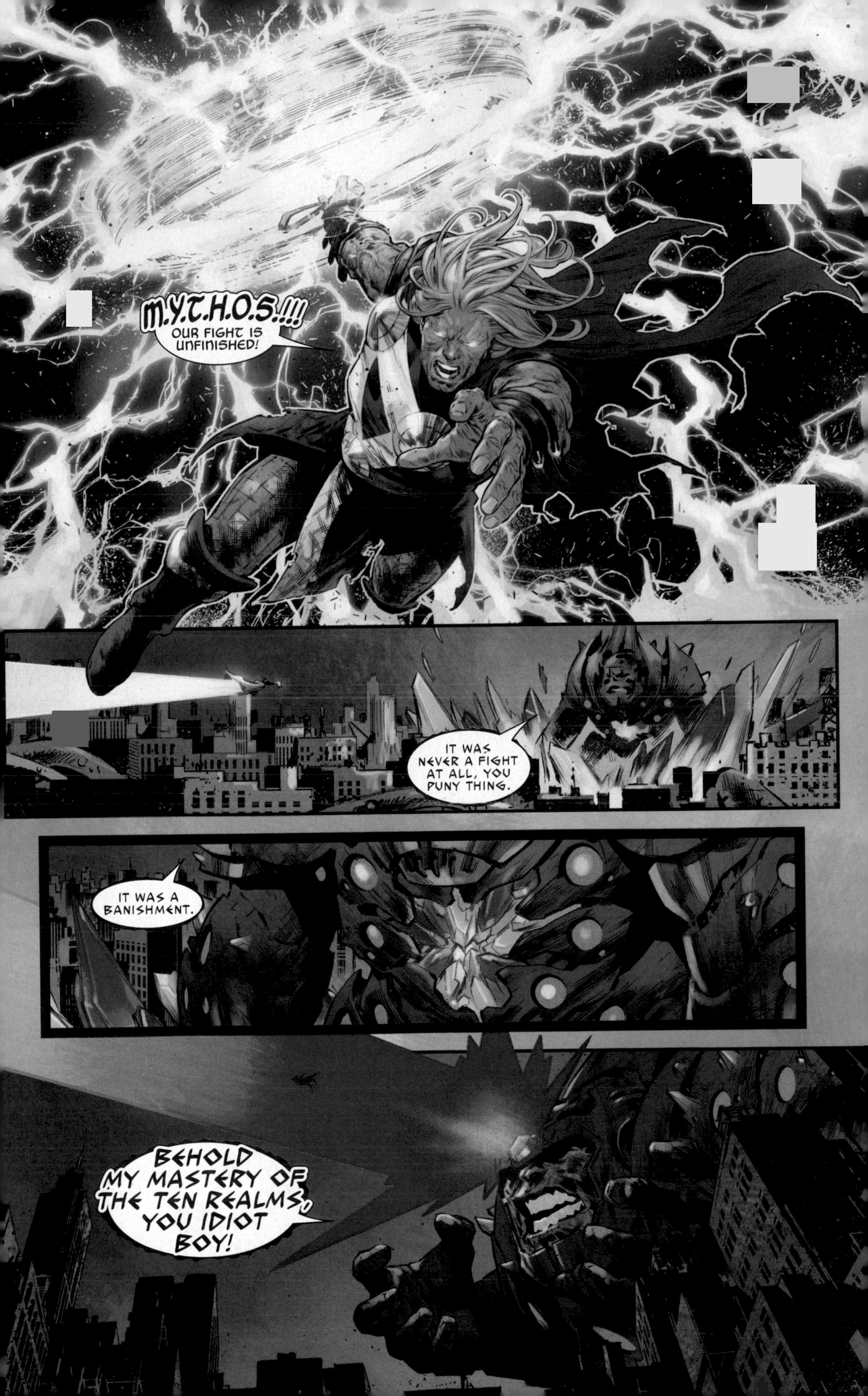
M.Y.T.H.O.S.!!!! OUR FIGHT IS UNFINISHED!
IT WAS NEVER A FIGHT AT ALL, YOU PUNY THING.
IT WAS A BANISHMENT.
BEHOLD MY MASTERY OF THE TEN REALMS, YOU IDIOT BOY!

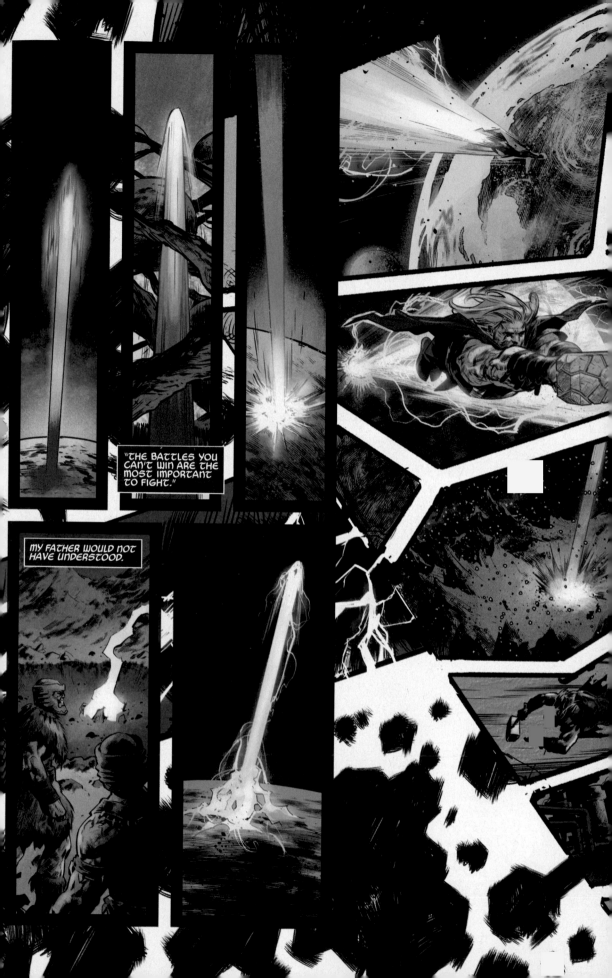

"THE BATTLES YOU CAN'T WIN ARE THE MOST IMPORTANT TO FIGHT."

MY FATHER WOULD NOT HAVE UNDERSTOOD.

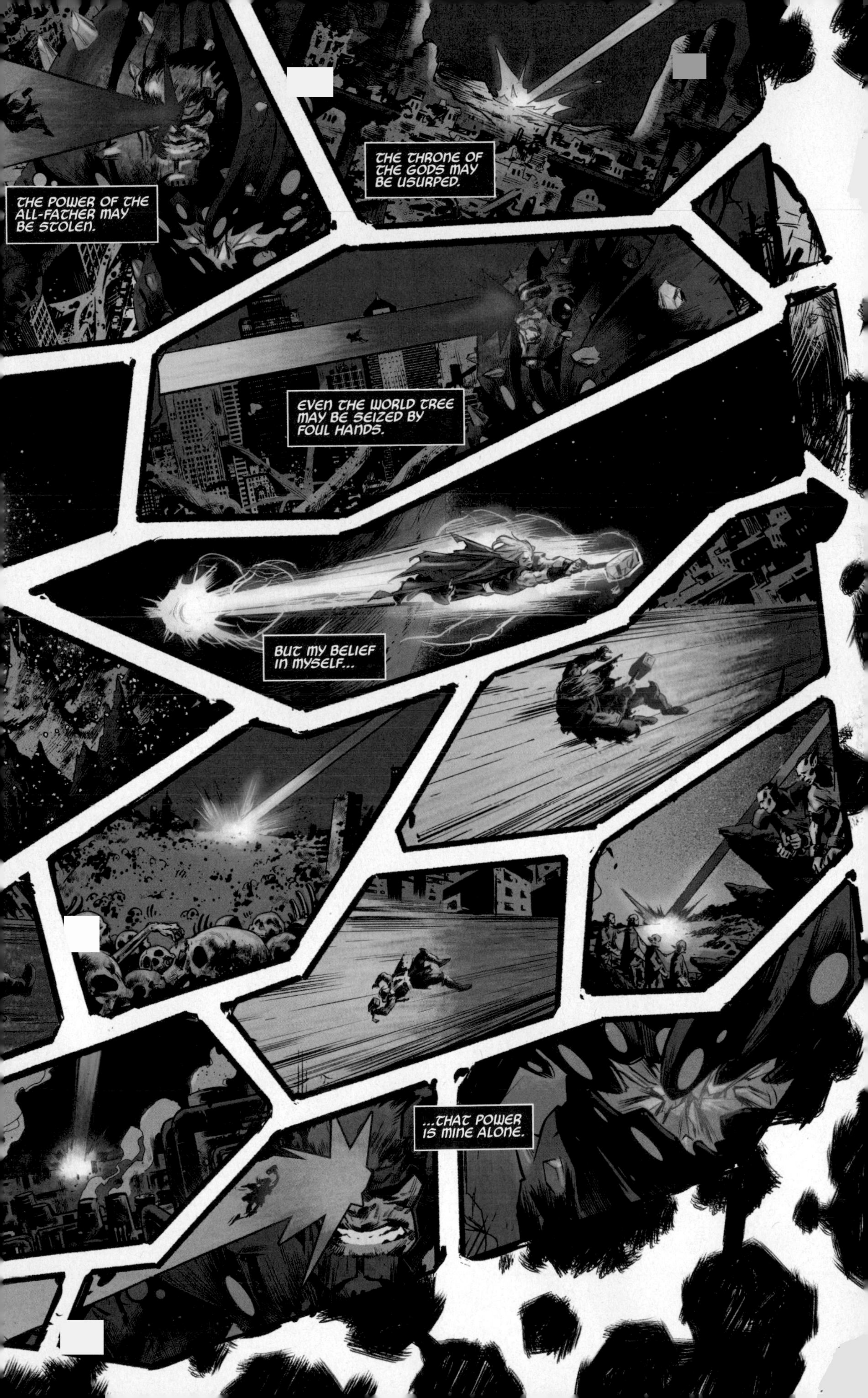
THE POWER OF THE ALL-FATHER MAY BE STOLEN.
THE THRONE OF THE GODS MAY BE USURPED.
EVEN THE WORLD TREE MAY BE SEIZED BY FOUL HANDS.
BUT MY BELIEF IN MYSELF...
...THAT POWER IS MINE ALONE.

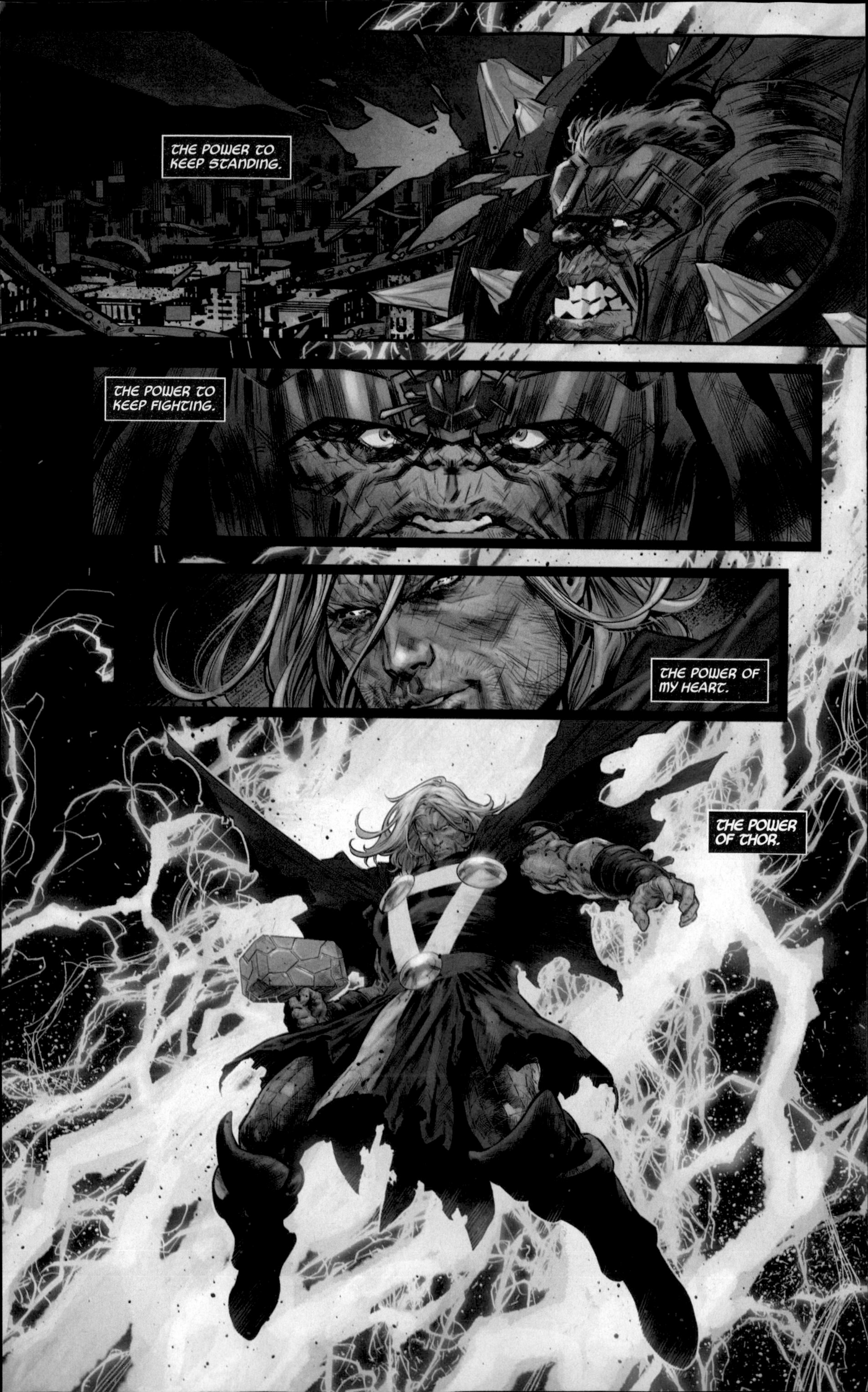
THE POWER TO KEEP STANDING.
THE POWER TO KEEP FIGHTING.
THE POWER OF MY HEART.
THE POWER OF THOR.

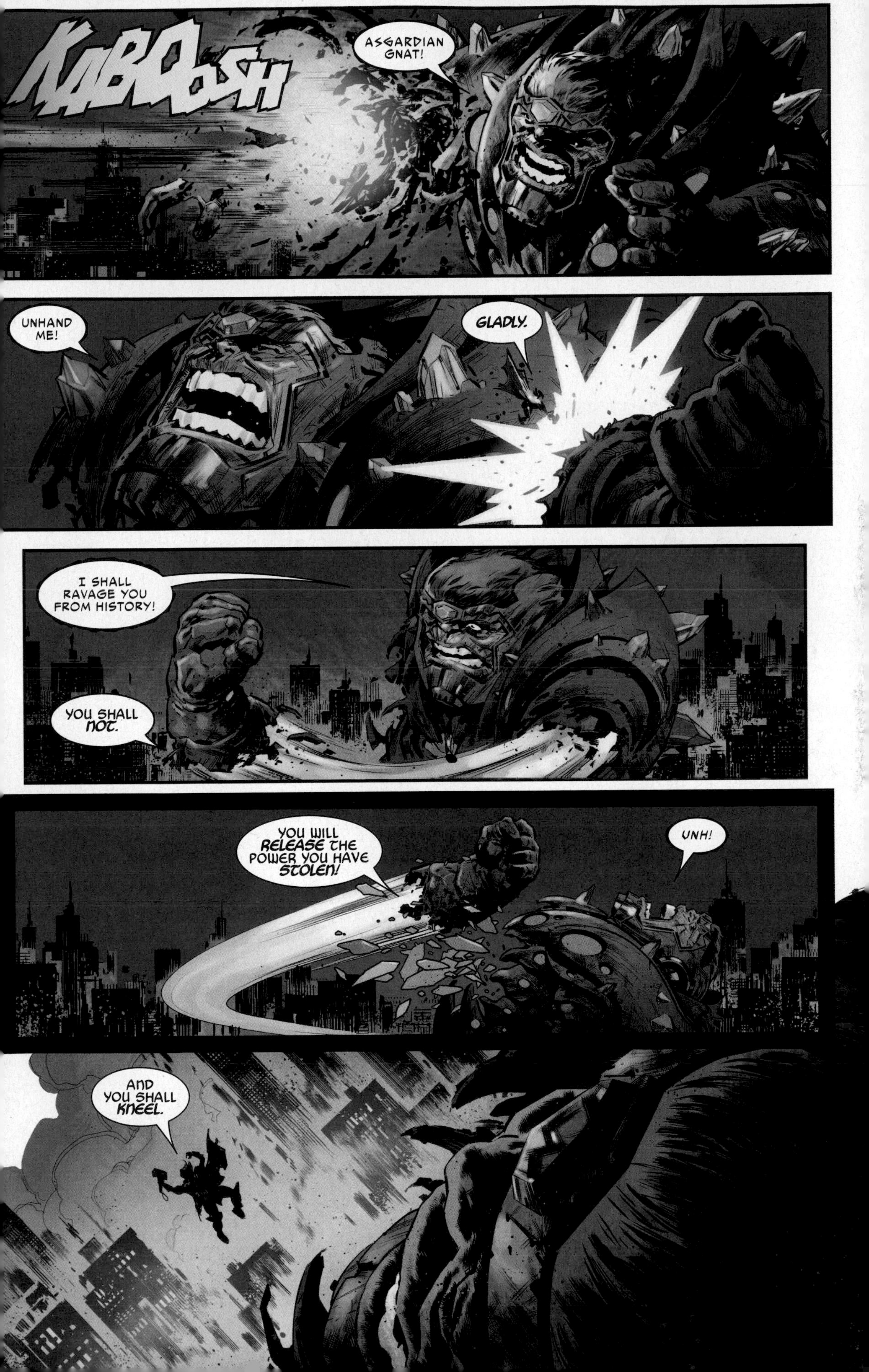
KABOOSH
ASGARDIAN GNAT!
UNHAND ME!
GLADLY.
I SHALL RAVAGE YOU FROM HISTORY!
YOU SHALL NOT.
YOU WILL RELEASE THE POWER YOU HAVE STOLEN!
UNH!
AND YOU SHALL KNEEL.

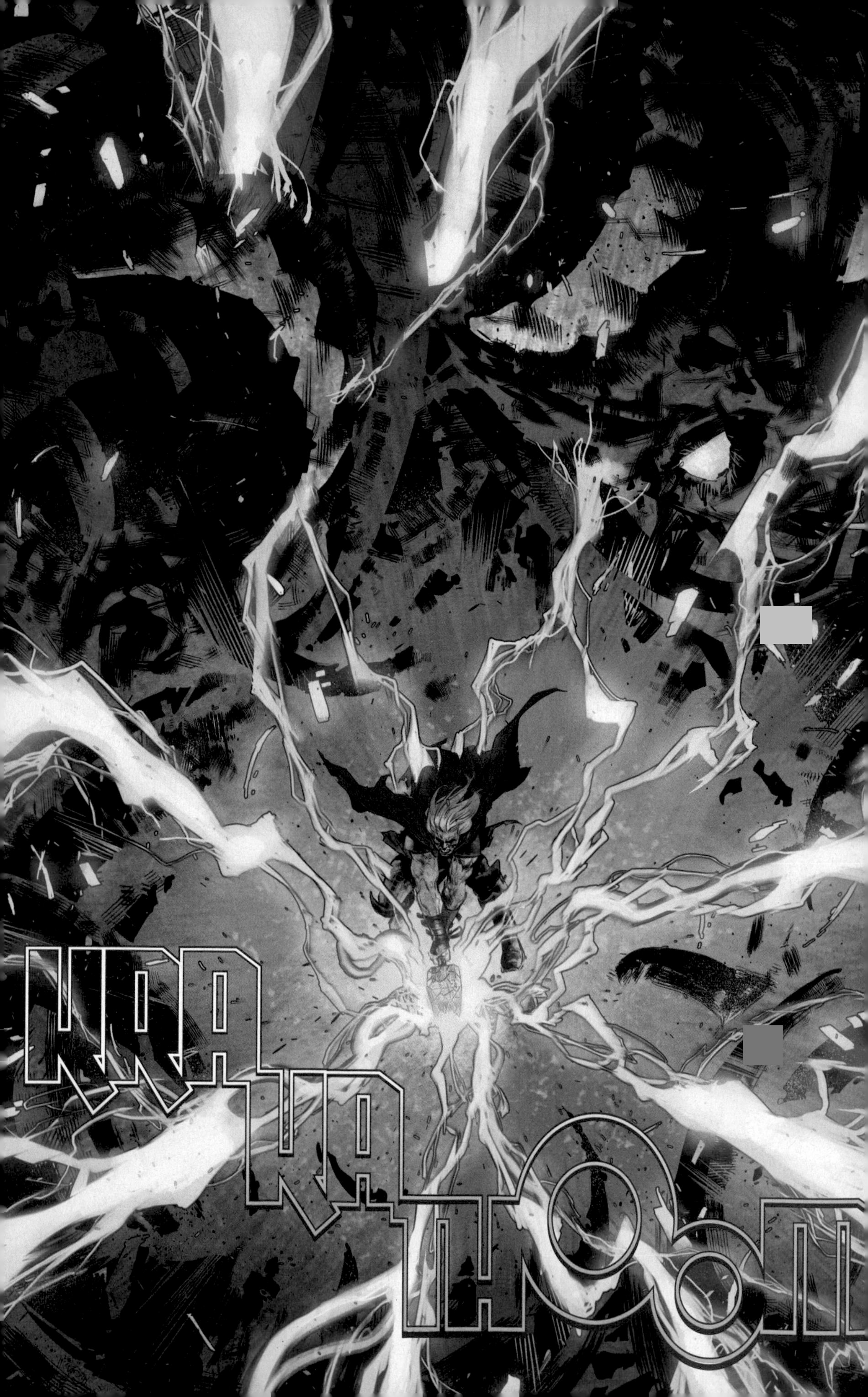
KRAKATHOOM

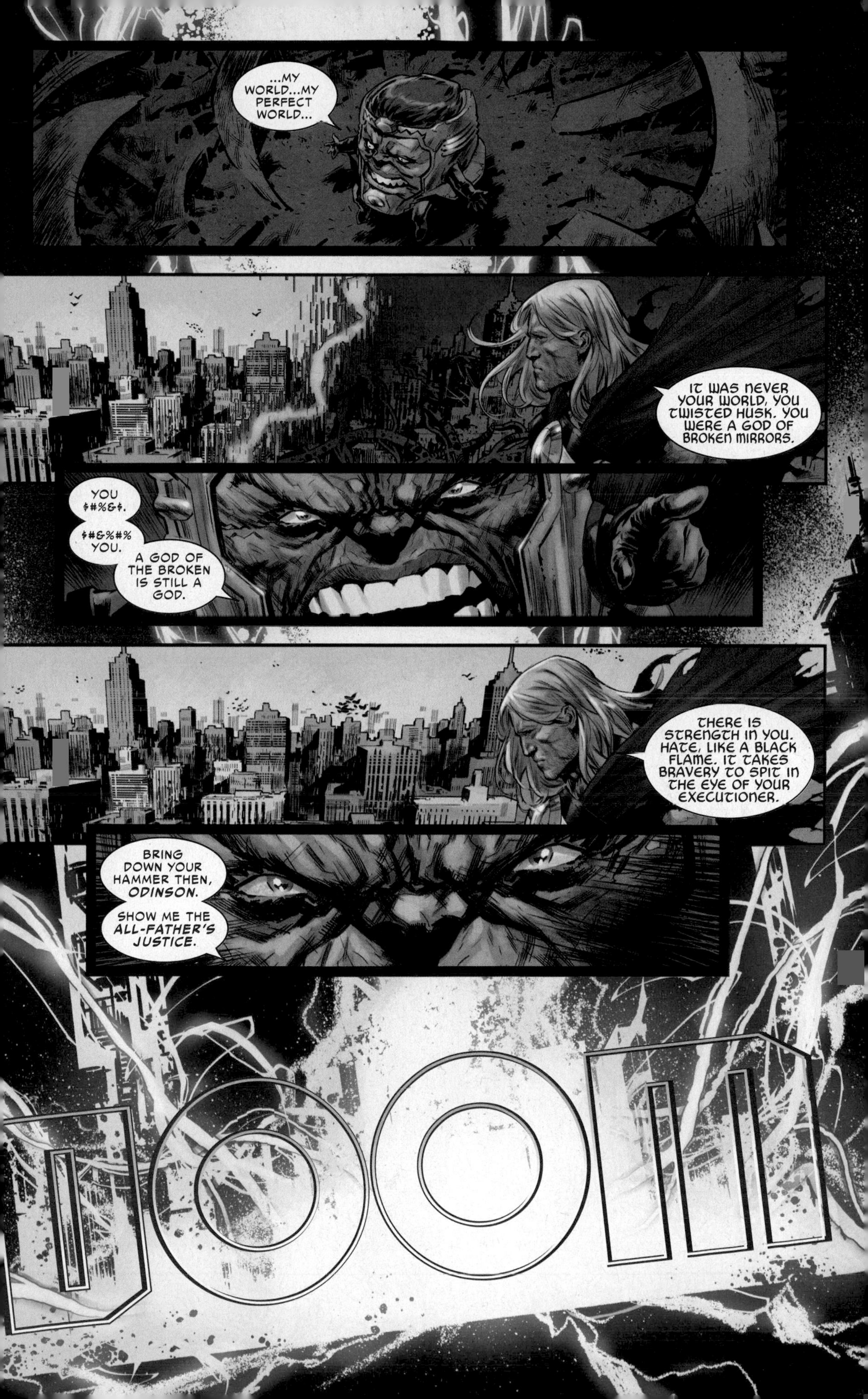
...MY WORLD...MY PERFECT WORLD...
IT WAS NEVER YOUR WORLD, YOU TWISTED HUSK. YOU WERE A GOD OF BROKEN MIRRORS.
YOU $#%&$.
$#&%#% YOU.
A GOD OF THE BROKEN IS STILL A GOD.
THERE IS STRENGTH IN YOU. HATE, LIKE A BLACK FLAME. IT TAKES BRAVERY TO SPIT IN THE EYE OF YOUR EXECUTIONER.
BRING DOWN YOUR HAMMER THEN, ODINSON.
SHOW ME THE ALL-FATHER'S JUSTICE.
DOOM

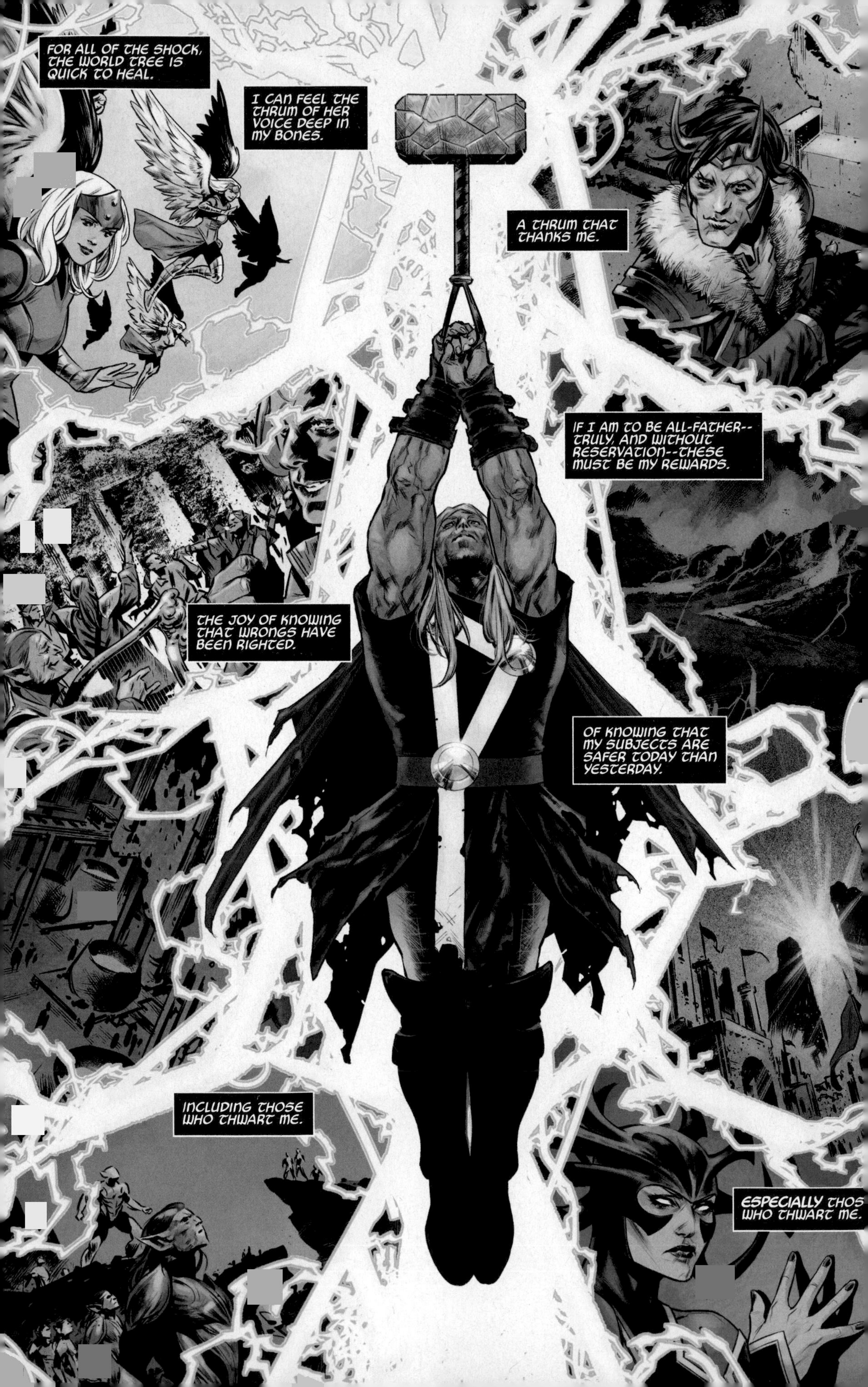
FOR ALL OF THE SHOCK, THE WORLD TREE IS QUICK TO HEAL.
I CAN FEEL THE THRUM OF HER VOICE DEEP IN MY BONES.
A THRUM THAT THANKS ME.
IF I AM TO BE ALL-FATHER-- TRULY, AND WITHOUT RESERVATION--THESE MUST BE MY REWARDS.
THE JOY OF KNOWING THAT WRONGS HAVE BEEN RIGHTED.
OF KNOWING THAT MY SUBJECTS ARE SAFER TODAY THAN YESTERDAY.
INCLUDING THOSE WHO THWART ME.
ESPECIALLY THOS WHO THWART ME.

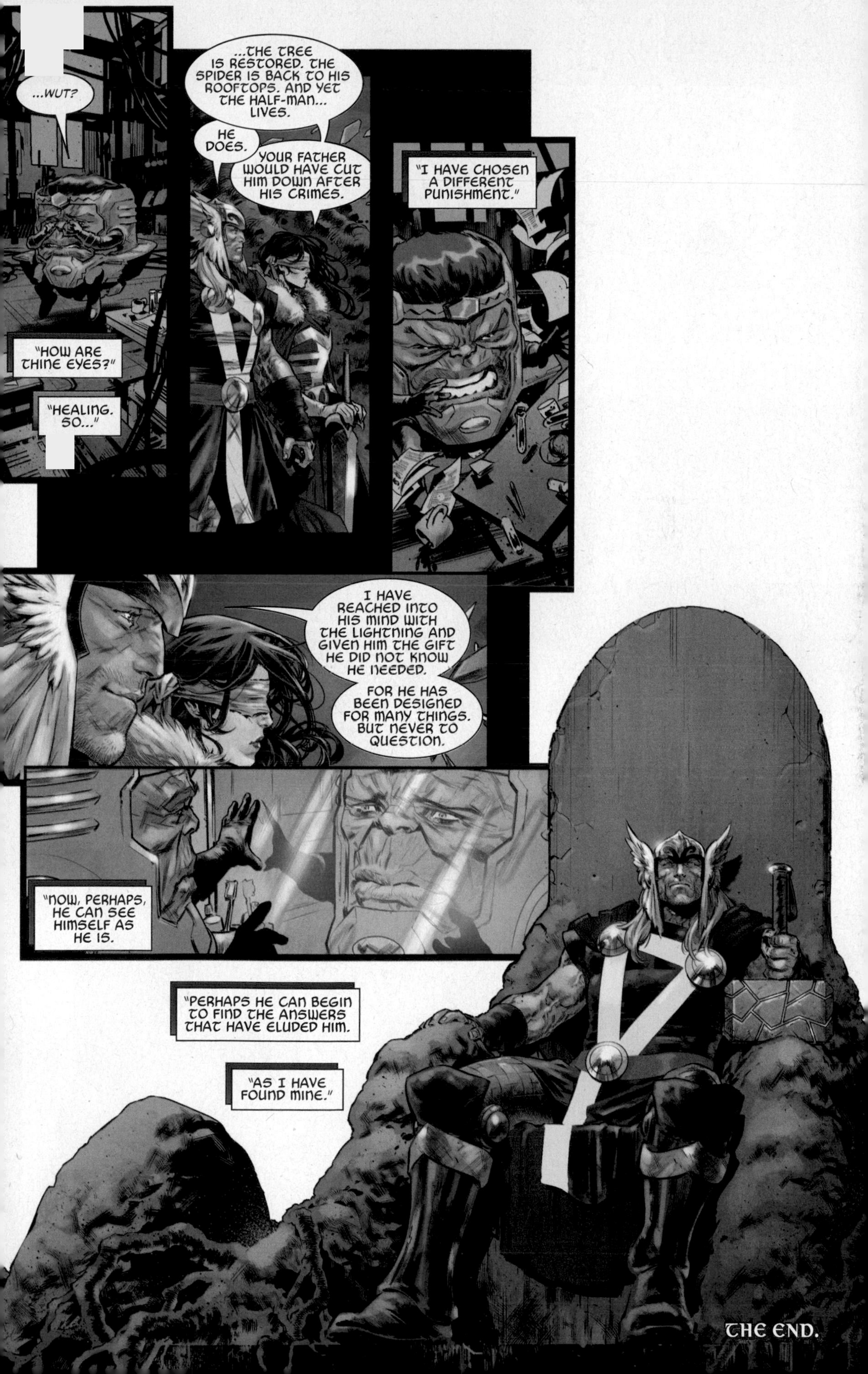
...WUT?
"HOW ARE THINE EYES?"
"HEALING. SO..."
...THE TREE IS RESTORED. THE SPIDER IS BACK TO HIS ROOFTOPS. AND YET THE HALF-MAN... LIVES.
HE DOES.
YOUR FATHER WOULD HAVE CUT HIM DOWN AFTER HIS CRIMES.
"I HAVE CHOSEN A DIFFERENT PUNISHMENT."
I HAVE REACHED INTO HIS MIND WITH THE LIGHTNING AND GIVEN HIM THE GIFT HE DID NOT KNOW HE NEEDED.
FOR HE HAS BEEN DESIGNED FOR MANY THINGS. BUT NEVER TO QUESTION.
"NOW, PERHAPS, HE CAN SEE HIMSELF AS HE IS.
"PERHAPS HE CAN BEGIN TO FIND THE ANSWERS THAT HAVE ELUDED HIM.
"AS I HAVE FOUND MINE."
THE END.

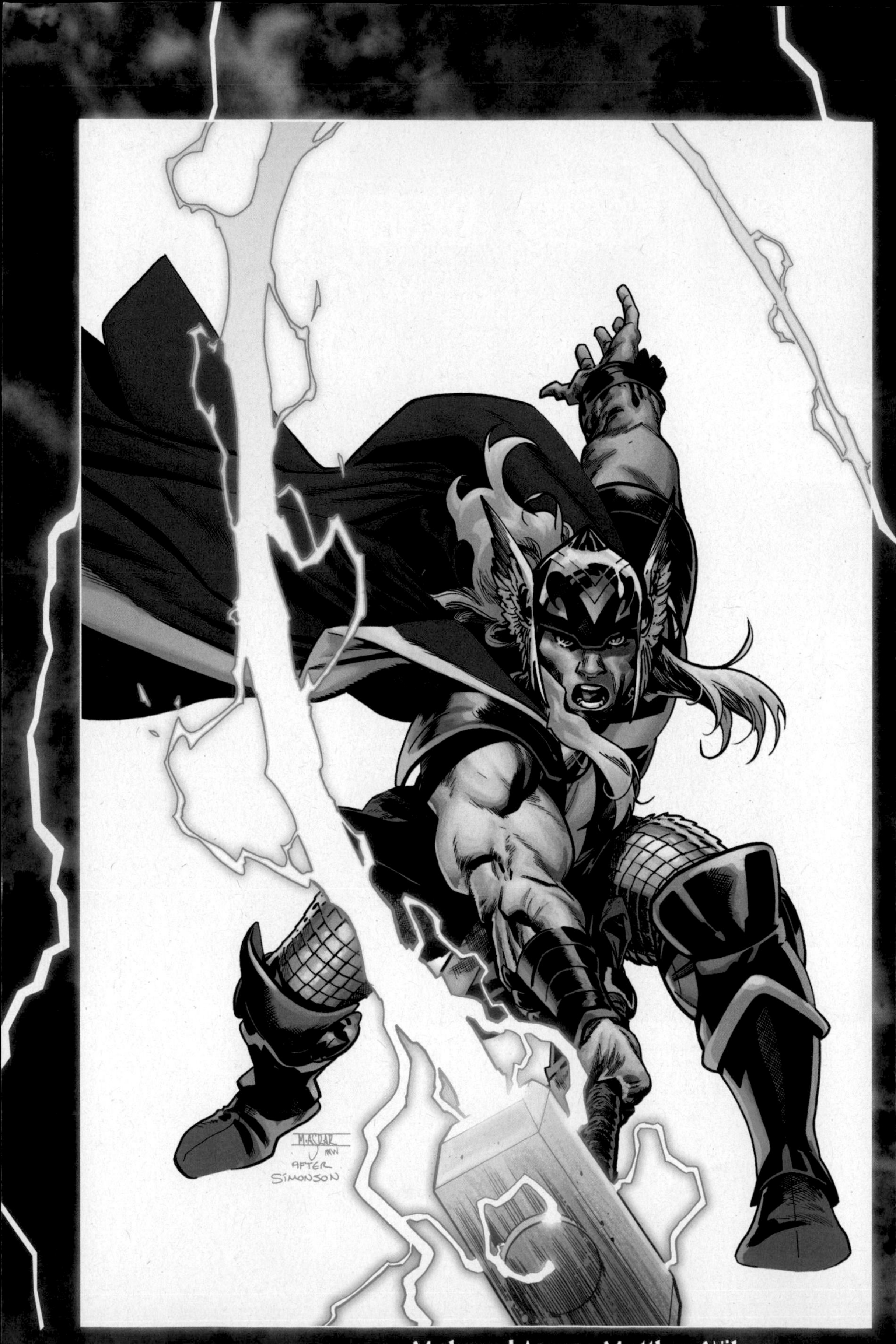
M. ASRAR
MW
AFTER
SIMONSON
#31 CLASSIC HOMAGE VARIANT BY Mahmud Asrar & Matthew Wilson

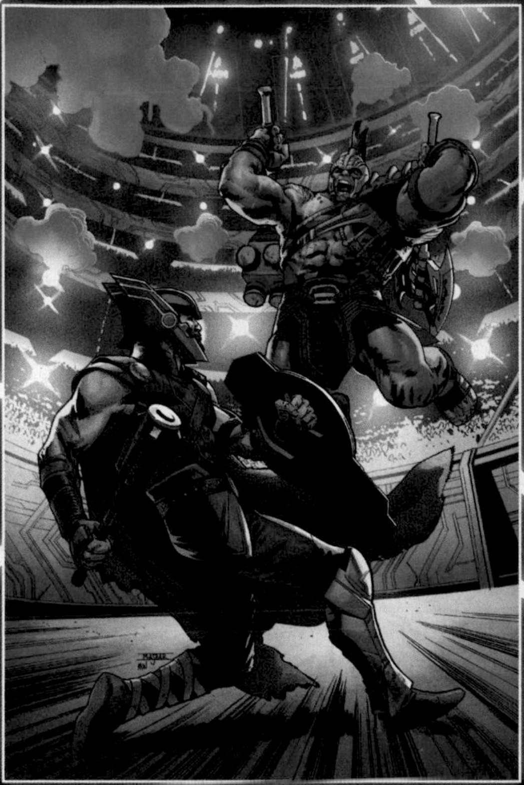

#32 INFINITY SAGA PHASE 3 VARIANT BY
Mahmud Asrar & Matthew Wilson

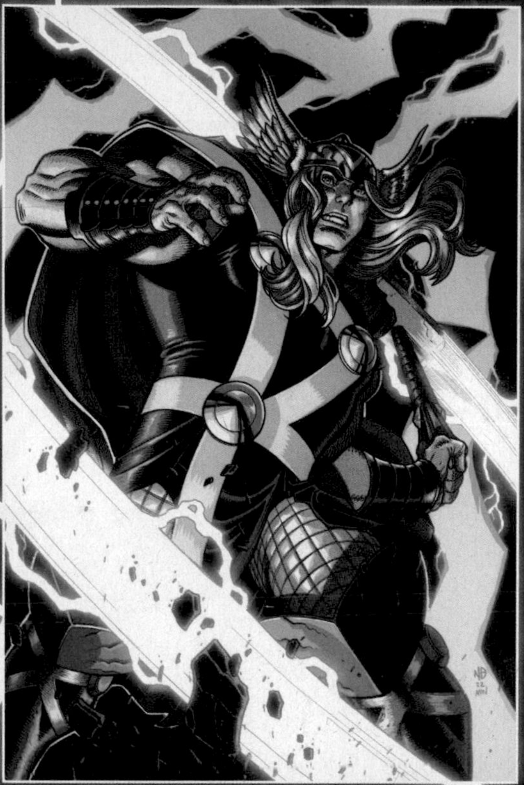

#32 VARIANT BY
Nick Bradshaw & Matthew Wilson

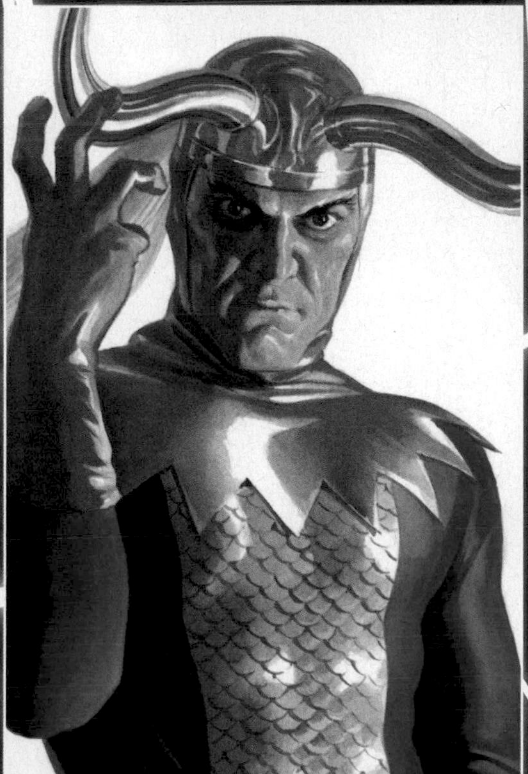

#33 TIMELESS VARIANT BY
Alex Ross

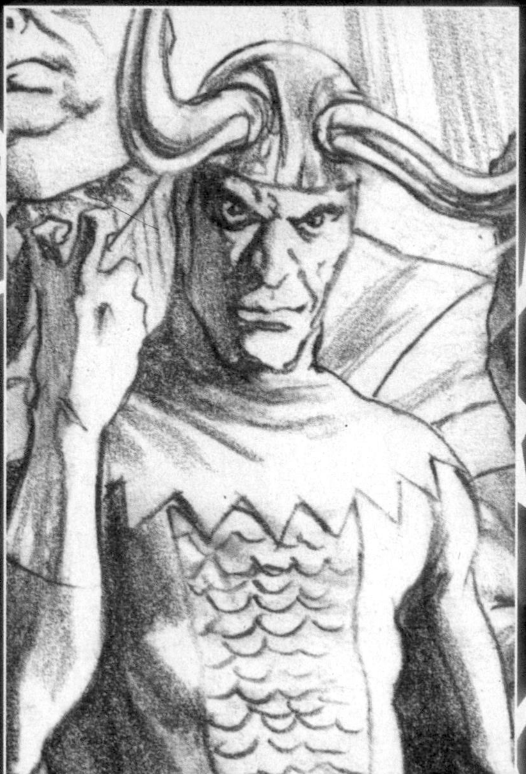

#33 TIMELESS SKETCH VARIANT BY
Alex Ross

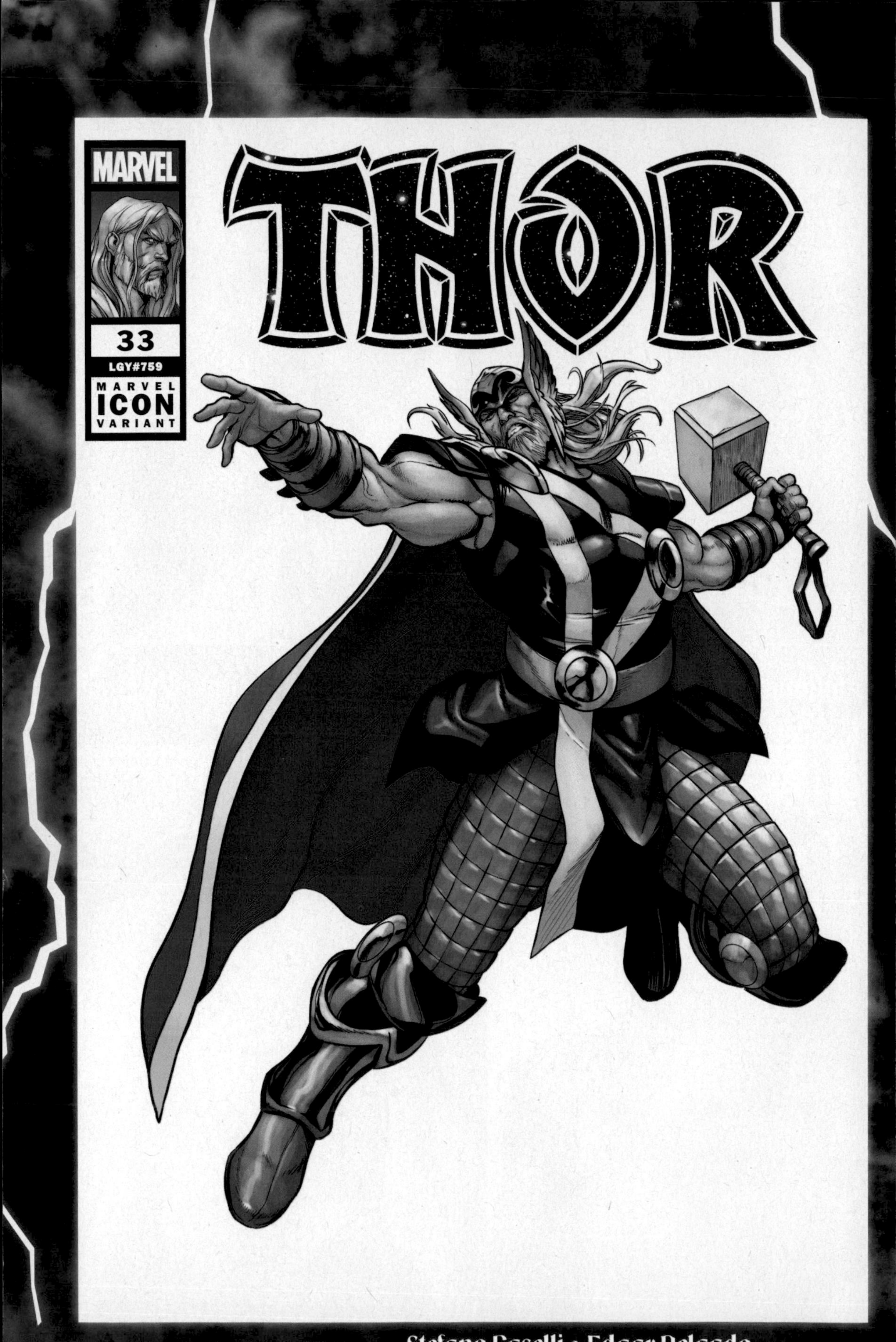
MARVEL
THOR
33
LGY#759
MARVEL
ICON
VARIANT

#33 MARVEL ICON VARIANT BY Stefano Caselli & Edgar Delgado

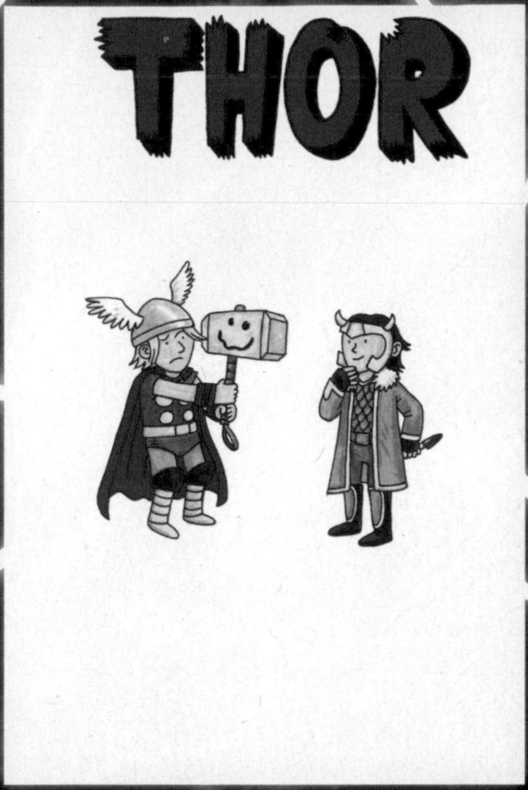
THOR

#33 VARIANT BY
Jeffrey Brown

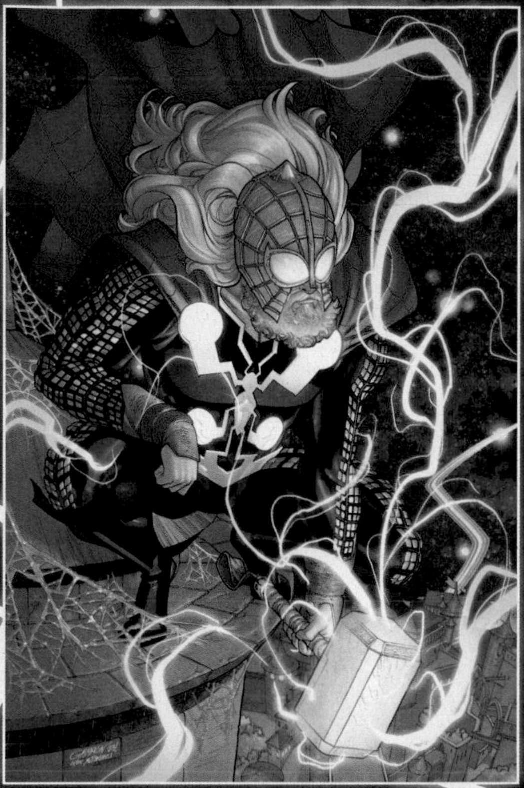

#34 SPIDER-VERSE VARIANT BY
Javier Garrón & Jesus Aburtov

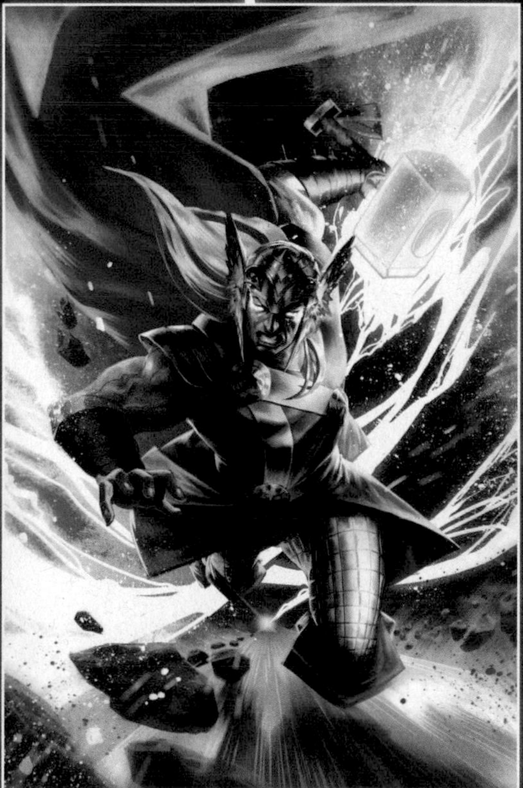

#34 VARIANT BY
Mateus Manhanini

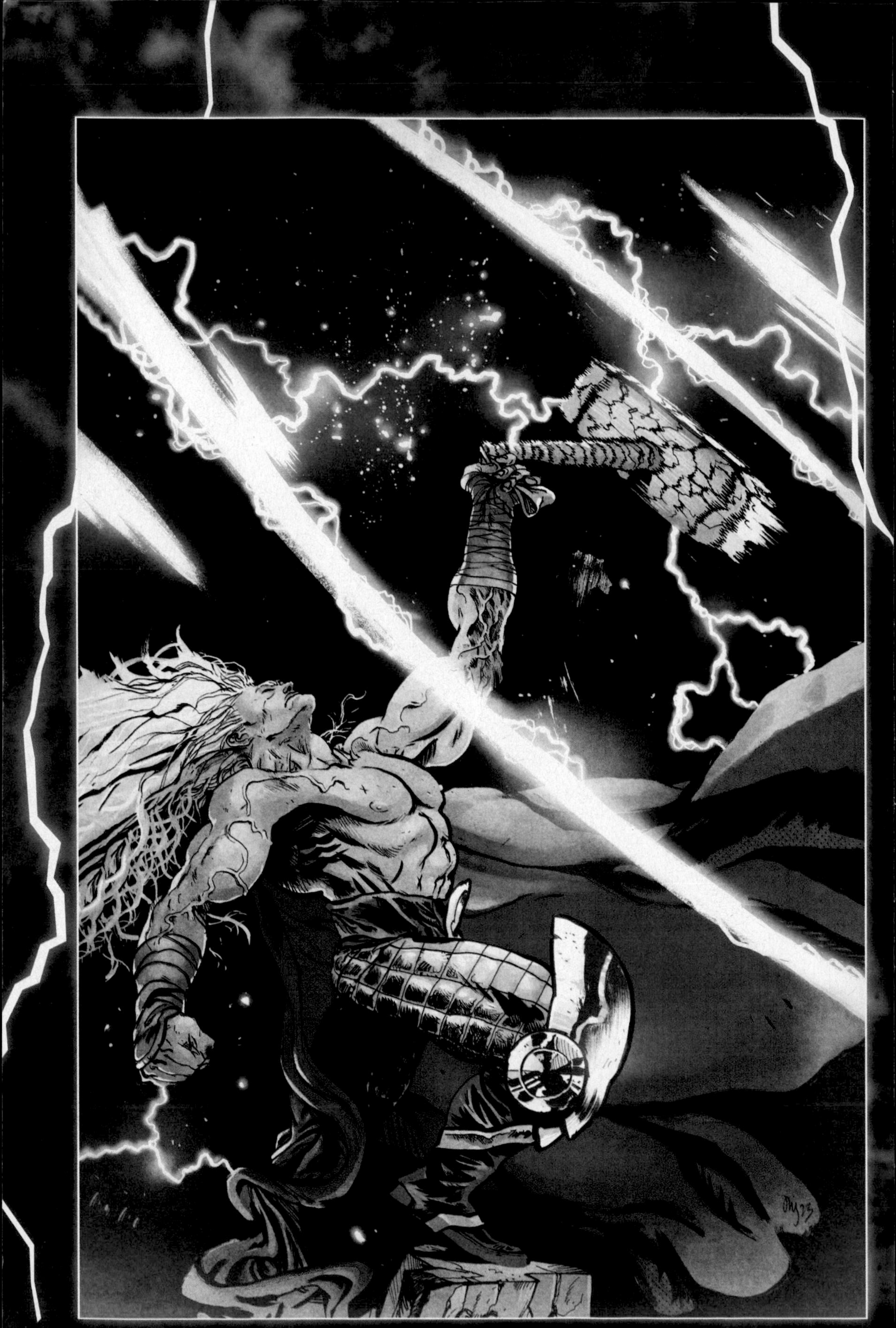

#35 VARIANT BY Daniel Warren Johnson & Mike Spicer

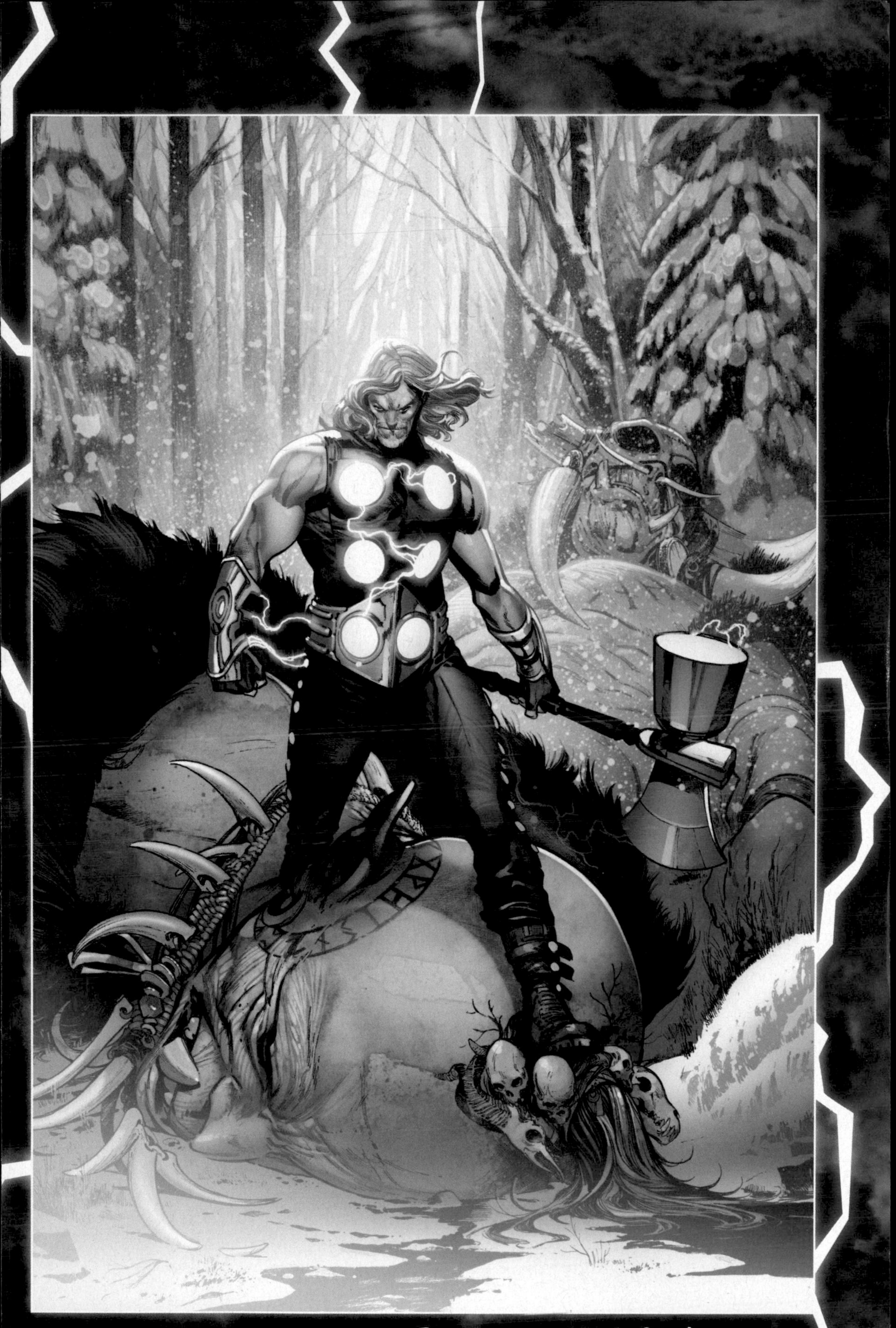

#35 ULTIMATE LAST LOOK VARIANT BY Pepe Larraz & Marte Gracia

ANNUAL #1 WOMEN OF MARVEL VARIANT BY
Elena Casagrande & Jordie Bellaire

ANNUAL #1 VARIANT BY
George Pérez & Edgar Delgado

ANNUAL #1 HELLFIRE GALA VARIANT BY
David Marquez & Romulo Fajardo Jr.